Illustrated Microsoft® Office 365 & Office 2016

Introductory

Custom Edition

Beskeen/Cram/Duffy/Friedrichsen/Reding

CENGAGE
Learning·

Australia • Brazil • Japan • Korea • Mexico • Singapore • Spain • United Kingdom • United States

**Illustrated Microsoft® Office 365 &
Office 2016—Introductory; Custom Edition**

Illustrated Microsoft® Office 365 & Office 2016—Introductory
Beskeen/Cram/Duffy/Friedrichsen/Reding

© 2017 Cengage Learning. All rights reserved.

For product information and technology assistance, contact us at
Cengage Learning Customer & Sales Support, 1-800-354-9706

For permission to use material from this text or product,
submit all requests online at **cengage.com/permissions**
Further permissions questions can be emailed to
permissionrequest@cengage.com

This book contains select works from existing Cengage Learning resources and was produced by Cengage Learning Custom Solutions for collegiate use. As such, those adopting and/or contributing to this work are responsible for editorial content accuracy, continuity and completeness.

Compilation © 2017 Cengage Learning

ISBN: 9781337708258

Cengage Learning
20 Channel Center Street
Boston, MA 02210
USA

Cengage Learning is a leading provider of customized learning solutions with office locations around the globe, including Singapore, the United Kingdom, Australia, Mexico, Brazil, and Japan. Locate your local office at:
www.**international.cengage.com/region**.

Cengage Learning products are represented in Canada by Nelson Education, Ltd.

For your lifelong learning solutions, visit www.**cengage.com/custom**.

Visit our corporate website at www.**cengage.com**.

Brief Contents

Getting Started with Microsoft Office 2016

CASE This module introduces you to the most frequently used programs in Office, as well as common features they all share.

Module Objectives

After completing this module, you will be able to:

- Understand the Office 2016 suite
- Start an Office app
- Identify Office 2016 screen elements
- Create and save a file

- Open a file and save it with a new name
- View and print your work
- Get Help, close a file, and exit an app

Files You Will Need

OF 1-1.xlsx

Understand the Office 2016 Suite

Learning Outcomes
- Identify Office suite components
- Describe the features of each app

Microsoft Office 2016 is a group of programs—which are also called applications or apps—designed to help you create documents, collaborate with coworkers, and track and analyze information. You use different Office programs to accomplish specific tasks, such as writing a letter or producing a presentation, yet all the programs have a similar look and feel. Microsoft Office 2016 apps feature a common, context-sensitive user interface, so you can get up to speed faster and use advanced features with greater ease. The Office apps are bundled together in a group called a **suite**. The Office suite is available in several configurations, but all include Word, Excel, PowerPoint, and OneNote. Some configurations include Access, Outlook, Publisher, Skype, and OneDrive. **CASE** ▶ *As part of your job, you need to understand how each Office app is best used to complete specific tasks.*

DETAILS

The Office apps covered in this book include:

QUICK TIP

In this book, the terms "program" and "app" are used interchangeably.

- **Microsoft Word 2016**

  When you need to create any kind of text-based document, such as a memo, newsletter, or multipage report, Word is the program to use. You can easily make your documents look great by using formatting tools and inserting eye-catching graphics. The Word document shown in **FIGURE 1-1** contains a company logo and simple formatting.

- **Microsoft Excel 2016**

  Excel is the perfect solution when you need to work with numeric values and make calculations. It puts the power of formulas, functions, charts, and other analytical tools into the hands of every user, so you can analyze sales projections, calculate loan payments, and present your findings in a professional manner. The Excel worksheet shown in **FIGURE 1-1** tracks checkbook transactions. Because Excel automatically recalculates results whenever a value changes, the information is always up to date. A chart illustrates how the monthly expenses are broken down.

- **Microsoft PowerPoint 2016**

  Using PowerPoint, it's easy to create powerful presentations complete with graphics, transitions, and even a soundtrack. Using professionally designed themes and clip art, you can quickly and easily create dynamic slide shows such as the one shown in **FIGURE 1-1**.

- **Microsoft Access 2016**

  Access is a relational database program that helps you keep track of large amounts of quantitative data, such as product inventories or employee records. The form shown in **FIGURE 1-1** can be used to generate reports on customer invoices and tours.

Microsoft Office has benefits beyond the power of each program, including:

- **Note-taking made simple; available on all devices**

  Use OneNote to take notes (organized in tabbed pages) on information that can be accessed on your computer, tablet, or phone. Share the editable results with others. Contents can include text, web page clips (using OneNote Clipper), email contents (directly inserted into a default section), photos (using Office Lens), and web pages.

- **Common user interface: Improving business processes**

  Because the Office suite apps have a similar **interface**, your experience using one app's tools makes it easy to learn those in the other apps. Office documents are **compatible** with one another, so you can easily **integrate**, or combine, elements—for example, you can add an Excel chart to a PowerPoint slide, or an Access table to a Word document.

  Most Office programs include the capability to incorporate feedback—called **online collaboration**—across the Internet or a company network.

FIGURE 1-1: Microsoft Office 2016 documents

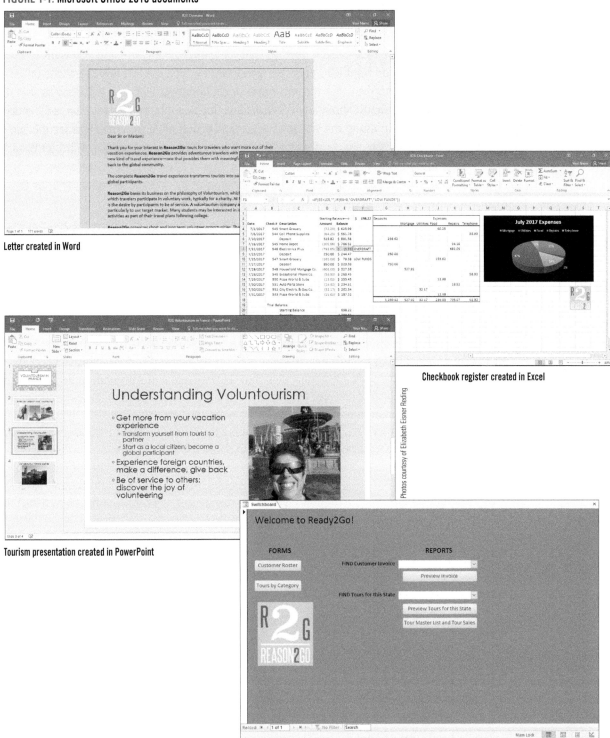

Letter created in Word

Checkbook register created in Excel

Tourism presentation created in PowerPoint

Form created in Access

Office 2016

Photos courtesy of Elizabeth Eisner Reding

What is Office 365?

Until recently, most consumers purchased Microsoft Office in a traditional way: by buying a retail package from a store or downloading it from Microsoft.com. You can still purchase Microsoft Office 2016 in this traditional way—but you can also now purchase it as a subscription service called Microsoft Office 365, which is available in a wide variety of configurations.

Depending on which configuration you purchase, you will always have access to the most up-to-date versions of the apps in your package and, in many cases, can install these apps on multiple computers, tablets, and phones. And if you change computers or devices, you can easily uninstall the apps from an old device and install them on a new one.

Start an Office App

Learning
Outcomes
• Start an Office app
• Explain the purpose
of a template
• Start a new blank
document

To get started using Microsoft Office, you need to start, or **launch**, the Office app you want to use. An easy way to start the app you want is to press the Windows key, type the first few characters of the app name you want to search for, then click the app name In the Best match list. You will discover that there are many ways to accomplish just about any Windows task; for example, you can also see a list of all the apps on your computer by pressing the Windows key, then clicking All Apps. When you see the app you want, click its name. **CASE** *You decide to familiarize yourself with Office by starting Microsoft Word.*

STEPS

QUICK TIP
You can also press
the Windows key on
your keyboard to
open the Start menu.

QUICK TIP
In Word, Excel, and
PowerPoint, the
interface can be
modified to automat-
ically open a blank
document, work-
book, or presenta-
tion. To do this, click
the File tab, click
Options, in the Start
up options section
click Show the Start
screen when this
application starts
(to deselect it), then
click OK. The next
time the program
opens, it will open a
blank document.

1. **Click the Start button ⊞ on the Windows taskbar**

   The Start menu opens, listing the most used apps on your computer. You can locate the app you want to open by clicking the app name if you see it, or you can type the app name to search for it.

2. **Type word**

   Your screen now displays "Word 2016" under "Best match", along with any other app that has "word" as part of its name (such as WordPad). See **FIGURE 1-2**.

3. **Click Word 2016**

   Word 2016 launches, and the Word **start screen** appears, as shown in **FIGURE 1-3**. The start screen is a landing page that appears when you first start an Office app. The left side of this screen displays recent files you have opened. (If you have never opened any files, then there will be no files listed under Recent.) The right side displays images depicting different templates you can use to create different types of documents. A **template** is a file containing professionally designed content and formatting that you can easily customize for your own needs. You can also start from scratch using the Blank Document template, which contains only minimal formatting settings.

Enabling touch mode

If you are using a touch screen with any of the Office 2016 apps, you can enable the touch mode to give the user interface a more spacious look, making it easier to navigate with your fingertips. Enable touch mode by clicking the Quick Access toolbar list arrow, then clicking Touch/Mouse Mode to select it. Then you'll see the Touch Mode button 👆 in the Quick Access toolbar. Click 👆, and you'll see the interface spread out.

Using shortcut keys to move between Office programs

You can switch between open apps using a keyboard shortcut. The [Alt][Tab] keyboard combination lets you either switch quickly to the next open program or file or choose one from a gallery. To switch immediately to the next open program or file, press [Alt][Tab]. To choose from all open programs and files, press and hold [Alt], then press and release [Tab] without releasing [Alt]. A gallery opens on screen, displaying the filename and a thumbnail image of each open program and file, as well as of the desktop. Each time you press [Tab] while holding [Alt], the selection cycles to the next open file or location. Release [Alt] when the program, file, or location you want to activate is selected.

FIGURE 1-2: Searching for the Word app

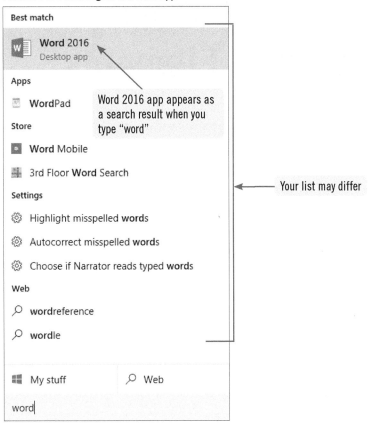

FIGURE 1-3: Word start screen

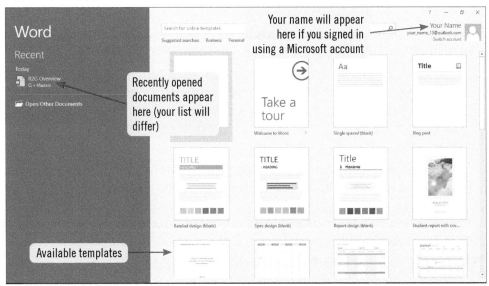

Using the Office Clipboard

You can use the Office Clipboard to cut and copy items from one Office program and paste them into others. The Office Clipboard can store a maximum of 24 items. To access it, open the Office Clipboard task pane by clicking the dialog box launcher 🖬 in the Clipboard group on the Home tab. Each time you copy a selection, it is saved in the Office Clipboard. Each entry in the Office Clipboard includes an icon that tells you the program it was created in. To paste an entry, click in the document where you want it to appear, then click the item in the Office Clipboard. To delete an item from the Office Clipboard, right-click the item, then click Delete.

Identify Office 2016 Screen Elements

Learning Outcomes
• Identify basic components of the user interface
• Display and use Backstage view
• Adjust the zoom level

One of the benefits of using Office is that its apps have much in common, making them easy to learn and making it simple to move from one to another. All Office 2016 apps share a similar user interface, so you can use your knowledge of one to get up to speed in another. A **user interface** is a collective term for all the ways you interact with a software program. The user interface in Office 2016 provides intuitive ways to choose commands, work with files, and navigate in the program window. **CASE** *Familiarize yourself with some of the common interface elements in Office by examining the PowerPoint program window.*

STEPS

1. **Click the Start button ⊞ on the Windows taskbar, type** pow, **click** PowerPoint 2016, **then click** Blank Presentation

   PowerPoint starts and opens a new file, which contains a blank slide. Refer to **FIGURE 1-4** to identify common elements of the Office user interface. The **document window** occupies most of the screen. At the top of every Office program window is a **title bar** that displays the document name and program name. Below the title bar is the **Ribbon**, which displays commands you're likely to need for the current task. Commands are organized onto **tabs**. The tab names appear at the top of the Ribbon, and the active tab appears in front. The **Share button** in the upper-right corner lets you invite other users to view your cloud-stored Word, Excel, or Powerpoint file.

QUICK TIP

The Ribbon in every Office program includes tabs specific to the program, but all Office programs include a File tab and Home tab on the left end of the Ribbon. Just above the File tab is the **Quick Access toolbar**, which also includes buttons for common Office commands.

2. **Click the** File tab

   The File tab opens, displaying **Backstage view**. It is called Backstage view because the commands available here are for working with the files "behind the scenes." The navigation bar on the left side of Backstage view contains commands to perform actions common to most Office programs.

3. **Click the** Back button ⊙ **to close Backstage** view **and return to the document** window, **then click the** Design tab **on the Ribbon**

   To display a different tab, click its name. Each tab contains related commands arranged into **groups** to make features easy to find. On the Design tab, the Themes group displays available design themes in a **gallery**, or visual collection of choices you can browse. Many groups contain a **launcher**, which you can click to open a dialog box or pane from which to choose related commands.

4. **Move the mouse pointer ⌖ over the** Ion Boardroom theme **in the Themes group as shown in** FIGURE 1-5, **but** *do not click* **the mouse button**

   The Ion Boardroom theme is temporarily applied to the slide in the document window. However, because you did not click the theme, you did not permanently change the slide. With the **Live Preview** feature, you can point to a choice, see the results, then decide if you want to make the change. Live Preview is available throughout Office.

TROUBLE

If you accidentally click a theme, click the Undo button on the Quick Access toolbar.

5. **Move ⌖ away from the Ribbon and towards the slide**

   If you had clicked the Ion theme, it would be applied to this slide. Instead, the slide remains unchanged.

QUICK TIP

You can also use the Zoom button in the Zoom group on the View tab to enlarge or reduce a document's appearance.

6. **Point to the** Zoom slider `— ——|—— + 100%` **on the status bar, then drag to the right until the Zoom level reads** 166%

   The slide display is enlarged. Zoom tools are located on the status bar. You can drag the slider or click the Zoom In or Zoom Out buttons to zoom in or out on an area of interest. **Zooming in** (a higher percentage), makes a document appear bigger on screen but less of it fits on the screen at once; **zooming out** (a lower percentage) lets you see more of the document at a reduced size.

7. **Click the** Zoom Out button `—` **on the status bar to the left of the Zoom slider until the Zoom level reads** 120%

FIGURE 1-4: PowerPoint program window

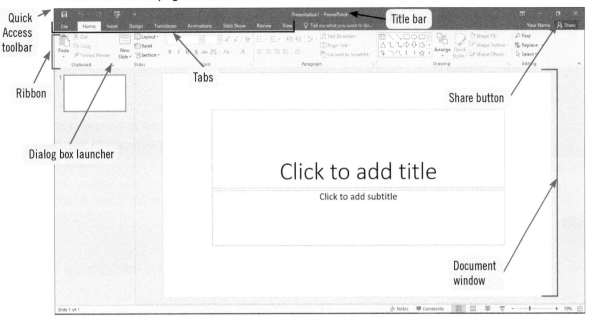

FIGURE 1-5: Viewing a theme with Live Preview

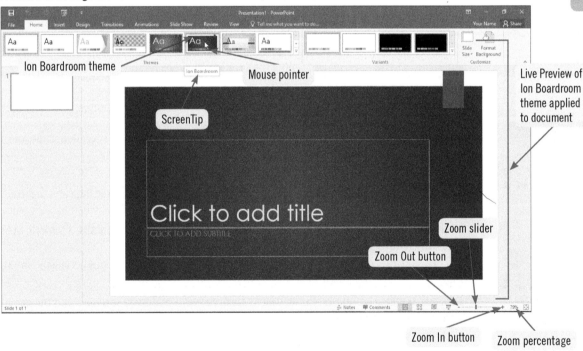

Using Backstage view

Backstage view in each Microsoft Office app offers "one stop shopping" for many commonly performed tasks, such as opening and saving a file, printing and previewing a document, defining document properties, sharing information, and exiting a program. Backstage view opens when you click the File tab in any Office app, and while features such as the Ribbon, Mini toolbar, and Live Preview all help you work *in* your documents, the File tab and Backstage view help you work *with* your documents. You can click commands in the navigation pane to open different places for working with your documents, such as the Open place, the Save place, and so on. You can return to your active document by clicking the Back button.

Create and Save a File

Learning
Outcomes
• Create a file
• Save a file
• Explain OneDrive

When working in an Office app, one of the first things you need to do is to create and save a file. A **file** is a stored collection of data. Saving a file enables you to work on a project now, then put it away and work on it again later. In some Office programs, including Word, Excel, and PowerPoint, you can open a new file when you start the app, then all you have to do is enter some data and save it. In Access, you must create a file before you enter any data. You should give your files meaningful names and save them in an appropriate location, such as a folder on your hard drive or OneDrive so they're easy to find. **OneDrive** is a Microsoft cloud storage system that lets you easily save, share, and access your files from anywhere you have Internet access. **CASE** *Use Word to familiarize yourself with creating and saving a document. First you'll type some notes about a possible location for a corporate meeting, then you'll save the information for later use.*

STEPS

1. **Click the** Word button 📖 **on the taskbar, click** Blank document, **then click the** Zoom In button ➕ **until the level is** 120%, **if necessary**

2. **Type** Locations for Corporate Meeting, **then press** [Enter] **twice**
   The text appears in the document window, and the **insertion point** blinks on a new blank line. The insertion point indicates where the next typed text will appear.

3. **Type** Las Vegas, NV, **press** [Enter], **type** Chicago, IL, **press** [Enter], **type** Seattle, WA, **press** [Enter] **twice, then type your name**

4. **Click the** Save button 💾 **on the Quick Access toolbar**
   Because this is the first time you are saving this new file, the Save place in Backstage view opens, showing various options for saving the file. See **FIGURE 1-6**. Once you save a file for the first time, clicking 💾 saves any changes to the file *without* opening the Save As dialog box.

5. **Click** Browse
   The Save As dialog box opens, as shown in **FIGURE 1-7**, where you can browse to the location where you want to save the file. The Address bar in the Save As dialog box displays the default location for saving the file, but you can change it to any location. The File name field contains a suggested name for the document based on text in the file, but you can enter a different name.

6. **Type** OF 1-Possible Corporate Meeting Locations
   The text you type replaces the highlighted text. (The "OF 1-" in the filename indicates that the file is created in Office Module 1. You will see similar designations throughout this book when files are named.)

7. **In the Save As dialog box, use the Address bar or Navigation Pane to navigate to the location where you store your Data Files**
   You can store files on your computer, a network drive, your OneDrive, or any acceptable storage device.

8. **Click** Save
   The Save As dialog box closes, the new file is saved to the location you specified, and the name of the document appears in the title bar, as shown in **FIGURE 1-8**. (You may or may not see the file extension ".docx" after the filename.) See **TABLE 1-1** for a description of the different types of files you create in Office, and the file extensions associated with each.

TABLE 1-1: Common filenames and default file extensions

file created in	is called a	and has the default extension
Word	document	.docx
Excel	workbook	.xlsx
PowerPoint	presentation	.pptx
Access	database	.accdb

FIGURE 1-6: Save place in Backstage view

Saves to your OneDrive account

Click to display a list of recently accessed locations on this PC

Click to open the Save As dialog box

FIGURE 1-7: Save As dialog box

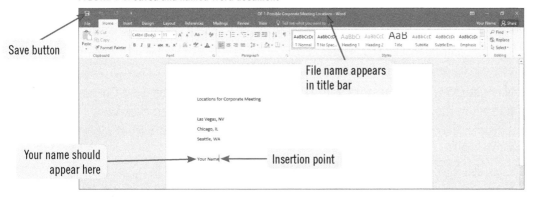

Address bar; your location may differ

Navigation pane; your links and folders may differ

File name field; your computer may not display file extensions

Save as type list

FIGURE 1-8: Saved and named Word document

Save button

File name appears in title bar

Your name should appear here

Insertion point

Saving files to OneDrive

All Office programs include the capability to incorporate feedback—called **online collaboration**—across the Internet or a company network. Using **cloud computing** (work done in a virtual environment), you can store your work in the cloud. Using OneDrive, a file storage service from Microsoft, you and your colleagues can create and store documents in the cloud and make the documents available anywhere there is Internet access to whomever you choose. To use OneDrive, you need a Microsoft Account, which you obtain at onedrive.live.com. Pricing and storage plans vary based on the type of Microsoft account you have. When you are logged into your Microsoft account and you save a file in any of the Office apps, the first option in the Save As screen is your OneDrive. Double-click your OneDrive option, and the Save As dialog box opens displaying a location in the address bar unique to your OneDrive account. Type a name in the File name text box, then click Save and your file is saved to your OneDrive. To sync your files with OneDrive, you'll need to download and install the OneDrive for Windows app. Then, when you open Explorer, you'll notice a new folder called OneDrive has been added to your folder. In this folder is a sub-folder called Documents. This means if your Internet connection fails, you can work on your files offline.

Office 2016

Open a File and Save It with a New Name

Learning
Outcomes
• Open an existing file
• Save a file with a new name

In many cases as you work in Office, you need to use an existing file. It might be a file you or a coworker created earlier as a work in progress, or it could be a complete document that you want to use as the basis for another. For example, you might want to create a budget for this year using the budget you created last year; instead of typing in all the categories and information from scratch, you could open last year's budget, save it with a new name, and just make changes to update it for the current year. By opening the existing file and saving it with the Save As command, you create a duplicate that you can modify to suit your needs, while the original file remains intact. **CASE** *Use Excel to open an existing workbook file, and save it with a new name so the original remains unchanged.*

STEPS

1. **Click the Start button ⊞ on the Windows taskbar, type** exc, **click** Excel 2016, **click** Open Other Workbooks, This PC, **then click** Browse

   The Open dialog box opens, where you can navigate to any drive or folder accessible to your computer to locate a file.

2. **In the Open dialog box, navigate to the location where you store your Data Files**

   The files available in the current folder are listed, as shown in **FIGURE 1-9**. This folder displays one file.

3. **Click** OF 1-1.xlsx, **then click** Open

   The dialog box closes, and the file opens in Excel. An Excel file is an electronic spreadsheet, so the new file displays a grid of rows and columns you can use to enter and organize data.

4. **Click the** File tab, **click** Save As **on the navigation bar, then click** Browse

   The Save As dialog box opens, and the current filename is highlighted in the File name text box. Using the Save As command enables you to create a copy of the current, existing file with a new name. This action preserves the original file and creates a new file that you can modify.

5. **Navigate to where you store your Data Files if necessary, type** OF 1-Corporate Meeting Budget **in the File name text box, as shown in FIGURE 1-10, then click** Save

   A copy of the existing workbook is created with the new name. The original file, OF 1-1.xlsx, closes automatically.

6. **Click cell** A18, **type your name, then press** [Enter], **as shown in FIGURE 1-11**

   In Excel, you enter data in cells, which are formed by the intersection of a row and a column. Cell A18 is at the intersection of column A and row 18. When you press [Enter], the cell pointer moves to cell A19.

7. **Click the** Save button 🖫 **on the Quick Access toolbar**

   Your name appears in the workbook, and your changes to the file are saved.

Exploring File Open options

You might have noticed that the Open button in the Open dialog box includes a list arrow to the right of the button. In a dialog box, if a button includes a list arrow you can click the button to invoke the command, or you can click the list arrow to see a list of related commands that you can apply to the currently selected file. The Open list arrow includes several related commands, including Open Read-Only and Open as Copy.

Clicking Open Read-Only opens a file that you can only save with a new name; you cannot make changes to the original file. Clicking Open as Copy creates and opens a copy of the selected file and inserts the word "Copy" in the file's title. Like the Save As command, these commands provide additional ways to use copies of existing files while ensuring that original files do not get changed by mistake.

FIGURE 1-9: Open dialog box

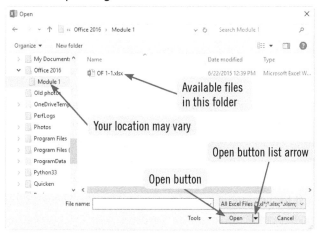

Available files in this folder

Your location may vary

Open button list arrow

Open button

FIGURE 1-10: Save As dialog box

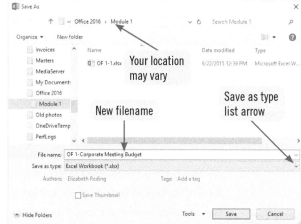

Your location may vary

New filename

Save as type list arrow

FIGURE 1-11: Your name added to the workbook

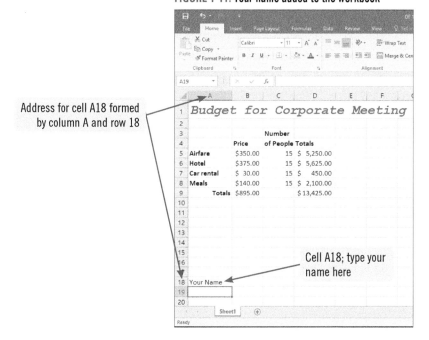

Address for cell A18 formed by column A and row 18

Cell A18; type your name here

Working in Compatibility Mode

Not everyone upgrades to the newest version of Office. As a general rule, new software versions are **backward compatible**, meaning that documents saved by an older version can be read by newer software. To open documents created in older Office versions, Office 2016 includes a feature called Compatibility Mode. When you use Office 2016 to open a file created in an earlier version of Office, "Compatibility Mode" appears in the title bar, letting you know the file was created in an earlier but usable version of the program. If you are working with someone who may not be using the newest version of the software, you can avoid possible incompatibility problems by saving your file in another, earlier format. To do this in an Office program, click the File tab, click Save As on the navigation bar, then click Browse. In the Save As dialog box, click the Save as type list arrow in the Save As dialog box, then click an option in the list. For example, if you're working in Excel, click Excel 97-2003 Workbook format in the Save as type list to save an Excel file so it can be opened in Excel 97 or Excel 2003.

View and Print Your Work

Learning
Outcomes
• Describe and
  change views in
  an app
• Print a document

Each Microsoft Office program lets you switch among various **views** of the document window to show more or fewer details or a different combination of elements that make it easier to complete certain tasks, such as formatting or reading text. Changing your view of a document does not affect the file in any way, it affects only the way it looks on screen. If your computer is connected to a printer or a print server, you can easily print any Office document using the Print button in the Print place in Backstage view. Printing can be as simple as **previewing** the document to see exactly what the printed version will look like and then clicking the Print button. Or, you can customize the print job by printing only selected pages. You can also use the Share place in Backstage view or the Share button on the Ribbon (if available) to share a document, export to a different format, or save it to the cloud. **CASE** *Experiment with changing your view of a Word document, and then preview and print your work.*

STEPS

1. **Click the** Word program button ▥ **on the taskbar**
   Word becomes active, and the program window fills the screen.

2. **Click the** View tab **on the Ribbon**
   In most Office programs, the View tab on the Ribbon includes groups and commands for changing your view of the current document. You can also change views using the View buttons on the status bar.

3. **Click the** Read Mode button **in the Views group on the View tab**
   The view changes to Read Mode view, as shown in **FIGURE 1-12**. This view shows the document in an easy-to-read, distraction-free reading mode. Notice that the Ribbon is no longer visible on screen.

4. **Click the** Print Layout button ▤ **on the Status bar**
   You return to Print Layout view, the default view in Word.

5. **Click the** File tab, **then click** Print **on the navigation bar**
   The Print place opens. The preview pane on the right displays a preview of how your document will look when printed. Compare your screen to **FIGURE 1-13**. Options in the Settings section enable you to change margins, orientation, and related options before printing. To change a setting, click it, and then click a new setting. For instance, to change from Letter paper size to Legal, click Letter in the Settings section, then click Legal on the menu that opens. The document preview updates as you change the settings. You also can use the Settings section to change which pages to print. If your computer is connected to multiple printers, you can click the current printer in the Printer section, then click the one you want to use. The Print section contains the Print button and also enables you to select the number of copies of the document to print.

6. **If your school allows printing, click the** Print button **in the Print place (otherwise, click the** Back button ◔**)**
   If you chose to print, a copy of the document prints, and Backstage view closes.

QUICK TIP

To minimize the display of the buttons and commands on tabs, click the Collapse the Ribbon button ⌃ on the lower-right end of the Ribbon.

QUICK TIP

You can add the Quick Print button 🖫 to the Quick Access toolbar by clicking the Customize Quick Access Toolbar button, then clicking Quick Print. The Quick Print button prints one copy of your document using the default settings.

Customizing the Quick Access toolbar

You can customize the Quick Access toolbar to display your favorite commands. To do so, click the Customize Quick Access Toolbar button ▾ in the title bar, then click the command you want to add. If you don't see the command in the list, click More Commands to open the Quick Access Toolbar tab of the current program's Options dialog box. In the Options dialog box, use the Choose commands from list to choose a category, click the desired command in the list on the left, click Add to add it to the Quick Access toolbar, then click OK. To remove a button from the toolbar, click the name in the list on the right in the Options dialog box, then click Remove. To add a command to the Quick Access toolbar as you work, simply right-click the button on the Ribbon, then click Add to Quick Access Toolbar on the shortcut menu. To move the Quick Access toolbar below the Ribbon, click the Customize Quick Access Toolbar button, and then click Show Below the Ribbon.

FIGURE 1-12: Read Mode view

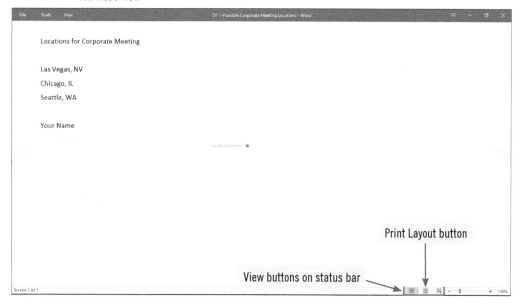

Print Layout button

View buttons on status bar

FIGURE 1-13: Print settings on the File tab

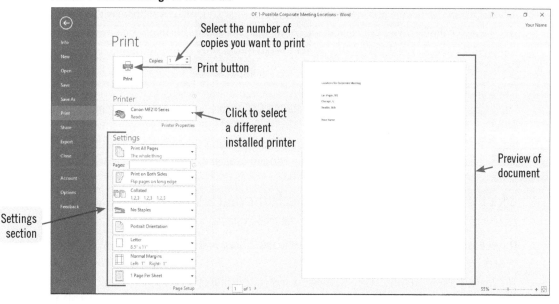

Select the number of copies you want to print

Print button

Click to select a different installed printer

Preview of document

Settings section

Creating a screen capture

A **screen capture** is a digital image of your screen, as if you took a picture of it with a camera. For instance, you might want to take a screen capture if an error message occurs and you want a Technical Support person to see exactly what's on the screen. You can create a screen capture using the Snipping Tool, an accessory designed to capture whole screens or portions of screens. To open the Snipping Tool, click the Start button on the Windows taskbar, type "sni", then click the Snipping Tool when it appears in the left panel. On the Snipping Tool toolbar, click New, then drag the pointer on the screen to select the area of the screen you want to capture. When you release the mouse button, the screen capture opens in the Snipping Tool window, and you can save, copy, or send it in an email. In Word, Excel, and PowerPoint 2016, you can capture screens or portions of screens and insert them in the current document using the Screenshot button in the Illustrations group on the Insert tab. Alternatively, you can create a screen capture by pressing [PrtScn]. (Keyboards differ, but you may find the [PrtScn] button in or near your keyboard's function keys.) Pressing this key places a digital image of your screen in the Windows temporary storage area known as the **Clipboard**. Open the document where you want the screen capture to appear, click the Home tab on the Ribbon (if necessary), then click the Paste button in the Clipboard group on the Home tab. The screen capture is pasted into the document.

Get Help, Close a File, and Exit an App

Learning
Outcomes
• Display a
  ScreenTip
• Use Help
• Close a file
• Exit an app

You can get comprehensive help at any time by pressing [F1] in an Office app or clicking the Help button on the title bar. You can also get help in the form of a ScreenTip by pointing to almost any icon in the program window. When you're finished working in an Office document, you have a few choices for ending your work session. You close a file by clicking the File tab, then clicking Close; you exit a program by clicking the Close button on the title bar. Closing a file leaves a program running, while exiting a program closes all the open files in that program as well as the program itself. In all cases, Office reminds you if you try to close a file or exit a program and your document contains unsaved changes. **CASE** *Explore the Help system in Microsoft Office, and then close your documents and exit any open programs.*

STEPS

1. **Point to the Zoom button in the Zoom group on the View tab of the Ribbon**
   A ScreenTip appears that describes how the Zoom button works and explains where to find other zoom controls.

   QUICK TIP
   You can also open Help (in any of the Office apps) by pressing [F1].

2. **Click the Tell me box above the Ribbon, then type Choose a template**
   As you type in the Tell me box, a Smart list anticipates what you might want help with. If you see the task you want to complete, you can click it and Word will take you to the dialog box or options you need to complete the task. If you don't see the answer to your query, you can use the bottom two options to search the database.

   QUICK TIP
   If you are not connected to the Internet, the Help window displays on the Help content available on your computer.

3. **Click Get Help on "choose a template"**
   The Word Help window opens, as shown in **FIGURE 1-14**, displaying help results for choosing a template in Word. Each entry is a hyperlink you can click to open a list of topics. The Help window also includes a toolbar of useful Help commands such as printing and increasing the font size for easier readability, and a Search field. Office.com supplements the help content available on your computer with a wide variety of up-to-date topics, templates, and training.

4. **Click the Where do I find templates link in the results list Word Help window**
   The Word Help window changes, and a more detailed explanation appears below the topic.

   QUICK TIP
   You can print the entire current topic by clicking the Print button 🖨 on the Help toolbar, then clicking Print in the Print dialog box.

5. **If necessary, scroll down until the Download Microsoft Office templates topic fills the Word Help window**
   The topic is displayed in the Help window, as shown in **FIGURE 1-15**. The content in the window explains that you can create a wide variety of documents using a template (a pre-formatted document) and that you can get many templates free of charge.

6. **Click the Keep Help on Top button 📌 in the lower-right corner of the window**
   The Pin Help button rotates so the pin point is pointed towards the bottom of the screen: this allows you to read the Help window while you work on your document.

7. **Click the Word document window, notice the Help window remains visible**

8. **Click a blank area of the Help window, click 📌 to Unpin Help, click the Close button ☒ in the Help window, then click the Close button ☒ in the Word program window**
   Word closes, and the Excel program window is active.

9. **Click the Close button ☒ in the Excel program window, click the PowerPoint app button 📷 on the taskbar if necessary, then click the Close button ☒ to exit PowerPoint**
   Excel and PowerPoint both close.

FIGURE 1-14: **Word Help window**

FIGURE 1-15: **Create a document Help topic**

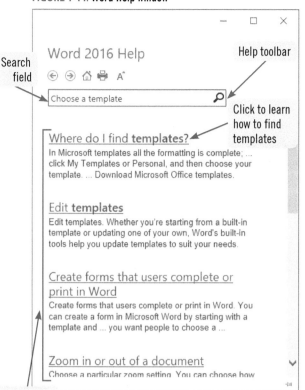

FIGURE 1-14: **Word Help window**

Search field

Help toolbar

Click to learn how to find templates

Help topics are updated frequently; your list may differ

FIGURE 1-15: **Create a document Help topic**

Print button

Drag scroll bar to read more

Keep Help on Top button

Using sharing features and co-authoring capabilities

If you are using Word, Excel, or PowerPoint, you can take advantage of the Share feature, which makes it easy to share your files that have been saved to OneDrive. When you click the Share button, you will be asked to invite others to share the file. To do this, type in the name or email addresses in the Invite people text box. When you invite others, you have the opportunity to give them different levels of permission. You might want some people to have read-only privileges; you might want others to be able to make edits. Also available in Word, Excel, and PowerPoint is real-time co-authoring capabilities for files stored on OneDrive. Once a file on OneDrive is opened and all the users have been given editing privileges, all the users can make edits simultaneously. On first use, each user will be prompted to automatically share their changes.

Recovering a document

Each Office program has a built-in recovery feature that allows you to open and save files that were open at the time of an interruption such as a power failure. When you restart the program(s) after an interruption, the Document Recovery task pane opens on the left side of your screen displaying both original and recovered versions of the files that were open. If you're not sure which file to open (original or recovered), it's usually better to open the recovered file because it will contain the latest information. You can, however, open and review all versions of the file that were recovered and save the best one. Each file listed in the Document Recovery task pane displays a list arrow with options that allow you to open the file, save it as is, delete it, or show repairs made to it during recovery.

Practice

Concepts Review

Label the elements of the program window shown in FIGURE 1-16.

FIGURE 1-16

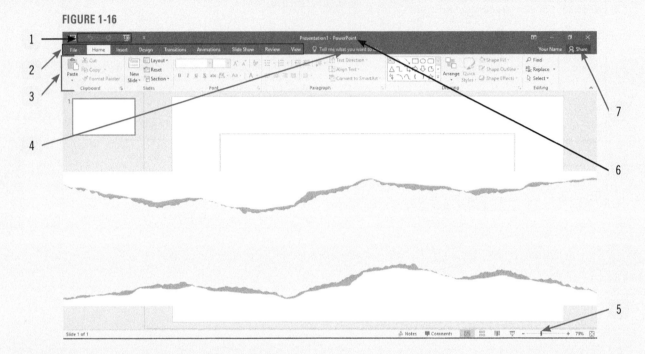

Match each project with the program for which it is best suited.

8. Microsoft PowerPoint
9. Microsoft Word
10. Microsoft Excel
11. Microsoft Access

a. Corporate convention budget with expense projections
b. Presentation for city council meeting
c. Business cover letter for a job application
d. Department store inventory

Independent Challenge 1

You just accepted an administrative position with a local independently owned insurance agent who has recently invested in computers and is now considering purchasing a subscription to Office 365. You have been asked to think of uses for the apps and you put your ideas in a Word document.

a. Start Word, create a new Blank document, then save the document as **OF 1-Microsoft Office Apps Uses** in the location where you store your Data Files.
b. Change the zoom factor to 120%, type **Microsoft Access**, press [Enter] twice, type **Microsoft Excel**, press [Enter] twice, type **Microsoft PowerPoint**, press [Enter] twice, type **Microsoft Word**, press [Enter] twice, then type your name.
c. Click the line beneath each program name, type at least two tasks you can perform using that program (each separated by a comma), then press [Enter].
d. Save the document, then submit your work to your instructor as directed.
e. Exit Word.

Creating Documents with Word 2016

CASE You have been hired to work in the Marketing Department at Reason2Go (R2G), a company that provides adventurous travelers with meaningful project options for giving back to the global community. Shortly after reporting to your new office, Mary Watson, the vice president of sales and marketing, asks you to use Word to create a memo to the marketing staff and a letter to one of the project hosts.

Module Objectives

After completing this module, you will be able to:

- Understand word processing software
- Explore the Word window
- Start a document
- Save a document
- Select text
- Format text using the Mini toolbar and the Ribbon
- Use a document template
- Navigate a document

Files You Will Need

WD 1-1.docx

Learning
Outcomes
• Identify the
  features of Word
• State the benefits
  of using a word
  processing
  program

Understand Word Processing Software

A **word processing program** is a software program that includes tools for entering, editing, and formatting text and graphics. Microsoft Word is a powerful word processing program that allows you to create and enhance a wide range of documents quickly and easily. FIGURE 1-1 shows the first page of a report created using Word and illustrates some of the Word features you can use to enhance your documents. The electronic files you create using Word are called **documents**. One of the benefits of using Word is that document files can be stored on a hard disk, flash drive, or other physical storage device, or to OneDrive or another Cloud storage place, making them easy to transport, share, and revise. **CASE** *Before beginning your memo to the marketing staff, you explore the editing and formatting features available in Word.*

DETAILS

You can use Word to accomplish the following tasks:

• **Type and edit text**

The Word editing tools make it simple to insert and delete text in a document. You can add text to the middle of an existing paragraph, replace text with other text, undo an editing change, and correct typing, spelling, and grammatical errors with ease.

• **Copy and move text from one location to another**

Using the more advanced editing features of Word, you can copy or move text from one location and insert it in a different location in a document. You also can copy and move text between documents. This means you don't have to retype text that is already entered in a document.

• **Format text and paragraphs with fonts, colors, and other elements**

The sophisticated formatting tools in Word allow you to make the text in your documents come alive. You can change the size, style, and color of text, add lines and shading to paragraphs, and enhance lists with bullets and numbers. Creatively formatting text helps to highlight important ideas in your documents.

• **Format and design pages**

The page-formatting features in Word give you power to design attractive newsletters, create powerful résumés, and produce documents such as research papers, business cards, brochures, and reports. You can change paper size, organize text in columns, and control the layout of text and graphics on each page of a document. For quick results, Word includes preformatted cover pages, pull quotes, and headers and footers, as well as galleries of coordinated text, table, and graphic styles. If you are writing a research paper, Word makes it easy to manage reference sources and create footnotes, endnotes, and bibliographies.

• **Enhance documents with tables, charts, graphics, screenshots, and videos**

Using the powerful graphics tools in Word, you can spice up your documents with pictures, videos, photographs, screenshots, lines, preset quick shapes, and diagrams. You also can illustrate your documents with tables and charts to help convey your message in a visually interesting way.

• **Use Mail Merge to create form letters and mailing labels**

The Word Mail Merge feature allows you to send personalized form letters to many different people. You can also use Mail Merge to create mailing labels, directories, e-mail messages, and other types of documents.

• **Share documents securely**

The security features in Word make it quick and easy to remove comments, tracked changes, and unwanted personal information from your files before you share them with others. You can also add a password or a digital signature to a document and convert a file to a format suitable for publishing on the web.

FIGURE 1-1: A report created using Word

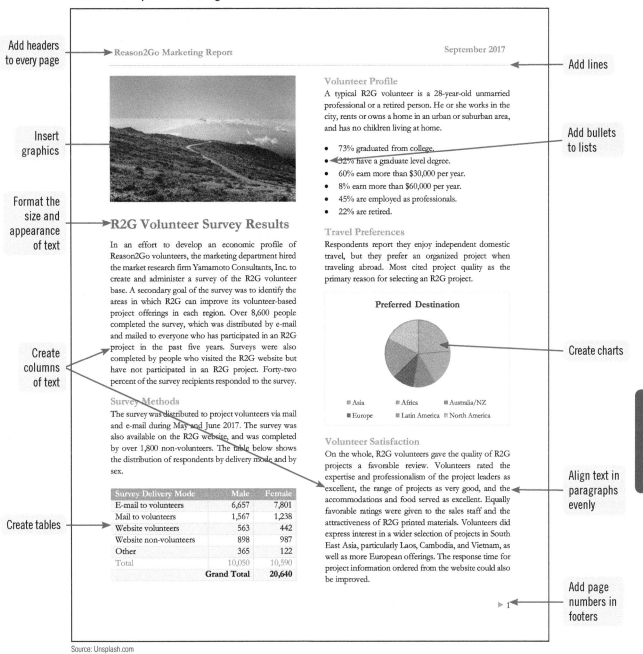

Add headers to every page →

Insert graphics →

Format the size and appearance of text →

Create columns of text →

Create tables →

Add lines ←

Add bullets to lists ←

Create charts ←

Align text in paragraphs evenly ←

Add page numbers in footers ←

Reason2Go Marketing Report — September 2017

Volunteer Profile

A typical R2G volunteer is a 28-year-old unmarried professional or a retired person. He or she works in the city, rents or owns a home in an urban or suburban area, and has no children living at home.

- 73% graduated from college.
- 52% have a graduate level degree.
- 60% earn more than $30,000 per year.
- 8% earn more than $60,000 per year.
- 45% are employed as professionals.
- 22% are retired.

R2G Volunteer Survey Results

In an effort to develop an economic profile of Reason2Go volunteers, the marketing department hired the market research firm Yamamoto Consultants, Inc. to create and administer a survey of the R2G volunteer base. A secondary goal of the survey was to identify the areas in which R2G can improve its volunteer-based project offerings in each region. Over 8,600 people completed the survey, which was distributed by e-mail and mailed to everyone who has participated in an R2G project in the past five years. Surveys were also completed by people who visited the R2G website but have not participated in an R2G project. Forty-two percent of the survey recipients responded to the survey.

Survey Methods

The survey was distributed to project volunteers via mail and e-mail during May and June 2017. The survey was also available on the R2G website, and was completed by over 1,800 non-volunteers. The table below shows the distribution of respondents by delivery mode and by sex.

Survey Delivery Mode	Male	Female
E-mail to volunteers	6,657	7,801
Mail to volunteers	1,567	1,238
Website volunteers	563	442
Website non-volunteers	898	987
Other	365	122
Total	10,050	10,590
	Grand Total	20,640

Travel Preferences

Respondents report they enjoy independent domestic travel, but they prefer an organized project when traveling abroad. Most cited project quality as the primary reason for selecting an R2G project.

Preferred Destination

- Asia
- Africa
- Australia/NZ
- Europe
- Latin America
- North America

Volunteer Satisfaction

On the whole, R2G volunteers gave the quality of R2G projects a favorable review. Volunteers rated the expertise and professionalism of the project leaders as excellent, the range of projects as very good, and the accommodations and food served as excellent. Equally favorable ratings were given to the sales staff and the attractiveness of R2G printed materials. Volunteers did express interest in a wider selection of projects in South East Asia, particularly Laos, Cambodia, and Vietnam, as well as more European offerings. The response time for project information ordered from the website could also be improved.

1

Planning a document

Before you create a new document, it's a good idea to spend time planning it. Identify the message you want to convey, the audience for your document, and the elements, such as tables or charts, you want to include. You should also think about the tone and look of your document—are you writing a business letter, which should be written in a pleasant, but serious, tone and have a formal appearance, or are you creating a flyer that must be colorful, eye-catching, and fun to read? The purpose and audience for your document determine the appropriate design. Planning the layout and design of a document involves deciding how to organize the text, selecting the fonts to use, identifying the graphics to include, and selecting the formatting elements that will enhance the message and appeal of the document. For longer documents, such as newsletters, it can be useful to sketch the layout and design of each page before you begin.

Explore the Word Window

When you start Word, the Word start screen opens. It includes a list of recently opened documents and a gallery of templates for creating a new document. **CASE** ▶ *You open a blank document and examine the elements of the Word program window.*

STEPS

1. **Start** Word, **then click** Blank document

   A blank document opens in the **Word program window**, as shown in FIGURE 1-2. The blinking vertical line in the document window is the **insertion point**. It indicates where text appears as you type.

2. **Move the mouse pointer around the Word program window**

   The mouse pointer changes shape depending on where it is in the Word program window. You use pointers to move the insertion point or to select text to edit. TABLE 1-1 describes common pointers in Word.

3. **Place the mouse pointer over a button on the Ribbon**

   When you place the mouse pointer over a button or some other elements of the Word program window, a ScreenTip appears. A **ScreenTip** is a label that identifies the name of the button or feature, briefly describes its function, conveys any keyboard shortcut for the command, and includes a link to associated help topics, if any.

DETAILS

Using FIGURE 1-2 **as a guide, find the elements described below in your program window:**

• The **title bar** displays the name of the document and the name of the program. Until you give a new document a different name, its temporary name is Document1. The left side of the title bar contains the **Quick Access toolbar**, which includes buttons for saving a document and for undoing, redoing, and repeating a change. The right side of the title bar contains the **Ribbon Display Options button**, which you use to hide or show the Ribbon and tabs, the resizing buttons, and the program Close button.

• The **File tab** provides access to **Backstage view** where you manage files and the information about them. Backstage view includes commands related to working with documents, such as opening, printing, and saving a document. The File tab also provides access to your account and to the Word Options dialog box, which is used to customize the way you use Word.

• The **Ribbon** contains the Word tabs. Each **tab** on the Ribbon includes buttons for commands related to editing and formatting documents. The commands are organized in **groups**. For example, the Home tab includes the Clipboard, Font, Paragraph, Styles, and Editing groups. The Ribbon also includes the **Tell Me box**, which you can use to find a command or access the Word Help system, and the **Share button**, which you can use to save a document to the Cloud.

• The **document window** displays the current document. You enter text and format your document in the document window.

• The rulers appear in the document window in Print Layout view. The **horizontal ruler** displays left and right document margins as well as the tab settings and paragraph indents, if any, for the paragraph in which the insertion point is located. The **vertical ruler** displays the top and bottom document margins.

• The **vertical** and **horizontal scroll bars** are used to display different parts of the document in the document window. The scroll bars include **scroll boxes** and **scroll arrows**, which you use to scroll.

• The **status bar** displays the page number of the current page, the total number of pages and words in the document, and the status of spelling and grammar checking. It also includes the view buttons, the Zoom slider, and the Zoom level button. You can customize the status bar to display other information.

• The **view buttons** on the status bar allow you to display the document in Read Mode, Print Layout, or Web Layout view. The **Zoom slider** and the **Zoom level button** provide quick ways to enlarge and decrease the size of the document in the document window, making it easy to zoom in on a detail of a document or to view the layout of the document as a whole.

Creating Documents with Word 2016

FIGURE 1-2: Elements of the Word program window

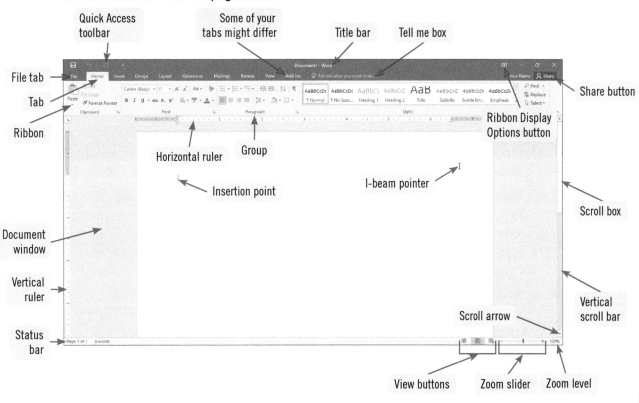

TABLE 1-1: Common mouse pointers in Word

name	pointer	use to
I-beam pointer	I	Move the insertion point in a document or to select text
Click and Type pointers, including left-align and center-align	I ≡ I	Move the insertion point to a blank area of a document in Print Layout or Web Layout view; double-clicking with a Click and Type pointer automatically applies the paragraph formatting (alignment and indentation) required to position text or a graphic at that location in the document
Selection pointer	⊳	Click a button or other element of the Word program window; appears when you point to elements of the Word program window
Right-pointing arrow pointer	⊲	Select a line or lines of text; appears when you point to the left edge of a line of text in the document window
Hand pointer	⊐	Open a hyperlink; appears when you point to a hyperlink in a task pane or when you press [Ctrl] and point to a hyperlink in a document
Hide white space pointer	⊥⊤	Hide the white space in the top and bottom margins of a document in Print Layout view
Show white space pointer	⊤⊥	Show the white space in the top and bottom margins of a document in Print Layout view

Start a Document

You begin a new document by simply typing text in a blank document in the document window. Word uses **word wrap**, a feature that automatically moves the insertion point to the next line of the document as you type. You only press [Enter] when you want to start a new paragraph or insert a blank line. **CASE** ▸ *You type a quick memo to the marketing staff.*

---

1. Type Reason2Go, **then press** [Enter] **twice**

Each time you press [Enter] the insertion point moves to the start of the next line.

2. Type TO:, **then press** [Tab] **twice**

Pressing [Tab] moves the insertion point several spaces to the right. You can use the [Tab] key to align the text in a memo header or to indent the first line of a paragraph.

3. Type R2G Managers, **then press** [Enter]

The insertion point moves to the start of the next line.

4. Type: FROM: [Tab] [Tab] Mary Watson [Enter]

DATE: [Tab] [Tab] March 13, 2017 [Enter]

RE: [Tab] [Tab] Marketing Meeting [Enter] [Enter]

Red or blue wavy lines may appear under the words you typed, indicating a possible spelling or grammar error. Spelling and grammar checking is one of the many automatic features you will encounter as you type. **TABLE 1-2** describes several of these automatic features. You can correct any typing errors you make later.

5. Type The next marketing staff meeting will be held on the 17th of March at 2 p.m. in the conference room on the ground floor., **then press** [Spacebar]

As you type, notice that the insertion point moves automatically to the next line of the document. You also might notice that Word automatically changed "17th" to "17th" in the memo. This feature is called **AutoCorrect**. AutoCorrect automatically makes typographical adjustments and detects and adjusts typing errors, certain misspelled words (such as "taht" for "that"), and incorrect capitalization as you type.

6. Type Heading the agenda will be the launch of our new Sea Turtle Conservation Project, a rewarding opportunity to supervise hatcheries, count and release baby turtles, and patrol the nighttime shores of Costa Rica. The project is scheduled for September 2017.

When you type the first few characters of "September," the Word AutoComplete feature displays the complete word in a ScreenTip. **AutoComplete** suggests text to insert quickly into your documents. You can ignore AutoComplete for now. Your memo should resemble **FIGURE 1-3**.

7. Press [Enter], **then type** Sam Roiphe is in Tamarindo hammering out the details. A preliminary draft of the project brochure is attached. Bring your creative ideas to the meeting.

When you press [Enter] and type the new paragraph, notice that Word adds more space between the paragraphs than it does between the lines in each paragraph. This is part of the default style for paragraphs in Word, called the **Normal style**.

8. Position the Ⅰ **pointer after** for **(but before the space) in the last sentence of the first paragraph, then click to move the insertion point after "for"**

9. Press [Backspace] **three times, then type** to begin in

Pressing [Backspace] removes the character before the insertion point.

10. Move the insertion point before staff **in the first sentence, then press** [Delete] **six times to remove the word "staff" and the space after it**

Pressing [Delete] removes the character after the insertion point. **FIGURE 1-4** shows the revised memo.

FIGURE 1-3: Memo text in the document window

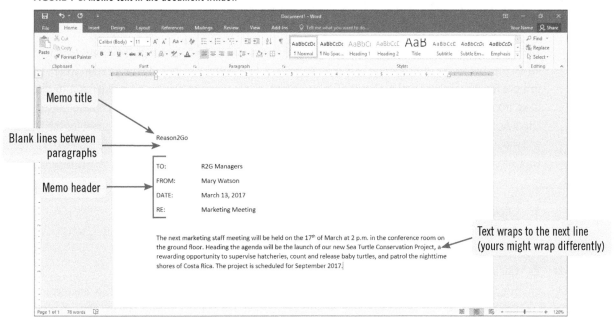

Memo title

Blank lines between paragraphs

Memo header

Text wraps to the next line (yours might wrap differently)

FIGURE 1-4: Edited memo text

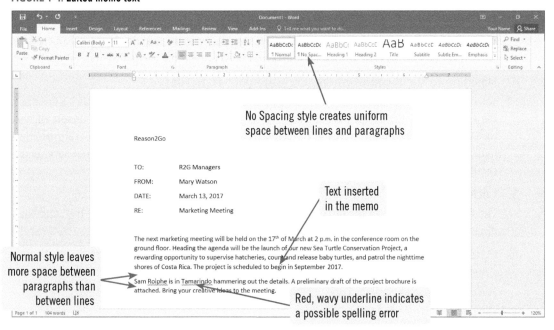

No Spacing style creates uniform space between lines and paragraphs

Text inserted in the memo

Normal style leaves more space between paragraphs than between lines

Red, wavy underline indicates a possible spelling error

TABLE 1-2: Automatic features that appear as you type in Word

feature	what appears	to use
AutoComplete	A ScreenTip suggesting text to insert appears as you type	Press [Enter] to insert the text suggested by the ScreenTip; continue typing to reject the suggestion
AutoCorrect	A small blue box appears when you place the pointer over text corrected by AutoCorrect; an AutoCorrect Options button appears when you point to the blue box	Word automatically corrects typos, minor spelling errors, and capitalization, and adds typographical symbols (such as © and ™) as you type; to reverse an AutoCorrect adjustment, click the AutoCorrect Options list arrow, then click the option that will undo the action
Spelling and Grammar	A red wavy line under a word indicates a possible misspelling or a repeated word; a blue wavy line under text indicates a possible grammar error	Right-click red- or blue-underlined text to display a shortcut menu of correction options; click a correction option to accept it and remove the wavy underline

Save a Document

Learning
Outcomes
• Save a file using
a descriptive
filename
• Use the Save As
dialog box

To store a document permanently so you can open it and edit it at another time, you must save it as a **file**. When you **save** a document you give it a name, called a **filename**, and indicate the location where you want to store the file. Files created in Word 2016 are automatically assigned the .docx file extension to distinguish them from files created in other software programs. You can save a document using the Save button on the Quick Access toolbar or the Save command on the File tab. Once you have saved a document for the first time, you should save it again every few minutes and always before printing so that the saved file is updated to reflect your latest changes. **CASE** *You save your memo using a descriptive filename and the default file extension.*

STEPS

1. **Click the** Save button 🖫 **on the Quick Access toolbar**

   The first time you save a document, the Save As screen opens. The screen displays all the places you can save a file to, including OneDrive, your PC, or a different location.

TROUBLE
If you don't see the
extension .docx as
part of the filename,
the setting in
Windows to display
file extensions is
not active.

2. **Click** Browse **in the Save As screen**

   The Save As dialog box opens, similar to **FIGURE 1-5**. The default filename, Reason2Go, appears in the File name text box. The default filename is based on the first few words of the document. The default file type, Word Document, appears in the Save as type list box. **TABLE 1-3** describes the functions of some of the buttons in the Save As dialog box.

3. **Type** WD 1-Sea Turtle Memo **in the File name text box**

   The new filename replaces the default filename. Giving your documents brief descriptive filenames makes it easier to locate and organize them later. You do not need to type .docx when you type a new filename.

4. **Navigate to the location where you store your Data Files**

   You can navigate to a different drive or folder in several ways. For example, you can click a drive or folder in the Address bar or the navigation pane to go directly to that location. You can also double-click a drive or folder in the folder window to change the active location. When you are finished navigating to the drive or folder where you store your Data Files, that location appears in the Address bar. Your Save As dialog box should resemble **FIGURE 1-6**.

5. **Click** Save

   The document is saved to the drive and folder you specified in the Save As dialog box, and the title bar displays the new filename, WD 1-Sea Turtles Memo.docx.

6. **Place the insertion point before** conference **in the first sentence, type** large, **then press** [Spacebar]

   You can continue to work on a document after you have saved it with a new filename.

7. **Click** 🖫

   Your change to the memo is saved. After you save a document for the first time, you must continue to save the changes you make to the document. You also can press [Ctrl][S] to save a document.

FIGURE 1-5: Save As dialog box

Active folder or
drive (yours might
differ)

Folders and files
in the active folder
or drive (yours
might differ)

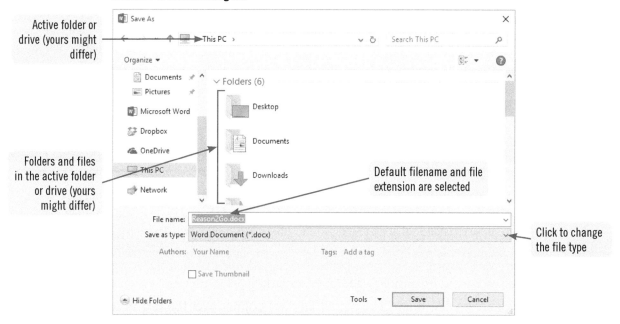

Default filename and file
extension are selected

Click to change
the file type

FIGURE 1-6: File to be saved to the Mod 1 folder

Click to create a new
folder in the active
folder or drive

Save location
(yours might differ)

New filename

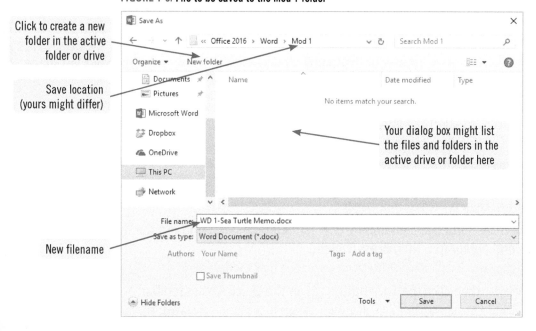

Your dialog box might list
the files and folders in the
active drive or folder here

TABLE 1-3: Save As dialog box buttons

button	use to
Back	Navigate back to the last location shown in the Address bar
Forward	Navigate to the location that was previously shown in the Address bar
Up to	Navigate to the location above the current location in the folder hierarchy
Organize	Open a menu of commands related to organizing the selected file or folder, including Cut, Copy, Delete, Rename, and Properties
New folder	Create a new folder in the current folder or drive
Change your view	Change the way folder and file information is shown in the folder window in the Save As dialog box; click the Change your view button to toggle between views, or click the list arrow to open a menu of view options

Select Text

Learning Outcomes
- Select text using the mouse
- Use formatting marks

Before deleting, editing, or formatting text, you must **select** the text. Selecting text involves clicking and dragging the I-beam pointer across the text to highlight it. You also can click in the margin to the left of text with the ⌐ pointer to select whole lines or paragraphs. TABLE 1-4 describes the many ways to select text. **CASE** *You revise the memo by selecting text and replacing it with new text.*

STEPS

1. **Click the** Show/Hide ¶ **button** ¶ **in the Paragraph group**

   Formatting marks appear in the document window. **Formatting marks** are special characters that appear on your screen but do not print. Common formatting marks include the paragraph symbol (¶), which shows the end of a paragraph—wherever you press [Enter]; the dot symbol (·), which represents a space—wherever you press [Spacebar]; and the arrow symbol (↦), which shows the location of a tab stop—wherever you press [Tab]. Working with formatting marks turned on can help you to select, edit, and format text with precision.

QUICK TIP
You deselect text by clicking anywhere in the document window.

2. **Click before** R2G Managers, **then drag the** ⌐ **pointer over the text to select it**

   The words are selected, as shown in FIGURE 1-7. For now, you can ignore the floating toolbar that appears over text when you first select it.

3. **Type** Marketing Staff

   The text you type replaces the selected text.

4. **Double-click** Mary, **type your first name, double-click** Watson, **then type your last name**

   Double-clicking a word selects the entire word.

TROUBLE
If you delete text by mistake, immediately click the Undo button on the Quick Access toolbar to restore the deleted text to the document.

5. **Place the pointer in the margin to the left of the RE: line so that the pointer changes to** ⌐, **click to select the line, then type** RE: [Tab] [Tab] Launch of new Sea Turtle Conservation Project

   Clicking to the left of a line of text with the ⌐ pointer selects the entire line.

6. **Select** supervise **in the third line of the first paragraph, type** build, **select** nighttime shores, **then type** moon-lit beaches

7. **Select the sentence** Sam Roiphe is in Tamarindo hammering out the details. **in the second paragraph, then press** [Delete]

   Selecting text and pressing [Delete] removes the text from the document.

QUICK TIP
Always save before and after editing text.

8. **Click** ¶, **then click the** Save **button** 🖫 **on the Quick Access toolbar**

   Formatting marks are turned off, and your changes to the memo are saved. The Show/Hide ¶ button is a **toggle button**, which means you can use it to turn formatting marks on and off. The edited memo is shown in FIGURE 1-8.

FIGURE 1-7: Text selected in the memo

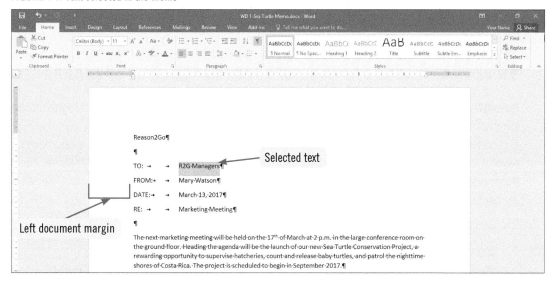

FIGURE 1-8: Edited memo with replacement text

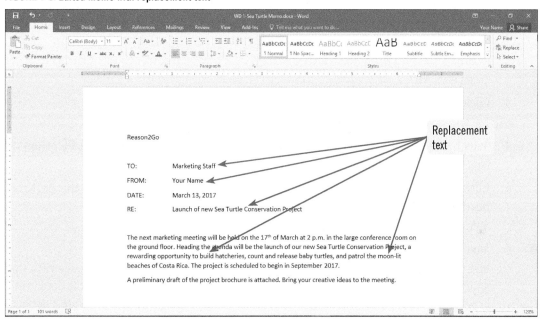

Word 2016

TABLE 1-4: Methods for selecting text

to select	use the pointer to
Any amount of text	Drag over the text
A word	Double-click the word
A line of text	Move the pointer to the left of the line, then click
A sentence	Press and hold [Ctrl], then click the sentence
A paragraph	Triple-click the paragraph or double-click with the pointer to the left of the paragraph
A large block of text	Click at the beginning of the selection, press and hold [Shift], then click at the end of the selection
Multiple nonconsecutive selections	Select the first selection, then press and hold [Ctrl] as you select each additional selection
An entire document	Triple-click with the pointer to the left of any text; press [Ctrl][A]; or click the Select button in the Editing group on the Home tab, and then click Select All

Learning
Outcomes
• Apply bold to text
• Increase the font
  size of text
• Print a document

Format Text Using the Mini Toolbar and the Ribbon

Formatting text is a fast and fun way to spruce up the appearance of a document and highlight important information. You can easily change the font, color, size, style, and other attributes of text by selecting the text and clicking a command on the Home tab. The **Mini toolbar**, which appears above text when you first select it, also includes commonly used text and paragraph formatting commands. **CASE** *You enhance the appearance of the memo by formatting the text using the Mini toolbar. When you are finished, you preview the memo for errors and then print it.*

STEPS

1. **Select** Reason2Go

   The Mini toolbar appears over the selected text, as shown in FIGURE 1-9. You click a formatting option on the Mini toolbar to apply it to the selected text. TABLE 1-5 describes the function of the buttons on the Mini toolbar. The buttons on the Mini toolbar are also available on the Ribbon.

2. **Click the** Increase Font Size button A˘ **on the Mini toolbar six times, then click the** Bold button B **on the Mini toolbar**

   Each time you click the Increase Font Size button the selected text is enlarged. Applying bold to the text makes it thicker.

3. **Click the** Center button **in the Paragraph group on the Home tab**

   The selected text is centered between the left and right margins.

4. **Select** TO:, **click** B, **select** FROM:, **click** B, **select** DATE:, **click** B, **select** RE:, **then click** B

   Bold is applied to the memo header labels.

5. **Click the blank line between the RE: line and the body text, then click the** Bottom Border button ⊞ **in the Paragraph group**

   A single-line border is added between the heading and the body text in the memo.

6. **Save the document, click the** File tab, **then click** Print

   Information related to printing the document appears on the Print screen in Backstage view. Options for printing the document appear on the left side of the Print screen and a preview of the document as it will look when printed appears on the right side, as shown in FIGURE 1-10. Before you print a document, it's a good habit to examine it closely so you can identify and correct any problems.

7. **Click the** Zoom In button ➕ **on the status bar five times, then proofread your document carefully for errors**

   The document is enlarged in print preview. If you notice errors in your document, you need to correct them before you print. To do this, press [Esc] or click the Back button in Backstage view, correct any mistakes, save your changes, click the File tab, and then click the Print command again to be ready to print the document.

8. **Click the** Print button **on the Print screen**

   A copy of the memo prints using the default print settings. To change the current printer, change the number of copies to print, select what pages of a document to print, or modify another print setting, you simply change the appropriate setting on the Print screen before clicking the Print button.

9. **Click the** File tab, **then click** Close

   The document closes, but the Word program window remains open.

FIGURE 1-9: Mini toolbar

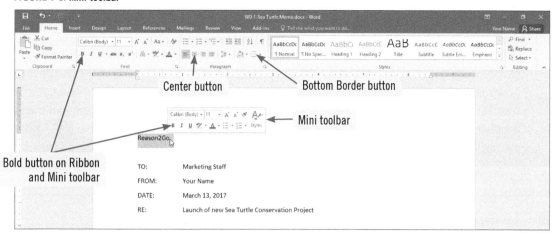

Center button

Bottom Border button

Mini toolbar

Bold button on Ribbon and Mini toolbar

FIGURE 1-10: Preview of the completed memo

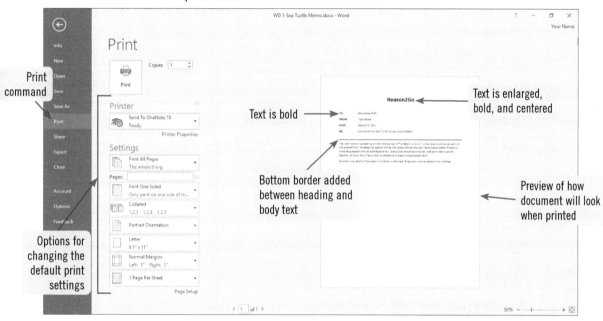

Print command

Text is bold

Text is enlarged, bold, and centered

Bottom border added between heading and body text

Preview of how document will look when printed

Options for changing the default print settings

TABLE 1-5: Buttons on the Mini toolbar

button	use to	button	use to
Calibri (Body) ▾	Change the font of text	**B**	Apply bold to text
11 ▾	Change the font size of text	*I*	Apply italic to text
A˄	Make text larger	U̲	Apply an underline to text
A˅	Make text smaller	aby ▾	Apply colored highlighting to text
✦	Copy the formats applied to selected text to other text	A ▾	Change the color of text
A̷	Apply a style to text	▤ ▾	Apply bullets to paragraphs
		▤ ▾	Apply numbering to paragraphs

Use a Document Template

Word includes many templates that you can use to create letters, reports, brochures, calendars, and other professionally designed documents quickly. A **template** is a formatted document that contains place-holder text and graphics, which you replace with your own text and graphics. To create a document that is based on a template, you use the New command on the File tab in Backstage view, and then select a template to use. You can then customize the document and save it with a new filename. **CASE** ▶ *You use a template to create a cover letter for a contract you will send to the Rainforest Hotel in Tamarindo.*

STEPS

1. **Click the** File tab, **then click** New

   The New screen opens in Backstage view, as shown in **FIGURE 1-11**. You can select a template from the gallery shown in this window, or use the search box and links in the Suggested Searches section to find other templates.

2. **Scroll down until you find the** Cover Letter (blue) **thumbnail on the New screen, click it, preview the template in the preview window that opens, then click** Create

   The Cover Letter (blue) template opens as a new document in the document window. It contains placeholder text, which you can replace with your own information. Your name might appear at the top of the document. Don't be concerned if it does not. When a document is created using this template, Word automatically enters the username from the Word Options dialog box at the top of the document and in the signature block.

3. **Click** [Date] **in the document**

   The placeholder text is selected and appears inside a content control. A **content control** is an interactive object that you use to customize a document with your own information. A content control might include placeholder text, a drop-down list of choices, or a calendar.

4. **Click the** [Date] list arrow

   A calendar opens below the content control. You use the calendar to select the date you want to appear on your document—simply click a date on the calendar to enter that date in the document.

5. **Click the** Today button **on the calendar**

   The current date replaces the placeholder text.

6. **Click** [Recipient Name], **type** Ms. Yana Roy, **press** [Enter], **type** Manager, **press** [Enter], **type** Rainforest Lodge, **press** [Enter], **type** P.O. Box 4397, **press** [Enter], **then type** Tamarindo 50309, COSTA RICA

   You do not need to drag to select the placeholder text in a content control, you can simply click it. The text you type replaces the placeholder text.

7. **Click** [Recipient], **then type** Ms. Roy

   The text you type replaces the placeholder text in the greeting line.

8. **Click the** File tab, **click** Save As, **then save the document as** WD 1-Rainforest Letter **to the location where you store your Data Files**

   The document is saved with the filename WD 1-Rainforest Letter, as shown in **FIGURE 1-12**.

FIGURE 1-11: New screen in Backstage view

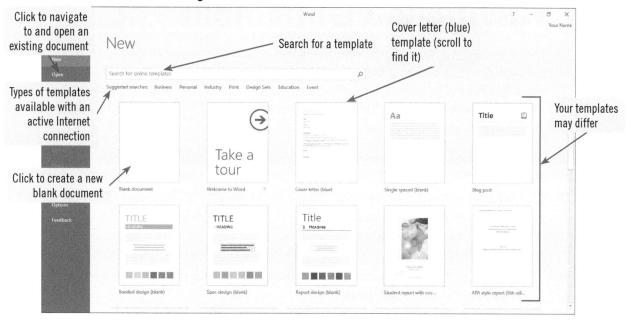

Click to navigate to and open an existing document

Types of templates available with an active Internet connection

Click to create a new blank document

Search for a template

Cover letter (blue) template (scroll to find it)

Your templates may differ

FIGURE 1-12: Document created using the Cover Letter (blue) template

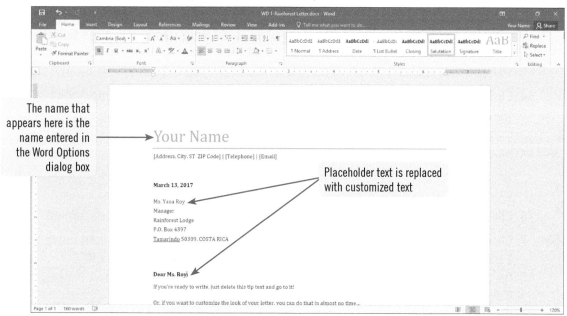

The name that appears here is the name entered in the Word Options dialog box

Placeholder text is replaced with customized text

Word 2016

Using the Undo, Redo, and Repeat commands

Word remembers the editing and formatting changes you make so that you can easily reverse or repeat them. You can reverse the last action you took by clicking the Undo button 🔄 on the Quick Access toolbar, or you can undo a series of actions by clicking the Undo list arrow 🔄 ▾ and selecting the action you want to reverse. When you undo an action using the Undo list arrow, you also undo all the actions above it in the list—that is, all actions that were performed after the action you selected. Similarly, you can keep the change you just reversed by using the Redo button ⤴

on the Quick Access toolbar. The Redo button appears only immediately after clicking the Undo button to undo a change.

If you want to repeat an action you just completed, you can use the Repeat button ⟳ on the Quick Access toolbar. For example, if you just typed "thank you," clicking ⟳ inserts "thank you" at the location of the insertion point. If you just applied bold, clicking ⟳ applies bold to the currently selected text. You also can repeat the last action you took by pressing [F4].

Navigate a Document

Learning Outcomes
- Remove a content control
- Zoom, scroll, and use Word views

The Zoom feature in Word lets you enlarge a document in the document window to get a close-up view of a detail or reduce the size of the document in the document window for an overview of the layout as a whole. You zoom in and out on a document using the tools in the Zoom group on the View tab or you can use the Zoom level buttons and Zoom slider on the status bar. **CASE** *You find it is helpful to zoom in and out on the document as you finalize the letter.*

STEPS

TROUBLE
If your name does not appear in the content control, replace the text that does.

1. **Click your name in the upper-left corner of the document, right-click the** Your Name **content control,** click Remove Content Control **on the menu that opens, select your name, then type** Reason2Go

   Removing the content control changes the text to static text that you can then replace with other text.

TROUBLE
If you do not see the vertical scroll box, move the pointer to the right side of the document window to display it.

2. **Drag the** vertical scroll box down **until the body of the letter and the signature block are visible in your document window**

   You **scroll** to display different parts of the document in the document window. You can also scroll by clicking the scroll arrows above and below the scroll bar, or by clicking the scroll bar.

3. **Select the** four paragraphs **of placeholder body text, type** Enclosed please find a copy of our contract for the Sea Turtle Conservation Project. We look forward to working with you., **then, if the name in the signature block is not your name, select the text in the content control and type your name**

   The text you type replaces the placeholder text, as shown in **FIGURE 1-13**.

4. **Click the** View tab, **then click the** Page Width button **in the Zoom group**

   The document is enlarged to the width of the document window. When you enlarge a document, the area where the insertion point is located appears in the document window.

QUICK TIP
You can also click the Zoom button in the Zoom group on the View tab to open the Zoom dialog box.

5. **Click the** Zoom level button 154% **on the status bar**

   The Zoom dialog box opens. You use the Zoom dialog box to select a zoom level for displaying the document in the document window.

6. **Click the** Whole page option button, **then click** OK **to view the entire document**

QUICK TIP
You can also move the Zoom slider by clicking a point on the Zoom slide, or by clicking the Zoom Out and Zoom In buttons.

7. **Click** Reason2Go **to move the insertion point to the top of the page, then move the Zoom slider to the right until the Zoom percentage is approximately 230%**

   Dragging the Zoom slider to the right enlarges the document in the document window. Dragging the zoom slider to the left allows you to see more of the page at a reduced size.

8. **Click the** [Address...] **content control, type** Travel, **click** [Telephone], **type** Volunteer, **click** [Email], **type** www.r2g.com, **then press** [Tab]

   You can replace placeholder text with information that is different from what is suggested in the content control.

9. **Click the** Read Mode button 📖 **on the status bar**

   The document appears in the document window in Read Mode view. Read Mode view hides the tabs and ribbon to make it easier to read documents on screen. Read Mode view is useful for reading long documents.

QUICK TIP
You can also click View on the menu bar, then click Edit Document to return to Print Layout view.

10. **Click the** Print Layout view button 📄 **on the status bar, click the** Zoom Out **button** ➖ **on the status bar until the zoom level is 100%, then save the document**

   The completed cover letter is displayed at 100% zoom level in Print Layout view, as shown in **FIGURE 1-14**.

11. **Submit the document to your instructor, close the file, then exit Word**

FIGURE 1-13: Replacement text and Zoom slider

Replace placeholder text with this text

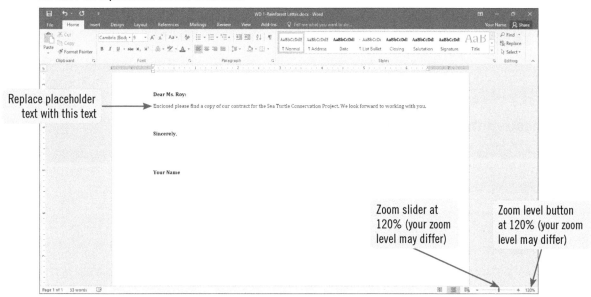

Zoom slider at 120% (your zoom level may differ)

Zoom level button at 120% (your zoom level may differ)

FIGURE 1-14: Completed letter

Using Word document views

Document **views** are different ways of displaying a document in the document window. Each Word view provides features that are useful for working on different types of documents. The default view, **Print Layout view**, displays a document as it will look on a printed page. Print Layout view is helpful for formatting text and pages, including adjusting document margins, creating columns of text, inserting graphics, and formatting headers and footers. Also useful is **Read Mode view**, which displays document text so that it is easy to read on screen. Other Word views are helpful for performing specialized tasks. **Web Layout view** allows you to format webpages or documents that will be viewed on a computer screen. In Web Layout view,

a document appears just as it will when viewed with a web browser. **Outline view** is useful for editing and formatting longer documents that include multiple headings. Outline view allows you to reorganize text by moving the headings. Finally, **Draft view**, shows a simplified layout of a document, without margins, headers and footers, or graphics. When you want to quickly type and edit text, it's often easiest to work in Draft View. You switch between views by clicking the view buttons on the status bar or by using the commands on the View tab. Changing views does not affect how the printed document will appear. It simply changes the way you view the document in the document window.

Practice

Concepts Review

Label the elements of the Word program window shown in FIGURE 1-15.

FIGURE 1-15

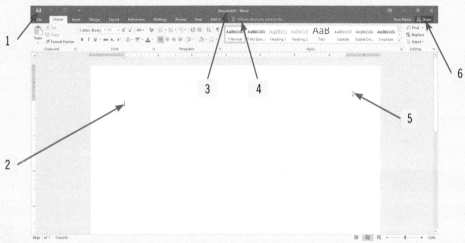

Match each term with the statement that best describes it.

7. **Ribbon**
8. **AutoCorrect**
9. **AutoComplete**
10. **Zoom slider**
11. **Status bar**
12. **Horizontal ruler**
13. **Template**
14. **Formatting marks**

a. A formatted document that contains placeholder text
b. Suggests text to insert into a document
c. Fixes certain errors as you type
d. Provides access to Word commands
e. Special characters that appear on screen but do not print
f. Displays tab settings and paragraph indents
g. Enlarges and reduces the document in the document window
h. Displays the number of pages in the current document

Select the best answer from the list of choices.

15. **Which of the following shows the number of words in the document?**
   a. The title bar
   b. The Ribbon
   c. The status bar
   d. The Mini toolbar

16. **Which tab includes buttons for formatting text?**
   a. View
   b. Page Layout
   c. Insert
   d. Home

17. **Which element of the Word window shows the top and bottom document margins settings?**
   a. Status bar
   b. View tab
   c. Vertical ruler
   d. Vertical scroll bar

18. **What is the default file extension for a document created in Word 2016?**
   a. .doc
   b. .dot
   c. .dotx
   d. .docx

19. Which of the following is not included in a ScreenTip for a command?

    a. Link to a help topic on the command   **c.** Keyboard shortcut for the command

    b. Alternative location of the command   **d.** Description of the function of the command

20. Which view is best for reading text onscreen?

    a. Print Layout view   **c.** Read Mode view

    b. Outline view   **d.** Draft view

Skills Review

1. Explore the Word program window.

    a. Start Word and open a new, blank document.

    b. Identify as many elements of the Word program window as you can without referring to the module material.

    c. Click the File tab, then click the Info, New, Save, Open, Save As, Print, Share, and Export commands.

    d. Click the Back button in Backstage view to return to the document window.

    e. Click each tab on the Ribbon, review the groups and buttons on each tab, then return to the Home tab.

    f. Point to each button on the Home tab and read its ScreenTip.

    g. Click the view buttons to view the blank document in each view, then return to Print Layout view.

    h. Use the Zoom slider to zoom all the way in and all the way out on the document, then return to 120%.

2. Start a document.

    a. In a new blank document, type **Summer of Music Festivals** at the top of the page, then press [Enter] two times.

    b. Type the following, pressing [Tab] as indicated and pressing [Enter] at the end of each line:

        To: [Tab] [Tab] **Michael Mellon**

        From: [Tab] [Tab] **Your Name**

        Date: [Tab] [Tab] **Today's date**

        Re: [Tab] [Tab] **Reservation confirmation**

        Pages: [Tab] [Tab] **1**

        Fax: [Tab] [Tab] **(603) 555-5478**

    c. Press [Enter] again, then type **Thank you for your interest in our summer music festival weekend package, which includes accommodations for three nights, continental breakfast, and a festival pass. Rooms are still available during the following festivals: International Jazz Festival, Americana Festival, Classical Fringe Festival, and the Festival of Arts. Please see the attached schedule for festival dates and details.**

    d. Press [Enter], then type **To make a reservation, please call me at (617) 555-7482 or visit our website. Payment must be received in full by the 3rd of June to hold a room. No one knows how to celebrate summer like music-lovers!**

    e. Insert **Summer Strings Festival,** before International Jazz Festival.

    f. Using the [Backspace] key, delete **1** in the Pages: line, then type **2**.

    g. Using the [Delete] key, delete **festival** in the last sentence of the first paragraph.

3. Save a document.

    a. Click the Save button on the Quick Access toolbar.

    b. Save the document as **WD 1-Mellon Fax** with the default file extension to the location where you store your Data Files.

    c. After your name, type a comma, press [Spacebar], then type **Reservations Manager**

    d. Save the document.

4. Select text.

    a. Turn on formatting marks.

    b. Select the **Re:** line, then type **Re:** [Tab] [Tab] **Summer Music Festival Weekend Package**

    c. Select **three** in the first sentence, then type **two**.

    d. Select **3rd of June** in the second sentence of the last paragraph, type **15th of May**, select **room**, then type **reservation**.

    e. Delete the sentence **No one knows how to celebrate summer like music-lovers!**

    f. Turn off the display of formatting marks, then save the document.

5. Format text using the Mini toolbar.

    a. Select **Summer of Music Festivals**, click the Increase Font Size button on the Mini toolbar six times, then apply bold.

    b. Center **Summer of Music Festivals** on the page.

    c. Apply a bottom border under **Summer of Music Festivals**.

    d. Apply bold to the following words in the fax heading: **To:**, **From:**, **Date:**, **Re:**, **Pages:**, and **Fax:**.

FIGURE 1-16

    e. Read the document using the Read Mode view.

    f. Return to Print Layout view, zoom in on the document, then proofread the fax.

    g. Correct any typing errors in your document, then save the document. Compare your document to FIGURE 1-16.

    h. Submit the fax to your instructor, then close the document.

6. Create a document using a template.

    a. Click the File tab, click New, then scroll the gallery of templates.

    b. Create a new document using the Fax cover sheet (Professional design) template.

    c. Click the "Company Name" placeholder text, type **Summer of Music Festivals**, delete the "Street Address" and "City..." content controls, click the "Phone number" placeholder text, type **Tel: 617-555-7482**, click the "Fax number" placeholder text, type **Fax: 617-555-1176**, click the website placeholder text, then type **www.summerofmusic.com**.

    d. Type **Jude Lennon** to replace the "To:" placeholder text; type **555-2119** to replace the "Fax:" placeholder text; click the "Phone:" placeholder text, then press [Delete]; then type **Summer of Music Festivals** to replace the "Re:" placeholder text.

    e. If your name is not on the From line, select the text in the From content control, then type your name.

    f. Insert today's date using the date content control.

    g. Delete the "Pages:" and "cc:" placeholder text.

    h. Save the document with the filename **WD 1-Lennon Fax** to the location where you store your Data Files, clicking OK if a warning box opens.

7. View and navigate a document.

    a. Scroll down until Comments is near the top of your document window.

    b. Replace the Comments placeholder text with the following text: **Packages for the following summer music festivals are sold out: Chamber Music Festival, Solstice Festival, and Dragonfly Festival. We had expected these packages to be less popular than those for the bigger festivals, but interest has been high. Next year, we will increase our bookings for these festivals by 30%.**

Summer of Music Festivals

To:	Michael Mellon
From:	Your Name, Reservations Manager
Date:	April 11, 2017
Re:	Summer Music Festival Weekend Package
Pages:	2
Fax:	(603) 555-5478

Thank you for your interest in our summer music festival weekend package, which includes accommodations for two nights, continental breakfast, and a festival pass. Rooms are still available during the following festivals: Summer Strings Festival, International Jazz Festival, Americana Festival, Classical Fringe Festival, and the Festival of Arts. Please see the attached schedule for dates and details.

To make a reservation, please call me at (617) 555-7482 or visit our website. Payment must be received in full by the 15th of May to hold a reservation.

Skills Review (continued)

c. Use the Zoom dialog box to view the Whole Page.

d. Use the Zoom slider to set the Zoom percentage at approximately 100%.

e. Read the document using the Read Mode view.

f. Return to Print Layout view, zoom in on the document, then proofread the fax.

g. Preview the document, then correct any errors, saving changes if necessary. Compare your document to FIGURE 1-17. Submit the document to your instructor, close the file, then exit Word.

FIGURE 1-17

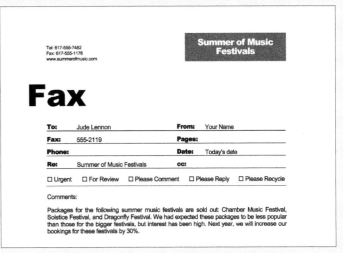

Independent Challenge 1

Yesterday you interviewed for a job as marketing director at Rose Design Services. You spoke with several people at the company, including Yuko Picard, chief executive officer, whose business card is shown in FIGURE 1-18. You need to write a follow-up letter to Ms. Picard, thanking her for the interview and expressing your interest in the company and the position. She also asked you to send her some samples of your marketing work, which you will enclose with the letter.

a. Start Word and save a new blank document as **WD 1-Picard Letter** to the location where you store your Data Files.

b. Begin the letter by clicking the No Spacing button in the Styles group. You use this button to apply the No Spacing style to the document so that your document does not include extra space between paragraphs.

c. Type a personal letterhead for the letter that includes your name, address, telephone number, and e-mail address. If Word formats your e-mail address as a hyperlink, right-click your e-mail address, then click Remove Hyperlink. (*Note: Format the letterhead after you finish typing the letter.*)

FIGURE 1-18

d. Three lines below the bottom of the letterhead, type today's date.

e. Four lines below the date, type the inside address, referring to FIGURE 1-18 for the information. Include the recipient's title, company name, and full mailing address.

f. Two lines below the inside address, type **Dear Ms. Picard:** for the salutation.

g. Two lines below the salutation, type the body of the letter according to the following guidelines:

- In the first paragraph, thank her for the interview. Then restate your interest in the position and express your desire to work for the company. Add any specific details you think will enhance the power of your letter.

- In the second paragraph, note that you are enclosing three samples of your work, and explain something about the samples you are enclosing.

- Type a short final paragraph.

h. Two lines below the last body paragraph, type a closing, then four lines below the closing, type the signature block. Be sure to include your name in the signature block.

i. Two lines below the signature block, type an enclosure notation. (*Hint:* An enclosure notation usually includes the word "Enclosures" or the abbreviation "Enc." followed by the number of enclosures in parentheses.)

j. Format the letterhead with bold, centering, and a bottom border.

k. Save your changes, preview the letter, submit it to your instructor, then close the document and exit Word.

Independent Challenge 2

Your company has recently installed Word 2016 on its company network. As the training manager, it's your responsibility to teach employees how to use the new software productively. Now that they have begun working with Word 2016, several employees have asked you about sharing documents with colleagues using OneDrive. In response, you wrote a memo to all employees explaining the Share feature. You now need to format the memo before distributing it.

a. Start Word, open the file **WD 1-1.docx** from the location where you store your Data Files, clicking the Enable Editing button if prompted to do so, then read the memo to get a feel for its contents. Switch to Print Layout view if the document is not already displayed in Print Layout view.

b. Save the file as **WD 1-Share Memo** to the location where you store your Data Files.

c. Replace the information in the memo header with the information shown in FIGURE 1-19. Make sure to include your name in the From line and the current date in the Date line.

d. Apply bold to **To:**, **From:**, **Date:**, and **Re:**.

e. Increase the size of **WORD TRAINING MEMORANDUM** to match FIGURE 1-19, center the text on the page, add a border below it, then save your changes.

FIGURE 1-19

WORD TRAINING MEMORANDUM

To:	All employees
From:	Your Name, Training Manager
Date:	Today's date
Re:	Sharing documents

f. Preview the memo, submit it to your instructor, then close the document and exit Word.

Independent Challenge 3

You are an expert on climate change. The president of the National Parks Association, Isabella Meerts, has asked you to be the keynote speaker at an upcoming conference on the impact of climate change on the national parks, to be held in Grand Teton National Park. You use one of the Word letter templates to write a letter to Ms. Meerts accepting the invitation and confirming the details. Your letter to Ms. Meerts should reference the following information:

- The conference will be held September 17–19, 2017, at the Jackson Lake Lodge in the park.
- You have been asked to speak for an hour on Saturday, September 18, followed by one-half hour for questions.
- Ms. Meerts suggested the lecture topic "Melting Glaciers, Changing Ecosystems."
- Your talk will include a 45-minute slide presentation.
- The National Parks Association will make your travel arrangements.
- Your preference is to arrive at Jackson Hole Airport on the morning of Friday, September 17, and to depart on Monday, September 20. You would like to rent a car at the airport for the drive to the Jackson Lake Lodge.
- You want to fly in and out of the airport closest to your home.

a. Start Word, click the File tab, click New, and then search for and select an appropriate letter template. Save the document as **WD 1-Meerts Letter** to the location where you store your Data Files.

b. Replace the placeholders in the letterhead with your personal information. Include your name, address, phone number, and e-mail address. Delete any placeholders that do not apply. (*Hints:* Depending on the template you choose, the letterhead might be located at the top or on the side of the document. You can press [Enter] when typing in a placeholder to add an additional line of text. You can also change the format of text typed in a placeholder. If your e-mail address appears as a hyperlink, right-click the e-mail address and click Remove Hyperlink.)

Independent Challenge 3 (continued)

c. Use the [Date] content control to select the current date.

d. Replace the placeholders in the inside address. Be sure to include Ms. Meerts title and the name of the organization. Make up a street address and zip code.

e. Type **Dear Ms. Meerts:** for the salutation.

f. Using the information listed previously, type the body of the letter:

- In the first paragraph, accept the invitation to speak.
- In the second paragraph, confirm the important conference details, confirm your lecture topic, and provide any relevant details.
- In the third paragraph, state your travel preferences.
- Type a short final paragraph.

g. Type **Sincerely**, for the closing, then include your name in the signature block.

h. Adjust the formatting of the letter as necessary. For example, remove bold formatting or change the font color of text to a more appropriate color.

i. Proofread your letter, make corrections as needed, then save your changes.

j. Submit the letter to your instructor, close the document, then exit Word.

Independent Challenge 4: Explore

Word includes a wide variety of templates that can help you create professional-looking documents quickly, including business letters, business cards, résumés, calendars, faxes, memos, labels, reports, blog posts, posters, invitations, certificates, newsletters, and holiday and party cards. In this independent challenge, you will explore the variety of Word templates available to you, and use a template to make a document that is helpful to you in your business or personal life. You might create business cards for yourself, a poster for an event, a letter for a job search, a new résumé, or an invitation to a party. Choose a template that allows you to personalize the text.

a. Start Word, click the File tab, click New, then click each link after Suggested searches: (Business, Personal, Industry, Print, Design Sets, Education, Event) to explore the templates available to you.

b. Preview all the templates for the type of document you want to create, and then select one to create a new document.

c. Save the document as **WD 1-Template Document** to the location where you store your Data Files.

d. Replace the placeholders in the document with your personal information. Delete any placeholders that do not apply. (*Hints:* You can press [Enter] when typing in a placeholder to add an additional line of text. If an e-mail or web address appears as a hyperlink in your document, right-click the e-mail or web address and then click Remove Hyperlink.)

e. Use the [Pick the date] content control to select a date if your document includes a date placeholder.

f. Experiment with changing the font of the text in your document by using the Font list arrow on the Mini toolbar or in the Font group on the Home tab. (*Note:* Remember to use the Undo button immediately after you make the change if you do not like the change and want to remove it.)

g. Experiment with changing the font size of the text in your document by using the Font Size list arrow on the Mini toolbar or in the Font group on the Home tab.

h. Experiment with changing the color of text in your document using the Font Color button on the Mini toolbar or in the Font group on the Home tab.

i. Make other adjustments to the document as necessary, using the Undo button to remove a change you decide you do not want to keep.

j. Save your changes to the document, preview it, submit it to your instructor, then close the document and exit Word.

Visual Workshop

Create the cover letter shown in FIGURE 1-20. Before beginning to type, click the No Spacing button in the Styles group on the Home tab. Add the bottom border to the letterhead after typing the letter. Save the document as **WD 1-Davidson Cover Letter** to the location where you store your Data Files, submit the letter to your instructor, then close the document and exit Word.

FIGURE 1-20

Your Name
82 Genesee Street, Madison, WI 53701
Tel: 608-555-7283; E-mail: yourname@gmail.com

November 8, 2017

Ms. Marta Davidson
Davidson Associates
812 Jefferson Street
Suite 300
Madison, WI 53704

Dear Ms. Davidson:

I read of the opening for a public information assistant in the November 4 edition of wisconsinjobs.com, and I would like to be considered for the position. I am a recent graduate of the University of Wisconsin-Madison (UW), and I am interested in pursuing a career in public relations.

My interest in a public relations career springs from my publicly acknowledged writing and journalism abilities. For example, at UW, I was a reporter for the student newspaper and frequently wrote press releases for campus and community events.

I have a wealth of experience using Microsoft Word in professional settings. Last summer, I worked as an office assistant for the architecture firm Mason & Greenbush, where I used Word to create newsletters, brochures, and financial reports. During the school year, I also worked part-time in the UW Office of Community Relations, where I used the Word mail merge feature to create form letters and mailing labels.

My enclosed resume details my skills and experience. I welcome the opportunity to discuss the position and my qualifications with you. I can be reached at 608-555-7283.

Sincerely,

Your Name

Enc.

Editing Documents

CASE ▶ You have been asked to edit and finalize a press release for an R2G promotional lecture series. The press release should provide information about the series so that newspapers, radio stations, and other media outlets can announce it to the public. R2G press releases are disseminated via the website and by e-mail. Before distributing the file electronically to your lists of press contacts and local R2G clients, you add several hyperlinks and then strip the file of private information.

Module Objectives

After completing this module, you will be able to:

- Cut and paste text
- Copy and paste text
- Use the Office Clipboard
- Find and replace text
- Check spelling and grammar
- Research information
- Add hyperlinks
- Work with document properties

Files You Will Need

WD 2-1.docx	WD 2-5.docx
WD 2-2.docx	WD 2-6.docx
WD 2-3.docx	WD 2-7.docx
WD 2-4.docx	

Cut and Paste Text

The editing features in Word allow you to move text from one location to another in a document. Moving text is often called **cut and paste**. When you **cut** text, it is removed from the document and placed on the **Clipboard**, a temporary storage area for text and graphics that you cut or copy from a document. You can then **paste**, or insert, text that is stored on the Clipboard in the document at the location of the insertion point. You cut and paste text using the Cut and Paste buttons in the Clipboard group on the Home tab. You also can move selected text by dragging it to a new location using the mouse. This operation is called **drag and drop**. **CASE** ▶ *You open the press release, save it with a new filename, and then reorganize the information in the press release using the cut-and-paste and drag-and-drop methods.*

STEPS

1. **Start Word, click Blank document, click the File tab, click This PC on the Open screen, click Browse to open the Open dialog box, navigate to the location where you store your Data Files, click WD 2-1.docx, then click Open**

   The document opens in Print Layout view. Once you have opened a file, you can edit it and use the Save or the Save As command to save your changes. You use the **Save** command when you want to save the changes you make to a file, overwriting the stored file. You use the **Save As** command when you want to leave the original file intact and create a duplicate file with a different filename, file extension, or location.

2. **Click the File tab, click Save As, click Computer, click Browse to open the Save As dialog box, type WD 2-Lecture PR in the File name text box, then click Save**

   You can now make changes to the press release file without affecting the original file.

3. **Replace Mary Watson with your name, scroll down until the headline "Pedro Soares to Speak..." is at the top of your document window, then click the Show/Hide ¶ button ¶ in the Paragraph group on the Home tab to display formatting marks**

4. **Select Alaskan guide Michael Coonan, (including the comma and the space after it) in the third body paragraph, then click the Cut button in the Clipboard group**

   The text is removed from the document and placed on the Clipboard. Word uses two different clipboards: the **system clipboard**, which holds just one item, and the **Office Clipboard** (the Clipboard), which holds up to 24 items. The last item you cut or copy is always added to both clipboards.

5. **Place the insertion point before African (but after the space) in the first line of the third paragraph, then click the Paste button in the Clipboard group**

   The text is pasted at the location of the insertion point, as shown in **FIGURE 2-1**. The Paste Options button appears below text when you first paste it in a document. For now you can ignore the Paste Options button.

6. **Press and hold [Ctrl], click the sentence Ticket prices include lunch. in the fourth paragraph, then release [Ctrl]**

   The entire sentence is selected. You will drag the selected text to a new location using the mouse.

7. **Press and hold the mouse button over the selected text, then drag the pointer's vertical line to the end of the fifth paragraph (between the period and the paragraph mark) as shown in FIGURE 2-2**

   You drag the insertion point to where you want the text to be inserted when you release the mouse button.

8. **Release the mouse button**

   The selected text is moved to the location of the insertion point. Text is not placed on the Clipboard when you drag and drop it.

9. **Deselect the text, then click the Save button ⊟ on the Quick Access toolbar**

Editing Documents

FIGURE 2-1: Moved text with Paste Options button

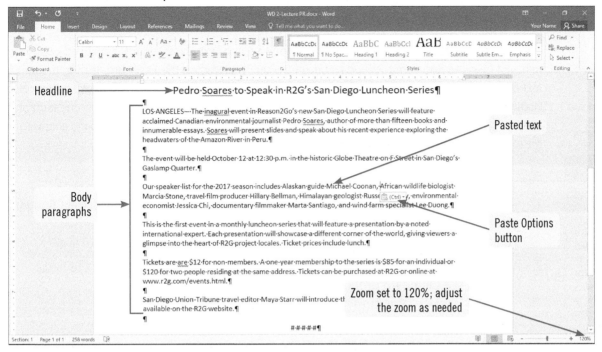

FIGURE 2-2: Dragging and dropping text in a new location

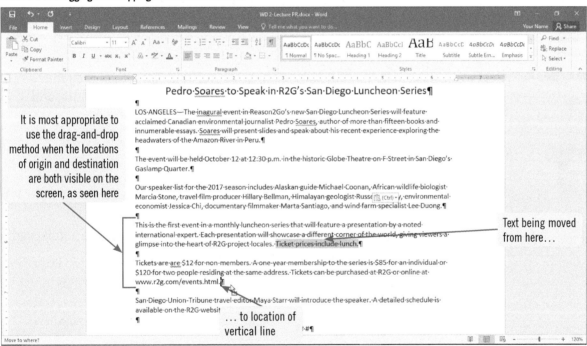

Using keyboard shortcuts

A **shortcut key** is a function key, such as [F1], or a combination of keys, such as [Ctrl][S], that you press to perform a command. For example, instead of using the Cut, Copy, and Paste commands on the Ribbon or the Mini toolbar, you can use the **keyboard shortcuts** [Ctrl][X] to cut text, [Ctrl][C] to copy text, and [Ctrl][V] to paste text. You can also press [Ctrl][S] to save changes to a document instead of clicking the Save button on the Quick Access toolbar or clicking Save on the File tab. Becoming skilled at using keyboard shortcuts can help you quickly accomplish many of the tasks you perform in Word. If a keyboard shortcut is available for a command, then it is listed in the ScreenTip for that command.

Copy and Paste Text

Learning
Outcomes
• Copy and paste
  text
• Format pasted text
  with the Paste
  Options button

Copying and pasting text is similar to cutting and pasting text, except that the text you **copy** is not removed from the document. Rather, a copy of the text is placed on the Clipboard, leaving the original text in place. You can copy text to the Clipboard using the Copy button in the Clipboard group on the Home tab, or you can copy text by pressing [Ctrl] as you drag the selected text from one location to another. **CASE** *You continue to edit the press release by copying text from one location to another using the copy-and-paste and drag-and-drop methods.*

STEPS

QUICK TIP
You can also cut or copy text by right-clicking the selected text, and then clicking the Cut or Copy command on the menu that opens.

1. **Select** San Diego Luncheon **in the headline, then click the** Copy button **in the Clipboard group on the Home tab**

   A copy of the selected text is placed on the Clipboard, leaving the original text you copied in place.

2. **Place the insertion point before** season **in the third paragraph, then click the** Paste button **in the Clipboard group**

   "San Diego Luncheon" is inserted before "season," as shown in FIGURE 2-3. Notice that the pasted text is formatted differently than the paragraph in which it was inserted.

3. **Click the** Paste Options button, **move the mouse over each button on the menu that opens to read its ScreenTip, then click the** Keep Text Only (T) button

   The formatting of "San Diego Luncheon" is changed to match the rest of the paragraph. The buttons on the Paste Options menu allow you to change the formatting of pasted text. You can choose to keep the original formatting (Keep Source Formatting), match the destination formatting (Merge Formatting), or paste as unformatted text (Keep Text Only).

TROUBLE
Be sure you can see the last two paragraphs on your screen before completing this step.

4. **Select** www.r2g.com **in the fifth paragraph, press and hold** [Ctrl], **then drag the** pointer's vertical line **to the end of the last paragraph, placing it between** site **and the period**

   As you drag, the pointer changes to ⬚, indicating that the selected text is being copied and moved.

TROUBLE
If you move the text instead of copying it, click the Undo button ↶ on the Quick Access toolbar and repeat Steps 4 and 5.

5. **Release the mouse button, then release** [Ctrl]

   The text is copied to the last paragraph. Since the formatting of the text you copied is the same as the formatting of the destination paragraph, you can ignore the Paste Options button. Text is not copied to the Clipboard when you copy it using the drag-and-drop method.

6. **Place the insertion point before** www.r2g.com **in the last paragraph, type** at **followed by a space, then save the document**

   Compare your document with FIGURE 2-4.

Splitting the document window to copy and move items in a long document

If you want to copy or move items between parts of a long document, it can be useful to split the document window into two panes. This allows you to display the item you want to copy or move in one pane and the destination for the item in the other pane. To split a window, click the Split button in the Window group on the View tab, and then drag the horizontal split bar that appears to the location you want to split the window. Once the document window is split into two panes, you can use the scroll bars in each pane to display different parts of the document. To copy or move an item from one pane to another, you can use the Cut, Copy, and Paste commands, or you can drag the item between the panes. When you are finished editing the document, double-click the split bar to restore the window to a single pane, or click the Remove Split button in the Window group on the View tab.

Editing Documents

FIGURE 2-3: Text pasted in document

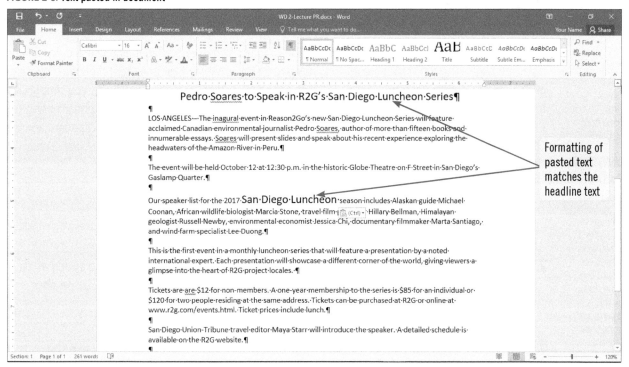

FIGURE 2-4: Copied text in document

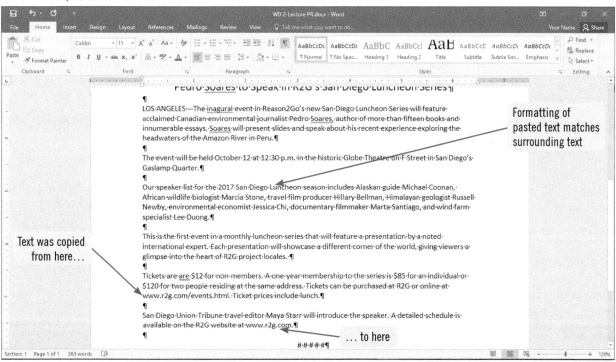

Use the Office Clipboard

Learning
Outcomes
• Copy and cut
items to the
Clipboard
• Paste items from
the Clipboard

The Office Clipboard allows you to collect text and graphics from files created in any Office program and insert them into your Word documents. It holds up to 24 items and, unlike the system clipboard, the items on the Office Clipboard can be viewed. To display the Office Clipboard (the Clipboard), you simply click the launcher in the Clipboard group on the Home tab. You add items to the Office Clipboard using the Cut and Copy commands. The last item you collect is always added to both the system clipboard and the Office Clipboard. **CASE** ▸ *You use the Office Clipboard to move several sentences in your press release.*

STEPS

QUICK TIP

You can set the Clipboard pane to open automatically when you cut or copy two items consecutively by clicking Options on the Clipboard pane, and then selecting Show Office Clipboard Automatically.

1. **Click the launcher 🔲 in the Clipboard group on the Home tab**

   The Office Clipboard opens in the Clipboard pane. It contains the San Diego Luncheon item you copied in the last lesson.

2. **Select the sentence San Diego Union-Tribune travel editor... (including the space after the period) in the last paragraph, right-click the selected text, then click Cut on the menu that opens**

   The sentence is cut to the Clipboard.

3. **Select the sentence A detailed schedule is... (including the ¶ mark), right-click the selected text, then click Cut**

   The Clipboard displays the items you cut or copied, as shown in **FIGURE 2-5**. The icon next to each item indicates the items are from a Word document. The last item collected is displayed at the top of the Clipboard pane. As new items are collected, the existing items move down the Clipboard.

QUICK TIP

If you add a 25th item to the Clipboard, the first item you collected is deleted.

4. **Place the insertion point at the end of the second paragraph (after "Quarter." but before the ¶ mark), then click the San Diego Union-Tribune... item on the Clipboard**

   Clicking an item on the Clipboard pastes the item in the document at the location of the insertion point. Items remain on the Clipboard until you delete them or close all open Office programs.

5. **Place the insertion point at the end of the third paragraph (after "Duong."), then click the A detailed schedule is... item on the Clipboard**

   The sentence is pasted into the document.

6. **Select the fourth paragraph, which begins with the sentence This is the first event... (including the ¶ mark), right-click the selected text, then click Cut**

   The paragraph is cut to the Clipboard.

7. **Place the insertion point at the beginning of the third paragraph (before "Our..."), click the Paste button in the Clipboard group on the Home tab, then press [Backspace]**

   The sentences from the "This is the first..." paragraph are pasted at the beginning of the "Our speaker list..." paragraph. You can paste the last item collected using either the Paste command or the Clipboard.

8. **Place the insertion point at the end of the third paragraph (after "www.r2g.com." and before the ¶ mark), then press [Delete] twice**

   Two ¶ symbols and the corresponding blank lines between the third and fourth paragraphs are deleted.

9. **Click the Show/Hide ¶ button ¶ on in the Paragraph group**

   Compare your press release with **FIGURE 2-6**. Note that many Word users prefer to work with formatting marks on at all times. Experiment to see which method you prefer.

QUICK TIP

To delete an individual item from the Clipboard, click the list arrow next to the item, then click Delete.

10. **Click the Clear All button on the Clipboard pane to remove the items from the Clipboard, click the Close button 🗙 on the Clipboard pane, press [Ctrl][Home], then save the document**

    Pressing [Ctrl][Home] moves the insertion point to the top of the document.

FIGURE 2-5: Office Clipboard in Clipboard pane

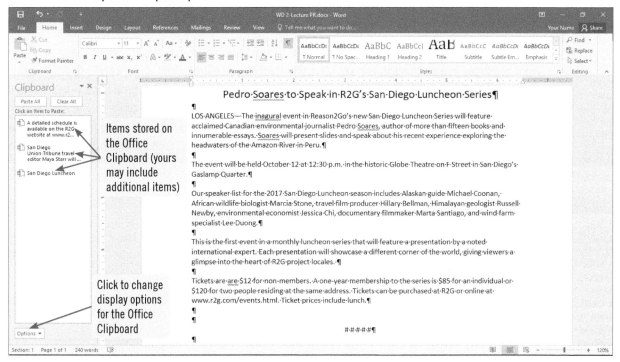

FIGURE 2-6: Revised press release

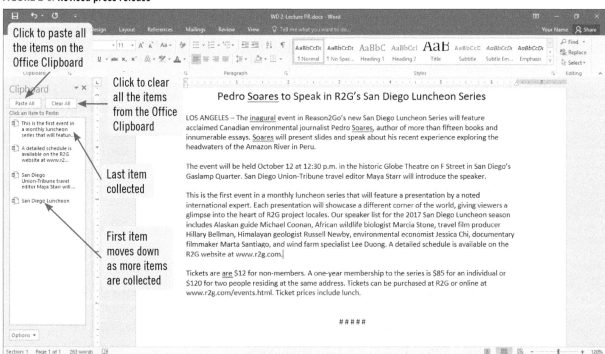

Copying and moving items between documents

You can also use the Clipboard to copy and move items between documents. To do this, open both documents and the Clipboard pane. With multiple documents open, copy or cut an item from one document and then switch to the other document and paste the item. To switch between open documents, point to the Word icon [W] on the taskbar, and then click the document you want to appear in the document window. You can also display more than one document at the same time by clicking the Arrange All button or the View Side by Side button in the Window group on the View tab.

Find and Replace Text

Learning Outcomes
• Replace text
• Find text with the Navigation pane
• Navigate a document

The Find and Replace feature in Word allows you to automatically search for and replace all instances of a word or phrase in a document. For example, you might need to substitute "tour" for "trip." To manually locate and replace each instance of "trip" in a long document would be very time-consuming. Using the Replace command, you can find and replace all occurrences of specific text at once, or you can choose to find and review each occurrence individually. Using the Find command, you can locate and highlight every occurrence of a specific word or phrase in a document. **CASE** ▶ *R2G management has decided to change the name of the lecture series from "Travel Luncheon Series" to "Travel Lecture Series." You use the Replace command to search the document for all instances of "Luncheon" and replace them with "Lecture."*

STEPS

TROUBLE
If any of the Search Options check boxes are selected in your Find and Replace dialog box, deselect them. If Format appears under the Find what or Replace with text box, click in the text box, then click the No Formatting button.

1. **Click the** Replace button **in the Editing group, then click** More **in the Find and Replace dialog box**

   The Find and Replace dialog box opens and expands, as shown in FIGURE 2-7.

2. **Type** Luncheon **in the Find what text box**

   "Luncheon" is the text that will be replaced.

3. **Press [Tab], then type** Lecture **in the Replace with text box**

   "Lecture" is the text that will replace "Luncheon."

4. **Click the** Match case check box **in the Search Options section to select it**

   Selecting the Match case check box tells Word to find only exact matches for the uppercase and lowercase characters you entered in the Find what text box. You want to replace all instances of "Luncheon" in the proper name "San Diego Luncheon Series." You do not want to replace "luncheon" when it refers to a lunchtime event.

QUICK TIP
To find, review, and replace each occurrence individually, click Find Next.

5. **Click** Replace All

   Clicking Replace All changes all occurrences of "Luncheon" to "Lecture" in the press release. A message box reports three replacements were made.

6. **Click** OK **to close the message box, then click the** Close button **in the Find and Replace dialog box**

   Word replaced "Luncheon" with "Lecture" in three locations, but did not replace "luncheon."

QUICK TIP
Alternately, you can also use the Find tab in the Find and Replace dialog box to find text in a document.

7. **Click the** Find button **in the Editing group**

   Clicking the Find button opens the Navigation pane, which is used to browse a longer document by headings, by pages, or by specific text. The Find command allows you to quickly locate all instances of text in a document. You use it to verify that Word did not replace "luncheon."

8. **Type** luncheon **in the search text box in the Navigation pane, then scroll up until the headline is at the top of the document window**

   The word "luncheon" is highlighted and selected in the document, as shown in FIGURE 2-8.

9. **Click the** Close button **in the Navigation pane**

   The highlighting is removed from the text when you close the Navigation pane.

10. **Press [Ctrl][Home], then save the document**

FIGURE 2-7: Find and Replace dialog box

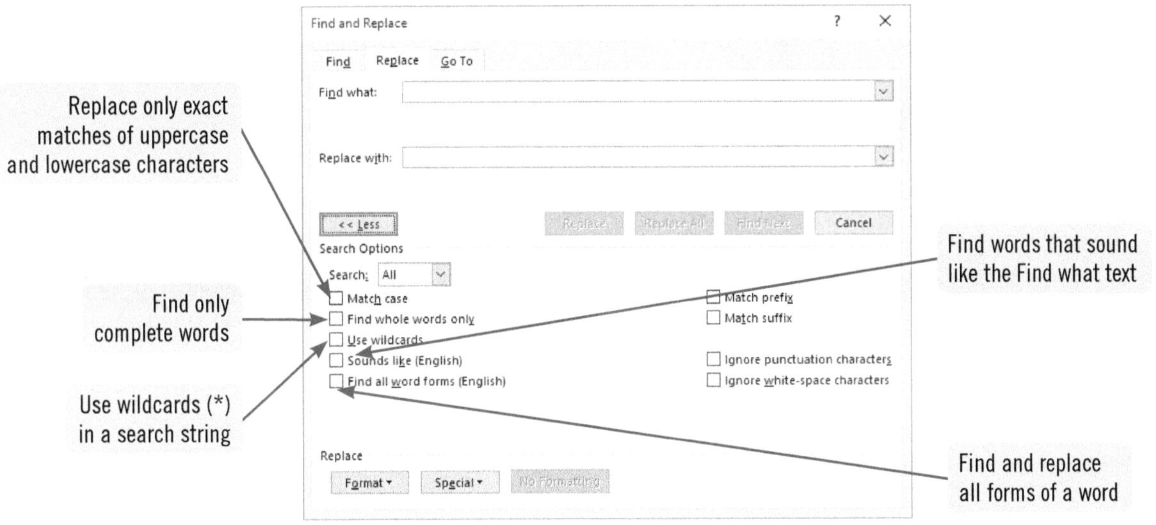
Replace only exact matches of uppercase and lowercase characters
Find only complete words
Use wildcards (*) in a search string
Find words that sound like the Find what text
Find and replace all forms of a word
Find and Replace
Find
Replace
Go To
Find what:
Replace with:
<< Less
Replace
Replace All
Find Next
Cancel
Search Options
Search: All
Match case
Find whole words only
Use wildcards
Sounds like (English)
Find all word forms (English)
Match prefix
Match suffix
Ignore punctuation characters
Ignore white-space characters
Replace
Format
Special
No Formatting

FIGURE 2-8: Found text highlighted in document

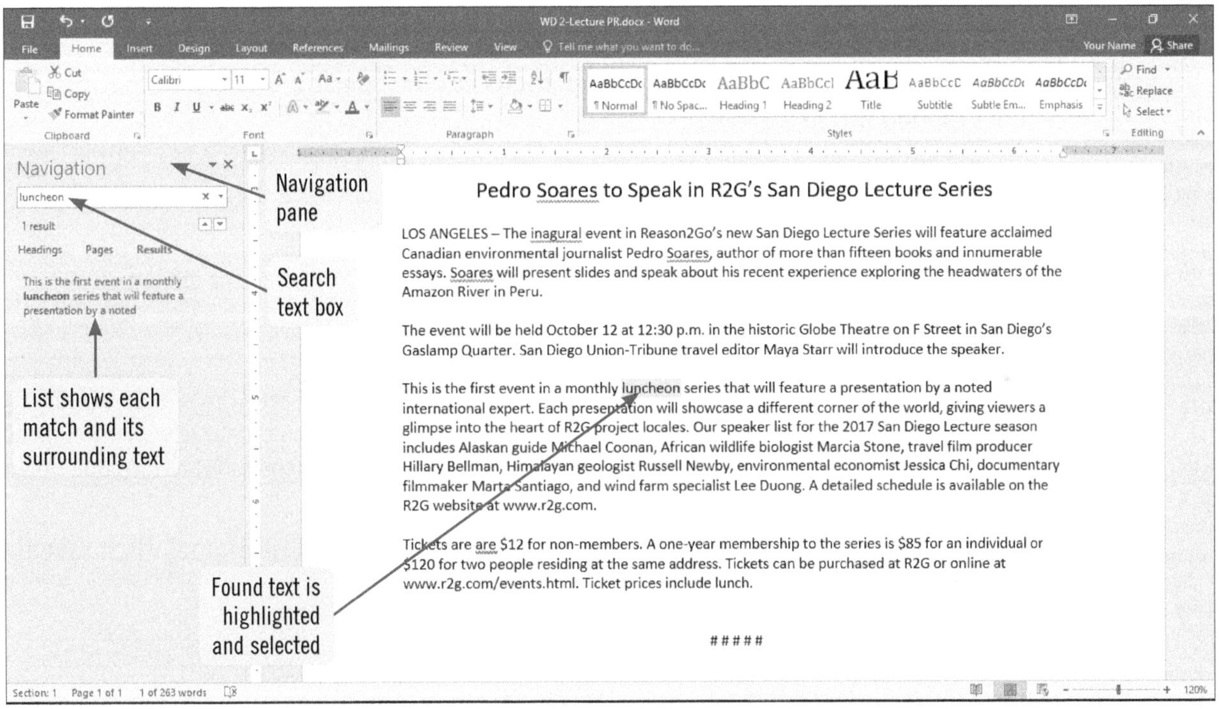
Navigation pane
Search text box
List shows each match and its surrounding text
Found text is highlighted and selected
WD 2-Lecture PR.docx - Word
Navigation
luncheon
1 result
Headings
Pages
Results
This is the first event in a monthly luncheon series that will feature a presentation by a noted
Pedro Soares to Speak in R2G's San Diego Lecture Series
LOS ANGELES – The inagural event in Reason2Go's new San Diego Lecture Series will feature acclaimed Canadian environmental journalist Pedro Soares, author of more than fifteen books and innumerable essays. Soares will present slides and speak about his recent experience exploring the headwaters of the Amazon River in Peru.
The event will be held October 12 at 12:30 p.m. in the historic Globe Theatre on F Street in San Diego's Gaslamp Quarter. San Diego Union-Tribune travel editor Maya Starr will introduce the speaker.
This is the first event in a monthly luncheon series that will feature a presentation by a noted international expert. Each presentation will showcase a different corner of the world, giving viewers a glimpse into the heart of R2G project locales. Our speaker list for the 2017 San Diego Lecture season includes Alaskan guide Michael Coonan, African wildlife biologist Marcia Stone, travel film producer Hillary Bellman, Himalayan geologist Russell Newby, environmental economist Jessica Chi, documentary filmmaker Marta Santiago, and wind farm specialist Lee Duong. A detailed schedule is available on the R2G website at www.r2g.com.
Tickets are are $12 for non-members. A one-year membership to the series is $85 for an individual or $120 for two people residing at the same address. Tickets can be purchased at R2G or online at www.r2g.com/events.html. Ticket prices include lunch.
#####
Section: 1
Page 1 of 1
1 of 263 words

Navigating a document using the Navigation pane and the Go To command

Rather than scrolling to move to a different place in a longer document, you can use the Navigation pane to quickly move the insertion point to a specific page or a specific heading. One way to open the Navigation pane is by clicking the Page number button on the status bar, then clicking the link in the Navigation pane for the type of item you want to use to navigate the document.

To move to a specific page, section, line, table, graphic, or other item in a document, you use the Go To tab in the Find and Replace dialog box. On the Go To tab in the Find and Replace dialog box, select the type of item you want to find in the Go to what list box, enter the relevant information about that item, and then click Next to move the insertion point to the item.

Check Spelling and Grammar

Learning
Outcomes
• Ignore correctly
  spelled words
• Correct spelling
  errors
• Correct grammar
  errors

When you finish typing and revising a document, you can use the Spelling and Grammar command to search the document for misspelled words and grammar errors. The Spelling and Grammar checker flags possible mistakes, suggests correct spellings, and offers remedies for grammar errors such as subject–verb agreement, repeated words, and punctuation. **CASE** ➤ *You use the Spelling and Grammar checker to search your press release for errors. Before beginning the search, you set the Spelling and Grammar checker to ignore words, such as Soares, that you know are spelled correctly.*

STEPS

1. **Right-click** Soares **in the headline**

   A menu that includes suggestions for correcting the spelling of "Soares" opens. You can correct individual spelling and grammar errors by right-clicking text that is underlined with a red or blue wavy line and selecting a correction. Although "Soares" is not in the Word dictionary, it is spelled correctly in the document.

2. **Click** Ignore All

   Clicking Ignore All tells Word not to flag "Soares" as misspelled.

3. **Press** [Ctrl][Home]**, click the** Review tab**, then click the** Spelling & Grammar button **in the Proofing group**

   The Spelling pane opens, as shown in **FIGURE 2-9**. The pane identifies "inagural" as misspelled and suggests a possible correction for the error. The word selected in the suggestions box is the correct spelling.

4. **Click** Change

   Word replaces the misspelled word with the correctly spelled word. Next, the pane indicates that "are" is repeated in a sentence.

5. **Click** Delete

   Word deletes the second occurrence of the repeated word, and the Spelling pane closes. Keep in mind that the Spelling and Grammar checker identifies many common errors, but you cannot rely on it to find and correct all spelling and grammar errors in your documents, or to always suggest a valid correction. Always proofread your documents carefully.

6. **Click** OK **to complete the spelling and grammar check, press** [Ctrl][Home]**, then save the document**

Using Smart Lookup

The Smart Lookup feature gives you quick access to information about document text, including definitions, images, and other material from online sources. For example, you might use Smart Lookup to see the definition of a word used in a document or to hear the word pronounced. To use Smart Lookup, select the text you want to look up in your document, then click the Smart Lookup button in the Insights group on the Review tab. The Insights pane opens and includes the Explore and Define tabs. The Explore tab includes images and web links related to the selected text. The Define tab includes a dictionary definition of the selected text and a link you can click to hear the selected text pronounced.

FIGURE 2-9: Spelling pane

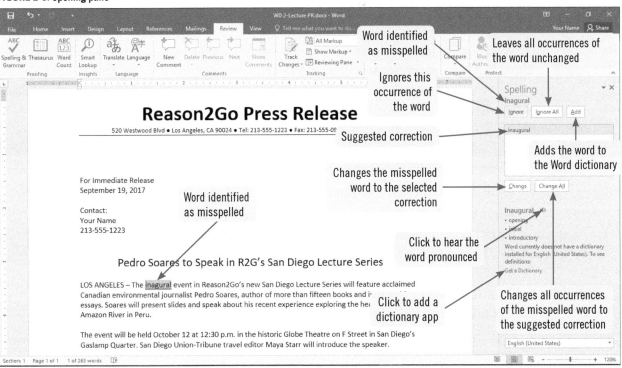

Inserting text with AutoCorrect

As you type, AutoCorrect automatically corrects many commonly misspelled words. By creating your own AutoCorrect entries, you can set Word to insert text that you type often, such as your name or contact information, or to correct words you misspell frequently. For example, you could create an AutoCorrect entry so that the name "Mary T. Watson" is automatically inserted whenever you type "mtw" followed by a space. You create AutoCorrect entries and customize other AutoCorrect and AutoFormat options using the AutoCorrect dialog box. To open the AutoCorrect dialog box, click the File tab, click Options, click Proofing in the Word Options dialog box that opens, and then click AutoCorrect Options. On the AutoCorrect tab in the AutoCorrect dialog box, type the text you want to be corrected automatically in the Replace text box (such as "mtw"), type the text you want to be inserted in its place automatically in the With text box (such as "Mary T. Watson"), and then click Add. The AutoCorrect entry is added to the list. Click OK to close the AutoCorrect dialog box, and then click OK to close the Word Options dialog box. Word inserts an AutoCorrect entry in a document when you press [Spacebar] or a punctuation mark after typing the text you want Word to correct. For example, Word inserts "Mary T. Watson" when you type "mtw" followed by a space. If you want to remove an AutoCorrect entry you created, simply open the AutoCorrect dialog box, select the AutoCorrect entry you want to remove in the list, click Delete, click OK, and then click OK to close the Word Options dialog box.

Research Information

The Word research features allow you to quickly search reference sources and the web for information related to a word or phrase. Among the reference sources available are a Thesaurus, which you can use to look up synonyms for awkward or repetitive words, as well as dictionary and translation sources. **CASE** ▶ *After proofreading your document for errors, you decide the press release would read better if several adjectives were more descriptive. You use the Thesaurus to find synonyms.*

STEPS

1. **Scroll until the headline is displayed at the top of your screen**

2. **Select noted in the first sentence of the third paragraph, then click the Thesaurus button in the Proofing group on the Review tab**
   The Thesaurus pane opens, as shown in FIGURE 2-10. "Noted" appears in the search text box, and possible synonyms for "noted" are listed under the search text box.

3. **Point to prominent in the list of synonyms**
   A shaded box containing a list arrow appears around the word.

4. **Click the list arrow, click Insert on the menu that opens, then close the Thesaurus pane**
   "Prominent" replaces "noted" in the press release.

5. **Right-click innumerable in the first sentence of the first paragraph, point to Synonyms on the menu that opens, then click numerous**
   "Numerous" replaces "innumerable" in the press release.

6. **Select the four paragraphs of body text, then click the Word Count button in the Proofing group**
   The Word Count dialog box opens, as shown in FIGURE 2-11. The dialog box lists the number of pages, words, characters, paragraphs, and lines included in the selected text. Notice that the status bar also displays the number of words included in the selected text and the total number of words in the entire document. If you want to view the page, character, paragraph, and line count for the entire document, make sure nothing is selected in your document, and then click Word Count in the Proofing group.

7. **Click Close, press [Ctrl][Home], then save the document**

8. **Click the File tab, click Save As, navigate to the location where you store your files, type WD 2-Lecture PR Public in the File name text box, then click Save**
   The WD 2-Lecture PR file closes, and the WD 2-Lecture PR Public file is displayed in the document window. You will modify this file to prepare it for electronic release to the public.

Publishing a blog directly from Word

A **blog**, which is short for weblog, is an informal journal that is created by an individual or a group and available to the public on the Internet. A blog usually conveys the ideas, comments, and opinions of the blogger and is written using a strong personal voice. The person who creates and maintains a blog, the **blogger**, typically updates the blog regularly. If you have or want to start a blog, you can configure Word to link to your blog site so that you can write, format, and publish blog entries directly from Word.

To create a new blog post, click the File tab, click New, then double-click Blog post to open a predesigned blog post document that you can customize with your own text, formatting, and images. You can also publish an existing document as a blog post by opening the document, clicking the File tab, clicking Share, and then clicking Post to Blog. In either case, Word prompts you to log onto your personal blog account. To blog directly from Word, you must first obtain a blog account with a blog service provider. Resources, such as the Word Help system and online forums, provide detailed information on obtaining and registering your personal blog account with Word.

FIGURE 2-10: Thesaurus pane

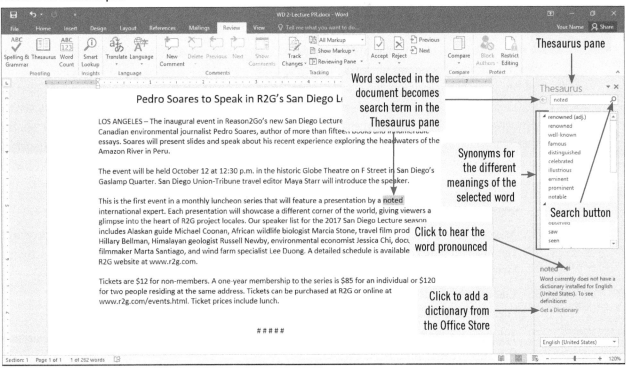

FIGURE 2-11: Word Count dialog box

Word Count	? ✕
Statistics:	
Pages	1
Words	217
Characters (no spaces)	1,189
Characters (with spaces)	1,403
Paragraphs	4
Lines	19

☑ Include textboxes, footnotes and endnotes

Close

Using a dictionary and other add-ins for Word

Instead of a built-in dictionary, Word includes the ability to install a free dictionary add-in from the Office Store that you can use to see definitions of words. A dictionary add-in is just one of many add-ins that are available in Word. **Add-ins** are small programs embedded in Word that allow you to access information on the web without having to leave Word. For example, you can look up something on Wikipedia, insert an online map in one of your documents, or access dictionaries and other reference sources, all from within Word using an add-in. To install a free dictionary add-in from the Office Store, click the Thesaurus button In the Proofing group on the Review tab, click the Get a Dictionary link to open the Dictionaries pane, decide which dictionary you want, review the Terms & Conditions as well as the Privacy Policy associated with the add-in you want, and then click the Download button associated with the dictionary you want in order to install that dictionary. If you want to download other dictionaries or other add-ins, click the Store button in the Add-ins group on the Insert tab, find the add-in you want, and then follow the prompts to install the add-in. Some add-ins are free, and some require purchase. To use an add-in, click the My Add-ins button in the Add-ins group to see your list of add-ins, and then click the add-in you want to use.

Add Hyperlinks

Learning
Outcomes
• Insert a hyperlink
• Test hyperlinks
• E-mail a document
  from Word

A **hyperlink** is text or a graphic that, when clicked, "jumps" the viewer to a different location or program. When a document is viewed on screen, hyperlinks allow readers to link (or jump) to a webpage, an e-mail address, a file, or a specific location in a document. When you create a hyperlink in a document, you select the text or graphic you want to use as a hyperlink and then you specify the location you want to jump to when the hyperlink is clicked. You create a hyperlink using the Hyperlink button in the Links group on the Insert tab. Text that is formatted as a hyperlink appears as colored, underlined text.   **CASE**   ▸ *Hundreds of people on your lists of press and client contacts will receive the press release by e-mail or view it on your website. To make it easier for these people to access additional information about the series, you add several hyperlinks to the press release.*

STEPS

QUICK TIP
By default, Word
automatically creates
a hyperlink to an
e-mail address or
URL when you type
an e-mail address or
a URL in a document.

1. **Select** your name, **click the** Insert tab, **then click the** Hyperlink button **in the Links group**

   The Insert Hyperlink dialog box opens, as shown in **FIGURE 2-12**. You use this dialog box to specify the location you want to jump to when the hyperlink—in this case, your name—is clicked.

2. **Click** E-mail Address **in the Link to section**

   The Insert Hyperlink dialog box changes so you can create a hyperlink to your e-mail address.

3. **Type your e-mail address in the E-mail address text box, type** San Diego Lecture Series **in the Subject text box, then click** OK

   As you type, Word automatically adds mailto: in front of your e-mail address. After you close the dialog box, the hyperlink text—your name—is formatted in blue and underlined.

TROUBLE
If an e-mail message
does not open, close
the window that
opens and continue
with step 6.

4. **Press and hold** [Ctrl], **then click the** your name hyperlink

   An e-mail message addressed to you with the subject "San Diego Lecture Series" opens in the default e-mail program. People can use this hyperlink to send you an e-mail message.

5. **Close the e-mail message window, clicking** No **if you are prompted to save**

   The hyperlink text changes to purple, indicating the hyperlink has been followed.

QUICK TIP
To remove a hyper-
link, right-click it,
then click Remove
Hyperlink. Removing
a hyperlink removes
the link, but the text
remains.

6. **Scroll down, select** Gaslamp Quarter **in the second paragraph, click the** Hyperlink button, **click** Existing File or Web Page **in the Link to section, type** www.gaslamp.org **in the Address text box, then click** OK

   As you type the web address, Word automatically adds "http://" in front of "www." The text "Gaslamp Quarter" is formatted as a hyperlink to the Gaslamp Quarter Association home page at www.gaslamp.org. When clicked, the hyperlink will open the webpage in the default browser window. If you point to a hyperlink in Word, the link to location appears in a ScreenTip. You can edit ScreenTip text to make it more descriptive.

QUICK TIP
You can also edit the
hyperlink destination
or the hyperlink text.

7. **Right-click** Quarter **in the Gaslamp Quarter hyperlink, click** Edit Hyperlink, **click** ScreenTip **in the Edit Hyperlink dialog box, type** Map, parking, and other information about the Gaslamp Quarter **in the ScreenTip text box, click** OK, **click** OK, **save your changes, then point to the** Gaslamp Quarter hyperlink **in the document**

   The ScreenTip you created appears above the Gaslamp Quarter hyperlink, as shown in **FIGURE 2-13**.

TROUBLE
If you are not working
with an active
Internet connection,
skip this step.

8. **Press** [Ctrl], **click the** Gaslamp Quarter hyperlink, **verify the link opened in your browser, then click the** Word icon 📄 **on the taskbar to return to the press release**

   Before distributing a document, it's important to test each hyperlink to verify it works as you intended.

FIGURE 2-12: Insert Hyperlink dialog box

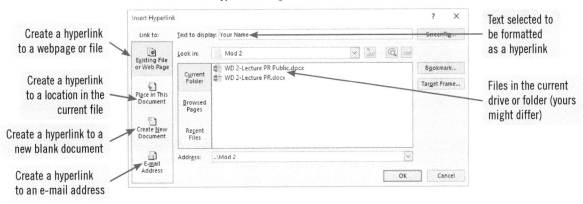

Create a hyperlink to a webpage or file

Create a hyperlink to a location in the current file

Create a hyperlink to a new blank document

Create a hyperlink to an e-mail address

Text selected to be formatted as a hyperlink

Files in the current drive or folder (yours might differ)

FIGURE 2-13: Hyperlinks in the document

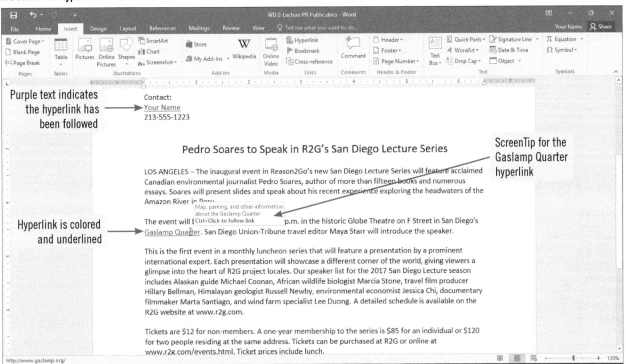

Purple text indicates the hyperlink has been followed

ScreenTip for the Gaslamp Quarter hyperlink

Hyperlink is colored and underlined

Word 2016

Sharing documents directly from Word, including e-mailing

Word includes several options for distributing and sharing documents over the Internet directly from within Word, including saving a document to OneDrive for others to view and edit, e-mailing a document, presenting a document online so others can view it in a web browser, sending it by Instant Message, and posting a document to a blog. To share a document, open the file in Word, click the File tab, click Share, and then click one of the Share options. You can also use the Share button on the title bar to save a document to an online location.

When you e-mail a document from within Word, the document is sent as an attachment to an e-mail message using your default e-mail program. You can choose to attach the document as a Word file, a .pdf file, or an .xps file, or to send it as an Internet fax. When you click an option, a message window opens that includes the filename of the current file as the message subject and the file as an attachment. Type the e-mail address(es) of the recipient(s) in the To and Cc text boxes, any message you want in the message window, and then click Send to send the message. The default e-mail program sends a copy of the document to each recipient. Note that faxing a document directly from Word requires registration with a third-party Internet fax service.

Work with Document Properties

Learning Outcomes
• Edit document properties
• Remove document properties
• Modify advanced document properties

Before you distribute a document electronically to people outside your organization, it's wise to make sure the file does not include embedded private or confidential information. The Info screen in Backstage view includes tools for stripping a document of sensitive information, for securing its authenticity, and for guarding it from unwanted changes once it is distributed to the public. One of these tools, the Document Inspector, detects and removes unwanted private or confidential information from a document. **CASE** ▸ *Before sending the press release to the public, you remove all identifying information from the file.*

STEPS

1. **Press [Ctrl][Home], then click the File tab**
   Backstage view opens with the Info screen displayed. The left side of the Info screen includes options related to stripping the file of private information. See **TABLE 2-1**. The right side of the Info screen displays basic information about the document. Notice that the file contains document properties. You want to remove these before you distribute the press release to the public.

2. **Click the Show All Properties link at the bottom of the Info screen**
   The Properties section expands on the Info screen. It shows the document properties for the press release. **Document properties** are user-defined details about a file that describe its contents and origin, including the name of the author, the title of the document, and keywords that you can assign to help organize and search your files. You decide to remove this information from the file before you distribute it electronically.

3. **Click the Check for Issues button on the Info screen, then click Inspect Document, clicking Yes if prompted to save changes**
   The Document Inspector dialog box opens. You use this dialog box to indicate which private or identifying information you want to search for and remove from the document.

4. **Make sure all the check boxes are selected, then click Inspect**
   After a moment, the Document Inspector dialog box indicates the file contains document properties, as shown in **FIGURE 2-14**.

5. **Click Remove All next to Document Properties and Personal Information, then click Close**
   The document property information is removed from the press release document, but the change will not be reflected on the Info screen until you close the document and reopen it.

6. **Click Save on the Info screen, close the document, open the document again in Word, then click the File tab**
   The Info screen shows the document properties have been removed from the file.

7. **Save the document, submit it to your instructor, close the file, then exit Word**
   The completed press release is shown in **FIGURE 2-15**.

TABLE 2-1: Options on the Info screen

option	use to
Protect Document	Mark a document as final so that it is read-only and cannot be edited; encrypt a document so that a password is required to open it; restrict what kinds of changes can be made to a document and by whom; restrict access to editing, copying, and printing a document and add a digital signature to a document to verify its integrity
Check for Issues	Detect and remove unwanted information from a document, including document properties and comments; check for content that people with disabilities might find difficult to read; and check the document for features that are not supported by previous versions of Microsoft Word
Manage Document	Browse and recover draft versions of unsaved files

FIGURE 2-14: **Results after inspecting a document**

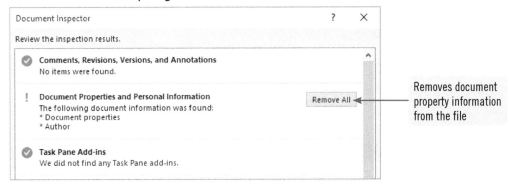

FIGURE 2-15: **Completed press release for electronic distribution**

Viewing and modifying advanced document properties

The Properties section of the Info screen includes summary information about the document that you enter. To view more detailed document properties, click the Properties button on the Info screen, and then click Advanced Properties to open the Properties dialog box. The General, Statistics, and Contents tabs of the Properties dialog box display information about the file that is automatically created and updated by Word. The General tab shows the file type, location, size, and date and time the file was created and last modified; the Statistics tab displays information about revisions to the document along with the number of pages, words, lines, paragraphs, and characters in the file; and the Contents tab shows the title of the document.

You can define other document properties using the Summary and Custom tabs in the Properties dialog box. The Summary tab shows information similar to the information shown on the Info screen. The Custom tab allows you to create new document properties, such as client, project, or date completed. To create a custom property, select a property name in the Name list box on the Custom tab, use the Type list arrow to select the type of data you want for the property, type the identifying detail (such as a project name) in the Value text box, and then click Add. When you are finished viewing or modifying the document properties, click OK to close the Properties dialog box.

Practice

Concepts Review

Label the elements of the Word program window shown in FIGURE 2-16.

FIGURE 2-16

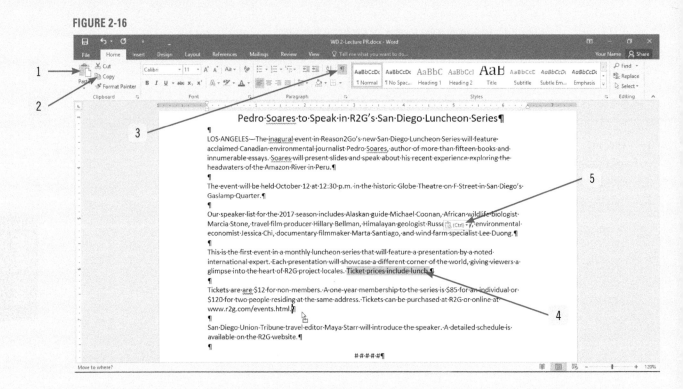

Match each term with the statement that best describes it.

6. Office Clipboard
7. Paste
8. Hyperlink
9. Thesaurus
10. Shortcut Key
11. Smart Lookup
12. Cut
13. System clipboard
14. Document properties

a. Command used to insert text stored on the Clipboard into a document
b. Temporary storage area for up to 24 items collected from Office files
c. Temporary storage area for only the last item cut or copied from a document
d. A function key or a combination of keys that perform a command when pressed
e. Text or a graphic that jumps the reader to a different location or program when clicked
f. A program that accesses information on the web from within Word
g. User-defined details about a file that describe its contents and origin
h. Feature used to suggest synonyms for words
i. Command used to remove text from a document and place it on the Clipboard

Select the best answer from the list of choices.

15. **What is the keyboard shortcut for the Cut command?**
    a. [Ctrl][V]
    b. [Ctrl][C]
    c. [Ctrl][P]
    d. [Ctrl][X]

16. **Which command is used to display a document in two panes in the document window?**
    a. Split
    b. New Window
    c. Arrange All
    d. Two pages

17. **Which of the following statements is *not* true?**
    a. You can view the contents of the Office Clipboard.
    b. The last item cut or copied from a document is stored on the system clipboard.
    c. The Office Clipboard can hold more than one item.
    d. When you move text by dragging it, a copy of the text you move is stored on the system clipboard.

18. **To locate and select all instances of a word in a document, which command do you use?**
    a. Highlight
    b. Show/Hide
    c. Find
    d. Search

19. **Which of the following is an example of a document property?**
    a. URL
    b. Keyword
    c. Permission
    d. Language

20. **A hyperlink *cannot* be linked to which of the following?**
    a. Document
    b. E-mail address
    c. ScreenTip
    d. Webpage

Skills Review

1. **Cut and paste text.**
   a. Start Word, click the Open Other Documents link, open the file WD 2-2.docx from the location where you store your Data File, then save the document with the filename **WD 2-MATOS 2017 PR**.
   b. Select **Your Name** and replace it with your name.
   c. Display paragraph and other formatting marks in your document if they are not already displayed.
   d. Use the Cut and Paste buttons to switch the order of the two sentences in the fourth body paragraph (which begins New group shows…).
   e. Use the drag-and-drop method to switch the order of the second and third paragraphs.
   f. Adjust the spacing if necessary so that there is one blank line between paragraphs, then save your changes.

2. **Copy and paste text.**
   a. Use the Copy and Paste buttons to copy **MATOS 2015** from the headline and paste it before the word **map** in the third paragraph.
   b. Change the formatting of the pasted text to match the formatting of the third paragraph, then insert a space between **2015** and **map** if necessary.
   c. Use the drag-and-drop method to copy **MATOS** from the third paragraph and paste it before the word **group** in the second sentence of the fourth paragraph, then save your changes.

3. **Use the Office Clipboard.**
   a. Use the launcher in the Clipboard group to open the Clipboard pane.
   b. Scroll so that the first body paragraph is displayed at the top of the document window.
   c. Select the fifth paragraph (which begins Studio location maps…) and cut it to the Clipboard.
   d. Select the third paragraph (which begins Manchester is easily accessible…) and cut it to the Clipboard.
   e. Use the Clipboard to paste the Studio location maps… item as the new fourth paragraph.
   f. Use the Clipboard to paste the Manchester is easily accessible… item as the new fifth paragraph.
   g. Adjust the spacing if necessary so there is one blank line between each of the six body paragraphs.
   h. Turn off the display of formatting marks, clear and close the Clipboard pane, then save your changes.

4. Find and replace text.

  a. Using the Replace command, replace all instances of **2015** with **2017**.

  b. Replace all instances of **tenth** with **twelfth**.

  c. Replace all instances of the abbreviation **st** with **street**, taking care to replace whole words only when you perform the replace. (*Hint*: Deselect Match case if it is selected.)

  d. Click the Find tab, deselect the Find whole words only check box, click the Reading Highlight button, click Highlight All, close the dialog box, then view all instances of **st** in the document to make sure no errors occurred when you replaced st with street.

  e. Click the Find button to open the Navigation pane, notice the results and the highlighted text, close the Navigation pane, then save your changes to the press release. (*Note: You can see the highlighted results using either the Reading Highlight button in the Find and Replace dialog box or the Navigation pane.*)

5. Check spelling and grammar and research information.

  a. Switch to the Review tab.

  b. Move the insertion point to the top of the document, then use the Spelling & Grammar command to search for and correct any spelling and grammar errors in the press release.

  c. Use the Thesaurus to replace **thriving** in the second paragraph with a different suitable word, then close the Thesaurus pane.

  d. Check the word count of the press release.

  e. Proofread your press release, correct any errors, then save your changes.

6. Add hyperlinks.

  a. Save the document as **WD 2-MATOS 2017 PR Public**, then switch to the Insert tab.

  b. Select your name, then open the Insert Hyperlink dialog box.

  c. Create a hyperlink to your e-mail address with the subject **MATOS 2017**.

  d. Test the your name hyperlink, then close the message window that opens and click No if a message window opens. (*Hint*: Press [Ctrl], then click the hyperlink.)

  e. Select **NEA** in the last paragraph of the press release, then create a hyperlink to the webpage with the URL **www.nea.gov**.

  f. Right-click the NEA hyperlink, then edit the hyperlink ScreenTip to become **Information on the National Endowment for the Arts**.

  g. Point to the NEA hyperlink to view the new ScreenTip, then save your changes.

  h. If you are working with an active Internet connection, press [Ctrl], click the NEA hyperlink, view the NEA home page in the browser window, then close the browser window and return to Word. The finished press release is shown in **FIGURE 2-17**.

FIGURE 2-17

PRESS RELEASE

FOR IMMEDIATE RELEASE
September 7, 2017

Contact:
Your Name
910-555-2938

MATOS 2017
Manchester Artists Open Their Studios to the Public

MANCHESTER, NH – The fall 2017 Open Studios season kicks off with Manchester Art/Tech Open Studios (MATOS) on Saturday and Sunday, October 13 and 14, from 11 a.m. to 6 p.m. More than 60 Manchester artists will open their studios and homes to the public for this annual event, now in its twelfth year.

Manchester is a historic and diverse city, long home to a flourishing community of artists. Quiet residential streets lined with charming Victorians edge a vibrant commercial and industrial zone, all peppered with the studios of printmakers, sculptors, painters, glass and jewelry makers, illustrators, potters, photographers, watercolorists, and other artists working in a wide range of digital mediums.

Internationally celebrated sculptor Mara Currier will display her new work in the rotunda of City Library. New MATOS group shows will open at the Art 5 Gallery and at the Fisher Café, both on Hanover Street.

Studio location maps will be available prior to the opening at businesses and public libraries, and on the days of the event in Victory Park. Victory Park is located at the junction of Amherst Street and Chestnut Street in downtown Manchester.

Manchester is easily accessible from all points in New England by car or bus, and from other cities by air. On Saturday, non-Manchester residents may park in permit-only areas provided they display a copy of the MATOS 2017 map on the dashboard. There are no parking restrictions on Sundays in Manchester.

MATOS 2017 receives funds from participating artists and from the Manchester Arts Council, the North Hampshire Cultural Council, and the NEA, with valuable support from local universities and businesses.

#####

Skills Review (continued)

7. Work with document properties.

  a. Click the File tab, click the Properties button on the Info screen, then click Advanced Properties to open the Properties dialog box and view the document properties for the press release on the Summary tab.

  b. Close the Properties dialog box, then use the Check for Issues command to run the Document Inspector.

  c. Remove the document property and personal information data, close the Document Inspector, save your changes, then close the file.

  d. Open the file WD 2-MATOS 2017 PR Public, then verify that the document propertes have been removed both on the Info screen and in the Properties dialog box. Save the document, submit it to your instructor, close the file, then exit Word.

Independent Challenge 1

Because of your success in revitalizing a historic theatre in Auckland, New Zealand, you were hired as the director of The Adelaide Opera House in Adelaide, Australia, to breathe life into its revitalization efforts. After a year on the job, you are launching your first major fund-raising drive. You'll create a fund-raising letter for The Adelaide Opera House by modifying a letter you wrote for the Lyric Theatre in Auckland.

  a. Start Word, open the file WD 2-3.docx from the location where you store your Data Files, then save it as **WD 2-Fundraising Letter**.

  b. Replace the theatre name and address, the date, the inside address, and the salutation with the text shown in **FIGURE 2-18**.

  c. Use the Replace command to replace all instances of **Auckland** with **Adelaide**.

  d. Use the Replace command to replace all instances of **Lyric Theatre** with **Opera House**.

  e. Use the Replace command to replace all instances of **New Zealanders** with **Australians**.

  f. Use the Find command to locate the word **considerable**, then use the Thesaurus to replace the word with a synonym.

FIGURE 2-18

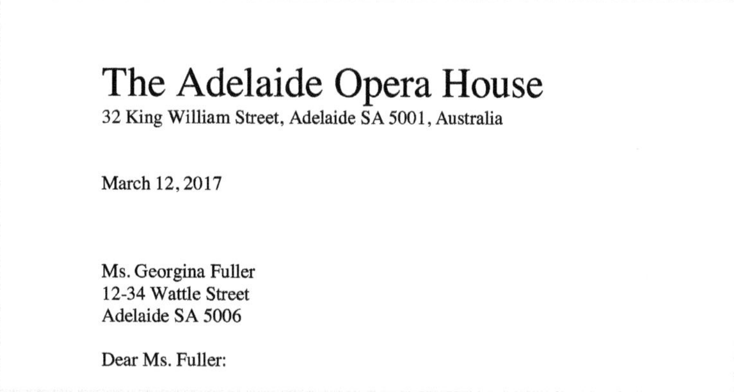

> ## The Adelaide Opera House
> 32 King William Street, Adelaide SA 5001, Australia
>
> March 12, 2017
>
> Ms. Georgina Fuller
> 12-34 Wattle Street
> Adelaide SA 5006
>
> Dear Ms. Fuller:

  g. Move the fourth body paragraph so that it becomes the second body paragraph.

  h. Create an AutoCorrect entry that inserts **Executive Director** whenever you type **exd**.

  i. Replace Your Name with your name in the signature block, select Title, then type **exd** followed by a space.

  j. Use the Spelling and Grammar command to check for and correct spelling and grammar errors.

  k. Delete the AutoCorrect entry you created for exd. (*Hint*: Open the AutoCorrect dialog box, select the AutoCorrect entry you created, then click [Delete].)

  l. Open the Properties dialog box, add your name as the author, change the title to **Adelaide Opera House**, add the keyword **fund-raising**, then add the comment **Letter for the capital campaign**.

  m. Review the paragraph, line, word, and character count on the Statistics tab.

  n. On the Custom tab, add a property named **Project** with the value **Capital Campaign**, then close the dialog box.

  o. Proofread the letter, correct any errors, save your changes, submit a copy to your instructor, close the document, then exit Word.

Independent Challenge 2

An advertisement for job openings in Chicago caught your eye and you have decided to apply. The ad, shown in FIGURE 2-19, was printed in last weekend's edition of your local newspaper. Instead of writing a cover letter from scratch, you revise a draft of a cover letter you wrote several years ago for a summer internship position.

FIGURE 2-19

ThinkPoint Technologies

Career Opportunities in Detroit

ThinkPoint Technologies, an established software development firm with offices in North America, Asia, and Europe, is seeking candidates for the following positions in its Detroit facility:

Instructor
Responsible for delivering software training to our expanding Midwestern customer base. Duties include delivering hands-on training, keeping up-to-date with product development, and working with the Director of Training to ensure the high quality of course materials. Successful candidate will have excellent presentation skills and be proficient in Microsoft PowerPoint and Microsoft Word. Position B12C6

Administrative Assistant
Proficiency with Microsoft Word a must! Administrative office duties include making travel arrangements, scheduling meetings, taking notes and publishing meeting minutes, handling correspondence, and ordering office supplies. Must have superb multitasking abilities, excellent communication, organizational, and interpersonal skills, and be comfortable working with e-mail and the Internet. Position B16F5

Copywriter
The ideal candidate will have marketing or advertising writing experience in a high tech environment, including collateral, newsletters, and direct mail. Experience writing for the Web, broadcast, and multimedia is a plus. Fluency with Microsoft Word required. Position C13D4

Positions offer salary, excellent benefits, and career opportunities.

Send resume and cover letter referencing position code to:

Selena Torres
Director of Recruiting
ThinkPoint Technologies
700 Woodward Ave.
Detroit, MI 48226

a. Read the ad shown in FIGURE 2-19 and decide which position to apply for. Choose the position that most closely matches your qualifications.

b. Start Word, open WD 2-4.docx from the location where you store your Data Files, then save it as **WD 2-ThinkPoint Cover Letter**.

c. Replace the name, address, telephone number, and e-mail address in the letterhead with your own information.

d. Remove the hyperlink from the e-mail address.

e. Replace the date with today's date, then replace the inside address and the salutation with the information shown in FIGURE 2-19.

f. Read the draft cover letter to get a feel for its contents.

g. Rework the text in the body of the letter to address your qualifications for the job you have chosen to apply for in the following ways:

- Delete the third paragraph.
- Adjust the first sentence of the first paragraph as follows: specify the job you are applying for, including the position code, and indicate where you saw the position advertised.
- Move the first sentence in the last paragraph, which briefly states your qualifications and interest in the position, to the end of the first paragraph, then rework the sentence to describe your current qualifications.
- Adjust the second paragraph as follows: describe your work experience and skills. Be sure to relate your experience and qualifications to the position requirements listed in the advertisement. Add a third paragraph if your qualifications are extensive.
- Adjust the final paragraph as follows: politely request an interview for the position and provide your phone number and e-mail address.

h. Include your name in the signature block.

i. When you are finished revising the letter, check it for spelling and grammar errors, and correct any mistakes. Make sure to remove any hyperlinks.

j. Save your changes to the letter, submit the file to your instructor, close the document, then exit Word.

Independent Challenge 3

As administrative director of continuing education, you drafted a memo to instructors asking them to help you finalize the course schedule for next semester. Today, you'll examine the draft and make revisions before distributing it as an e-mail attachment.

a. Start Word, open the file WD 2-5.docx from the drive and folder where you store your Data Files, then save it as **WD 2-Business Courses Memo**.

Independent Challenge 3 (continued)

b. Replace Your Name with your name in the From line, then scroll until the first body paragraph is at the top of the screen.

c. Use the Split command on the View tab to split the window under the first body paragraph, then scroll until the last paragraph of the memo is displayed in the bottom pane.

d. Use the Cut and Paste buttons to move the sentence **If you are planning to teach...** from the first body paragraph to become the first sentence in the last paragraph of the memo.

e. Double-click the split bar to restore the window to a single pane.

f. Use the [Delete] key to merge the first two paragraphs into one paragraph.

g. Use the Clipboard to reorganize the list of twelve-week courses so that the courses are listed in alphabetical order, then clear and close the Clipboard.

h. Use drag-and-drop to reorganize the list of one-day seminars so they are in alphabetical order.

i. Select the phrase "website" in the first paragraph, then create a hyperlink to the URL **www.course.com** with the ScreenTip **Spring 2018 Business Courses**.

j. Select "e-mail me" in the last paragraph, then create a hyperlink to your e-mail address with the subject **Final Business Course Schedule**.

k. Use the Spelling and Grammar command to check for and correct spelling and grammar errors.

l. Use the Document Inspector to strip the document of document property information, ignore any other content that is flagged by the Document Inspector, then close the Document Inspector.

m. Proofread the memo, correct any errors, save your changes, submit a copy to your instructor, close the document, then exit Word.

Independent Challenge 4: Explore

Reference sources—dictionaries, thesauri, style and grammar guides, and guides to business etiquette and procedure—are essential for day-to-day use in the workplace. Much of this reference information is available on the World Wide Web. In this independent challenge, you will locate reference sources that might be useful to you, including the Office Add-ins resources that are available for Word. Your goal is to familiarize yourself with online reference sources and Office Add-ins for Word so you can use them later in your work. You will insert a screenshot of an Office Add-in webpage in your document.

a. Start Word, open the file WD 2-6.docx from the location where you store your Data Files, then save it as **WD 2-References**. This document contains the questions you will answer about the web reference sources you find and Office Add-ins. You will type your answers to the questions in the document.

b. Replace the placeholder text at the top of the WD 2-References document with your name and the date.

c. Use your favorite search engine to search the web for grammar and style guides, dictionaries, and thesauri. Use the keywords **grammar**, **usage**, **dictionary**, **glossary**, or **thesaurus** to conduct your search.

d. Complete question 1 of the WD 2-References document, making sure to format each website name as a hyperlink to that website.

e. Read question 2 of the WD 2-References document, then move the insertion point under question 2.

f. Click the Store button in the Add-ins group on the Insert tab. Explore the add-ins available through the Office Add-ins window, click one add-in to select it, then click the hyperlink for that add-in to open it in a new browser window. (*Hint:* The hyperlink for an add-in is located under the icon for the add-in.)

g. Switch to the WD 2-References document in Word. Close the Office Add-ins window if it is still open.

h. With the insertion point below question 2, click the Screenshot button in the Illustrations group on the Insert tab. The Available Windows gallery opens.

i. Read the ScreenTip for each thumbnail in the gallery, find the Add-in browser window thumbnail in the gallery, click it, then click Yes in the dialog box that opens. A screenshot of the Add-in you selected is inserted in the WD 2-References document.

j. Save the document, submit a copy to your instructor, close the document, then exit Word.

Visual Workshop

Open WD 2-7.docx from the drive and folder where you store your Data Files, then save the document as **WD 2-Visa Letter**. Replace the placeholders for the date, letterhead, inside address, salutation, and closing with the information shown in FIGURE 2-20, then use the Office Clipboard to reorganize the sentences to match FIGURE 2-20. Correct spelling and grammar errors, remove the document property information from the file, then submit a copy to your instructor.

FIGURE 2-20

Your Name

863 East 18th Street, Apt. 4, New York, NY 20211; Tel: 212-555-9384

1/12/2017

Embassy of the Republic of Korea
2320 Massachusetts Avenue NW
Washington, DC 20008

Dear Sir or Madam:

I am applying for a long-stay tourist visa to South Korea, valid for four years. I am scheduled to depart for Seoul on March 9, 2017, returning to Chicago on September 22, 2017.

During my stay in South Korea, I will be interviewing musicians and recording footage for a film I am making on contemporary Korean music. I would like a multiple entry visa valid for four years so I can return to South Korea after this trip to follow up on my initial research. I will be based in Seoul, but I will be traveling frequently to record performances and to meet with musicians and producers.

Included with this letter are my completed visa application form, my passport, a passport photo, a copy of my return air ticket, and the visa fee. Please contact me if you need further information.

Sincerely,

Your Name

Enc: 5

Formatting Text and Paragraphs

CASE You have finished drafting the text for a two-page flyer advertising last minute specials for R2G October projects. Now, you need to format the flyer so it is attractive and highlights the significant information.

Module Objectives

After completing this module, you will be able to:

- Format with fonts
- Use the Format Painter
- Change line and paragraph spacing
- Align paragraphs
- Work with tabs

- Work with indents
- Add bullets and numbering
- Add borders and shading
- Insert online pictures

Files You Will Need

WD 3-1.docx	WD 3-4.docx
WD 3-2.docx	WD 3-5.docx
WD 3-3.docx	WD 3-6.docx

Format with Fonts

Formatting text with fonts is a quick and powerful way to enhance the appearance of a document. A **font** is a complete set of characters with the same typeface or design. Arial, Times New Roman, Courier, Tahoma, and Calibri are some of the more common fonts, but there are hundreds of others, each with a specific design and feel. Another way to change the appearance of text is to increase or decrease its **font size**. Font size is measured in points. A **point** is 1/72 of an inch. **CASE** *You change the font and font size of the body text, title, and headings in the flyer. You select fonts and font sizes that enhance the positive tone of the document and help to structure the flyer visually for readers.*

STEPS

1. **Start Word, open the file** WD 3-1.docx **from the location where you store your Data Files, save it as** WD 3-October Projects, **then change the zoom level to 120%**

   Notice that the name of the font used in the document, Calibri, is displayed in the Font list box in the Font group. The word "(Body)" in the Font list box indicates Calibri is the font used for body text in the current theme, the default theme. A **theme** is a related set of fonts, colors, styles, and effects that is applied to an entire document to give it a cohesive appearance. The font size, 11, appears in the Font Size list box in the Font group.

2. **Scroll the document to get a feel for its contents, press [Ctrl][Home], press [Ctrl][A] to select the entire document, then click the** Font list arrow **in the Font group**

   The Font list, which shows the fonts available on your computer, opens as shown in FIGURE 3-1. The font names are formatted in the font. Font names can appear in more than one location on the Font list.

3. **Drag the pointer slowly down the font names in the Font list, drag the scroll box to scroll down the Font list, then click** Garamond

   As you drag the pointer over a font name, a preview of the font is applied to the selected text. Clicking a font name applies the font. The font of the flyer changes to Garamond.

4. **Click the** Font Size list arrow **in the Font group, drag the pointer slowly up and down the Font Size list, then click** 12

   As you drag the pointer over a font size, a preview of the font size is applied to the selected text. Clicking 12 increases the font size of the selected text to 12 points.

5. **Select the title** Reason2Go October Projects, **click the** Font list arrow, **scroll to and click** Trebuchet MS, **click the** Font Size list arrow, **click** 22, **then click the** Bold button **B** in the **Font group**

   The title is formatted in 22-point Trebuchet MS bold.

6. **Click the** Font Color list arrow **A ⁃ in the Font group**

   A gallery of colors opens. It includes the set of theme colors in a range of tints and shades as well as a set of standard colors. You can point to a color in the gallery to preview it applied to the selected text.

7. **Click the** Green, Accent 6 **color as shown in** FIGURE 3-2, **then deselect the text**

   The color of the title text changes to green. The active color on the Font Color button also changes to green.

8. **Scroll down, select the heading** Animal Care Rajasthan, **then, using the Mini toolbar, click the** Font list arrow, **click** Trebuchet MS, **click the** Font Size list arrow, **click** 14, **click** **B**, **click** **A**, **then deselect the text**

   The heading is formatted in 14-point Trebuchet MS bold with a green color.

9. **Press [Ctrl][Home], then click the** Save button **on the Quick Access toolbar**

   Compare your document to FIGURE 3-3.

FIGURE 3-1: Font list

Fonts used in the default theme

List of recently used fonts (your list may differ)

Alphabetical list of all fonts on your computer (your list may differ)

Font Size list arrow

Font list arrow

FIGURE 3-2: Font Color Palette

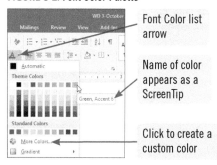

Font Color list arrow

Name of color appears as a ScreenTip

Click to create a custom color

FIGURE 3-3: Document formatted with fonts

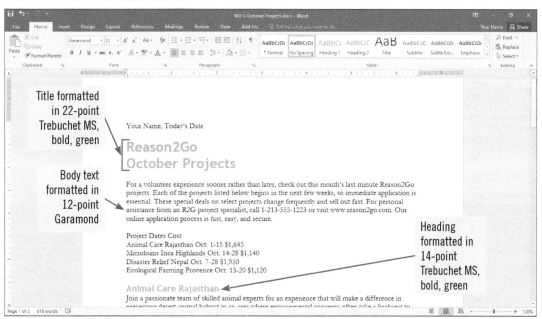

Title formatted in 22-point Trebuchet MS, bold, green

Body text formatted in 12-point Garamond

Heading formatted in 14-point Trebuchet MS, bold, green

Adding a drop cap

A fun way to illustrate a document with fonts is to add a drop cap to a paragraph. A **drop cap** is a large initial capital letter, often used to set off the first paragraph of an article. To create a drop cap, place the insertion point in the paragraph you want to format, click the Insert tab, and then click the Drop Cap button in the Text group to open a menu of Drop cap options. Preview and select one of the options on the menu, or click Drop Cap Options to open the Drop Cap dialog box, shown in FIGURE 3-4. In the Drop Cap dialog box, select the position, font, number of lines to drop, and the distance you want the drop cap to be from the paragraph text, and then click OK. The drop cap is added to the paragraph as a graphic object.

Once a drop cap is inserted in a paragraph, you can modify it by selecting it and then changing the settings in the Drop Cap dialog box. For even more interesting effects, you can enhance a drop cap with font color, font styles, or font effects. You can also fill the graphic object with shading or add a border around it. To enhance a drop cap, first select it, and then experiment with the formatting options available in the Font dialog box and in the Borders and Shading dialog box.

FIGURE 3-4: Drop Cap dialog box

Use the Format Painter

Learning
Outcomes
• Apply font styles
  and effects
• Add a shadow to
  text
• Change character
  spacing

You can dramatically change the appearance of text by applying different font styles, font effects, and character-spacing effects. For example, you can use the buttons in the Font group to make text darker by applying **bold** or to make text slanted by applying *italic*. When you are satisfied with the formatting of certain text, you can quickly apply the same formats to other text using the Format Painter. The **Format Painter** is a powerful Word feature that allows you to copy all the format settings applied to selected text to other text that you want to format the same way. **CASE** *You spice up the appearance of the text in the document by applying different font styles and text effects.*

STEPS

1. **Select** immediate application is essential **in the first body paragraph, click the** Bold **button** B **on the Mini toolbar, select the entire** paragraph, **then click the** Italic button I

   The phrase "immediate application is essential" is bold, and the entire paragraph is italic.

2. **Select** October Projects, **then click the** launcher ⌐ **in the Font group**

   The Font dialog box opens, as shown in FIGURE 3-5. You can use the options on the Font tab to change the font, font style, size, and color of text, and to add an underline and apply font effects to text.

3. **Scroll down the Size list, click** 48, **click the** Font color list arrow, **click the** Orange, Accent 2 color **in the Theme Colors, then click the** Text Effects button

   The Format Text Effects dialog box opens with the options for Text Fill & Outline active. You can also use this dialog box to apply text effects, such as shadow, reflection, and 3-D effects to selected text.

4. **Click the white** Text Effects icon **in the dialog box, click** Shadow, **click the** Presets list arrow, **click** Offset Diagonal Bottom Right **in the Outer section, click** OK, **click** OK, **then deselect the text**

   The text is larger, orange, and has a shadow effect.

5. **Select** October Projects, **right-click, click** Font **on the menu that opens, click the** Advanced tab, **click the** Scale list arrow, **click** 80%, **click** OK, **then deselect the text**

   You use the Advanced tab in the Font dialog box to change the scale, or width, of the selected characters, to alter the spacing between characters, or to raise or lower the characters. Decreasing the scale of the characters makes them narrower and gives the text a tall, thin appearance, as shown in FIGURE 3-6.

6. **Scroll down, select the subheading** Wildlife Refuge, **then, using the Mini toolbar, click the** Font list arrow, **click** Trebuchet MS, **click** B, **click** I, **click the** Font Color list arrow A ▾, **click the** Orange, Accent 2 color **in the Theme Colors, then deselect the text**

   The subheading is formatted in Trebuchet MS, bold, italic, and orange.

7. **Select** Wildlife Refuge, **then click the** Format Painter button **in the Clipboard group**

   The pointer changes to 🖌I.

8. **Scroll down, select** Animal Shelter **with the** 🖌I **pointer, then deselect the text**

   The subheading is formatted in Trebuchet MS, bold, italic, and orange, as shown in FIGURE 3-7.

9. **Scroll up, select** Animal Care Rajasthan, **then double-click the** Format Painter button

   Double-clicking the Format Painter button allows the Format Painter to remain active until you turn it off. By keeping the Format Painter active, you can apply formatting to multiple items.

10. **Scroll down, select the headings** Microloans Inca Highlands, Disaster Relief Nepal, **and** Ecological Farming Provence **with the pointer, click the** Format Painter **button to turn off the Format Painter, then save your changes**

    The headings are formatted in 14-point Trebuchet MS bold with a green font color.

FIGURE 3-5: Font tab in Font dialog box

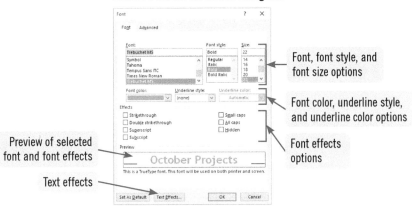

Font, font style, and font size options

Font color, underline style, and underline color options

Font effects options

Preview of selected font and font effects

Text effects

FIGURE 3-6: Font and character spacing effects applied to text

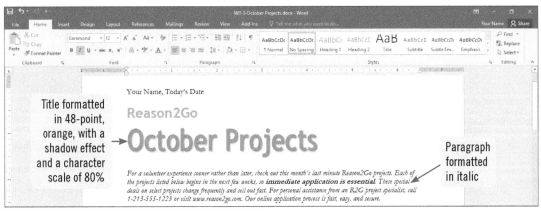

Title formatted in 48-point, orange, with a shadow effect and a character scale of 80%

Paragraph formatted in italic

FIGURE 3-7: Formats copied and applied using the Format Painter

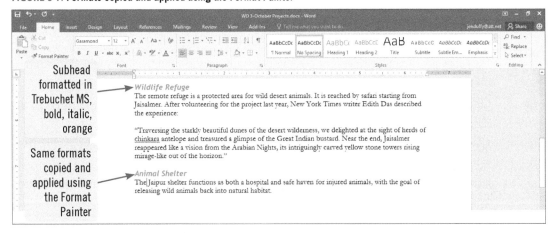

Subhead formatted in Trebuchet MS, bold, italic, orange

Same formats copied and applied using the Format Painter

Underlining text

Another creative way to call attention to text and to jazz up the appearance of a document is to apply an underline style to words you want to highlight. The Underline list arrow in the Font group displays straight, dotted, wavy, dashed, and mixed underline styles, along with a gallery of colors to choose from. To apply an underline to text, simply select it, click the Underline list arrow, and then select an underline style from the list. For a wider variety of underline styles, click More Underlines in the list, and then select an underline style in the Font dialog box. You can change the color of an underline at any time by selecting the underlined text, clicking the Underline list arrow, pointing to Underline Color, and then choosing from the options in the color gallery. If you want to remove an underline from text, select the underlined text, and then click the Underline button.

Word 2016

Change Line and Paragraph Spacing

Learning
Outcomes
• Add spacing under
paragraphs
• Change line spac-
ing in paragraphs
• Apply styles to text

Increasing the amount of space between lines adds more white space to a document and can make it easier to read. Adding space before and after paragraphs can also open up a document and improve its appearance. You use the Line and Paragraph Spacing list arrow in the Paragraph group on the Home tab to quickly change line spacing. To change paragraph spacing, you use the Spacing options in the Paragraph group on the Layout tab. Both line and paragraph spacing are measured in points. **CASE** *You increase the line spacing of several paragraphs and add extra space under each heading to give the flyer a more open feel. You work with formatting marks turned on, so you can see the paragraph marks (¶).*

STEPS

1. **Press [Ctrl][Home], click the** Show/Hide ¶ button ¶ **in the Paragraph group, place the insertion point in the italicized paragraph under the title, then click the** Line and Paragraph Spacing list arrow ⬛ **in the Paragraph group on the Home tab**
   The Line Spacing list opens. This list includes options for increasing the space between lines. The check mark on the Line Spacing list indicates the current line spacing.

2. **Click** 1.15
   The space between the lines in the paragraph increases to 1.15 lines. Notice that you do not need to select an entire paragraph to change its paragraph formatting; simply place the insertion point in the paragraph.

QUICK TIP
Word recognizes any string of text that ends with a para-graph mark as a paragraph, including titles, headings, and single lines in a list.

3. **Scroll down, select the** five-line list **that begins with "Project Dates Cost", click** ⬛, **then click** 1.5
   The line spacing between the selected paragraphs changes to 1.5. To change the paragraph-formatting features of more than one paragraph, you must select the paragraphs.

4. **Scroll down, place the insertion point in the heading** Animal Care Rajasthan, **then click the** Layout tab
   The paragraph spacing settings for the active paragraph are shown in the Before and After text boxes in the Paragraph group on the Layout tab.

QUICK TIP
You can also type a number in the Before and After text boxes.

5. **Click the** After up arrow **in the Spacing section in the Paragraph group until 6 pt appears**
   Six points of space are added after the Animal Care Rajasthan heading paragraph.

TROUBLE
If your [F4] key does not work, use the After up arrow to apply 6 pts of space to the headings listed in Steps 6 and 7, then continue with Step 8.

6. **Scroll down, place the insertion point in** Microloans Inca Highlands, **then press** [F4]
   Pressing [F4] repeats the last action you took. In this case, six points of space are added after the Microloans Inca Highlands heading. Note that using [F4] is not the same as using the Format Painter. Pressing [F4] repeats only the last action you took, and using the Format Painter applies multiple format settings at the same time.

7. **Scroll down, select** Disaster Relief Nepal, **press and hold** [Ctrl], **select** Ecological Farming Provence, **release** [Ctrl], **then press** [F4]
   When you press [Ctrl] as you select items, you can select and format multiple items at once. Six points of space are added after each heading.

QUICK TIP
Adjusting the space between paragraphs is a more precise way to add white space to a document than inserting blank lines.

8. **Press [Ctrl][Home], place the insertion point in** October Projects, **then click the** Before up arrow **in the Spacing section in the Paragraph group twice so that 12 pt appears**
   The second line of the title has 12 points of space before it, as shown in FIGURE 3-8.

9. **Click the** Home tab, **click** ¶, **then save your changes**

Formatting Text and Paragraphs

FIGURE 3-8: Line and paragraph spacing applied to document

12 points of space added before October Projects heading

Insertion point (your placement may vary)

6 points of space added after the heading

Spacing section shows paragraph spacing for the paragraph where the insertion point is located

Line spacing is 1.15

Line spacing is 1.5

Word 2016

Formatting with Quick Styles

You can also apply multiple format settings to text in one step by applying a style. A **style** is a set of formats, such as font, font size, and paragraph alignment, that is named and stored together. Formatting a document with styles is a quick and easy way to give it a professional appearance. To make it even easier, Word includes sets of styles, called **Quick Styles**, that are designed to be used together in a document to make it attractive and readable. A Quick Style set includes styles for a title, several heading levels, body text, quotes, and lists. The styles in a Quick Style set use common fonts, colors, and formats so that using the styles together in a document gives the document a cohesive look.

To view the active set of Quick Styles, click the More button in the Styles group on the Home tab to expand the Quick Styles gallery, shown in FIGURE 3-9. As you move the pointer over each style in the gallery, a preview of the style is applied to the selected text. To apply a style to the selected text, you simply click the style in the Quick Styles gallery. To remove a style from

FIGURE 3-9: Quick Styles gallery

| AaBbCcDc ¶ Normal | AaBbCcDc No Spacing | AaBbCc Heading 1 | AaBbCcD Heading 2 | AaB Title | AaBbCcD Subtitle | AaBbCcDc Subtle Em... | AaBbCcDc Emphasis |
| AaBbCcDc Intense E... | AaBbCcDc Strong | AaBbCcDc Quote | AaBbCcDc Intense Q... | AABBCCDC Subtle Ref... | AABBCCDC Intense R... | AaBbCcDc Book Title | AaBbCcDc ¶ List Para... |

Create a Style
Clear Formatting
Apply Styles...

selected text, you click the Clear All Formatting button in the Font group or the Clear Formatting command in the Quick Styles gallery.

If you want to change the active set of Quick Styles to a Quick Style set with a different design, click the Design tab, click the More button in the Document Formatting group, and then select the Quick Style set that best suits your document's content, tone, and audience. When you change the Quick Style set, a complete set of new fonts and colors is applied to the entire document. You can also change the color scheme or font used in the active Quick Style set by clicking the Colors or Fonts buttons, and then selecting from the available color schemes or font options.

Align Paragraphs

Changing paragraph alignment is another way to enhance a document's appearance. Paragraphs are aligned relative to the left and right margins in a document. By default, text is **left-aligned**, which means it is flush with the left margin and has a ragged right edge. Using the alignment buttons in the Paragraph group, you can **right-align** a paragraph—make it flush with the right margin—or **center** a paragraph so that it is positioned evenly between the left and right margins. You can also **justify** a paragraph so that both the left and right edges of the paragraph are flush with the left and right margins. **CASE** *You change the alignment of several paragraphs at the beginning of the flyer to make it more visually interesting.*

STEPS

1. **Replace** Your Name, Today's Date **with your name, a comma, and the date**

2. **Select your name, the comma, and the date, then click the** Align Right button ≣ **in the Paragraph group**

   The text is aligned with the right margin. In Page Layout view, the place where the white and shaded sections on the horizontal ruler meet shows the left and right margins.

3. **Place the insertion point between your name and the comma, press** [Delete] **to delete the comma, then press** [Enter]

   The new paragraph containing the date is also right-aligned. Pressing [Enter] in the middle of a paragraph creates a new paragraph with the same text and paragraph formatting as the original paragraph.

4. **Select the** two-line title, **then click the** Center button ≣ **in the Paragraph group**

   The two paragraphs that make up the title are centered between the left and right margins.

5. **Scroll down as needed, place the insertion point in the** Animal Care Rajasthan **heading, then click** ≣

   The Animal Care Rajasthan heading is centered.

6. **Place the insertion point in the italicized paragraph under the title, then click the** Justify button ≣ **in the Paragraph group**

   The paragraph is aligned with both the left and right margins, as shown in FIGURE 3-10. When you justify a paragraph, Word adjusts the spacing between words so that each line in the paragraph is flush with the left and the right margins.

7. **Scroll down, place the insertion point in** Animal Care Rajasthan, **then click the** launcher ⬚ **in the Paragraph group**

   The Paragraph dialog box opens, as shown in FIGURE 3-11. The Indents and Spacing tab shows the paragraph format settings for the paragraph where the insertion point is located. You can check or change paragraph format settings using this dialog box.

8. **Click the** Alignment list arrow, **click** Left, **click** OK, **then save your changes**

   The Animal Care Rajasthan heading is left-aligned.

FIGURE 3-10: Modified paragraph alignment

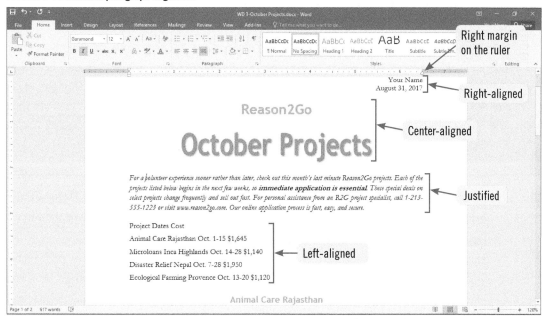

FIGURE 3-11: Indents and Spacing tab in the Paragraph dialog box

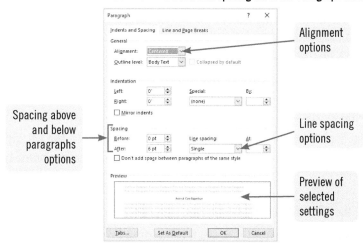

Formatting a document using themes

Changing the theme applied to a document is another powerful and efficient way to tailor a document's look and feel, particularly when a document is formatted with a Quick Style set. By default, all documents created in Word are formatted with the default Office theme—which uses Calibri as the font for the body text— but you can change the theme at any time to fit the content, tone, and purpose of a document. When you change the theme for a document, a complete set of new theme colors, fonts, and effects is applied to the whole document.

To preview how various themes look when applied to the current document, click the Themes button in the Document Formatting group on the Design tab, and then move the pointer over each theme in the gallery and notice how the document changes. When you click the theme you like, all document content that uses theme colors, all text that is formatted with a style,

including default body text, and all table styles and graphic effects change to the colors, fonts, and effects used by the theme. In addition, the gallery of colors changes to display the set of theme colors, and the active Quick Style set changes to employ the theme colors and fonts. Note that changing the theme does not change the non-theme-based font formatting that has already been applied. For example, if you changed the font of text, applied bold to text, or changed the font color of text to a standard or custom color, that formatting remains in place.

If you want to tweak the document design further, you can modify it by applying a different set of theme colors, heading and body text fonts, or graphic effects. To do this, simply click the Colors, Fonts, or Effects button in the Document Formatting group, move the pointer over each option in the gallery to preview it in the document, and then click the option you like best.

Work with Tabs

Learning
Outcomes
• Set tab stops and
  tab leaders
• Modify tabs
• Use tabs to align
  text

Tabs allow you to align text at a specific location in a document. A **tab stop** is a point on the horizontal ruler that indicates the location at which to align text. By default, tab stops are located every 1/2" from the left margin, but you can also set custom tab stops. Using tabs, you can align text to the left, right, or center of a tab stop, or you can align text at a decimal point or insert a bar character. TABLE 3-1 describes the different types of tab stops. You set tabs using the horizontal ruler or the Tabs dialog box. **CASE** ▶ *You use tabs to format the summary information on last minute projects so it is easy to read.*

STEPS

QUICK TIP
To remove a tab
stop, drag it off the
ruler.

1. **Scroll as needed, then select the five-line list beginning with "Project Dates Cost"**
   Before you set tab stops for existing text, you must select the paragraphs for which you want to set tabs.

2. **Point to the tab indicator 🔲 at the left end of the horizontal ruler**
   The icon that appears in the tab indicator indicates the active type of tab; pointing to the tab indicator displays a ScreenTip with the name of the active tab type. By default, left tab is the active tab type. Clicking the tab indicator scrolls through the types of tabs and indents.

3. **Click the tab indicator to see each of the available tab and indent types, make Left Tab 🔲 the active tab type, click the 1" mark on the horizontal ruler, then click the 3½" mark on the horizontal ruler**
   A left tab stop is inserted at the 1" mark and the 3½" mark on the horizontal ruler. Clicking the horizontal ruler inserts a tab stop of the active type for the selected paragraph or paragraphs.

4. **Click the tab indicator twice so the Right Tab icon 🔲 is active, then click the 5" mark on the horizontal ruler**
   A right tab stop is inserted at the 5" mark on the horizontal ruler, as shown in FIGURE 3-12.

5. **Place the insertion point before Project in the first line in the list, press [Tab], place the insertion point before Dates, press [Tab], place the insertion point before Cost, then press [Tab]**
   Inserting a tab before "Project" left-aligns the text at the 1" mark, inserting a tab before "Dates" left-aligns the text at the 3½" mark, and inserting a tab before "Cost" right-aligns "Cost" at the 5" mark.

6. **Insert a tab at the beginning of each remaining line in the list**
   The paragraphs left-align at the 1" mark.

QUICK TIP
Place the insertion
point in a paragraph
to see the tab stops
for that paragraph
on the horizontal
ruler.

7. **Insert a tab before each Oct. in the list, then insert a tab before each $ in the list**
   The dates left-align at the 3½" mark. The prices right-align at the 5" mark.

8. **Select the five lines of tabbed text, drag the right tab stop to the 5½" mark on the horizontal ruler, then deselect the text**
   Dragging the tab stop moves it to a new location. The prices right-align at the 5½" mark.

QUICK TIP
Double-click a tab
stop on the ruler
to open the Tabs
dialog box.

9. **Select the last four lines of tabbed text, click the launcher 🔲 in the Paragraph group, then click the Tabs button at the bottom of the Paragraph dialog box**
   The Tabs dialog box opens, as shown in FIGURE 3-13. You can use the Tabs dialog box to set tab stops, change the position or alignment of existing tab stops, clear tab stops, and apply tab leaders to tabs. **Tab leaders** are lines that appear in front of tabbed text.

10. **Click 3.5" in the Tab stop position list box, click the 2 option button in the Leader section, click Set, click 5.5" in the Tab stop position list box, click the 2 option button in the Leader section, click Set, click OK, deselect the text, then save your changes**
    A dotted tab leader is added before each 3.5" and 5.5" tab stop in the last four lines of tabbed text, as shown in FIGURE 3-14.

Formatting Text and Paragraphs

FIGURE 3-12: Left and right tab stops on the horizontal ruler

Right Tab icon in tab indicator

Left tab stops

Right tab stop

FIGURE 3-13: Tabs dialog box

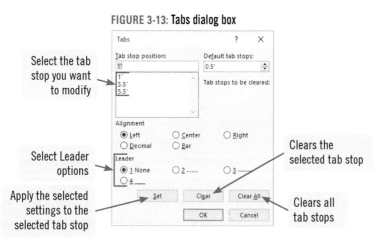

Select the tab stop you want to modify

Select Leader options

Apply the selected settings to the selected tab stop

Clears the selected tab stop

Clears all tab stops

FIGURE 3-14: Tab leaders

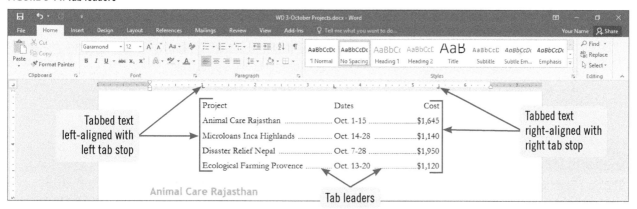

Tabbed text left-aligned with left tab stop

Tabbed text right-aligned with right tab stop

Tab leaders

TABLE 3-1: Types of tabs

tab	use to
Left tab	Set the start position of text so that text runs to the right of the tab stop as you type
Center tab	Set the center align position of text so that text stays centered on the tab stop as you type
Right tab	Set the right or end position of text so that text moves to the left of the tab stop as you type
Decimal tab	Set the position of the decimal point so that numbers align around the decimal point as you type
Bar tab	Insert a vertical bar at the tab position

Work with Indents

Learning Outcomes
- Indent a paragraph
- Indent the first line of a paragraph

When you **indent** a paragraph, you move its edge in from the left or right margin. You can indent the entire left or right edge of a paragraph, just the first line, or all lines except the first line. The **indent markers** on the horizontal ruler indicate the indent settings for the paragraph in which the insertion point is located. Dragging an indent marker to a new location on the ruler is one way to change the indentation of a paragraph; changing the indent settings in the Paragraph group on the Layout tab is another; and using the indent buttons in the Paragraph group on the Home tab is a third. TABLE 3-2 describes different types of indents and some of the methods for creating each. **CASE** *You indent several paragraphs in the flyer.*

STEPS

1. **Press [Ctrl][Home], place the insertion point in the italicized paragraph under the title, then click the Increase Indent button ▣ in the Paragraph group on the Home tab**

   The entire paragraph is indented ½" from the left margin, as shown in FIGURE 3-15. The indent marker also moves to the ½" mark on the horizontal ruler. Each time you click the Increase Indent button, the left edge of a paragraph moves another ½" to the right.

2. **Click the Decrease Indent button ▣ in the Paragraph group**

   The left edge of the paragraph moves ½" to the left, and the indent marker moves back to the left margin.

3. **Drag the First Line Indent marker ▽ to the ¼" mark on the horizontal ruler**

   FIGURE 3-16 shows the First Line Indent marker being dragged. The first line of the paragraph is indented ¼". Dragging the First Line Indent marker indents only the first line of a paragraph.

4. **Scroll to the bottom of page 1, place the insertion point in the quotation, click the Layout tab, click the Indent Left text box in the Paragraph group, type .5, click the Indent Right text box, type .5, then press [Enter]**

   The left and right edges of the paragraph are indented ½" from the margins, as shown in FIGURE 3-17.

5. **Press [Ctrl][Home], place the insertion point in the italicized paragraph, then click the launcher ▣ in the Paragraph group**

   The Paragraph dialog box opens. You can use the Indents and Spacing tab to check or change the alignment, indentation, and paragraph and line spacing settings applied to a paragraph.

6. **Click the Special list arrow, click (none), click OK, then save your changes**

   The first line indent is removed from the paragraph.

Applying text effects and clearing formatting

The Word Text Effects and Typography feature allows you to add visual appeal to your documents by adding special text effects to text, including outlines, shadows, reflections, and glows. The feature also includes a gallery of preformatted combined text effect styles, called **WordArt**, that you can apply to your text to format it quickly and easily. To apply a WordArt style or a text effect to text, simply select the text, click the Text Effects and Typography button in the Font group on the Home tab, and select a WordArt style from the gallery or point to a type of text effect, such as reflection or shadow, to open a gallery of styles related to that type of text effect. Experiment with combining text effect styles to give your text a striking appearance.

If you are unhappy with the way text is formatted, you can use the Clear All Formatting command to return the text to the default format settings. The default format includes font and paragraph formatting: text is formatted in 11-point Calibri, and paragraphs are left-aligned with 1.08 point line spacing, 8 points of space after, and no indents. To clear formatting from text and return it to the default format, select the text you want to clear, and then click the Clear All Formatting button in the Font group on the Home tab. If you prefer to return the text to the default font and remove all paragraph formatting, making the text 11-point Calibri, left-aligned, single spaced, with no paragraph spacing or indents, select the text and then simply click the No Spacing button in the Styles group on the Home tab.

FIGURE 3-15: Indented paragraph

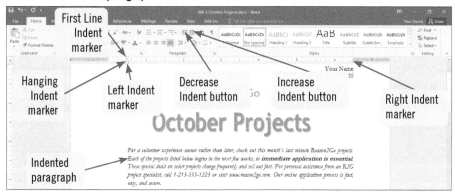

FIGURE 3-16: Dragging the First Line Indent marker

FIGURE 3-17: Paragraph indented from the left and right

TABLE 3-2: Types of indents

indent type: description	to create
Left indent: The left edge of a paragraph is moved in from the left margin	Drag the Left Indent marker ▢ on the ruler to the right to the position where you want the left edge of the paragraph to align; when you drag the left indent marker, all the indent markers move as one
Right indent: The right edge of a paragraph is moved in from the right margin	Drag the Right Indent marker △ on the ruler to the left to the position where you want the right edge of the paragraph to align
First line indent: The first line of a paragraph is indented more than the subsequent lines	Drag the First Line Indent marker ▽ on the ruler to the right to the position where you want the first line of the paragraph to begin; or activate the First Line Indent marker ▽ in the tab indicator, and then click the ruler at the position where you want the first line of the paragraph to begin
Hanging indent: The subsequent lines of a paragraph are indented more than the first line	Drag the Hanging Indent marker △ on the ruler to the right to the position where you want the hanging indent to begin; or activate the Hanging Indent marker △ in the tab indicator, and then click the ruler at the position where you want the second and remaining lines of the paragraph to begin; when you drag the hanging indent marker, the left indent marker moves with it
Negative indent (or Outdent): The left edge of a paragraph is moved to the left of the left margin	Drag the Left Indent marker ▢ on the ruler left to the position where you want the negative indent to begin; when you drag the left indent marker, all markers move as one

Formatting Text and Paragraphs

Add Bullets and Numbering

Learning Outcomes
- Apply bullets or numbering to lists
- Renumber a list
- Change bullet or numbering styles

Formatting a list with bullets or numbering can help to organize the ideas in a document. A **bullet** is a character, often a small circle, that appears before the items in a list to add emphasis. Formatting a list as a numbered list helps illustrate sequences and priorities. You can quickly format a list with bullets or numbering by using the Bullets and Numbering buttons in the Paragraph group on the Home tab. **CASE** *You format the lists in your flyer with numbers and bullets.*

STEPS

1. **Scroll until the** Disaster Relief Nepal heading **is at the top of your screen**

2. **Select the** three-line list **of 3-day add-ons, click the** Home tab, **then click the** Numbering list arrow ▦ ▾ **in the Paragraph group**

   The Numbering Library opens, as shown in FIGURE 3-18. You use this list to choose or change the numbering style applied to a list. You can drag the pointer over the numbering styles to preview how the selected text will look if the numbering style is applied.

3. **Click the numbering style called out in** FIGURE 3-18

   The paragraphs are formatted as a numbered list.

4. **Place the insertion point after** Pokhara — Valley of Lakes, **press [Enter], then type** Temples of Janakpur

   Pressing [Enter] in the middle of the numbered list creates a new numbered paragraph and automatically renumbers the remainder of the list. Similarly, if you delete a paragraph from a numbered list, Word automatically renumbers the remaining paragraphs.

5. **Click** 1 **in the list**

   Clicking a number in a list selects all the numbers, as shown in FIGURE 3-19.

6. **Click the** Bold button ☐B **in the Font group**

   The numbers are all formatted in bold. Notice that the formatting of the items in the list does not change when you change the formatting of the numbers. You can also use this technique to change the formatting of bullets in a bulleted list.

7. **Select the list of items under "Last minute participants in the Disaster Relief Nepal project...", then click the** Bullets button ▦ **in the Paragraph group**

   The four paragraphs are formatted as a bulleted list using the most recently used bullet style.

8. **Click a** bullet **in the list to select all the bullets, click the** Bullets list arrow ▦ ▾ **in the Paragraph group, click the** check mark bullet style, **click the** document **to deselect the text, then save your changes**

   The bullet character changes to a check mark, as shown in FIGURE 3-20.

Creating multilevel lists

You can create lists with hierarchical structures by applying a multilevel list style to a list. To create a **multilevel list**, also called an outline, begin by applying a multilevel list style using the Multilevel List list arrow ▦ ▾ in the Paragraph group on the Home tab, then type your outline, pressing [Enter] after each item. To demote items to a lower level of importance in the outline, place the insertion point in the item, then click the Increase Indent button ▦ in the Paragraph group on the Home tab. Each time you indent a paragraph, the item is demoted to a lower level in the outline. Similarly, you can use the Decrease Indent button ▦ to promote an item to a higher level in the outline. You can also create a hierarchical structure in any bulleted or numbered list by using ▦ and ▦ to demote and promote items in the list. To change the multilevel list style applied to a list, select the list, click ▦ ▾ and then select a new style.

Formatting Text and Paragraphs

FIGURE 3-18: Numbering Library

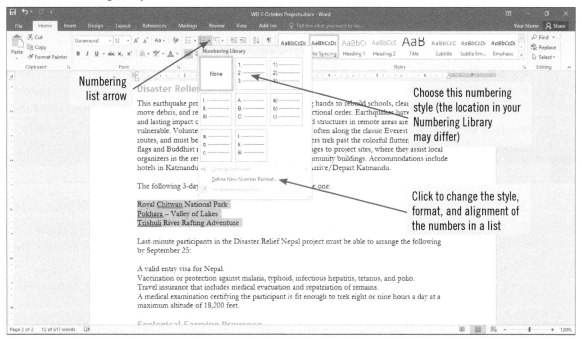

FIGURE 3-19: Numbered list

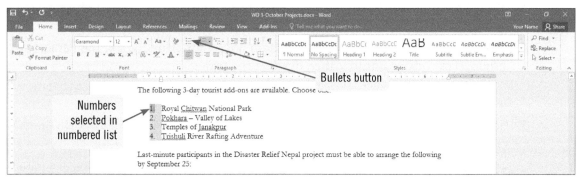

FIGURE 3-20: Check mark bullets applied to list

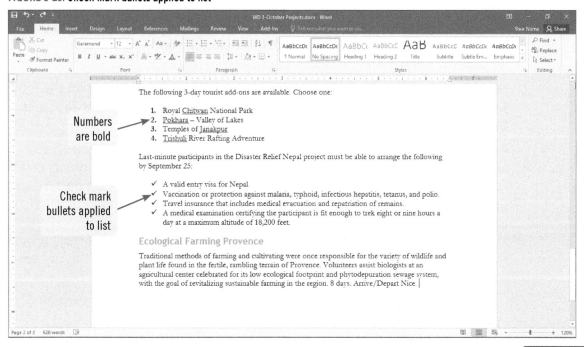

Add Borders and Shading

Learning
Outcomes
• Apply shading to text
• Apply borders to text
• Highlight text

Borders and shading can add color and splash to a document. **Borders** are lines you add above, below, to the side, or around words or paragraphs. You can format borders using different line styles, colors, and widths. **Shading** is a color or pattern you apply behind words or paragraphs to make them stand out on a page. You apply borders and shading using the Borders button and the Shading button in the Paragraph group on the Home tab. **CASE** *You enhance the tabbed text of the last minute projects schedule by adding shading to it. You also apply a border around the tabbed text to set it off from the rest of the document.*

STEPS

1. **Press [Ctrl][Home], then scroll down until the tabbed text is at the top of your screen**

2. **Select the** five paragraphs **of tabbed text, click the** Shading list arrow 🔲 **in the Paragraph group on the Home tab, click the** Green, Accent 6, Lighter 60% **color, then deselect the text**
   Light green shading is applied to the five paragraphs. Notice that the shading is applied to the entire width of the paragraphs, despite the tab settings.

3. **Select the** five paragraphs, **drag the** Left Indent marker 🔲 **to the ¾" mark on the horizontal ruler, drag the** Right Indent marker △ **to the 5¾" mark, then deselect the text**
   The shading for the paragraphs is indented from the left and right, which makes it look more attractive, as shown in **FIGURE 3-21**.

4. **Select the** five paragraphs, **click the** Bottom Border list arrow 🔲 **in the Paragraph group, click** Outside Borders, **then deselect the text**
   A black outside border is added around the selected text. The style of the border added is the most recently used border style, in this case the default, a thin black line.

5. **Select the** five paragraphs, **click the** Outside Borders list arrow 🔲, **click** No Border, **click the** No Border list arrow 🔲, **then click** Borders and Shading
   The Borders and Shading dialog box opens, as shown in **FIGURE 3-22**. You use the Borders tab to change the border style, color, and width, and to add boxes and lines to words or paragraphs.

6. **Click the** Box icon **in the Setting section, scroll down the Style list, click the** double-line style, **click the** Color list arrow, **click the** Green, Accent 6, Darker 25% **color, click the** Width list arrow, **click** 1½ pt, **click** OK, **then deselect the text**
   A 1½-point dark green double-line border is added around the tabbed text.

7. **Select the** five paragraphs, **click the** Bold button **B** **in the Font group, click the** Font Color list arrow 🔠 **in the Font group, click the** Green, Accent 6, Darker 25% **color, then deselect the text**
   The text changes to bold dark green.

8. **Select the** first line **in the tabbed text, click the** launcher 🔲 **in the Font group, click the** Font tab **if it is not the active tab, scroll and click** 14 **in the Size list, click the** Font color list arrow, **click the** Orange, Accent 2, Darker 25% **color, click the** Small caps check box **in the Effects section, click** OK, **deselect the text, then save your changes**
   The text in the first line of the tabbed text is enlarged and changed to orange small caps, as shown in **FIGURE 3-23**. When you change text to small caps, the lowercase letters are changed to uppercase letters in a smaller font size.

FIGURE 3-21: Shading applied to the tabbed text

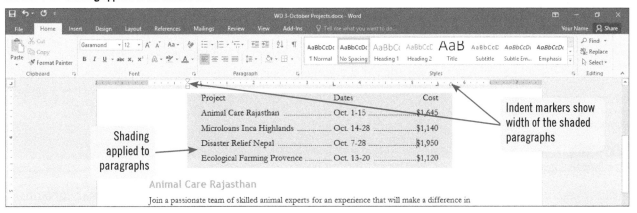

Shading applied to paragraphs

Indent markers show width of the shaded paragraphs

FIGURE 3-22: Borders tab in Borders and Shading dialog box

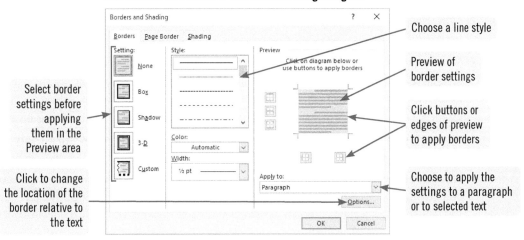

Select border settings before applying them in the Preview area

Click to change the location of the border relative to the text

Choose a line style

Preview of border settings

Click buttons or edges of preview to apply borders

Choose to apply the settings to a paragraph or to selected text

FIGURE 3-23: Borders and shading applied to the document

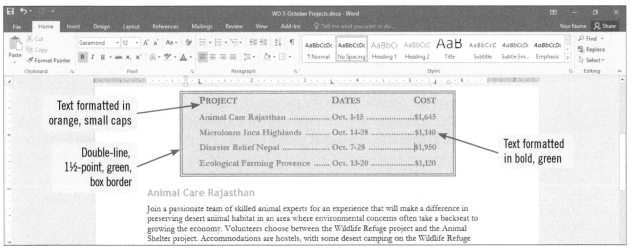

Text formatted in orange, small caps

Double-line, 1½-point, green, box border

Text formatted in bold, green

Highlighting text in a document

The Highlight tool allows you to mark and find important text in a document. **Highlighting** is transparent color that is applied to text using the Highlight pointer. To highlight text, click the Text Highlight Color list arrow in the Font group on the Home tab, select a color, then use the I-beam part of the pointer to select the text you want to highlight. Click to turn off the Highlight pointer. To remove highlighting, select the highlighted text, click then click No Color. Highlighting prints, but it is used most effectively when a document is viewed on screen.

Insert Online Pictures

Learning
Outcomes
• Insert images
• Resize images
• Wrap text and
  position images

Clip art is a collection of graphic images that you can insert into a document. Bing Image Search clip art images are images that you can add to a document using the Online Pictures command on the Insert tab. Once you insert a clip art image, you can wrap text around it, resize it, enhance it, and move it to a different location. **CASE** ▶ *You illustrate the second page of the document with an online clip art image.*

STEPS

QUICK TIP
To complete these steps, your computer must be connected to the Internet.

1. **Scroll to the top of page 2, place the insertion point before** Microloans Inca Highlands, **click the** Insert tab, **then click the** Online Pictures button **in the Illustrations group**

   The Insert Pictures window opens. You can use this to search for images related to a keyword.

2. **Type** Inca **in the Bing Image Search text box, then press** [Enter]

   Images that have the keyword "Inca" associated with them appear in the Bing Image Search window.

TROUBLE
Select a different clip if the clip shown in FIGURE 3-24 is not available to you. You can also click the Show all web results button to see more clip art options.

3. **Scroll down the gallery of images, click the clip called out in** FIGURE 3-24, **then click** Insert

   The clip is inserted at the location of the insertion point. When a graphic is selected, the active tab changes to the Picture Tools Format tab. This tab contains commands used to adjust, enhance, arrange, and size graphics. The white circles that appear on the square edges of the graphic are the **sizing handles**.

4. **Type** 1.8 **in the Shape Height text box in the Size group on the Picture Tools Format tab, then press** [Enter]

   The size of the graphic is reduced. When you decreased the height of the graphic, the width decreased proportionally. You can also resize a graphic proportionally by dragging a corner sizing handle. Until you apply text wrapping to a graphic, it is part of the line of text in which it was inserted (an **inline graphic**). To move a graphic independently of text, you must make it a **floating graphic**.

QUICK TIP
To position a graphic using precise measurements, click the Position button, click More Layout Options, then adjust the settings on the Position tab in the Layout dialog box.

5. **Click the** Position button **in the Arrange group, then click** Position in Middle Center with Square Text Wrapping

   The graphic is moved to the middle of the page and the text wraps around it. Applying text wrapping to the graphic made it a floating graphic. A floating graphic can be moved anywhere on a page. You can also wrap text around a graphic using the Layout Options button.

6. **Scroll up until the Microloans Inca Highlands heading is at the top of your screen, position the pointer over the graphic, when the pointer changes to** ⬩↖, **drag the graphic up and to the right so its edges align with the right margin and the top of the paragraph under the Microloans Inca Highlands heading as shown in** FIGURE 3-25, **then release the mouse button**

   The graphic is moved to the upper-right corner of the page. Green alignment guides may appear to help you align the image with the margins.

7. **Click the** Position button **in the Arrange group, then click** Position in Top Left with Square Text Wrapping

   The graphic is moved to the upper-left corner of the page.

TROUBLE
If your document is longer than two pages, reduce the size of the graphic by dragging the lower-right corner sizing handle up and to the left.

8. **Click the** Picture Effects button **in the Picture Styles group, point to** Shadow, **point to each style to see a preview of the style applied to the graphic, then click** Offset Left

   A shadow effect is applied to the graphic.

9. **Press** [Ctrl][Home], **click the** View tab, **then click the** Multiple Pages button **in the Zoom group to view the completed document as shown in** FIGURE 3-26.

10. **Save your changes, submit the document to your instructor, then close the document and exit Word**

Formatting Text and Paragraphs

FIGURE 3-24: Insert Pictures window

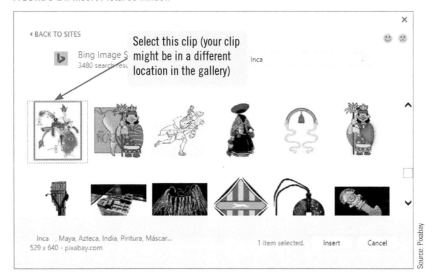

FIGURE 3-25: Graphic being moved to a new location

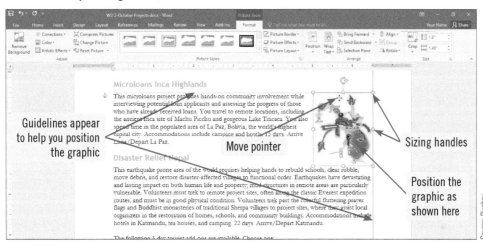

FIGURE 3-26: Completed Document

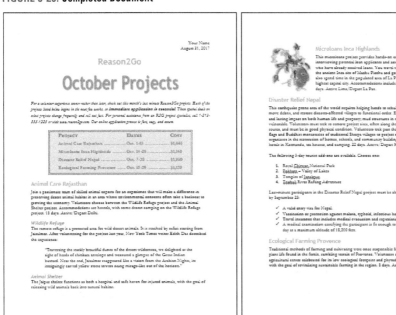

Formatting Text and Paragraphs

Practice

Concepts Review

Label each element of the Word program window shown in FIGURE 3-27.

FIGURE 3-27

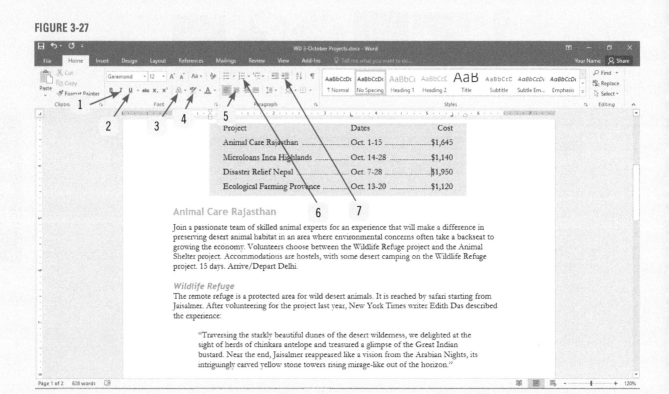

Match each term with the statement that best describes it.

8. Inline graphic

9. Style

10. Shading

11. Border

12. Floating graphic

13. Highlight

14. Point

15. Bullet

a. A graphic symbol that appears at the beginning of a paragraph in a list

b. Transparent color that is applied to text to mark it in a document

c. A set of format settings

d. An image that text wrapping has been applied to

e. An image that is inserted as part of a line of text

f. A line that can be applied above, below, or to the sides of a paragraph

g. A unit of measurement equal to $1/72$ of an inch

h. Color or pattern that is applied behind text to make it look attractive

Formatting Text and Paragraphs

Select the best answer from the list of choices.

16. **Which dialog box is used to change the scale of characters?**
    a. Paragraph
    b. Font
    c. Tabs
    d. Borders and Shading

17. **What is Calibri?**
    a. A font
    b. A style
    c. A text effect
    d. A character format

18. **What is the most precise way to increase the amount of white space between two paragraphs?**
    a. Indent the paragraphs
    b. Change the line spacing of the paragraphs
    c. Change the before spacing for the second paragraph
    d. Change the font size

19. **Which type of indent results in subsequent lines of a paragraph being indented more than the first line?**
    a. Right indent
    b. First line indent
    c. Negative indent
    d. Hanging indent

20. **Which command is used to add a reflection or an outline to text?**
    a. Underline
    b. Text Effects and Typography
    c. Strikethrough
    d. Change Case

Skills Review

1. **Format with fonts.**
   a. Start Word, open the file WD 3-2.docx from the location where you store your Data Files, save it as **WD 3-Manchester EDA Report**, then scroll through the document to get a feel for its contents.
   b. Press [Ctrl][A], then format the text in 12-point Californian FB. Choose a different serif font if Californian FB is not available to you.
   c. Press [Ctrl][Home], format the report title **City of Manchester** in 28-point Berlin Sans FB Demi. Choose a different sans serif font if Berlin Sans FB Demi is not available to you.
   d. Change the font color of the report title to Blue, Accent 5, Darker 25%.
   e. Format the subtitle **Economic Development Authority Report Executive Summary** in 16-point Berlin Sans FB Demi, then press [Enter] before Executive in the subtitle.
   f. Format the heading **Mission Statement** in 14-point Berlin Sans FB Demi with a Gold, Accent 4, Darker 25% font color.
   g. Press [Ctrl][Home], then save your changes to the report.

2. **Copy formats using the Format Painter.**
   a. Use the Format Painter to copy the format of the Mission Statement heading to the following headings: **Guiding Principles, Issues, Proposed Actions**.
   b. Show formatting marks, then format the paragraph under the Mission Statement heading in italic.
   c. Format **Years Population Growth**, the first line in the four-line list under the Issues heading, in bold, small caps, with a Blue, Accent 5, Darker 25% font color.
   d. Change the font color of the next two lines under Years Population Growth to Blue, Accent 5, Darker 25%.
   e. Format the line **Source: Office of State Planning** in italic, then save your changes.

3. **Change line and paragraph spacing.**
   a. Change the line spacing of the three-line list under the first body paragraph to 1.5 lines.
   b. Add 6 points of space after the title City of Manchester. Add 18 points of space before and 6 points of space after the Executive Summary line in the subtitle.
   c. Add 12 points of space after the Mission Statement heading, then add 12 points of space after each additional heading in the report (Guiding Principles, Issues, Proposed Actions).

    d. Add 6 points of space after each paragraph in the list under the Guiding Principles heading.

    e. Change the line spacing of the four-line list under the Issues heading that begins with Years Population Growth to 1.15.

    f. Add 6 points of space after each paragraph under the Proposed Actions heading.

    g. Press [Ctrl][Home], then save your changes to the report.

4. Align paragraphs.

    a. Press [Ctrl][A] to select the entire document, then justify all the paragraphs.

    b. Center the three-line report title.

    c. Press [Ctrl][End], press [Enter], type your name, press [Enter], type the current date, then right-align your name and the date.

    d. Save your changes to the report.

5. Work with tabs.

    a. Scroll up and select the four-line list of population information under the Issues heading.

    b. Set left tab stops at the 2" mark and the 3¾" mark.

    c. Insert a tab at the beginning of each line in the list.

    d. In the first line, insert a tab before Population. In the second line, insert a tab before 4.5%. In the third line, insert a tab before 53%.

    e. Select the first three lines, then drag the second tab stop to the 3" mark on the horizontal ruler.

    f. Press [Ctrl][Home], then save your changes to the report.

6. Work with indents.

    a. Indent the first line of the paragraph under the Mission Statement heading ½".

    b. Indent the first line of the paragraph under the Guiding Principles heading ½".

    c. Indent the first line of each of the three body paragraphs under the Issues heading ½".

    d. Press [Ctrl][Home], then save your changes to the report.

7. Add bullets and numbering.

    a. Apply bullets to the three-line list under the first body paragraph. Change the bullet style to small black circles if that is not the current bullet symbol.

    b. Change the font color of the bullets to Blue, Accent 5, Darker 25%.

    c. Scroll down until the Guiding Principles heading is at the top of your screen.

    d. Format the six-paragraph list under Guiding Principles as a numbered list.

    e. Format the numbers in 14-point Berlin Sans FB Demi, then change the font color to Blue, Accent 5, Darker 25%.

    f. Scroll down until the Proposed Actions heading is at the top of your screen, then format the paragraphs under the heading as a bulleted list using check marks as the bullet style.

    g. Change the font color of the bullets to Blue, Accent 5, Darker 25%, press [Ctrl][Home], then save your changes to the report.

8. Add borders and shading.

    a. Add a 1-point Blue, Accent 5, Darker 25% bottom border below the Mission Statement heading.

    b. Use the Format Painter or the [F4] keys to add the same border to the other headings in the report (Guiding Principles, Issues, Proposed Actions).

    c. Under the Issues heading, select the first three lines of tabbed text, which are formatted in blue, then apply Gold, Accent 4, Lighter 60% shading to the paragraphs.

    d. Select the first three lines of tabbed text again if necessary, then add a 1½ -point Blue, Accent 5, Darker 25% single line box border around the paragraphs.

    e. Indent the shading and border around the paragraphs 1¾" from the left and 1¾" from the right.

    f. Turn off formatting marks, then save your changes.

Skills Review (continued)

9. **Insert online pictures.** *(Note: To complete these steps, your computer must be connected to the Internet.)*

   a. Press [Ctrl][Home], then open the Insert Pictures window.

   b. Search using Bing Image Search to find images related to the keyword **buildings**.

   c. Insert the image shown in **FIGURE 3-28**. *(Note:* Select a different image if this one is not available to you. It is best to select an image that is similar in shape to the image shown in **FIGURE 3-28**.)

   d. Use the Shape Width text box in the Size group on the Picture Tools Format tab to change the width of the image to 1.5".

   e. Use the Position command to position the image in the top right with square text wrapping.

   f. Apply an Offset Diagonal Bottom Left shadow style to the image.

   g. View your document in two-page view and compare it to the document shown in **FIGURE 3-28**. Adjust the size or position of the image as needed to so that your document resembles the document shown in the figure.

   h. Save your changes to the document, submit it to your instructor, close the file, and then exit Word.

FIGURE 3-28

City of Manchester
Economic Development Authority Report
Executive Summary

The City of Manchester Economic Development Authority (EDA) has written an economic policy plan for the city of Manchester. The plan is intended to advance dynamic and interactive discussion. It will be used to continuously assess and foster decision-making about the following in the city of Manchester:

- Development
- Infrastructure
- Quality of life

Mission Statement

The purpose of the EDA is to foster a sustainable economy consistent with the city's planning objectives. The mix of industry, commerce, open space, residential development, and the arts in Manchester results in the city's vitality and an excellent quality of life for its citizens. Maintaining this balance is important.

Guiding Principles

Six basic principles guide Manchester's economic policy. These principles seek to safeguard the special features that give the city its character while embracing appropriate economic opportunities.

1. Manchester should remain a major economic center of the region.
2. Economic activity must respect Manchester's natural, cultural, and historic heritage.
3. A pedestrian-friendly commercial center is essential.
4. Sustained economic prosperity requires a balance between residential development, industrial/commercial development, and open space.
5. Open space in the rural district must be preserved.
6. Investing in the infrastructure is necessary to maintain and expand the existing tax and job base.

Issues

Of Manchester's approximately 64,000 acres of land, 12% is zoned for business, commercial, or industrial use, and 88% for residential development. Historically the city has relied upon business and industry to provide 35%-40% of the tax base, as well as employment opportunities. Non-residential development has traditionally been the backbone of the Manchester economy. Today, however, Manchester does not have a great deal of non-residential development potential.

The population of Manchester is expected to rise dramatically over the next few decades. The following chart shows the expected change:

Years	Population Growth
2020-2040	4.5%
2040-2060	53% (projected)

Source: Office of State Planning

At issue is the city's ability to continue to support increasing public costs (most importantly, education) with a tax base shifting toward residential taxpayers. The EDA believes Manchester should remain the market center of the region and avoid becoming a bedroom community. Manchester has maintained a sense of community in part because more than 50% of working residents are able to earn a living within the city. Jobs must be continuously created to sustain the percentage of residents who live and work in Manchester.

Proposed Actions

- Implement a business retention program that focuses on the growth and expansion of businesses already operating in Manchester.
- Build a consortium of technical and skill development resources to assist companies with educational and training needs.
- Sponsor a green business workshop.
- Allocate funds for expanded downtown parking.
- Develop a strategic open space plan.

Your Name
Today's Date

Source: Pixabay

Independent Challenge 1

You are an estimator for Sustainable Life Design | Build in Jackson, Illinois. You have drafted an estimate for a home renovation job and you need to format it. It's important that your estimate have a clean, striking design, and reflect your company's professionalism.

a. Start Word, open the file WD 3-3.docx from the drive and folder where you store your Data Files, save it as

FIGURE 3-29

SustainableLIFE Design | Build

482 North Street, Jackson, IL 62705; Tel: 217-555-3202; www.sustainablelifedesignbuild.com

WD 3-Chou Birch Estimate, then read the document to get a feel for its contents. FIGURE 3-29 shows how you will format the letterhead.

b. Select the entire document, change the style to No Spacing, then change the font to 11-point Calibri Light.

c. In the first line of the letterhead, format **Sustainable Life** in 30-point Arial Black, then apply all caps to Life. Format **Sustainable** with the Green, Accent 6, Darker 25% font color, format **LIFE** with the Green, Accent 6 font color, then delete the space between the two words. Format **Design | Build** in 30-point Arial with a Green, Accent 6, Darker 25% font color. (*Hint*: Type 30 in the Font Size text box, then press [Enter].)

d. Format the next line in 10-point Arial with a Green, Accent 6, Darker 25% font color.

e. Center the two-line letterhead.

f. Add a 2¼-point dotted Green, Accent 6, Darker 25% border below the address line paragraph.

g. With the insertion point in the address line, open the Borders and Shading dialog box, click Options to open the Border and Shading Options dialog box, change the Bottom setting to **5** points, then click OK twice to close the dialog boxes and to adjust the location of the border relative to the line of text.

h. Format the title **Proposal of Renovation** in 14-point Arial, then center the title.

i. Format the following headings (including the colons) in 11-point Arial: **Date, Work to be performed for and at, Scope of work, Payment schedule**, and **Agreement**.

j. Select the 14-line list under **Scope of work** that begins with **Demo of all…**, then change the paragraph spacing to add 4 points of space after each paragraph in the list. (*Hint*: Select 0 pt in the After text box, type 4, then press Enter.)

k. With the list selected, set a right tab stop at the 6¼" mark, insert tabs before every price in the list, then apply dotted line tab leaders.

l. Format the list as a numbered list, then apply bold to the numbers.

m. Apply bold and italic to the two lines, **Total estimated job cost…** and **Approximate job time…** below the list.

n. Replace Your Name with your name in the signature block, select the signature block (Respectfully submitted through your name), set a left tab stop at the 3¼" mark, then indent the signature block using tabs.

o. Examine the document carefully for formatting errors, and make any necessary adjustments.

p. Save the document, submit it to your instructor, then close the file and exit Word.

Independent Challenge 2

Your employer, the Mission Center for Contemporary Arts in Guelph, Ontario, is launching a membership drive. Your boss has written the text for a flyer advertising Mission membership, and asks you to format it so that it is eye catching and attractive.

a. Open the file WD 3-4.docx from the drive and folder where you store your Data Files, save it as **WD 3-Mission 2017**, then read the document. FIGURE 3-30 shows how you will format the first several paragraphs of the flyer.

FIGURE 3-30

What we do for ARTISTS

Since 1982, the artist residency program at the Mission Center for Contemporary Arts has supported the work of more than 1500 artists from all over Canada and from 40 other nations. The residency awards include studio and living space, a monthly stipend to help artists with their expenses, and use of specialized equipment for all types of visual and performance art. Each artist gives a public lecture or performance at the Mission.

b. Select the entire document, change the style to No Spacing, then change the font to 10-point Calibri Light.

c. Center the first line, **MEMBERSHIP DRIVE**, and apply shading to the paragraph. Choose a dark custom shading color of your choice for the shading color. (*Hint*: Click More Colors, then select a color from the Standard or Custom tab.) Format the text in 24-point Calibri Light, bold, with a white font color. Expand the character spacing by 10 points. (*Hint*: Use the Advanced tab in the Font dialog box. Set the Spacing to Expanded, and then type **10** in the By text box.)

d. Format the second line, **2017**, in 48-point Broadway, bold. Apply the Fill - White, Outline - Accent 2, Hard Shadow - Accent 2 text effect style to the text. (*Hint*: Use the Text Effects and Typography button.) Expand the character spacing by 10 points, and change the character scale to 250%. Center the line.

e. Format each **What we do for...** heading in 11-point Calibri Light, bold. Change the font color to the same custom color used for shading the title. (*Note*: The color now appears in the Recent Colors section of the Font Color gallery.) Add a single-line ½-point black border under each heading.

f. Format each subheading (**Gallery**, **Lectures**, **Library**, **All members...**, and **Membership Levels**) in 10-point Calibri Light, bold. Add 3 points of spacing before each paragraph. (*Hint*: Select 0 in the Before text box, type 3, then press Enter.)

g. Indent each body paragraph ¼", except for the lines under the **What we do for YOU** heading.

h. Format the four lines under the **All members...** subheading as a bulleted list. Use a bullet symbol of your choice, and format the bullets in the custom font color.

i. Indent the five lines under the **Membership Levels** heading ¼". For these five lines, set left tab stops at the 1¼" mark and the 2¼" mark on the horizontal ruler. Insert tabs before the price and before the word All in each of the five lines.

j. Format the name of each membership level (**Artistic**, **Conceptual**, etc.) in 10-point Calibri Light, bold, italic, with the custom font color.

k. Format the **For more information...** heading in 14-point Calibri Light, bold, with the custom font color, then center the heading.

l. Center the last two lines, replace Your Name with your name, then apply bold to your name.

m. Examine the document carefully for formatting errors, and make any necessary adjustments.

n. Save the flyer, submit it to your instructor, then close the file and exit Word.

Independent Challenge 3

One of your responsibilities as program coordinator at Alpine Vistas Resort is to develop a program of winter outdoor learning and adventure workshops. You have drafted a memo to your boss to update her on your progress. You need to format the memo so it is professional looking and easy to read.

a. Start Word, open the file WD 3-5.docx from the drive and folder where you store your Data Files, then save it as **WD 3-Alpine Vistas Memo**.

b. Select the **Alpine Vistas Resort Memorandum** heading, apply the Quick Style Title to it, then center the heading. (*Hint*: Open the Quick Style gallery, then click the Title style.)

c. In the memo header, replace Today's Date and Your Name with the current date and your name.

d. Select the four-line memo header, set a left tab stop at the ¾" mark, then insert tabs before the date, the recipient's name, your name, and the subject of the memo.

e. Apply the Quick Style Strong to **Date:**, **To:**, **From:**, and **Re:**.

f. Apply the Quick Style Heading 2 to the headings **Overview**, **Workshops**, **Accommodations**, **Fees**, and **Proposed winter programming**.

g. Under the Fees heading, apply the Quick Style Emphasis to the words **Workshop fees** and **Accommodations fees**.

h. On the second page of the document, format the list under the **Proposed winter programming** heading as a multilevel list. FIGURE 3-31 shows the hierarchical structure of the outline. (*Hints*: The list is on pages 2 and 3 so be sure to select the entire list before applying the multilevel style. Apply a multilevel list style, then use the Increase Indent and Decrease Indent buttons to change the level of importance of each item.)

i. Change the outline numbering style to the bullet numbering style shown in FIGURE 3-31 if a different style is used in your outline.

j. Change the font color of each bullet level in the list to a theme font color of your choice. (*Hint*: Select one bullet of each level to select all the bullets at that level, then apply a font color.)

k. Zoom out on the memo so that two pages are displayed in the document window, then, using the Change Case button, change the title Alpine Vistas Resort Memorandum so that only the initial letter of each word is capitalized.

l. Using the Fonts button on the Design tab, change the fonts to a font set of your choice. Choose fonts that allow the document to fit on two pages.

m. Using the Colors button on the Design tab, change the colors to a color palette of your choice.

n. Apply different styles and adjust other formatting elements as necessary to make the memo attractive, eye catching, and readable. The finished memo should fit on two pages.

o. Save the document, submit it to your instructor, then close the file and exit Word.

FIGURE 3-31

Proposed winter programming

❖ Skiing, Snowboarding, and Snowshoeing
  ➢ Skiing and Snowboarding
    ▪ Cross-country skiing
      • Cross-country skiing for beginners
      • Intermediate cross-country skiing
      • Inn-to-inn ski touring
      • Moonlight cross-country skiing
    ▪ Telemarking
      • Basic telemark skiing
      • Introduction to backcountry skiing
      • Exploring on skis
    ▪ Snowboarding
      • Backcountry snowboarding
  ➢ Snowshoeing
    ▪ Beginner
      • Snowshoeing for beginners
      • Snowshoeing and winter ecology
    ▪ Intermediate and Advanced
      • Intermediate snowshoeing
      • Guided snowshoe trek
      • Above tree line snowshoeing
❖ Winter Hiking, Camping, and Survival
  ➢ Hiking
    ▪ Beginner
      • Long-distance hiking
      • Winter summits
      • Hiking for women
  ➢ Winter camping and survival
    ▪ Beginner
      • Introduction to winter camping
      • Basic winter mountain skills
      • Building snow shelters
    ▪ Intermediate
      • Basic winter mountain skills II
      • Ice climbing
      • Avalanche awareness and rescue

Independent Challenge 4: Explore

The fonts you choose for a document can have a major effect on the document's tone. Not all fonts are appropriate for use in a business document, and some fonts, especially those with a definite theme, are appropriate only for specific purposes. In this Independent Challenge, you will use font formatting and other formatting features to design a letterhead and a fax coversheet for yourself or your business. The letterhead and coversheet should not only look professional and attract interest, but also say something about the character of your business or your personality. FIGURE 3-32 shows an example of a business letterhead.

a. Start Word, and save a new blank document as **WD 3-Personal Letterhead** to the drive and folder where you store your Data Files.

b. Type your name or the name of your business, your address, your phone number, your fax number, and your website or e-mail address.

c. Format your name or the name of your business in a font that expresses your personality or says something about the nature of your business. Use fonts, font colors, text effects and typography, borders, shading, paragraph formatting, and other formatting features to design a letterhead that is appealing and professional.

d. Save your changes, submit the document to your instructor, then close the file.

e. Open a new blank document, and save it as **WD 3-Personal Fax Coversheet**. Type FAX, your name or the name of your business, your address, your phone number, your fax number, and your website or e-mail address at the top of the document.

f. Type a fax header that includes the following: Date:, To:, From:, Re:, Pages:, and Comments:.

g. Format the information in the fax coversheet using fonts, font effects, borders, paragraph formatting, and other formatting features. Since a fax coversheet is designed to be faxed, all fonts and other formatting elements should be black or grey.

h. Save your changes, submit the document to your instructor, close the file, then exit Word.

FIGURE 3-32

Rebecca Valerino Interior Design

443 Sanchez Street, 6th floor, Santa Fe, NM 87501 Tel: 505-555-9767 Fax: 505-555-2992 www.valerino.com

Visual Workshop

Open the file WD 3-6.docx from the drive and folder where you store your Data Files. Create the menu shown in FIGURE 3-33. (*Hints*: Use the sizing handles to resize the graphic to be approximately 1.4" tall and 6.5" wide. Use Californian FB or a similar font for the text. Add color, bold, and italic as shown in the figure. Change the font size of the café name to 28 points, the font size of Today's Specials to 14 points, the font size of the menu to 12 points, and the font size of the italicized text at the bottom to 10 points. Format the prices using tabs and leader lines. Use paragraph spacing to adjust the spacing between paragraphs so that all the text fits on one page. Make other adjustments as needed so your menu is similar to the one shown in FIGURE 3-33.) Save the menu as **WD 3-Todays Specials**, then submit a copy to your instructor.

FIGURE 3-33

City Beach Café

Today's Specials

Strawberry Summer Salad

Arugula and baby spinach topped with sliced strawberries, goat cheese, sunflower seeds, and croutons, served with a strawberry vinaigrette. Add shrimp or lobster. $9.00

Shrimp and Avocado Salad

Shrimp and avocado salad over mixed greens with sliced tomatoes, cucumbers, and corn salsa, served with cilantro lime vinaigrette. $12.00

Lobster Tacos

Generous chunks of lobster over ginger slaw with chipotle crema and pickled onions. Served with cilantro lime rice and beans. $15.00

Coconut Encrusted Haddock

Filet of haddock lighted breaded with panko and coconut. Oven baked and served with cilantro lime rice and beans and corn on the cob. $16.00

Tropical Grilled Swordfish

Seasoned swordfish grilled and finished with citrus pineapple salsa. Served with cilantro lime rice and beans, and ginger slaw. $18.00

Shrimp Burrito

Tender grilled shrimp served with cilantro rice, black beans, romaine lettuce, cheese, salsa verde, pico de gallo, and corn on the cob. $11.00

Scallop Kebob

Ginger lime drenched scallops grilled and served with tropical macaroni salad, citrus pineapple salsa, and corn on the cob. $15.00

We serve only fresh, local, sustainably farmed and harvested ingredients.

Chef: Your Name

Source: Stocksnap.io

Formatting Documents

CASE You have written and formatted the text for an informational report for Reason2Go volunteers about staying healthy while traveling. You are now ready to format the pages. You plan to organize the text in columns, to illustrate the report with a table, and to add footnotes and a bibliography.

Module Objectives

After completing this module, you will be able to:

- Set document margins
- Create sections and columns
- Insert page breaks
- Insert page numbers
- Add headers and footers

- Insert a table
- Add footnotes and endnotes
- Insert citations
- Manage sources and create a bibliography

Files You Will Need

WD 4-1.docx	WD 4-5.docx
WD 4-2.docx	WD 4-6.docx
WD 4-3.docx	WD 4-7.docx
WD 4-4.docx	

Set Document Margins

Learning Outcomes
- Set custom margins
- Change paper size
- Change page orientation

Changing a document's margins is one way to change the appearance of a document and control the amount of text that fits on a page. The **margins** of a document are the blank areas between the edge of the text and the edge of the page. When you create a document in Word, the default margins are 1" at the top, bottom, left, and right sides of the page. You can adjust the size of a document's margins using the Margins command on the Layout tab or using the rulers. **CASE** *The report should be a four-page document when finished. You begin by reducing the size of the document margins so that more text fits on each page.*

STEPS

1. **Start Word, open the file** WD 4-1.docx **from the location where you store your Data Files, then save it as** WD 4-Travel Health 2Go

   The report opens in Print Layout view.

2. **Scroll through the report to get a feel for its contents, then press** [Ctrl][Home]

   The report is currently five pages long. Notice that the status bar indicates the page where the insertion point is located and the total number of pages in the document.

3. **Click the** Layout tab, **then click the** Margins button **in the Page Setup group**

   The Margins menu opens. You can select predefined margin settings from this menu, or you can click Custom Margins to create different margin settings.

4. **Click** Custom Margins

   The Page Setup dialog box opens with the Margins tab displayed, as shown in **FIGURE 4-1**. You can use the Margins tab to change the top, bottom, left, or right document margin, to change the orientation of the pages from portrait to landscape, and to alter other page layout settings. **Portrait orientation** means a page is taller than it is wide; **landscape orientation** means a page is wider than it is tall. This report uses portrait orientation. You can also use the Orientation button in the Page Setup group on the Layout tab to change the orientation of a document.

5. **Click the** Top down arrow **three times until** 0.7" **appears, then click the** Bottom down arrow **until** 0.7" **appears**

   The top and bottom margins of the report will be .7".

6. **Press** [Tab], **type** .7 **in the Left text box, press** [Tab], **then type** .7 **in the Right text box**

   The left and right margins of the report will also be .7". You can change the margin settings by using the arrows or by typing a value in the appropriate text box.

7. **Click** OK

   The document margins change to .7", as shown in **FIGURE 4-2**. The location of each margin (right, left, top, and bottom) is shown on the horizontal and vertical rulers at the intersection of the white and shaded areas. You can also change a margin setting by using the [icon] pointer to drag the intersection to a new location on the ruler.

8. **Click the** View tab, **then click the** Multiple Pages button **in the Zoom group**

   The first three pages of the document appear in the document window.

9. **Scroll down to view all five pages of the report, press** [Ctrl][Home], **click the** 100% button **in the Zoom group, then save your changes**

FIGURE 4-1: Margins tab in Page Setup dialog box

FIGURE 4-1: Margins tab in Page Setup dialog box

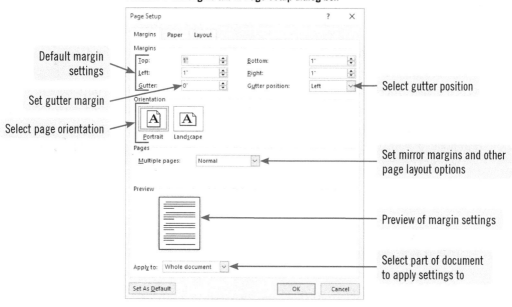

Default margin settings
Set gutter margin
Select page orientation

Select gutter position
Set mirror margins and other page layout options
Preview of margin settings
Select part of document to apply settings to

FIGURE 4-2: Report with smaller margins

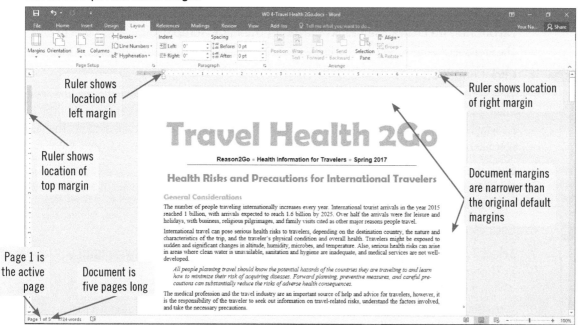

Ruler shows location of left margin
Ruler shows location of top margin
Page 1 is the active page
Document is five pages long

Ruler shows location of right margin
Document margins are narrower than the original default margins

Changing orientation, margin settings, and paper size

By default, the documents you create in Word use an 8½" x 11" paper size in portrait orientation with the default margin settings. You can change the orientation, margin settings, and paper size to common settings using the Orientation, Margins, and Size buttons in the Page Setup group on the Layout tab. You can also adjust these settings and others in the Page Setup dialog box. For example, to change the layout of multiple pages, use the Multiple pages list arrow on the Margins tab to create pages that use mirror margins, that include two pages per sheet of paper, or that are formatted using a book fold. **Mirror margins** are used in a document with facing pages, such as a magazine, where the margins on the left page of the document are a mirror image of the margins on the right page. Documents with mirror margins have inside and outside margins, rather than right and left margins. Another type of margin is a gutter margin, which is used in documents that are bound, such as books. A **gutter** adds extra space to the left, top, or inside margin to allow for the binding. Add a gutter to a document by adjusting the setting in the Gutter position text box on the Margins tab. To change the size of the paper used, use the Paper size list arrow on the Paper tab to select a standard paper size, or enter custom measurements in the Width and Height text boxes.

Create Sections and Columns

Learning
Outcomes
• Customize the
status bar
• Insert section
breaks
• Format text in
columns

Dividing a document into sections allows you to format each section of the document with different page layout settings. A **section** is a portion of a document that is separated from the rest of the document by section breaks. **Section breaks** are formatting marks that you insert in a document to show the end of a section. Once you have divided a document into sections, you can format each section with different column, margin, page orientation, header and footer, and other page layout settings. By default, a document is formatted as a single section, but you can divide a document into as many sections as you like. **CASE** *You insert a section break to divide the document into two sections, and then format the text in the second section in two columns. First, you customize the status bar to display section information.*

STEPS

QUICK TIP
Use the Customize
Status Bar menu to
turn on and off the
display of informa-
tion in the status bar.

1. **Right-click the** status bar, **click** Section **on the Customize Status Bar menu that opens (if it is not already checked), then click the document to close the menu**
   The status bar indicates the insertion point is located in section 1 of the document.

2. **Click the** Home tab, **then click the** Show/Hide ¶ button ¶ **in the Paragraph group**
   Turning on formatting marks allows you to see the section breaks you insert in a document.

3. **Place the insertion point before the heading** General Considerations, **click the** Layout tab, **then click the** Breaks button **in the Page Setup group**
   The Breaks menu opens. You use this menu to insert different types of section breaks. See **TABLE 4-1**.

QUICK TIP
A section break
stores the formatting
information for the
preceding section.

4. **Click** Continuous
   Word inserts a continuous section break, shown as a dotted double line, above the heading. When you insert a section break at the beginning of a paragraph, Word inserts the break at the end of the previous paragraph. The section break stores the formatting information for the previous section. The document now has two sections. Notice that the status bar indicates the insertion point is in section 2.

5. **Click the** Columns button **in the Page Setup group**
   The columns menu opens. You use this menu to format text using preset column formats or to create custom columns.

6. **Click** More Columns **to open the Columns dialog box**

QUICK TIP
When you delete a
section break, you
delete the section
formatting of the
text before the
break. That text
becomes part of the
following section,
and it assumes the
formatting of that
section.

7. **Select** Two **in the Presets section, click the** Spacing down arrow **twice until** 0.3" **appears as shown in** FIGURE 4-3, **then click** OK
   Section 2 is formatted in two columns of equal width with .3" of spacing between, as shown in **FIGURE 4-4**. Formatting text in columns is another way to increase the amount of text that fits on a page.

8. **Click the** View tab, **click the** Multiple Pages button **in the Zoom group, scroll down to examine all four pages of the document, press** [Ctrl][Home], **then save the document**
   The text in section 2—all the text below the continuous section break—is formatted in two columns. Text in columns flows automatically from the bottom of one column to the top of the next column.

TABLE 4-1: Types of section breaks

section	function
Next page	Begins a new section and moves the text following the break to the top of the next page
Continuous	Begins a new section on the same page
Even page	Begins a new section and moves the text following the break to the top of the next even-numbered page
Odd page	Begins a new section and moves the text following the break to the top of the next odd-numbered page

FIGURE 4-3: Columns dialog box

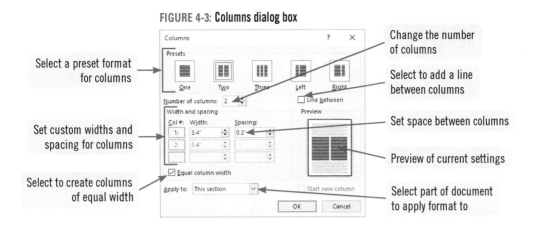

Select a preset format for columns

Change the number of columns

Select to add a line between columns

Set custom widths and spacing for columns

Set space between columns

Preview of current settings

Select to create columns of equal width

Select part of document to apply format to

FIGURE 4-4: Continuous section break and columns

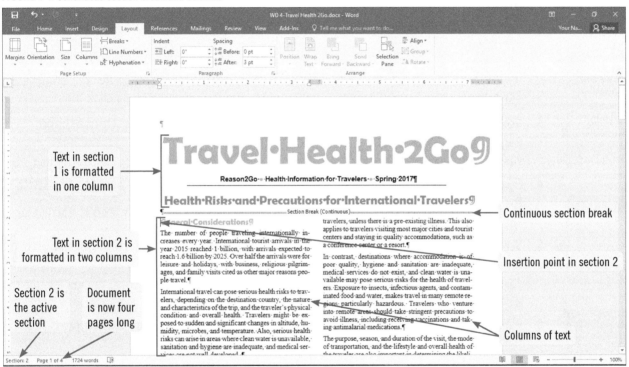

Text in section 1 is formatted in one column

Text in section 2 is formatted in two columns

Section 2 is the active section

Document is now four pages long

Continuous section break

Insertion point in section 2

Columns of text

Changing page layout settings for a section

Dividing a document into sections allows you to vary the layout of a document. In addition to applying different column settings to sections, you can apply different margins, page orientation, paper size, vertical alignment, header and footer, page numbering, footnotes, endnotes, and other page layout settings. For example, if you are formatting a report that includes a table with many columns, you might want to change the table's page orientation to landscape so that it is easier to read. To do this, you would insert a section break before and after the table to create a section that contains only the table, and then you would change the page orientation of the section that contains the table to landscape. If the table does not fill the page, you could also change the vertical alignment of the table so that it is centered vertically on the page. To do this, use the Vertical alignment list arrow on the Layout tab of the Page Setup dialog box.

To check or change the page layout settings for an individual section, place the insertion point in the section, then open the Page Setup dialog box. Select any options you want to change, click the Apply to list arrow, click This section, then click OK. When you select This section in the Apply to list box, the settings are applied to the current section only. When you select This point forward, the settings are applied to the current section and all sections that follow it. If you select Whole document in the Apply to list box, the settings are applied to all the sections in the document. Use the Apply to list arrow in the Columns dialog box or the Footnote and Endnote dialog box to change those settings for a section.

Insert Page Breaks

Learning
Outcomes
• Insert and delete
  page breaks
• Insert a column
  break
• Balance columns

As you type text in a document, Word inserts an **automatic page break** (also called a soft page break) when you reach the bottom of a page, allowing you to continue typing on the next page. You can also force text onto the next page of a document by using the Breaks command to insert a **manual page break** (also called a hard page break). Another way to control the flow of text is to apply pagination settings using the Line and Page Breaks tab in the Paragraph dialog box. **CASE** ▶ *You insert manual page breaks where you know you want to begin each new page of the report.*

STEPS

1. **Click the** 100% button, **scroll to the bottom of page 1, place the insertion point before the heading** Malaria: A Serious..., **click the** Layout tab, **then click the** Breaks button **in the Page Setup group**

   The Breaks menu opens. You also use this menu to insert page, column, and text-wrapping breaks. **TABLE 4-2** describes these types of breaks.

QUICK TIP
To control the flow
of text between
columns, insert a
column break to
force the text after
the break to the top
of the next column.

2. **Click** Page

   Word inserts a manual page break before "Malaria: A Serious Health Risk for Travelers" and moves all the text following the page break to the beginning of the next page, as shown in **FIGURE 4-5**.

3. **Scroll down, place the insertion point before the heading** Preventive Options... **on page 2, press and hold** [Ctrl], **then press** [Enter]

   Pressing [Ctrl][Enter] is a fast way to insert a manual page break. The heading is forced to the top of the third page.

4. **Scroll to the bottom of page 3, place the insertion point before the heading** Insurance for Travelers **on page 3, then press** [Ctrl][Enter]

   The heading is forced to the top of the fourth page.

QUICK TIP
You can also
double-click a page
break to select it,
and then press
[Delete] to delete it.

5. **Scroll up, click to the left of the page break on page 2 with the selection pointer** 𝒜 **to select the page break, then press** [Delete]

   The manual page break is deleted and the text from pages 2 and 3 flows together. You can also use the selection pointer to click to the left of a section or a column break to select it.

6. **Place the insertion point before the heading** Medical Kit... **on page 2, then press** [Ctrl] [Enter]

   The heading is forced to the top of the third page.

QUICK TIP
You can balance
columns of unequal
length on a page
by inserting a con-
tinuous section break
at the end of the last
column on the page.

7. **Click the** View tab, **click the** Multiple Pages button **in the Zoom group, scroll to view all four pages of the document, then save your changes**

   Pages 1, 2, and 3 are shown in **FIGURE 4-6**. Your screen might show a different number of pages.

Controlling automatic pagination

Another way to control the flow of text between pages (or between columns) is to apply pagination settings to specify where Word positions automatic page breaks. To apply automatic pagination settings, simply select the paragraphs(s) or line(s) you want to control, click the launcher in the Paragraph group on the Home or Layout tab, click the Line and Page Breaks tab in the Paragraph dialog box, and then select one or more of the following settings in the Pagination section before clicking OK.

• Keep with next: Apply to any paragraph you want to appear together with the next paragraph in order to prevent the page or column from breaking between the paragraphs.

• Keep lines together: Apply to selected paragraph or lines to prevent a page or column from breaking in the middle of a paragraph or between certain lines.

• Page break before: Apply to add an automatic page break before a specific paragraph.

• Widow/Orphan control: Turned on by default; ensures at least two lines of a paragraph appear at the top and bottom of every page or column by preventing a page or column from beginning with only the last line of a paragraph (a **widow**), or ending with only the first line of a new paragraph (an **orphan**).

FIGURE 4-5: Manual page break in document

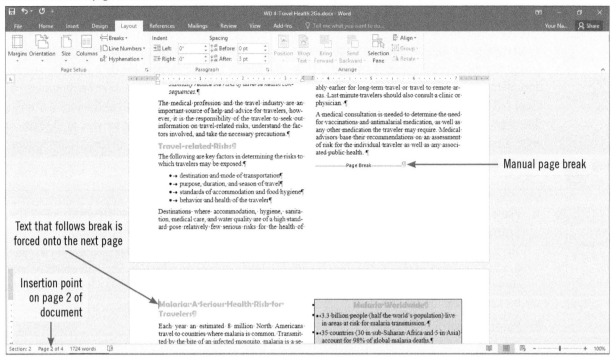

Manual page break

Text that follows break is forced onto the next page

Insertion point on page 2 of document

FIGURE 4-6: Pages 1, 2, and 3

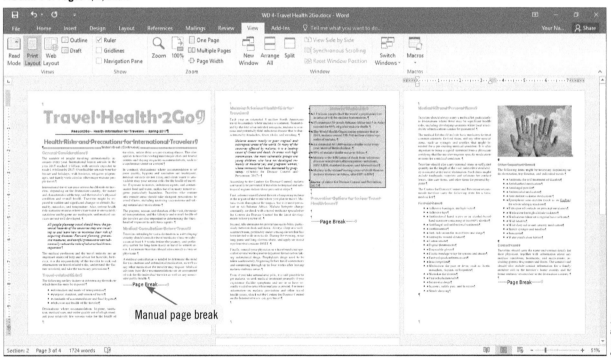

Manual page break

Source: Pixabay

TABLE 4-2: Types of breaks

break	function
Page	Forces the text following the break to begin at the top of the next page
Column	Forces the text following the break to begin at the top of the next column
Text Wrapping	Forces the text following the break to begin at the beginning of the next line

Insert Page Numbers

If you want to number the pages of a multiple-page document, you can insert a page number field to add a page number to each page. A **field** is a code that serves as a placeholder for data that changes in a document, such as a page number or the current date. When you use the Page Number button on the Insert tab to add page numbers to a document, you insert the page number field at the top, bottom, or side of any page, and Word automatically numbers all the pages in the document for you. **CASE** *You insert a page number field so that page numbers will appear centered between the margins at the bottom of each page in the document.*

STEPS

1. **Press [Ctrl][Home], click the 100% button in the Zoom group on the View tab, click the Insert tab, then click the Page Number button in the Header & Footer group**

   The Page Number menu opens. You use this menu to select the position for the page numbers. If you choose to add a page number field to the top, bottom, or side of a document, a page number will appear on every page in the document. If you choose to insert it in the document at the location of the insertion point, the field will appear on that page only.

2. **Point to Bottom of Page**

   A gallery of formatting and alignment options for page numbers to be inserted at the bottom of a page opens, as shown in **FIGURE 4-7**.

3. **Scroll down the gallery to view the options, scroll to the top of the gallery, then click Plain Number 2 in the Simple section**

   A page number field containing the number 1 is centered in the Footer area at the bottom of page 1 of the document, as shown in **FIGURE 4-8**. The document text is gray, or dimmed, because the Footer area is open. Text that is inserted in a Footer area appears at the bottom of every page in a document.

4. **Double-click the document text**

   Double-clicking the document text closes the Footer area. The page number is now dimmed because it is located in the Footer area, which is no longer the active area. When the document is printed, the page numbers appear as normal text. You will learn more about working with the Footer area in the next lesson.

5. **Scroll down the document to see the page number at the bottom of each page**

   Word numbered each page of the report automatically, and each page number is centered at the bottom of the page. If you want to change the numbering format or start page numbering with a different number, you can simply click the Page Number button, click Format Page Numbers, and then choose from the options in the Page Number Format dialog box.

6. **Press [Ctrl][Home], click the View tab, click the Page Width button in the Zoom group, then save the document**

Moving around in a long document

Rather than scrolling to move to a different place in a long document, you can use the Navigation pane to move the insertion point to the top of a specific page. To open the Navigation pane, click the Find button in the Editing group on the Home tab, and then click Pages to display a thumbnail of each page in the document in the Navigation pane. Use the scroll box in the Navigation pane to scroll through the thumbnails. Click a thumbnail in the Navigation pane to move the insertion point to the top of that page in the document window.

FIGURE 4-7: Page Number gallery

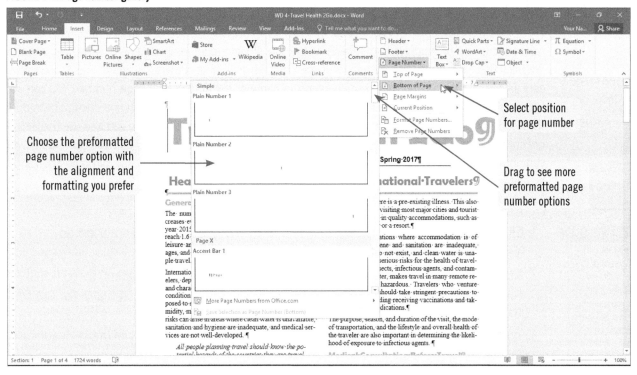

Choose the preformatted page number option with the alignment and formatting you prefer

Select position for page number

Drag to see more preformatted page number options

FIGURE 4-8: Page number in document

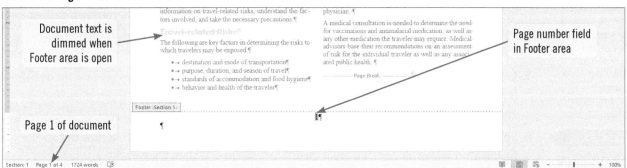

Document text is dimmed when Footer area is open

Page number field in Footer area

Page 1 of document

Inserting Quick Parts

The Word Quick Parts feature makes it easy to insert reusable pieces of content into a document quickly. The **Quick Parts** items you can insert include fields, such as for the current date or the total number of pages in a document; document property information, such as the author and title of a document; and building blocks, which are customized content that you create, format, and save for future use.

To insert a Quick Part into a document at the location of the insertion point, click the Quick Parts button in the Text group on the Insert tab (or, if headers and footers are open, click the Quick Parts button in the Insert group on the Header & Footer Tools Design tab), and then select the type of Quick Part you want to insert. To insert a field into a document, click Field on the Quick Parts menu that opens, click the name of the field you want to insert in the Field dialog box, and then click OK. Field information is updated automatically each time the document is opened or saved.

To insert a document property, point to Document Property on the Quick Parts menu, and then click the property you want to insert. The property is added to the document as a content control and contains the document property information shown in the Properties dialog box. If you did not assign a document property, the content control contains a placeholder, which you can replace with your own text. Once you replace the placeholder text—or edit the document property information that appears in the content control—this text replaces the property information in the Properties dialog box.

To insert a building block, click Building Blocks Organizer on the Quick Parts menu, select the building block you want, and then click Insert. You will learn more about working with building blocks in later lessons.

Add Headers and Footers

A **header** is text or graphics that appears at the top of every page of a document. A **footer** is text or graphics that appears at the bottom of every page. In longer documents, headers and footers often contain the title of the publication or chapter, the name of the author, or a page number. You can add headers and footers to a document by double-clicking the top or bottom margin of a document to open the Header and Footer areas, and then inserting text and graphics into them. You can also use the Header or Footer command on the Insert tab to insert predesigned headers and footers that you can modify with your information. When the header and footer areas are open, the document text is dimmed and cannot be edited. **CASE** *You create a header that includes the name of the report.*

STEPS

1. **Click the** Insert tab, **then click the** Header button **in the Header & Footer group**
   A gallery of built-in header designs opens.

2. **Scroll down the gallery to view the header designs, scroll up the gallery, then click** Blank
   The Header & Footer Tools Design tab opens and is the active tab, as shown in **FIGURE 4-9**. This tab is available whenever the Header and Footer areas are open.

3. **Type** Reason2Go Health Information for Travelers **in the content control in the Header area**
   This text will appear at the top of every page in the document.

4. **Select the header text (but not the paragraph mark below it), click the** Home tab, **click the** Font list arrow **in the Font group, click** Berlin Sans FB Demi, **click the** Font Color list arrow **A ·, click** Blue, Accent 5, **click the** Center button **in the Paragraph group, click the** Bottom Border button **, then click in the Header area to deselect the text**
   The text is formatted in blue Berlin Sans FB Demi and centered in the Header area with a bottom border.

5. **Click the** Header & Footer Tools Design tab, **then click the** Go to Footer button **in the Navigation group**
   The insertion point moves to the Footer area, where a page number field is centered in the Footer area.

6. **Select the** page number field **in the footer, use the Mini toolbar to change the formatting to** Berlin Sans FB Demi **and** Blue, Accent 5, **then click in the Footer area to deselect the text and field**
   The footer text is formatted in blue Berlin Sans FB Demi.

7. **Click the** Close Header and Footer button **in the Close group, then scroll down until the bottom of page 1 and the top of page 2 appear in the document window**
   The Header and Footer areas close, and the header and footer text is dimmed, as shown in **FIGURE 4-10**.

8. **Press** [Ctrl][Home]
   The report already includes the company information at the top of the first page, making the header information redundant. You can modify headers and footers so that the header and footer text does not appear on the first page of a document.

9. **Position the pointer over the header text at the top of page 1, then double-click**
   The Header and Footer areas open. The Options group on the Header & Footer Tools Design tab includes options for creating a different header and footer for the first page of a document, and for creating different headers and footers for odd- and even-numbered pages.

10. **Click the** Different First Page check box **to select it, click the** Close Header and Footer button, **scroll to see the header and footer on pages 2, 3, and 4, then save the document**
    The header and footer text is removed from the Header and Footer areas on the first page.

FIGURE 4-9: Header area

- Header area is open
- Header & Footer Tools Design tab active
- Tab stops for the header are set for the default document margins
- Content control
- Document text is dimmed

FIGURE 4-10: Header and footer in document

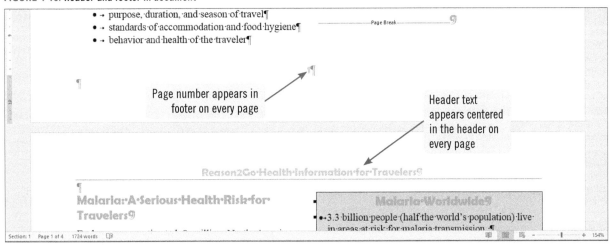

- Page number appears in footer on every page
- Header text appears centered in the header on every page

Adding a custom header or footer to the gallery

When you design a header that you want to use again in other documents, you can add it to the Header gallery by saving it as a building block. **Building blocks** are reusable pieces of formatted content or document parts, including headers and footers, page numbers, and text boxes, that are stored in galleries. Building blocks include predesigned content that comes with Word, as well as content that you create and save for future use. For example, you might create a custom header that contains your company name and logo and is formatted using the fonts, border, and colors you use in all company documents.

To add a custom header to the Header gallery, select all the text in the header, including the last paragraph mark, click the Header button, and then click Save Selection to Header Gallery.

In the Create New Building Block dialog box that opens, type a unique name for the header in the Name text box, click the Gallery list arrow and select the appropriate gallery, verify that the Category is General, and then type a brief description of the new header design in the Description text box. This description appears in a ScreenTip when you point to the custom header in the gallery. When you are finished, click OK. The new header appears in the Header gallery under the General category.

To remove a custom header from the Header gallery, right-click it, click Organize and Delete, make sure the appropriate building block is selected in the Building Blocks Organizer that opens, click Delete, click Yes, and then click Close. You can follow the same process to add or remove a custom footer to the Footer gallery.

Insert a Table

Learning Outcomes
• Create a table
• Delete a table
• Apply a table style

Adding a table to a document is a useful way to illustrate information that is intended for quick reference and analysis. A **table** is a grid of columns and rows that you can fill with text and graphics. A **cell** is the box formed by the intersection of a column and a row. The lines that divide the columns and rows of a table and help you see the grid-like structure of the table are called **borders**. A simple way to insert a table into a document is to use the Insert Table command on the Insert tab. **CASE** ▸ *You add a table to page 2 showing the preventive options for serious travel health diseases.*

STEPS

1. **Scroll until the heading** Preventive Options... **is at the top of your document window**

2. **Select the heading** Preventive Options... **and the two paragraph marks below it, click the** Layout tab, **click the** Columns button **in the Page Setup group, click** One, **click the** heading **to deselect the text, then scroll down to see the bottom half of page 2**

   A continuous section break is inserted before the heading and after the second paragraph mark, creating a new section, section 3, as shown in **FIGURE 4-11**. The document now includes four sections, with the heading Preventive Options... in Section 3. Section 3 is formatted as a single column.

3. **Place the insertion point before the first paragraph mark below the heading, click the** Insert tab, **click the** Table button **in the Tables group, then click** Insert Table

   The Insert Table dialog box opens. You use this dialog box to create a blank table.

4. **Type** 5 **in the Number of columns text box, press** [Tab], **type** 6 **in the Number of rows text box, make sure the** Fixed column width option button **is selected, then click** OK

   A blank table with five columns and six rows is inserted in the document. The insertion point is in the upper-left cell of the table, and the Table Tools Design tab becomes the active tab.

5. **Click the** Home tab, **click the** Show/Hide ¶ button ¶ **in the Paragraph group, type** Disease **in the first cell in the first row, press** [Tab], **type** Vaccine, **press** [Tab], **type** Prophylaxis Drug, **press** [Tab], **type** Eat and Drink Safely, **press** [Tab], **type** Avoid Insects, **then press** [Tab]

   Don't be concerned if the text wraps to the next line in a cell as you type. Pressing [Tab] moves the insertion point to the next cell in the row or to the first cell in the next row.

6. **Type** Malaria, **press** [Tab][Tab], **click the** Bullets list arrow ▤ ▾ **in the Paragraph group, click the** check mark style, **press** [Tab][Tab], **then click the** Bullets button ▤

   The active bullet style, a check mark, is added to a cell when you click the Bullets button.

7. **Type the text shown in** FIGURE 4-12 **in the table cells**

8. **Click the** Table Tools Layout tab, **click the** AutoFit button **in the Cell Size group, click** AutoFit Contents, **click the** AutoFit button **again, then click** AutoFit Window

   The width of the table columns is adjusted to fit the text and then the window.

9. **Click the** Select button **in the Table group, click** Select Table, **click the** Align Center button ▤ **in the Alignment group, click** Disease **in the table, click the** Select button, **click** Select Column, **click the** Align Center Left button ▤, **then click in the table to deselect the column**

   The text in the table is centered in each cell, and then the text in the first column is left-aligned.

10. **Click the** Table Tools Design tab, **click the** More button ▾ **in the Table Styles group, scroll down, click the** List Table 3 – Accent 5 style, **then save your changes**

    The List Table 3 - Accent 5 table style is applied to the table, as shown in **FIGURE 4-13**. A **table style** includes format settings for the text, borders, and shading in a table.

FIGURE 4-11: New section

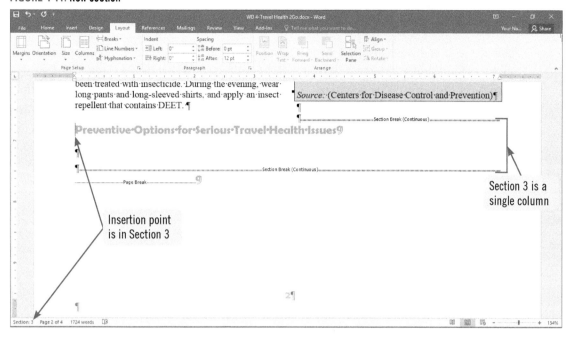

FIGURE 4-12: Text in table

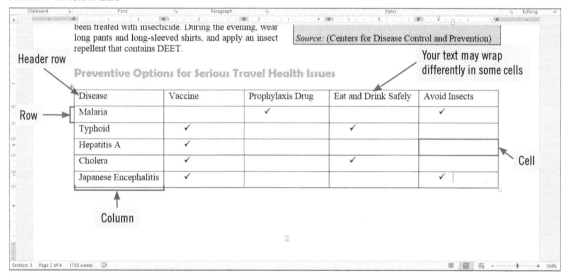

FIGURE 4-13: Completed table

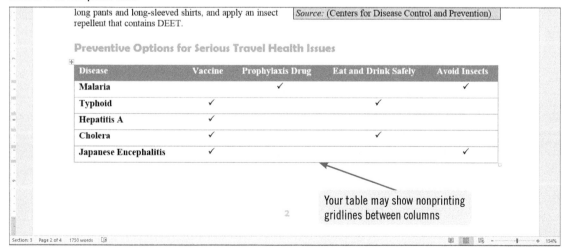

Add Footnotes and Endnotes

Footnotes and endnotes are used in documents to provide further information, explanatory text, or references for text in a document. A **footnote** or **endnote** is an explanatory note that consists of two linked parts: the **note reference mark** that appears next to text to indicate that additional information is offered in a footnote or endnote, and the corresponding footnote or endnote text. Word places footnotes at the end of each page and endnotes at the end of the document. You insert and manage footnotes and endnotes using the tools in the Footnotes group on the References tab. **CASE** *You add several footnotes to the report.*

STEPS

1. **Press [Ctrl][Home], place the insertion point at the end of the first body paragraph in the second column of text (after "resort."), click the References tab, then click the Insert Footnote button in the Footnotes group**

   A note reference mark, in this case a superscript 1, appears after "resort.", and the insertion point moves below a separator line at the bottom of the page. A note reference mark can be a number, a symbol, a character, or a combination of characters.

2. **Type Behavior is a critical factor. For example, going outdoors in a malaria-endemic area could result in becoming infected., place the insertion point at the end of the second column of text (after "health."), click the Insert Footnote button, then type It is best to consult a travel medicine specialist.**

   The footnote text appears below the separator line at the bottom of page 1, as shown in **FIGURE 4-14**.

3. **Scroll down until the bottom half of page 3 appears in the document window, place the insertion point at the end of "Medications taken on a regular basis at home" in the second column, click the Insert Footnote button, then type All medications should be stored in carry-on luggage, in their original containers and labeled clearly.**

   The footnote text for the third footnote appears at the bottom of the first column on page 3.

4. **Place the insertion point at the end of "Sunscreen" in the bulleted list in the second column, click the Insert Footnote button, then type SPF 15 or greater.**

   The footnote text for the fourth footnote appears at the bottom of page 3.

5. **Place the insertion point after "Disposable gloves" in the first column, click the Insert Footnote button, type At least two pairs., place the insertion point after "Scissors, safety pins, and tweezers" in the first column, click the Insert Footnote button, then type Pack these items in checked luggage.**

   Notice that when you inserted new footnotes between existing footnotes, Word automatically renumbered the footnotes and wrapped the footnote text to the next column. The new footnotes appear at the bottom of the first column on page 3, as shown in **FIGURE 4-15**.

6. **Press [Ctrl][Home], then click the Next Footnote button in the Footnotes group**

   The insertion point moves to the first reference mark in the document.

7. **Click the Next Footnote button twice, press [Delete] to select the number 3 reference mark, then press [Delete] again**

   The third reference mark and associated footnote are deleted from the document and the footnotes are renumbered automatically. You must select a reference mark to delete a footnote; you can not simply delete the footnote text itself.

8. **Press [Ctrl][Home], then save your changes**

FIGURE 4-14: Footnotes in the document

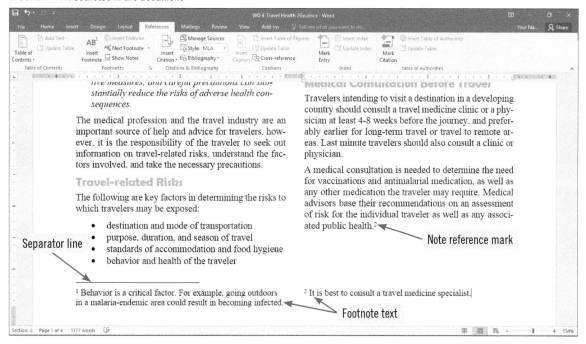

Separator line

Note reference mark

Footnote text

FIGURE 4-15: Renumbered footnotes in the document

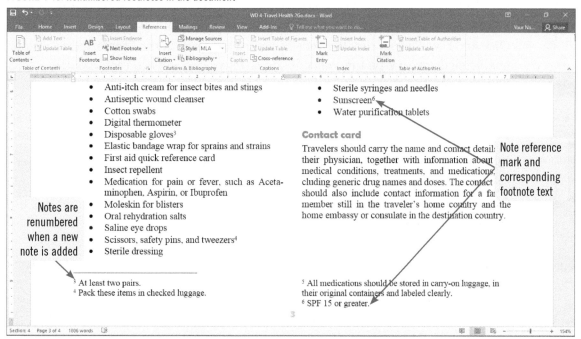

Notes are renumbered when a new note is added

Note reference mark and corresponding footnote text

Customizing the layout and formatting of footnotes and endnotes

You can change the location, formatting, and numbering options for footnotes and endnotes in a document using the Footnote and Endnote dialog box. To open the dialog box, click the launcher in the Footnotes group on the References tab. Use the list arrows in the Location section of the dialog box to locate footnotes at the bottom of the page (the default) or directly below the text on a page, and to locate endnotes at the end of a document or at the end of a section. Use the Columns list arrow in the Footnote layout section to format footnote text in one or more columns, or to match section layout (the default). Use the options in the Format section of the dialog box to change the number format of the note reference marks, to use a symbol instead of a character, and to change the numbering of footnotes and endnotes. You can choose to apply the settings to a section or to the document as a whole. When you are finished, click Apply.

Insert Citations

The Word References feature allows you to keep track of the reference sources you consult when writing research papers, reports, and other documents, and makes it easy to insert a citation in a document. A **citation** is a parenthetical reference in the document text that gives credit to the source for a quotation or other information used in a document. Citations usually include the name of the author and, for print sources, a page number. When you insert a citation you can use an existing source or create a new source. Each time you create a new source, the source information is saved on your computer so that it is available for use in any document. **CASE** ▶ *The report already includes two citations. You add several more citations to the report.*

STEPS

1. **Scroll down, place the insertion point after "people travel" but before the period at the end of the first paragraph in the first column of text, click the Style list arrow in the Citations & Bibliography group, then click MLA Seventh Edition**

   You will format the sources and citations in the report using the style recommended by the Modern Language Association (MLA).

2. **Click the Insert Citation button in the Citations & Bibliography group**

   A list of the sources already used in the document opens. You can choose to cite one of these sources, create a new source, or add a placeholder for a source. When you add a new citation to a document, the source is added to the list of master sources that is stored on the computer. The new source is also associated with the document.

3. **Click Add New Source, click the Type of Source list arrow in the Create Source dialog box, scroll down to view the available source types, click Report, then click the Corporate Author check box**

   You select the type of source and enter the source information in the Create Source dialog box. The fields available in the dialog box change, depending on the type of source selected.

4. **Enter the data shown in FIGURE 4-16 in the Create Source dialog box, then click OK**

   The citation (World Tourism Organization) appears at the end of the paragraph. Because the source is a print publication, it needs to include a page number.

5. **Click the citation to select it, click the Citation Options list arrow on the right side of the citation, then click Edit Citation**

   The Edit Citation dialog box opens, as shown in FIGURE 4-17.

6. **Type 19 in the Pages text box, then click OK**

   The page number 19 is added to the citation.

7. **Scroll down, place the insertion point at the end of the quotation (after ...consequences.), click the Insert Citation button, click Add New Source, enter the information shown in FIGURE 4-18, then click OK**

   A citation for the Web publication that the quotation was taken from is added to the report. No page number is used in this citation because the source is a Web site.

8. **Scroll to the bottom of page 2, click under the table, type Source:, italicize Source:, click after Source:, click the Insert Citation button, then click Johnson, Margaret in the list of sources**

   The citation (Johnson) appears under the table.

9. **Click the citation, click the Citation Options list arrow, click Edit Citation, type 55 in the Pages text box, click OK, then save your changes**

   The page number 55 is added to the citation.

FIGURE 4-16: Adding a Report source

Create Source   ?   ✕

Type of Source | Report ▾ |

Bibliography Fields for MLA

Author | | Edit

☑ Corporate Author | World Tourism Organization |

Title | Tourism Highlights |

Year | 2017 |

Publisher | World Tourism Organization |

City | Madrid |

Report Type | White Paper |

Medium | Print |

☐ Show All Bibliography Fields

Tag name   Example: Document   **Your tag name may differ**

| Wor17 ← |

OK   Cancel

FIGURE 4-17: Edit Citation dialog box

Selected citation appears in a content control

Citation Options list arrow

FIGURE 4-18: Adding a Web publication source

Create Source   ?   ✕

Type of Source | Document From Web site ▾ |

Bibliography Fields for MLA

Author | | Edit

☑ Corporate Author | World Health Organization |

Name of Web Page | International Travel and Health 2017 Edition |

Name of Web Site | World Health Organization Web site |

Year | 2017 |

Month | January |

Day | 10 |

Year Accessed | 2017 |

Month Accessed | March |

Day Accessed | 11 |

Medium | Web |

☐ Show All Bibliography Fields

Tag name   Example: Document

| Wor171 |

OK   Cancel

Manage Sources and Create a Bibliography

Learning Outcomes
• Add and delete sources
• Edit a source
• Insert a bibliography field

Many documents require a **bibliography**, a list of sources that you used in creating the document. The list of sources can include only the works cited in your document (a **works cited** list) or both the works cited and the works consulted (a bibliography). The Bibliography feature in Word allows you to generate a works cited list or a bibliography automatically based on the source information you provide for the document. The Source Manager dialog box helps you to organize your sources. **CASE** *You add a bibliography to the report. The bibliography is inserted as a field and it can be formatted any way you choose.*

STEPS

1. **Press [Ctrl][End] to move the insertion point to the end of the document, then click the Manage Sources button in the Citations & Bibliography group**

   The Source Manager dialog box opens, as shown in FIGURE 4-19. The Master List shows the two sources you added and any other sources available on your computer. The Current List shows the sources available in the current document. A check mark next to a source indicates the source is cited in the document. You use the tools in the Source Manager dialog box to add, edit, and delete sources from the lists, and to copy sources between the Master and Current Lists. The sources that appear in the Current List will appear in the bibliography.

2. **Click the Baker, Mary source in the Current List**

   A preview of the citation and bibliographical entry for the source in MLA style appears in the Preview box. You do not want this source to be included in your bibliography for the report.

3. **Click Delete**

   The source is removed from the Current List but remains on the Master List on the computer where it originated.

4. **Click Close, click the Bibliography button in the Citations & Bibliography group, click References, then scroll up to see the heading References at the top of the field**

   A Bibliography field labeled "References" is added at the location of the insertion point. The bibliography includes all the sources associated with the document, formatted in the MLA style for bibliographies. The text in the Bibliography field is formatted with the default styles.

5. **Select References; apply the following formats: Berlin Sans FB Demi and the Green, Accent 6 font color; drag down the list of sources to select the entire list and change the font size to 11; then click outside the bibliography field to deselect it**

   The format of the bibliography text now matches the rest of the report.

6. **Press [Ctrl][End], type your name, click the View tab, click Multiple Pages, then scroll up and down to view each page in the report**

   The completed report is shown in FIGURE 4-20.

7. **Save your changes, submit your document, close the file, then exit Word**

Working with Web sources

Publications found on the Web can be challenging to document. Many Web sites can be accessed under multiple domains, URLs change, and electronic publications are often updated frequently, making each visit to a Web site potentially unique. For these reasons, it's best to rely on the author, title, and publication information for a Web publication when citing it as a source in a research document. If possible, you can include a URL as supplementary information only, along with the date the Web site was last updated and the date you accessed the site. Since Web sites are often removed, it's also a good idea to download or print any Web source you use so that it can be verified later.

FIGURE 4-19: Source Manager dialog box

Your Master List will contain the two sources you added and either no additional sources or different additional sources

Preview of the citation and bibliography entry for the selected source in MLA style (as defined by Word)

List of sources associated with the document

Sources with a check mark have a citation in the document

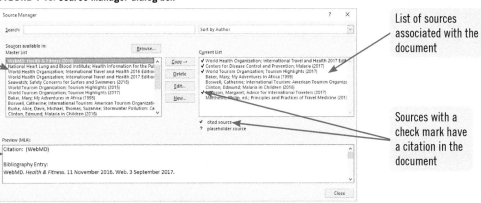

FIGURE 4-20: Completed report

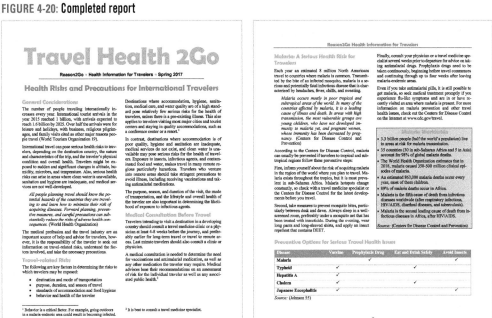

Source: Pixabay

Practice

Concepts Review

Label each element shown in FIGURE 4-21.

FIGURE 4-21

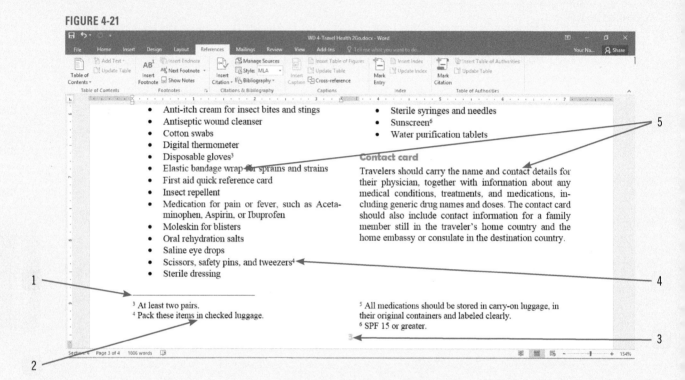

Match each term with the statement that best describes it.

6. **Bibliography**
7. **Header**
8. **Margin**
9. **Table**
10. **Citation**
11. **Manual page break**
12. **Field**
13. **Footer**
14. **Section break**

a. A grid of columns and rows that you can fill with text and graphics

b. A list of the sources used to create a document

c. Text or graphics that appear at the top of every page in a document

d. A formatting mark that forces the text following the mark to begin at the top of the next page

e. Text or graphics that appear at the bottom of every page in a document

f. A placeholder for information that changes

g. A formatting mark that divides a document into parts that can be formatted differently

h. The blank area between the edge of the text and the edge of the page

i. A parenthetical reference in the document text that gives credit to a source

Select the best answer from the list of choices.

15. **Which type of break can you insert if you want to force text to begin on the next page?**
    a. Column break
    c. Next page section break
    b. Continuous section break
    d. Text wrapping break

16. **Which type of break do you insert if you want to balance the columns in a section?**
    a. Text wrapping break
    c. Column break
    b. Manual page break
    d. Continuous section break

17. **Which of the following do documents with mirror margins always have?**
    a. Inside and outside margins
    c. Portrait orientation
    b. Sections
    d. Different first page headers and footers

18. **Which of the following cannot be inserted using the Quick Parts command?**
    a. AutoText building block
    c. Page break
    b. Page number field
    d. Document property

19. **Which appears at the end of a document?**
    a. Endnote
    c. Page break
    b. Citation
    d. Footnote

20. **What name describes formatted pieces of content that are stored in galleries?**
    a. Field
    c. Property
    b. Endnote
    d. Building Block

Skills Review

1. **Set document margins.**
    a. Start Word, open the file WD 4-2.docx from the location where you store your Data Files, then save it as **WD 4-Seaside Fitness**.
    b. Change the top and bottom margin settings to Moderate: 1" top and bottom, and .75" left and right.
    c. Save your changes to the document.

2. **Create sections and columns.**
    a. Turn on the display of formatting marks, then customize the status bar to display sections if they are not displayed already.
    b. Insert a continuous section break before the **Welcome to the Seaside Fitness Center** heading.
    c. Format the text in section 2 in two columns, then save your changes to the document.

3. **Insert page breaks.**
    a. Scroll to page 3, then insert a manual page break before the heading **Facilities and Services**. (*Hint*: The page break will appear at the bottom of page 2.)
    b. Scroll down and insert a manual page break before the heading **Membership**, then press [Ctrl][Home].
    c. On page 1, select the heading **Welcome to the Seaside Fitness Center** and the paragraph mark below it, use the Columns button to format the selected text as one column, then center the heading on the page.
    d. Follow the direction in step c to format the heading **Facilities and Services** and the paragraph mark below it on page 3, and the heading **Membership** and the paragraph mark below it on page 4, as one column, with centered text, then save your changes to the document.

4. **Insert page numbers.**
    a. Insert page numbers in the document at the bottom of the page. Select the Plain Number 2 page number style from the gallery.
    b. Close the Footer area, scroll through the document to view the page number on each page, then save your changes to the document.

Skills Review (continued)

5. Add headers and footers.

  a. Double-click the margin at the top of a page to open the Header and Footer areas.

  b. With the insertion point in the Header area, click the Quick Parts button in the Insert Group on the Header & Footer Tools Design tab, point to Document Property, then click Author.

  c. Replace the text in the Author content control with your name, press [End] to move the insertion point out of the content control, then press [Spacebar]. (*Note*: If your name does not appear in the header, right-click the Author content control, click Remove Content Control, then type your name in the header.)

  d. Click the Insert Alignment Tab button in the Position group, select the Right option button and keep the alignment relative to the margin, then click OK in the dialog box to close the dialog box and move the insertion point to the right margin.

  e. Use the Insert Date and Time command in the Insert group to insert the current date using a format of your choice as static text. (*Hint*: Be sure the Update automatically check box is not checked.)

  f. Apply italic to the text in the header.

  g. Move the insertion point to the Footer area.

  h. Double-click the page number to select it, then format the page number in bold and italic.

  i. Move the insertion point to the header on page 1, use the Header & Footer Tools Design tab to create a different header and footer for the first page of the document, type your name in the First Page Header area, then apply italic to your name.

  j. Close headers and footers, scroll to view the header and footer on each page, then save your changes to the document.

6. Insert a table.

  a. On page 4, double-click the word **Table** at the end of the Membership Rates section to select it, press [Delete], open the Insert Table dialog box, then create a table with two columns and five rows.

  b. Apply the List Table 2 table style to the table.

  c. Press [Tab] to leave the first cell in the header row blank, then type **Rate**.

  d. Press [Tab], then type the following text in the table, pressing [Tab] to move from cell to cell.

Enrollment/Individual	**$100**
Enrollment/Couple	**$150**
Monthly membership/Individual	**$125**
Monthly membership/Couple	**$200**

  e. Select the table, use the AutoFit command on the Table Tools Layout tab to select the AutoFit to Contents option, and then select the AutoFit to Window option. (*Note*: In this case, AutoFit to Window fits the table to the width of the column of text.)

  f. Save your changes to the document.

7. Add footnotes and endnotes.

  a. Press [Ctrl][Home], scroll down, place the insertion point at the end of the first body paragraph, insert a footnote, then type **People who are active live longer and feel better.**

  b. Place the insertion point at the end of the first paragraph under the Benefits of Exercise heading, insert a footnote, then type **There are 1,440 minutes in every day. Schedule 30 of them for physical activity.**

  c. Place the insertion point at the end of the first paragraph under the Tips for Staying Motivated heading, insert a footnote, type **Always consult your physician before beginning an exercise program.**, then save your changes.

8. Insert citations.

  a. Place the insertion point at the end of the second paragraph under the Benefits of Exercise heading (after "down from 52% in 2015" but before the period), then be sure the style for citations and bibliography is set to MLA Seventh Edition.

Skills Review (continued)

b. Insert a citation, add a new source, enter the source information shown in the Create Source dialog box in **FIGURE 4-22**, then click OK.

c. Place the insertion point at the end of the italicized quotation in the second column of text, insert a citation, then select Jason, Laura from the list of sources.

d. Edit the citation to include the page number **25**.

e. Scroll to page 2, place the insertion point at the end of the "Be a morning exerciser" paragraph but before the ending period, insert a citation for WebMD, then save your changes.

Word 2016

FIGURE 4-22

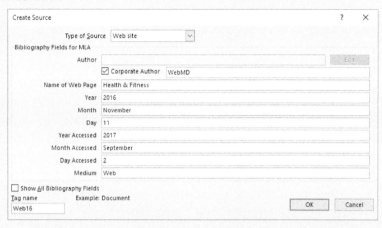

9. **Manage sources and create a bibliography.**

a. Press [Ctrl][End], then open the Source Manager dialog box.

b. Select the source Health, National Institute of: ... in the Current List, click Edit, click the Corporate Author check box, edit the entry so it reads **National Institute of Health**, click OK, then click Close.

c. Insert a bibliography labeled References.

d. Select References, then change the font to 14-point Tahoma with a black font color. Pages 1 and 4 of the formatted document are shown in **FIGURE 4-23**.

e. Save your changes to the document, submit it to your instructor, then close the document and exit Word.

FIGURE 4-23

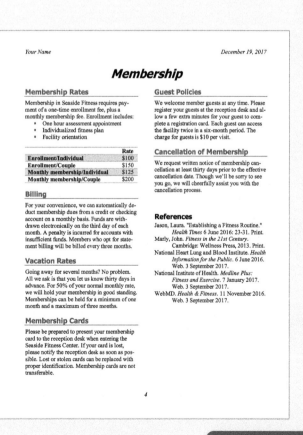

Independent Challenge 1

You are the owner of a small business called Lone Tree Catering. You have begun work on the text for a brochure advertising your business and you are now ready to lay out the pages and prepare the final copy. The brochure will be printed on both sides of an 8½" x 11" sheet of paper, and folded in thirds.

a. Start Word, open the file WD 4-3.docx from the location where you store your Data Files, then save it as **WD 4-Lone Tree Catering**. Read the document to get a feel for its contents.

b. Change the page orientation to landscape, and change all four margins to .6".

c. Format the document in three columns of equal width.

d. Insert a next page section break before the heading **Catering Services**.

e. On page 1, insert column breaks before the headings **Sample Tuscan Banquet Menu** and **Sample Indian Banquet Menu**.

f. Change the column spacing in section 1 (which is the first page) to .4", add lines between the columns on the first page, then select the text in the columns in section 1 and center it.

g. Double-click the bottom margin to open the footer area, create a different header and footer for the first page, then type **Call for custom menus designed to your taste and budget.** in the First Page Footer -Section 1- area.

FIGURE 4-24

h. Center the text in the footer area, format it in 20-point Papyrus, bold, with a Green, Accent 6 font color, then close headers and footers.

i. On page 2, insert a column break before Your Name, then press [Enter] 22 times to move the contact information to the bottom of the second column.

j. Replace Your Name with your name, then center the contact information in the column.

k. Press [Ctrl][End], insert a column break at the bottom of the second column. Type the text shown in FIGURE 4-24 in the third column, then apply the No Spacing style to the text. Refer to the figure as you follow the instructions for formatting the text in the third column.

l. Format Lone Tree Catering in 28-point Papyrus, bold, with a Green, Accent 6 font color.

m. Format the remaining text in 12-point Papyrus with a Green, Accent 6 font color. Center the text in the third column.

n. Insert an online picture of a tree, similar to the tree shown in FIGURE 4-24. Do not be concerned if the image you select is not the same tree image as that shown in the figure. Do not wrap text around the graphic.

o. Resize the graphic and add or remove blank paragraphs in the third column of your brochure so that the spacing between elements roughly matches the spacing shown in FIGURE 4-24.

p. Save your changes, then submit a copy to your instructor. If possible, you can print the brochure with the two pages back to back so that the brochure can be folded in thirds.

q. Close the document and exit Word.

Lone Tree Catering

Complete catering services available for all types of events. Menus and estimates provided upon request.

Source: Openclipart.org

Independent Challenge 2

You work in the Campus Safety Department at Valley State College. You have written the text for an informational flyer about parking regulations on campus, and now you need to format the flyer so it is attractive and readable.

a. Start Word, open the file WD 4-4.docx from the drive and folder where you store your Data Files, then save it as **WD 4-Valley Parking**. Read the document to get a feel for its contents.

b. Change all four margins to .7".

c. Insert a continuous section break before **1. May I bring a car to school?** (*Hint*: Place the insertion point before the word May.)

d. Scroll down and insert a next page section break before **Sample Parking Permit**.

e. Format the text in section 2 in three columns of equal width with .3" of space between the columns.

f. Hyphenate the document using the automatic hyphenation feature. (*Hint*: Use the Hyphenation button in the Page Setup group on the Layout tab.)

g. Add a 3-point dotted-line bottom border to the blank paragraph under Valley State College Department of Campus Safety. (*Hint*: Place the insertion point before the paragraph mark under Valley State College...)

h. Open the Header area, and type your name in the header. Right-align your name, and format it in 10-point Arial.

i. Add the following text to the footer, inserting symbols between words as indicated: **Parking and Shuttle Service Office • 54 Buckley Street • Valley State College • 942-555-2227**. (*Hint*: Click the Symbol command in the Symbols group on the Insert tab to insert a symbol. To find a small circle symbol, be sure the font is set to (normal text) and the subset is set to General Punctuation.)

j. Format the footer text in 9-point Arial Black, and center it in the footer.

k. Apply a 3-point dotted-line border above the footer text. Make sure to apply the border to the paragraph.

l. Add a continuous section break at the end of section 2 to balance the columns in section 2.

m. Place the insertion point on page 2 (which is section 4). Change the left and right margins in section 4 to 1". Also change the page orientation of section 4 to landscape.

n. Change the vertical alignment of section 4 to center. (*Hint*: Use the Vertical Alignment list arrow on the Layout tab in the Page Setup dialog box.)

o. Apply an appropriate table style to the table, such as the style shown in FIGURE 4-25. (*Hint*: Check and uncheck the options in the Table Style Options group on the Table Tools Design tab to customize the style so it enhances the table data.)

p. Save your changes, submit your work, close the document, then exit Word.

FIGURE 4-25

Sample Parking Permit

Valley State College
Office of Parking and Shuttle Service

2017-18 Student Parking Permit

License number:	VT 623 487
Make:	Subaru
Model:	Forester
Year:	2013
Color:	Silver
Permit Issue Date:	September 6, 2017
Permit Expiration Date:	June 4, 2018

Restrictions:
Parking is permitted in the Valley State College Greene Street lot 24 hours a day, 7 days a week. Shuttle service is available from the Greene Street lot to campus from 7 a.m. to 7 p.m. Monday through Friday. Parking is also permitted in any on-campus lot from 4:30 p.m. Friday to midnight Sunday.

Independent Challenge 3

A book publisher would like to publish an article you wrote on stormwater pollution in Australia as a chapter in a forthcoming book called *Environmental Issues for the New Millennium*. The publisher has requested that you format your article like a book chapter before submitting it for publication, and has provided you with a style sheet. According to the style sheet, the citations and bibliography should be formatted in Chicago style. You have already created the sources for the chapter, but you need to insert the citations.

a. Start Word, open the file WD 4-5.docx from the location where you store your Data Files, then save it as **WD 4-Chapter 8**. You will format the first page as shown in **FIGURE 4-26**.

FIGURE 4-26

b. Change the font of the entire document to 10-point Book Antigua. If this font is not available to you, select a different font suitable for the pages of a book. Change the alignment to justified.

c. Use the Page Setup dialog box to change the paper size to a custom setting of 6" x 9".

d. Create mirror margins. (*Hint:* Use the Multiple pages list arrow.) Change the top and bottom margins to .8", change the inside margin to .4", change the outside margin to .6", and create a .3" gutter to allow room for the book's binding.

e. Change the Zoom level to Page Width, open the Header and Footer areas, then apply the setting to create different headers and footers for odd- and even-numbered pages.

f. In the odd-page header, type **Chapter 8**, insert a symbol of your choice, type **The Silver Creek Catchment and Stormwater Pollution**, then format the header text in 9-point Book Antigua italic and right-align the text.

g. In the even-page header, type your name, then format the header text in 9-point Book Antigua italic. (*Note:* The even-page header should be left-aligned.)

h. Insert a left-aligned page number field in the even-page footer area, format it in 10-point Book Antigua, insert a right-aligned page number field in the odd-page footer area, then format it in 10-point Book Antigua.

i. Format the page numbers so that the first page of your chapter, which is Chapter 8 in the book, begins on page 167. (*Hint:* Select a page number field, click the Page Number button, then click Format Page Numbers.)

j. Go to the beginning of the document, press [Enter] 10 times, type **Chapter 8: The Silver Creek Catchment and Stormwater Pollution**, press [Enter] twice, type your name, then press [Enter] twice.

k. Format the chapter title in 16-point Book Antigua bold, format your name in 14-point Book Antigua, then left-align the title text and your name.

l. Click the References tab, make sure the citations and bibliography style is set to Chicago Sixteenth Edition, place the insertion point at the end of the first body paragraph on page 1 but before the ending period, insert a citation for Alice Burke, et. al., then add the page number **40** to the citation.

m. Add the citations listed in **TABLE 4-3** to the document using the sources already associated with the document.

TABLE 4-3

page	location for citation	source	page number
2	End of the first complete paragraph (after …WCSMP, but before the period)	City of Weston	3
3	End of the first complete paragraph (after …pollution, but before the colon)	Jensen	135
4	End of first paragraph (after …health effects, but before the period)	City of Weston	5
4	End of fourth bulleted list item (after 1 month.)	Seawatch	None
5	End of second paragraph (after …problem arises, but before the period)	Burke, et. al.	55
6	End of paragraph before Conclusion (after …stormwater system, but before the period)	City of Weston	7
6	End of first paragraph under Conclusion (after …include, but before the colon)	Jensen	142

Independent Challenge 3 (continued)

n. Press [Ctrl][End], insert a Works Cited list, format the Works Cited heading in 11-point Book Antigua, black font color, bold, then format the list of works cited in 10-point Book Antigua.

o. Scroll to page 4 in the document, place the insertion point at the end of the paragraph above the Potential health effects... heading, press [Enter] twice, type **Table 1: Total annual pollutant loads per year in the Silver Creek Catchment**, press [Enter] twice, then format the text you just typed as bold if it is not bold.

p. Insert a table with four columns and four rows.

q. Type the text shown in FIGURE 4-27 in the table. Do not be concerned when the text wraps to the next line in a cell.

FIGURE 4-27

Area	Nitrogen	Phosphorus	Suspended solids
Silver Creek	9.3 tonnes	1.2 tonnes	756.4 tonnes
Durras Arm	6.2 tonnes	.9 tonnes	348.2 tonnes
Cabbage Tree Creek	9.8 tonnes	2.3 tonnes	485.7 tonnes

r. Apply the Grid Table 1 Light table style. Make sure the text in the header row is bold, then remove any bold formatting from the text in the remaining rows.

s. Use AutoFit to make the table fit the contents, then use AutoFit to make the table fit the window.

t. Save your changes, submit your work, then close the document and exit Word.

Independent Challenge 4: Explore

One of the most common opportunities to use the page layout features of Word is when formatting a research paper. The format recommended by the *MLA Handbook for Writers of Research Papers*, a style guide that includes information on preparing, writing, and formatting research papers, is the standard format used by many schools, colleges, and universities. In this independent challenge, you will research the MLA guidelines for formatting a research paper and use the guidelines you find to format the pages of a sample research report.

a. Use your favorite search engine to search the Web for information on the MLA guidelines for formatting a research report. Use the keywords **MLA Style** and **research paper format** to conduct your search.

b. Look for information on the proper formatting for the following aspects of a research paper: paper size, margins, title page or first page of the report, line spacing, paragraph indentation, and page numbers. Also find information on proper formatting for citations and a works cited page. Print the information you find.

c. Start Word, open the file WD 4-6.docx from the drive and folder where you store your Data Files, then save it as **WD 4-Research Paper**. Using the information you learned, format this document as a research report.

d. Adjust the margins, set the line spacing, and add page numbers to the document in the format recommended by the MLA. Use **The Maori History of New Zealand** as the title for your sample report, use your name as the author name, and use the name of the course you are enrolled in currently as well as the instructor's name for that course. Make sure to format the title page exactly as the MLA style dictates.

e. Format the remaining text as the body of the research report. Indent the first line of each paragraph rather than use quadruple spacing between paragraphs.

f. Create three sources, insert three citations in the document—a book, a journal article, and a Web site—and create a works cited page, following MLA style. If necessary, edit the format of the citations and works cited page to conform to MLA format. (*Note*: For this practice document, you are allowed to make up sources. Never make up sources for real research papers.)

g. Save the document, submit a copy to your instructor, close the document, then exit Word.

Visual Workshop

Open the file WD 4-7.docx from the location where you store your Data Files, then modify it to create the article shown in FIGURE 4-28. (*Hint*: Change all four margins to .6". Add the footnotes as shown in the figure.) Save the document with the filename **WD 4-Garden**, then print a copy.

FIGURE 4-28

GARDENER'S NOTEBOOK

Preparing a Perennial Garden for Winter

By Your Name

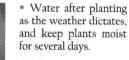

A sense of peace descends when a perennial garden is put to bed for the season. The plants are safely tucked in against the elements, and the garden is ready to welcome the winter. When the work is done, you can sit back and anticipate the bright blooms of spring. Many gardeners are uncertain about how to close a perennial garden. This week's column demystifies the process.

Clean up

Garden clean up can be a gradual process—plants will deteriorate at different rates, allowing you to do a little bit each week.

- Edge beds and borders and remove stakes, trellises, and other plant supports.
- Dig and divide irises, daylilies, and other early bloomers.
- Cut back plants when foliage starts to deteriorate, then rake all debris out of the garden and pull any weeds that remain.

Plant perennials

Fall is the perfect time to plant perennials.[1] The warm, sunny days and cool nights provide optimal conditions for new root growth, without the stress of summer heat.

- Dig deeply and enhance soil with organic matter.
- Use a good starter fertilizer to speed up new root growth and establish a healthy base.
- Untangle the roots of new plants before planting.

- Water after planting as the weather dictates, and keep plants moist for several days.

Add compost

Organic matter is the key ingredient to healthy garden soil. Composting adds nutrients to the soil, helps the soil retain water and nutrients, and keeps the soil well aerated. If you take care of the soil, your plants will become strong and disease resistant.[2]

Before adding compost, use an iron rake to loosen the top few inches of soil. Spread a one to two inch layer of compost over the entire garden—the best compost is made up of yard waste and kitchen scraps—and then refrain from stepping on the area and compacting the soil.

Winter mulch

Winter protection for perennial beds can only help plants survive the winter. Winter mulch prevents the freezing and thawing cycles, which cause plants to heave and eventually die. Here's what works and what doesn't:

- Always apply mulch after the ground is frozen.
- Never apply generic hay because it contains billions of weed seeds. Also, whole leaves and bark mulch hold too much moisture.[3]
- Use a loose material to allow air filtration. Straw and salt marsh hay are excellent choices for mulch.
- Remove the winter mulch in the spring as soon as new growth begins.

---

[1] Fall is also an excellent time to plant shrubs and trees.
[2] You can buy good compost, but it is easy and useful to make it at home. Composting kitchen scraps reduces household garbage by about one-third.

[3] If using leaves, use only stiff leaves, such as Oak or Beech. Soft leaves, such as Maple, make it difficult for air and water to filtrate.

Source: StockSnap

Getting Started with Excel 2016

CASE You have been hired as an assistant at Reason2Go (R2G), a company that allows travelers to make a difference in the global community through voluntourism, while having a memorable vacation experience. You report to Yolanda Lee, the vice president of finance. As Yolanda's assistant, you create worksheets to analyze data from various divisions of the company, so you can help her make sound decisions on company expansion, investments, and new voluntourism opportunities.

Module Objectives

After completing this module, you will be able to:

- Understand spreadsheet software
- Identify Excel 2016 window components
- Understand formulas
- Enter labels and values and use the AutoSum button
- Edit cell entries
- Enter and edit a simple formula
- Switch worksheet views
- Choose print options

Files You Will Need

EX 1-1.xlsx   EX 1-4.xlsx

EX 1-2.xlsx   EX 1-5.xlsx

EX 1-3.xlsx

Understand Spreadsheet Software

Learning
Outcomes
• Describe the
  uses of Excel
• Define key spread-
  sheet terms

Microsoft Excel is the electronic spreadsheet program within the Microsoft Office suite. An **electronic spreadsheet** is an app you use to perform numeric calculations and to analyze and present numeric data. One advantage of a spreadsheet program over pencil and paper is that your calculations are updated automatically, so you can change entries without having to manually recalculate. TABLE 1-1 shows some of the common business tasks people accomplish using Excel. In Excel, the electronic spreadsheet you work in is called a **worksheet**, and it is contained in a file called a **workbook**, which has the file extension .xlsx. **CASE** ▶ *At R2G, you use Excel extensively to track finances and manage corporate data.*

DETAILS

When you use Excel, you have the ability to:

• **Enter data quickly and accurately**

  With Excel, you can enter information faster and more accurately than with pencil and paper. FIGURE 1-1 shows a payroll worksheet created using pencil and paper. FIGURE 1-2 shows the same worksheet created using Excel. Equations were added to calculate the hours and pay. You can use Excel to recreate this information for each week by copying the worksheet's structure and the information that doesn't change from week to week, then entering unique data and formulas for each week.

• **Recalculate data easily**

  Fixing typing errors or updating data is easy in Excel. In the payroll example, if you receive updated hours for an employee, you just enter the new hours and Excel recalculates the pay.

• **Perform what-if analysis**

  The ability to change data and quickly view the recalculated results gives you the power to make informed business decisions. For instance, if you're considering raising the hourly rate for an entry-level tour guide from $12.50 to $15.00, you can enter the new value in the worksheet and immediately see the impact on the overall payroll as well as on the individual employee. Any time you use a worksheet to ask the question "What if?" you are performing **what-if analysis**. Excel also includes a Scenario Manager where you can name and save different what-if versions of your worksheet.

• **Change the appearance of information**

  Excel provides powerful features, such as the Quick Analysis tool, for making information visually appealing and easier to understand. Format text and numbers in different fonts, colors, and styles to make it stand out.

• **Create charts**

  Excel makes it easy to create charts based on worksheet information. Charts are updated automatically in Excel whenever data changes. The worksheet in FIGURE 1-2 includes a 3-D pie chart.

• **Share information**

  It's easy for everyone at R2G to collaborate in Excel using the company intranet, the Internet, or a network storage device. For example, you can complete the weekly payroll that your boss, Yolanda Lee, started creating. You can also take advantage of collaboration tools such as shared workbooks so that multiple people can edit a workbook simultaneously.

• **Build on previous work**

  Instead of creating a new worksheet for every project, it's easy to modify an existing Excel worksheet. When you are ready to create next week's payroll, you can open the file for last week's payroll, save it with a new filename, and modify the information as necessary. You can also use predesigned, formatted files called **templates** to create new worksheets quickly. Excel comes with many templates that you can customize.

FIGURE 1-1: Traditional paper worksheet

Reason2Go
Project Leader Divison Payroll Calculator

Name	Hours	O/T Hrs	Hrly Rate	Reg Pay	O/T Pay	Gross Pay
Brucker, Pieter	40	4	16.75	670	134	804
Cucci, Lucia	35	0	12	420	0	420
Klimt, Gustave	40	2	13.25	530	53	583
Lafontaine, Jeanne	29	0	15.25	442.25	0	442.25
Martinez, Juan	37	0	13.2	488.4	0	488.4
Mioshi, Keiko	39	0	21	819	0	819
Shernwood, Burt	40	0	16.75	670	0	670
Strano, Riccardo	40	8	16.25	650	260	910
Wadsworth, Alice	40	5	13.25	530	132.5	662.5
Yamamoto, Johji	38	0	15.5	589	0	589

FIGURE 1-2: Excel worksheet

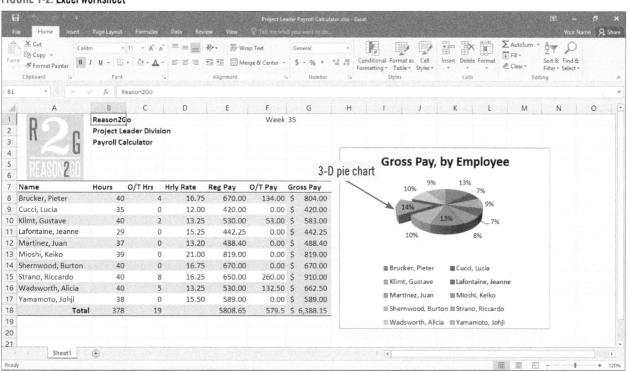

TABLE 1-1: Business tasks you can accomplish using Excel

you can use spreadsheets to	by
Perform calculations	Adding formulas and functions to worksheet data; for example, adding a list of sales results or calculating a car payment
Represent values graphically	Creating charts based on worksheet data; for example, creating a chart that displays expenses
Generate reports	Creating workbooks that combine information from multiple worksheets, such as summarized sales information from multiple stores
Organize data	Sorting data in ascending or descending order; for example, alphabetizing a list of products or customer names, or prioritizing orders by date
Analyze data	Creating data summaries and short lists using PivotTables or AutoFilters; for example, making a list of the top 10 customers based on spending habits
Create what-if data scenarios	Using variable values to investigate and sample different outcomes, such as changing the interest rate or payment schedule on a loan

Identify Excel 2016 Window Components

Learning Outcomes
• Open and save an Excel file
• Identify Excel window elements

To start Excel, Microsoft Windows must be running. Similar to starting any app in Office, you can use the Start button on the Windows taskbar, the Start button on your keyboard, or you may have a shortcut on your desktop you prefer to use. If you need additional assistance, ask your instructor or technical support person. **CASE** *You decide to start Excel and familiarize yourself with the worksheet window.*

STEPS

1. **Start Excel, click Open Other Workbooks on the navigation bar, click This PC, then click Browse to open the Open dialog box**

2. **In the Open dialog box, navigate to the location where you store your Data Files, click EX 1-1.xlsx, then click Open**

   The file opens in the Excel window.

3. **Click the File tab, click Save As on the navigation bar, then click Browse to open the Save As dialog box**

4. **In the Save As dialog box, navigate to the location where you store your Data Files if necessary, type EX 1-Project Leader Payroll Calculator in the File name text box, then click Save**

   Using **FIGURE 1-3** as a guide, identify the following items:

   • The **Name box** displays the active cell address. "A1" appears in the Name box.
   • The **formula bar** allows you to enter or edit data in the worksheet.
   • The **worksheet window** contains a grid of columns and rows. Columns are labeled alphabetically and rows are labeled numerically. The worksheet window can contain a total of 1,048,576 rows and 16,384 columns. The intersection of a column and a row is called a **cell**. Cells can contain text, numbers, formulas, or a combination of all three. Every cell has its own unique location or **cell address**, which is identified by the coordinates of the intersecting column and row. The column and row indicators are shaded to make identifying the cell address easy.
   • The **cell pointer** is a dark rectangle that outlines the cell you are working in. This cell is called the **active cell**. In **FIGURE 1-3**, the cell pointer outlines cell A1, so A1 is the active cell. The column and row headings for the active cell are highlighted, making it easier to locate.
   • **Sheet tabs** below the worksheet grid let you switch from sheet to sheet in a workbook. By default, a workbook file contains one worksheet—but you can have as many sheets as your computer's memory allows, in a workbook. The New sheet button to the right of Sheet 1 allows you to add worksheets to a workbook. **Sheet tab scrolling buttons** let you navigate to additional sheet tabs when available.
   • You can use the **scroll bars** to move around in a worksheet that is too large to fit on the screen at once.
   • The **status bar** is located at the bottom of the Excel window. It provides a brief description of the active command or task in progress. **The mode indicator** in the lower-left corner of the status bar provides additional information about certain tasks.

5. **Click cell A4**

   Cell A4 becomes the active cell. To activate a different cell, you can click the cell or press the arrow keys on your keyboard to move to it.

6. **Click cell B5, press and hold the mouse button, drag ⊕ to cell B14, then release the mouse button**

   You selected a group of cells and they are highlighted, as shown in **FIGURE 1-4**. A selection of two or more cells such as B5:B14 is called a **range**; you select a range when you want to perform an action on a group of cells at once, such as moving them or formatting them. When you select a range, the status bar displays the average, count (or number of items selected), and sum of the selected cells as a quick reference.

FIGURE 1-3: Open workbook

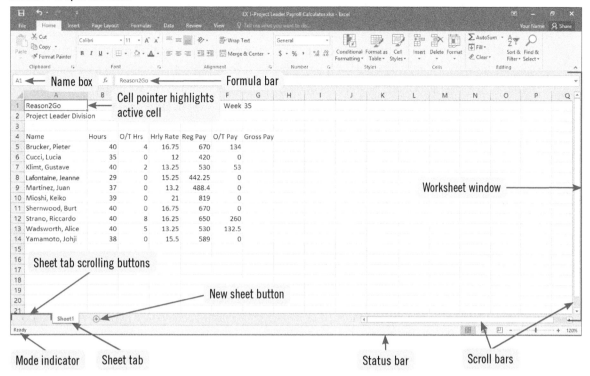

Name box — Formula bar — Cell pointer highlights active cell — Worksheet window — Sheet tab scrolling buttons — New sheet button — Mode indicator — Sheet tab — Status bar — Scroll bars

FIGURE 1-4: Selected range

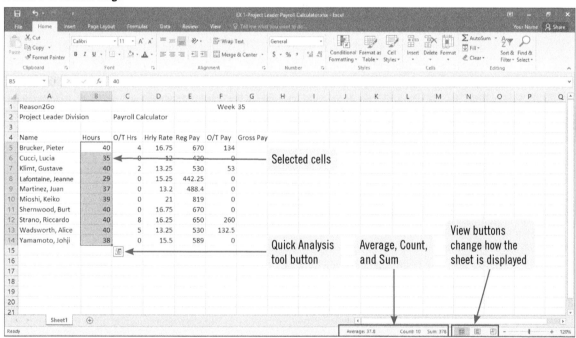

Selected cells — Quick Analysis tool button — Average, Count, and Sum — View buttons change how the sheet is displayed

Using OneDrive and Office Online

If you have a Microsoft account, you can save your Excel files and photos in OneDrive, a cloud-based service from Microsoft. When you save files in OneDrive, you can access them on other devices—such as a tablet or smartphone. OneDrive is available as an app on smartphones and tablets, making access simple. You can open files to view them on any device, and you can even make edits to them using **Office Online**, which includes simplified versions of the apps found in the Office 2016 suite. Because Office Online is web-based, the apps take up no computer disk space and you can use them on any Internet-connected device.

Understand Formulas

Learning
Outcomes
• Explain how a
  formula works
• Identify Excel
  arithmetic operators

Excel is a truly powerful program because users at every level of mathematical expertise can make calculations with accuracy. To do so, you use formulas. A **formula** is an equation in a worksheet. You use formulas to make calculations as simple as adding a column of numbers, or as complex as creating profit-and-loss projections for a global corporation. To tap into the power of Excel, you should understand how formulas work. **CASE** ▶ *Managers at R2G use the Project Leader Payroll Calculator workbook to keep track of employee hours prior to submitting them to the Payroll Department. You'll be using this workbook regularly, so you need to understand the formulas it contains and how Excel calculates the results.*

STEPS

1. **Click cell E5**

   The active cell contains a formula, which appears on the formula bar. All Excel formulas begin with the equal sign (=). If you want a cell to show the result of adding 4 plus 2, the formula in the cell would look like this: =4+2. If you want a cell to show the result of multiplying two values in your worksheet, such as the values in cells B5 and D5, the formula would look like this: =B5*D5, as shown in **FIGURE 1-5**. While you're entering a formula in a cell, the cell references and arithmetic operators appear on the formula bar. See **TABLE 1-2** for a list of commonly used arithmetic operators. When you're finished entering the formula, you can either click the Enter button on the formula bar or press [Enter].

2. **Click cell F5**

   This cell contains an example of a more complex formula, which calculates overtime pay. At R2G, overtime pay is calculated at twice the regular hourly rate times the number of overtime hours. The formula used to calculate overtime pay for the employee in row 5 is:

   O/T Hrs times (2 times Hrly Rate)

   In the worksheet cell, you would enter: =C5*(2*D5), as shown in **FIGURE 1-6**. The use of parentheses creates groups within the formula and indicates which calculations to complete first—an important consideration in complex formulas. In this formula, first the hourly rate is multiplied by 2, because that calculation is within the parentheses. Next, that value is multiplied by the number of overtime hours. Because overtime is calculated at twice the hourly rate, managers are aware that they need to closely watch this expense.

DETAILS

In creating calculations in Excel, it is important to:

- **Know where the formulas should be**

  An Excel formula is created in the cell where the formula's results should appear. This means that the formula calculating Gross Pay for the employee in row 5 will be entered in cell G5.

- **Know exactly what cells and arithmetic operations are needed**

  Don't guess; make sure you know exactly what cells are involved before creating a formula.

- **Create formulas with care**

  Make sure you know exactly what you want a formula to accomplish before it is created. An inaccurate formula may have far-reaching effects if the formula or its results are referenced by other formulas, as shown in the payroll example in **FIGURE 1-6**.

- **Use cell references rather than values**

  The beauty of Excel is that whenever you change a value in a cell, any formula containing a reference to that cell is automatically updated. For this reason, it's important that you use cell references in formulas, rather than actual values, whenever possible.

- **Determine what calculations will be needed**

  Sometimes it's difficult to predict what data will be needed within a worksheet, but you should try to anticipate what statistical information may be required. For example, if there are columns of numbers, chances are good that both column and row totals should be present.

FIGURE 1-5: Viewing a formula

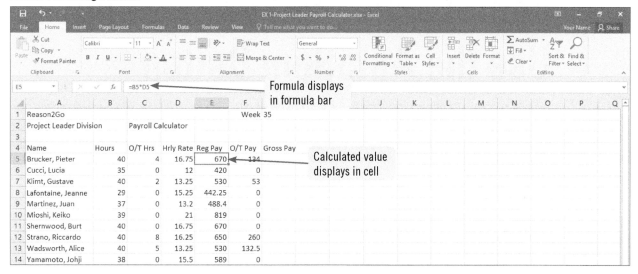

FIGURE 1-6: Formula with multiple operators

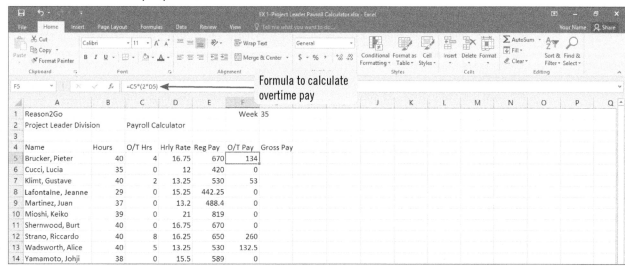

TABLE 1-2: Excel arithmetic operators

operator	purpose	example
+	Addition	=A5+A7
-	Subtraction or negation	=A5-10
*	Multiplication	=A5*A7
/	Division	=A5/A7
%	Percent	=35%
^ (caret)	Exponent	=6^2 (same as 6^2)

Enter Labels and Values and Use the AutoSum Button

Learning
Outcomes
• Build formulas with the AutoSum button
• Copy formulas with the fill handle

To enter content in a cell, you can type in the formula bar or directly in the cell itself. When entering content in a worksheet, you should start by entering all the labels first. **Labels** are entries that contain text and numerical information not used in calculations, such as "2019 Sales" or "Travel Expenses". Labels help you identify data in worksheet rows and columns, making your worksheet easier to understand. **Values** are numbers, formulas, and functions that can be used in calculations. To enter a calculation, you type an equal sign (=) plus the formula for the calculation; some examples of an Excel calculation are "=2+2" and "=C5+C6". Functions are built-in formulas; you learn more about them in the next module. **CASE** *You want to enter some information in the Project Leader Payroll Calculator workbook and use a very simple function to total a range of cells.*

STEPS

1. **Click cell A15, then click in the formula bar**

   Notice that the **mode indicator** on the status bar now reads "Edit," indicating you are in Edit mode. You are in Edit mode any time you are entering or changing the contents of a cell.

2. **Type Totals, then click the Enter button ✓ on the formula bar**

   Clicking the Enter button accepts the entry. The new text is left-aligned in the cell. Labels are left-aligned by default, and values are right-aligned by default. Excel recognizes an entry as a value if it is a number or it begins with one of these symbols: +, -, =, @, #, or $. When a cell contains both text and numbers, Excel recognizes it as a label.

3. **Click cell B15**

   You want this cell to total the hours worked by all the trip advisors. You might think you need to create a formula that looks like this: =B5+B6+B7+B8+B9+B10+B11+B12+B13+B14. However, there's an easier way to achieve this result.

4. **Click the AutoSum button Σ in the Editing group on the Home tab on the Ribbon**

   The SUM function is inserted in the cell, and a suggested range appears in parentheses, as shown in FIGURE 1-7. A **function** is a built-in formula; it includes the **arguments** (the information necessary to calculate an answer) as well as cell references and other unique information. Clicking the AutoSum button sums the adjacent range (that is, the cells next to the active cell) above or to the left, although you can adjust the range if necessary by selecting a different range before accepting the cell entry. Using the SUM function is quicker than entering a formula, and using the range B5:B14 is more efficient than entering individual cell references.

5. **Click ✓ on the formula bar**

   Excel calculates the total contained in cells B5:B14 and displays the result, 378, in cell B15. The cell actually contains the formula =SUM(B5:B14), and the result is displayed.

6. **Click cell C13, type 6, then press [Enter]**

   The number 6 replaces the cell's contents, the cell pointer moves to cell C14, and the value in cell F13 changes.

7. **Click cell C18, type Average Gross Pay, then press [Enter]**

   The new label is entered in cell C18. The contents appear to spill into the empty cells to the right.

8. **Click cell B15, position the pointer on the lower-right corner of the cell (the fill handle) so that the pointer changes to +, drag + to cell G15, then release the mouse button**

   Dragging the fill handle across a range of cells copies the contents of the first cell into the other cells in the range. In the range B15:G15, each filled cell now contains a function that sums the range of cells above, as shown in FIGURE 1-8.

9. **Save your work**

FIGURE 1-7: Creating a formula using the AutoSum button

Enter button — Selected cells in formula — =SUM(B5:B14)

AutoSum button, also referred to as the Sum button

Outline of cells included in formula

Name	Hours	O/T Hrs	Hrly Rate	Reg Pay	O/T Pay	Gross Pay
Brucker, Pieter	40	4	16.75	670	134	
Cucci, Lucia	35	0	12	420	0	
Klimt, Gustave	40	2	13.25	530	53	
Lafontaine, Jeanne	29	0	15.25	442.25	0	
Martinez, Juan	37	0	13.2	488.4	0	
Mioshi, Keiko	39	0	21	819	0	
Shernwood, Burt	40	0	16.75	670	0	
Strano, Riccardo	40	8	16.25	650	260	
Wadsworth, Alice	40	5	13.25	530	132.5	
Yamamoto, Johji	38	0	15.5	589	0	
Totals	=SUM(B5:B14)					

Reason2Go — Week 35
Project Leader Division — Payroll Calculator

SUM(number1, [number2], ...)

FIGURE 1-8: Results of copied SUM functions

B15 — =SUM(B5:B14)

Name	Hours	O/T Hrs	Hrly Rate	Reg Pay	O/T Pay	Gross Pay
Brucker, Pieter	40	4	16.75	670	134	
Cucci, Lucia	35	0	12	420	0	
Klimt, Gustave	40	2	13.25	530	53	
Lafontaine, Jeanne	29	0	15.25	442.25	0	
Martinez, Juan	37	0	13.2	488.4	0	
Mioshi, Keiko	39	0	21	819	0	
Shernwood, Burt	40	0	16.75	670	0	
Strano, Riccardo	40	8	16.25	650	260	
Wadsworth, Alice	40	6	13.25	530	159	
Yamamoto, Johji	38	0	15.5	589	0	
Totals	378	20	153.2	5808.65	606	0

Reason2Go — Week 35
Project Leader Division — Payroll Calculator

Auto Fill options button

Navigating a worksheet

With over a million cells available in a worksheet, it is important to know how to move around in, or **navigate**, a worksheet. You can use the arrow keys on the keyboard ,↑, ↓,→, or ← to move one cell at a time, or press [Page Up] or [Page Down] to move one screen at a time. To move one screen to the left, press [Alt][Page Up]; to move one screen to the right, press [Alt][Page Down]. You can also use the mouse pointer to click the desired cell. If the desired cell is not visible in the worksheet window, use the scroll bars or use the Go To command by clicking the Find & Select button in the Editing group on the Home tab on the Ribbon. To quickly jump to the first cell in a worksheet, press [Ctrl][Home]; to jump to the last cell, press [Ctrl][End].

Edit Cell Entries

Learning Outcomes
- Edit cell entries in the formula bar
- Edit cell entries in the cell

You can change, or **edit**, the contents of an active cell at any time. To do so, double-click the cell, and then click in the formula bar or just start typing. Excel switches to Edit mode when you are making cell entries. Different pointers, shown in TABLE 1-3, guide you through the editing process. **CASE** *You noticed some errors in the worksheet and want to make corrections. The first error is in cell A5, which contains a misspelled name.*

STEPS

1. **Click cell A5, then click to the right of P in the formula bar**

   As soon as you click in the formula bar, a blinking vertical line called the **insertion point** appears on the formula bar at the location where new text will be inserted. See FIGURE 1-9. The mouse pointer changes to I when you point anywhere in the formula bar.

2. **Press [Delete], then click the Enter button ✓ on the formula bar**

   Clicking the Enter button accepts the edit, and the spelling of the employee's first name is corrected. You can also press [Enter] or [Tab] to accept an edit. Pressing [Enter] to accept an edit moves the cell pointer down one cell, and pressing [Tab] to accept an edit moves the cell pointer one cell to the right.

3. **Click cell B6, then press [F2]**

   Excel switches to Edit mode, and the insertion point blinks in the cell. Pressing [F2] activates the cell for editing directly in the cell instead of the formula bar. Whether you edit in the cell or the formula bar is simply a matter of preference; the results in the worksheet are the same.

4. **Press [Backspace], type 8, then press [Enter]**

   The value in the cell changes from 35 to 38, and cell B7 becomes the active cell. Did you notice that the calculations in cells B15 and E15 also changed? That's because those cells contain formulas that include cell B6 in their calculations. If you make a mistake when editing, you can click the Cancel button ✗ on the formula bar *before* pressing [Enter] to confirm the cell entry. The Enter and Cancel buttons appear only when you're in Edit mode. If you notice the mistake *after* you have confirmed the cell entry, click the Undo button ↺ on the Quick Access toolbar.

5. **Click cell A9, then double-click the word Juan in the formula bar**

   Double-clicking a word in a cell selects it. When you selected the word, the Mini toolbar automatically displayed.

6. **Type Javier, then press [Enter]**

   When text is selected, typing deletes it and replaces it with the new text.

7. **Double-click cell C12, press [Delete], type 4, then click ✓**

   Double-clicking a cell activates it for editing directly in the cell. Compare your screen to FIGURE 1-10.

8. **Save your work**

Recovering unsaved changes to a workbook file

You can use Excel's AutoRecover feature to automatically save (Autosave) your work as often as you want. This means that if you suddenly lose power or if Excel closes unexpectedly while you're working, you can recover all or some of the changes you made since you saved it last. (Of course, this is no substitute for regularly saving your work: this is just added insurance.) To customize the AutoRecover settings, click the File tab, click Options, then click

Save. AutoRecover lets you decide how often and into which location it should Autosave files. When you restart Excel after losing power, a Document Recovery pane opens and provides access to the saved and Autosaved versions of the files that were open when Excel closed. You can also click the File tab, click Open on the navigation bar, then click any file in the Recover Unsaved Workbooks list to open Autosaved workbooks.

FIGURE 1-9: Worksheet in Edit mode

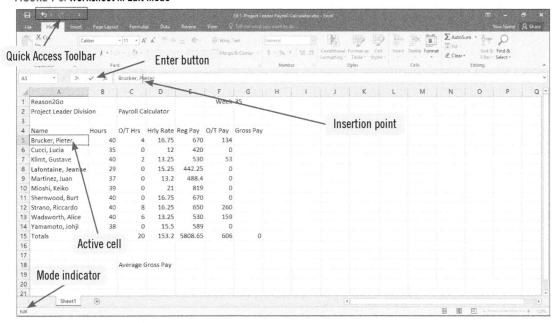

FIGURE 1-10: Edited worksheet

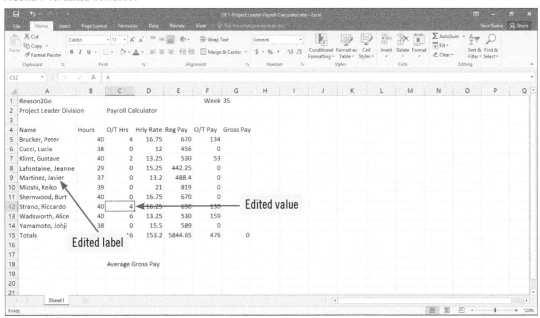

TABLE 1-3: Common pointers in Excel

name	pointer	use to	visible over the
Normal	⇧	Select a cell or range; indicates Ready mode	Active worksheet
Fill handle	+	Copy cell contents to adjacent cells	Lower right corner of the active cell or range
I-beam	I	Edit cell contents in active cell or formula bar	Active cell in Edit mode or over the formula bar
Move	⟡	Change the location of the selected cell(s)	Perimeter of the active cell(s)
Copy	⬡	Create a duplicate of the selected cell(s)	Perimeter of the active cell(s) when [Ctrl] is pressed
Column resize	↔	Change the width of a column	Border between column heading indicators

Enter and Edit a Simple Formula

You use formulas in Excel to perform calculations such as adding, multiplying, and averaging. Formulas in an Excel worksheet start with the equal sign (=), also called the **formula prefix**, followed by cell addresses, range names, values, and **calculation operators**. Calculation operators indicate what type of calculation you want to perform on the cells, ranges, or values. They can include **arithmetic operators**, which perform mathematical calculations (see TABLE 1-2 in the "Understand Formulas" lesson); **comparison operators**, which compare values for the purpose of true/false results; **text concatenation operators**, which join strings of text in different cells; and **reference operators**, which enable you to use ranges in calculations. **CASE** ▶ *You want to create a formula in the worksheet that calculates gross pay for each employee.*

STEPS

1. **Click cell G5**

   This is the first cell where you want to insert the formula. To calculate gross pay, you need to add regular pay and overtime pay. For employee Peter Brucker, regular pay appears in cell E5 and overtime pay appears in cell F5.

2. **Type =, click cell E5, type +, then click cell F5**

   Compare your formula bar to FIGURE 1-11. The blue and red cell references in cell G5 correspond to the colored cell outlines. When entering a formula, it's a good idea to use cell references instead of values whenever you can. That way, if you later change a value in a cell (if, for example, Peter's regular pay changes to 690), any formula that includes this information reflects accurate, up-to-date results.

3. **Click the Enter button ✔ on the formula bar**

   The result of the formula =E5+F5, 804, appears in cell G5. This same value appears in cell G15 because cell G15 contains a formula that totals the values in cells G5:G14, and there are no other values at this time.

4. **Click cell F5**

   The formula in this cell calculates overtime pay by multiplying overtime hours (C5) times twice the regular hourly rate (2*D5). You want to edit this formula to reflect a new overtime pay rate.

5. **Click to the right of 2 in the formula bar, then type .5 as shown in FIGURE 1-12**

   The formula that calculates overtime pay has been edited.

6. **Click ✔ on the formula bar**

   Compare your screen to FIGURE 1-13. Notice that the calculated values in cells G5, F15, and G15 have all changed to reflect your edits to cell F5.

7. **Save your work**

Understanding named ranges

It can be difficult to remember the cell locations of critical information in a worksheet, but using cell names can make this task much easier. You can name a single cell or range of contiguous, or touching, cells. For example, you might name a cell that contains data on average gross pay "AVG_GP" instead of trying to remember the cell address C18. A named range must begin with a letter or an underscore. It cannot contain any spaces or be the same as a built-in name, such as a function or another object (such as a different named range) in the workbook. To name a range, select the cell(s) you want to name, click the Name box in the formula bar, type the name you want to use, then press [Enter]. You can also name a range by clicking the Formulas tab, then clicking the Define Name button in the Defined Names group. Type the new range name in the Name text box in the New Name dialog box, verify the selected range, then click OK. When you use a named range in a formula, the named range appears instead of the cell address. You can also create a named range using the contents of a cell already in the range. Select the range containing the text you want to use as a name, then click the Create from Selection button in the Defined Names group. The Create Names from Selection dialog box opens. Choose the location of the name you want to use, then click OK.

FIGURE 1-11: Simple formula in a worksheet

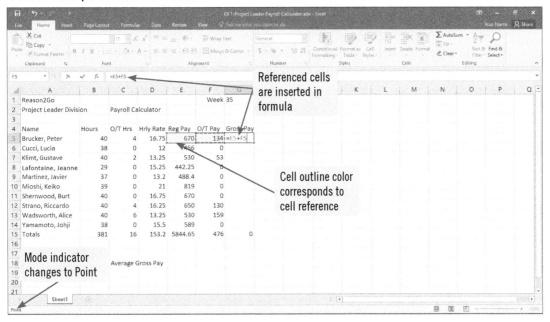

FIGURE 1-12: Edited formula in a worksheet

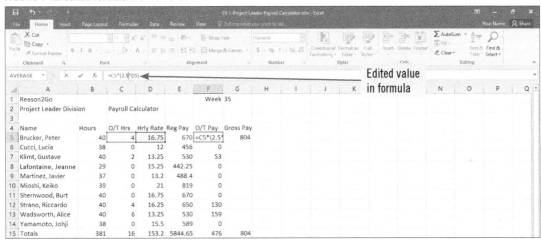

FIGURE 1-13: Edited formula with changes

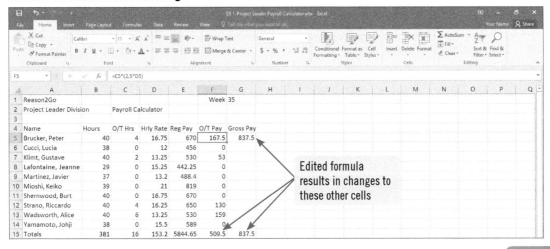

Switch Worksheet Views

Learning
Outcomes
• Change worksheet
  views
• Create a header/
  footer
• Select a range

You can change your view of the worksheet window at any time, using either the View tab on the Ribbon or the View buttons on the status bar. Changing your view does not affect the contents of a worksheet; it just makes it easier for you to focus on different tasks, such as entering content or preparing a worksheet for printing. The View tab includes a variety of viewing options, such as View buttons, zoom controls, and the ability to show or hide worksheet elements such as gridlines. The status bar offers fewer View options but can be more convenient to use. **CASE** ▶ *You want to make some final adjustments to your worksheet, including adding a header so the document looks more polished.*

STEPS

1. **Click the View tab on the Ribbon, then click the Page Layout button in the Workbook Views group**

   The view switches from the default view, Normal, to Page Layout view. **Normal view** shows the worksheet without including certain details like headers and footers, or tools like rulers and a page number indicator; it's great for creating and editing a worksheet, but may not be detailed enough when you want to put the finishing touches on a document. **Page Layout view** provides a more accurate view of how a worksheet will look when printed, as shown in **FIGURE 1-14**. The margins of the page are displayed, along with a text box for the header. A footer text box appears at the bottom of the page, but your screen may not be large enough to view it without scrolling. Above and to the left of the page are rulers. Part of an additional page appears to the right of this page, but it is dimmed, indicating that it does not contain any data. A page number indicator on the status bar tells you the current page and the total number of pages in this worksheet.

2. **Move the pointer 🔨 over the header *without clicking***

   The header is made up of three text boxes: left, center, and right. Each text box is outlined in green as you pass over it with the pointer.

3. **Click the left header text box, type Reason2Go, click the center header text box, type Project Leader Payroll Calculator, click the right header text box, then type Week 35**

   The new text appears in the text boxes, as shown in **FIGURE 1-15**. You can also press the [Tab] key to advance from one header box to the next.

4. **Select the range A1:G2, then press [Delete]**

   The duplicate information you just entered in the header is deleted from cells in the worksheet.

5. **Click the View tab if necessary, click the Ruler check box in the Show group, then click the Gridlines check box in the Show group**

   The rulers and the gridlines are hidden. By default, gridlines in a worksheet do not print, so hiding them gives you a more accurate image of your final document.

6. **Click the Page Break Preview button 🗗 on the status bar**

   Your view changes to Page Break Preview, which displays a reduced view of each page of your worksheet, along with page break indicators that you can drag to include more or less information on a page.

7. **Drag the pointer 🛪 from the bottom page break indicator to the bottom of row 20**

   See **FIGURE 1-16**. When you're working on a large worksheet with multiple pages, sometimes you need to adjust where pages break; in this worksheet, however, the information all fits comfortably on one page.

8. **Click the Page Layout button in the Workbook Views group, click the Ruler check box in the Show group, then click the Gridlines check box in the Show group**

   The rulers and gridlines are no longer hidden. You can show or hide View tab items in any view.

9. **Save your work**

FIGURE 1-14: Page Layout view

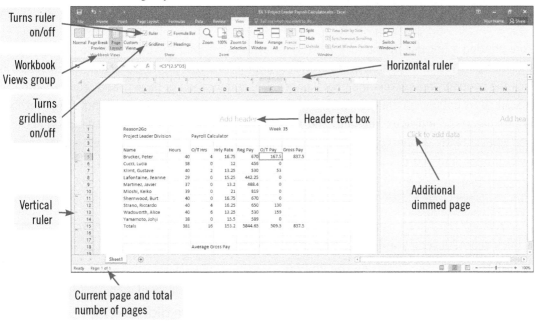

Turns ruler on/off

Workbook Views group

Turns gridlines on/off

Horizontal ruler

Header text box

Additional dimmed page

Vertical ruler

Current page and total number of pages

FIGURE 1-15: Header text entered

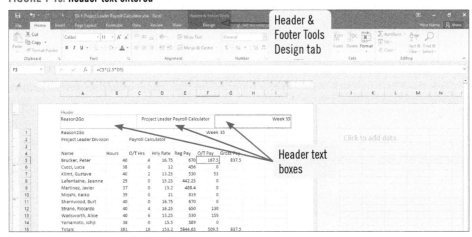

Header & Footer Tools Design tab

Header text boxes

FIGURE 1-16: Page Break Preview

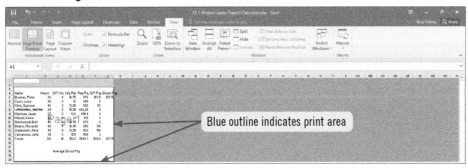

Blue outline indicates print area

Choose Print Options

Learning
Outcomes
• Change the page
  orientation
• Hide/view gridlines
  when printing
• Preview and print
  a worksheet

Before printing a document, you may want to review it using the Page Layout tab to fine-tune your printed output. You can use tools on the Page Layout tab to adjust print orientation (the direction in which the content prints across the page), paper size, and location of page breaks. You can also use the Scale to Fit options on the Page Layout tab to fit a large amount of data on a single page without making changes to individual margins, and to turn gridlines and column/row headings on and off. When you are ready to print, you can set print options such as the number of copies to print and the correct printer, and you can preview your document in Backstage view using the File tab. You can also adjust page layout settings from within Backstage view and immediately see the results in the document preview. **CASE** *You are ready to prepare your worksheet for printing.*

STEPS

1. **Click cell A20, type your name, then click ✓**

2. **Click the Page Layout tab on the Ribbon**
   Compare your screen to **FIGURE 1-17**. The solid outline indicates the default **print area**, the area to be printed.

QUICK TIP
You can use the Zoom slider on the status bar at any time to enlarge your view of specific areas of your worksheet.

3. **Click the Orientation button in the Page Setup group, then click Landscape**
   The paper orientation changes to **landscape**, so the contents will print across the length of the page instead of across the width. Notice how the margins of the worksheet adjust.

4. **Click the Orientation button in the Page Setup group, then click Portrait**
   The orientation returns to **portrait**, so the contents will print across the width of the page.

5. **Click the Gridlines View check box in the Sheet Options group on the Page Layout tab, click the Gridlines Print check box to select it if necessary, then save your work**
   Printing gridlines makes the data easier to read, but the gridlines will not print unless the Gridlines Print check box is checked.

QUICK TIP
To change the active printer, click the current printer in the Printer section in Backstage view, then choose a different printer.

6. **Click the File tab, click Print on the navigation bar, then select an active printer if necessary**
   The Print tab in Backstage view displays a preview of your worksheet exactly as it will look when it is printed. To the left of the worksheet preview, you can also change a number of document settings and print options. To open the Page Setup dialog box and adjust page layout options, click the Page Setup link in the Settings section. Compare your preview screen to **FIGURE 1-18**. You can print from this view by clicking the Print button, or return to the worksheet without printing by clicking the Back button ⬅. You can also print an entire workbook from the Backstage view by clicking the Print button in the Settings section, then selecting the active sheet or entire workbook.

QUICK TIP
If the Quick Print button 🖨 appears on the Quick Access Toolbar, you can click it to print a worksheet using the default settings.

7. **Compare your settings to FIGURE 1-18, then click the Print button**
   One copy of the worksheet prints.

8. **Submit your work to your instructor as directed, then exit Excel**

Printing worksheet formulas

Sometimes you need to keep a record of all the formulas in a worksheet. You might want to do this to see exactly how you came up with a complex calculation, so you can explain it to others. To prepare a worksheet to show formulas rather than results when printed, open the workbook containing the formulas you want to print. Click the Formulas tab, then click the Show Formulas button in the Formula Auditing group to select it. When the Show Formulas button is selected, formulas rather than resulting values are displayed in the worksheet on screen and when printed. (The Show Formulas button is a toggle: click it again to hide the formulas.)

FIGURE 1-17: Worksheet with Portrait orientation

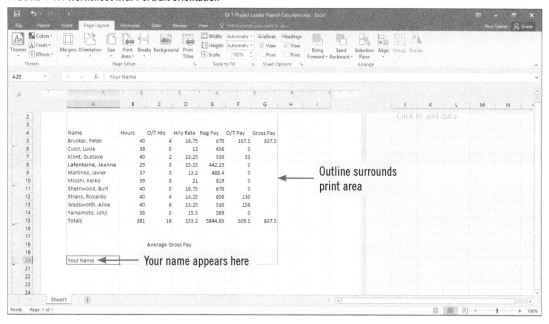

Outline surrounds print area

Your name appears here

FIGURE 1-18: Worksheet in Backstage view

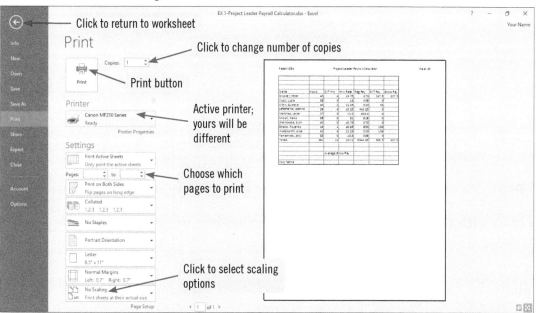

Click to return to worksheet

Click to change number of copies

Print button

Active printer; yours will be different

Choose which pages to print

Click to select scaling options

Scaling to fit

If you have a large amount of data that you want to fit to a single sheet of paper, but you don't want to spend a lot of time trying to adjust the margins and other settings, you have several options. You can easily print your work on a single sheet by clicking the No Scaling list arrow in the Settings section on the Print place in Backstage view, then clicking Fit Sheet in One Page. Another method for fitting worksheet content onto one page is to click the Page Layout tab, then change the Width and Height settings in the Scale to Fit group each to 1 Page. You can also use the Fit to option in the Page Setup dialog box to fit a worksheet on one page. To open the Page Setup dialog box, click the dialog box launcher in the Scale to Fit group on the Page Layout tab, or click the Page Setup link in the Print place in Backstage view. Make sure the Page tab is selected in the Page Setup dialog box, then click the Fit to option button.

Excel 2016

Practice

Concepts Review

Label the elements of the Excel worksheet window shown in FIGURE 1-19.

FIGURE 1-19

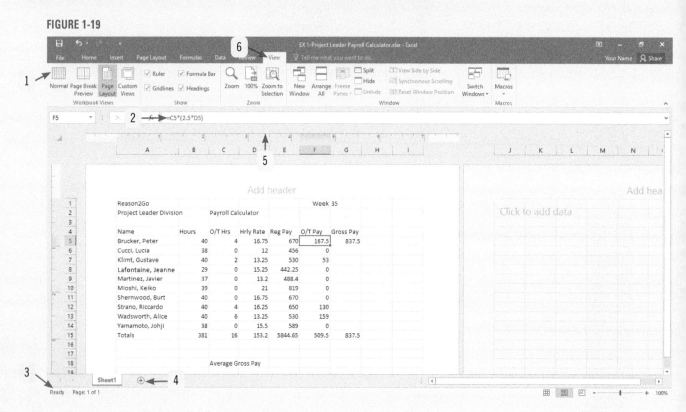

Match each term with the statement that best describes it.

7. **Name box**
8. **Workbook**
9. **Formula prefix**
10. **Orientation**
11. **Cell**
12. **Normal view**

a. Part of the Excel program window that displays the active cell address
b. Default view in Excel
c. Direction in which contents of page will print
d. Equal sign preceding a formula
e. File consisting of one or more worksheets
f. Intersection of a column and a row

Select the best answer from the list of choices.

13. Which feature could be used to print a very long worksheet on a single sheet of paper?
  a. Show Formulas
  b. Scale to Fit
  c. Page Break Preview
  d. Named Ranges

14. In which area can you see a preview of your worksheet?
  a. Page Setup
  b. Backstage view
  c. Printer Setup
  d. View tab

15. A selection of multiple cells is called a:
  a. Group.
  b. Range.
  c. Reference.
  d. Package.

16. Using a cell address in a formula is known as:
  a. Formularizing.
  b. Prefixing.
  c. Cell referencing.
  d. Cell mathematics.

17. Which worksheet view shows how your worksheet will look when printed?
  a. Page Layout
  b. Data
  c. Review
  d. View

18. Which key can you press to switch to Edit mode?
  a. [F1]
  b. [F2]
  c. [F4]
  d. [F6]

19. In which view can you see the header and footer areas of a worksheet?
  a. Normal view
  b. Page Layout view
  c. Page Break Preview
  d. Header/Footer view

20. Which view shows you a reduced view of each page of your worksheet?
  a. Normal
  b. Page Layout
  c. Thumbnail
  d. Page Break Preview

21. The maximum number of worksheets you can include in a workbook is:
  a. 3.
  b. 250.
  c. 255.
  d. Unlimited.

Skills Review

1. Understand spreadsheet software.
  a. What is the difference between a workbook and a worksheet?
  b. Identify five common business uses for electronic spreadsheets.
  c. What is what-if analysis?

2. Identify Excel 2016 window components.
  a. Start Excel.
  b. Open EX 1-2.xlsx from the location where you store your Data Files, then save it as **EX 1-Weather Data**.
  c. Locate the formula bar, the Sheet tabs, the mode indicator, and the cell pointer.

3. Understand formulas.
  a. What is the average high temperature of the listed cities? (*Hint*: Select the range B5:G5 and use the status bar.)
  b. What formula would you create to calculate the difference in altitude between Atlanta and Dallas? Enter your answer (as an equation) in cell D13.

Skills Review (continued)

4. **Enter labels and values and use the AutoSum button.**
   a. Click cell H8, then use the AutoSum button to calculate the total snowfall.
   b. Click cell H7, then use the AutoSum button to calculate the total rainfall.
   c. Save your changes to the file.

5. **Edit cell entries.**
   a. Use [F2] to correct the spelling of SanteFe in cell G3 (the correct spelling is Santa Fe).
   b. Click cell A17, then type your name.
   c. Save your changes.

6. **Enter and edit a simple formula.**
   a. Change the value 41 in cell C8 to **52**.
   b. Change the value 37 in cell D6 to **35.4**.
   c. Select cell J4, then use the fill handle to copy the formula in cell J4 to cells J5:J8.
   d. Save your changes.

7. **Switch worksheet views.**
   a. Click the View tab on the Ribbon, then switch to Page Layout view.
   b. Add the header **Average Annual Weather Data** to the center header text box.
   c. Add your name to the right header box.
   d. Delete the contents of cell A17.
   e. Delete the contents of cell A1.
   f. Save your changes.

8. **Choose print options.**
   a. Use the Page Layout tab to change the orientation to Portrait.
   b. Turn off gridlines by deselecting both the Gridlines View and Gridlines Print check boxes (if necessary) in the Sheet Options group.
   c. Scale the worksheet so all the information fits on one page. If necessary, scale the worksheet so all the information fits on one page. (*Hint*: Click the Width list arrow in the Scale to Fit group, click 1 page, click the Height list arrow in the Scale to Fit group, then click 1 page.) Compare your screen to FIGURE 1-20.
   d. Preview the worksheet in Backstage view, then print the worksheet.
   e. Save your changes, submit your work to your instructor as directed, then close the workbook and exit Excel.

FIGURE 1-20

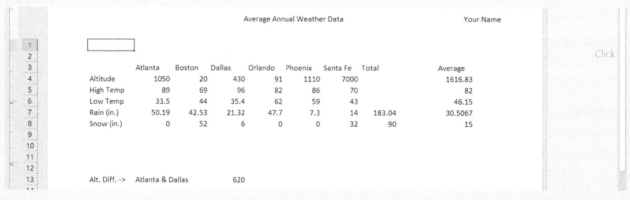

Independent Challenge 1

A real estate development company has hired you to help them make the transition to using Excel in their office. They would like to list properties they are interested in acquiring in a workbook. You've started a worksheet for this project that contains labels but no data.

   a. Open the file EX 1-3.xlsx from the location where you store your Data Files, then save it as **EX 1-Real Estate Acquisitions**.

   b. Enter the data shown in TABLE 1-4 in columns A, C, D, and E (the property address information should spill into column B).

TABLE 1-4

Property Address	Price	Bedrooms	Bathrooms	Area
1507 Pinon Lane	575000	4	2.5	NE
32 Zanzibar Way	429000	3	4	SE
60 Pottery Lane	526500	2	2	NE
902 Excelsior Drive	315000	4	3	NW

   c. Use Page Layout view to create a header with the following components: the title **Real Estate Acquisitions** in the center and your name on the right.

   d. Create formulas for totals in cells C6:E6.

   e. Save your changes, then compare your worksheet to FIGURE 1-21.

   f. Submit your work to your instructor as directed.

   g. Close the worksheet and exit Excel.

FIGURE 1-21

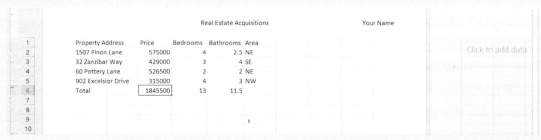

Independent Challenge 2

You are the general manager for Luxury Motors, a high-end auto reseller. Although the company is just five years old, it is expanding rapidly, and you are continually looking for ways to save time. You recently began using Excel to manage and maintain data on inventory and sales, which has greatly helped you to track information accurately and efficiently.

   a. Start Excel.

   b. Save a new workbook as **EX 1-Luxury Motors** in the location where you store your Data Files.

   c. Switch to an appropriate view, then add a header that contains your name in the left header text box and the title **Luxury Motors** in the center header text box.

Excel 2016

Independent Challenge 2 (continued)

d. Using FIGURE 1-22 as a guide, create labels for at least seven car manufacturers and sales for three months. Include other labels as appropriate. The car make should be in column A and the months should be in columns B, C, and D. A Total row should be beneath the data, and a Total column should be in column E.

FIGURE 1-22

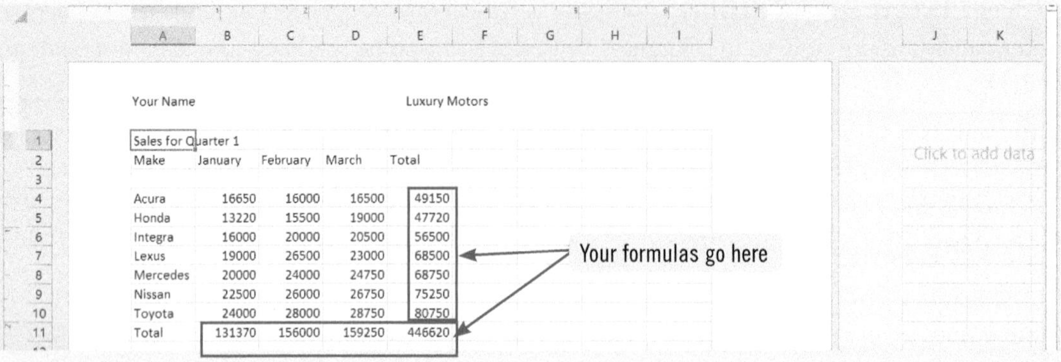

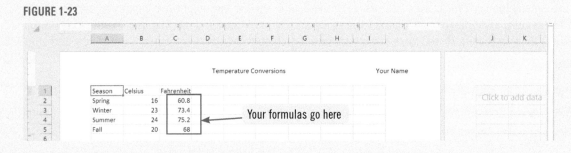

e. Enter values of your choice for the monthly sales for each make.

f. Add formulas in the Total column to calculate total quarterly sales for each make. Add formulas at the bottom of each column of values to calculate the total for that column. Remember that you can use the AutoSum button and the fill handle to save time.

g. Save your changes, preview the worksheet in Backstage view, then submit your work to your instructor as directed.

h. Close the workbook and exit Excel.

Independent Challenge 3

This Independent Challenge requires an Internet connection.

Your company, which is headquartered in Paris, is planning to open an office in New York City. You think it would be helpful to create a worksheet that can be used to convert Celsius temperatures to Fahrenheit, to help employees who are unfamiliar with this type of temperature measurement.

a. Start Excel, then save a blank workbook as **EX 1-Temperature Conversions** in the location where you store your Data Files.

b. Create column headings using FIGURE 1-23 as a guide. (*Hint*: You can widen column B by clicking cell B1, clicking the Format button in the Cells group on the Home tab, then clicking AutoFit Column Width.)

FIGURE 1-23

c. Create row labels for each of the seasons.

d. In the appropriate cells, enter what you determine to be a reasonable indoor temperature for each season.

e. Use your web browser to find out the conversion rate for Fahrenheit to Celsius. (*Hint*: Use your favorite search engine to search on a term such as **temperature conversion formula**.)

Independent Challenge 3 (continued)

f. In the appropriate cells, create a formula that calculates the conversion of the Fahrenheit temperature you entered into a Celsius temperature.

g. In Page Layout View, add your name and the title **Temperature Conversions** to the header.

h. Save your work, then submit your work to your instructor as directed.

i. Close the file, then exit Excel.

Independent Challenge 4: Explore

You've been asked to take over a project started by a co-worker whose Excel skills are not as good as your own. The assignment was to create a sample invoice for an existing client. The invoice will include personnel hours, supplies, and sales tax. Your predecessor started the project, including layout and initial calculations, but she has not made good use of Excel features and has made errors in her calculations. Complete the worksheet by correcting the errors and improving the design. Be prepared to discuss what is wrong with each of the items in the worksheet that you change.

a. Start Excel, open the file EX 1-4.xlsx from the location where you store your Data Files, then save it as **EX 1-Improved Invoice**.

b. There is an error in cell E5: please use the Help feature to find out what is wrong. If you need additional assistance, search Help on *overview of formulas*.

c. Correct the error in the formula in cell E5, then copy the corrected formula into cells E6:E7.

d. Correct the error in the formula in cell E11, then copy the corrected formula into cells E12 and E13.

e. Cells E8 and E14 also contain incorrect formulas. Cell E8 should contain a formula that calculates the total personnel expense, and cell E14 should calculate the total supplies used.

f. Cell G17 should contain a formula that adds the Invoice subtotal (total personnel and total supplies).

g. Cell G18 should calculate the sales tax by multiplying the Subtotal (G17) and the sales tax (cell G18).

h. The Invoice Total (cell G19) should contain a formula that adds the Invoice subtotal (cell G17) and Sales tax (cell G18).

i. Add the following to cell A21: **Terms**, then add the following to cell B21: **Net 10**.

j. Switch to Page Layout view and make the following changes to the Header: Improved Invoice for Week 22 (in the left header box), Client ABC (in the center header box), and your name (in the right header box).

k. Delete the contents of A1:A2, switch to Normal view, then compare your worksheet to FIGURE 1-24.

l. Save your work.

FIGURE 1-24

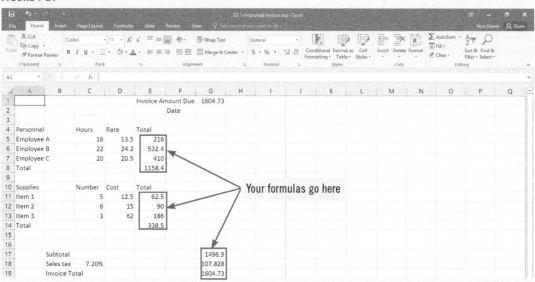

Excel 2016

Visual Workshop

Open the file EX 1-5.xlsx from the location where you store your Data Files, then save it as **EX 1-Project Tools**. Using the skills you learned in this module, modify your worksheet so it matches FIGURE 1-25. Enter formulas in cells D4 through D13 and in cells B14 and C14. Use the AutoSum button and fill handle to make entering your formulas easier. Add your name in the left header text box, then print one copy of the worksheet with the formulas displayed.

FIGURE 1-25

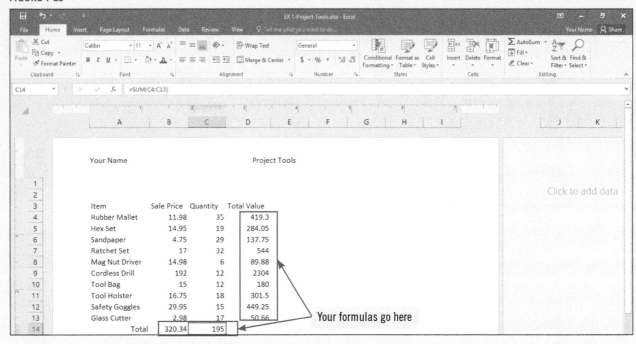

Working with Formulas and Functions

CASE ▶ Yolanda Lee, the vice president of finance at Reason2Go, needs to analyze tour expenses for the current year. She has asked you to prepare a worksheet that summarizes this expense data and includes some statistical analysis. She would also like you to perform some what-if analysis, to see what quarterly expenses would look like with various projected increases.

Module Objectives

After completing this module, you will be able to:

- Create a complex formula
- Insert a function
- Type a function
- Copy and move cell entries
- Understand relative and absolute cell references
- Copy formulas with relative cell references
- Copy formulas with absolute cell references
- Round a value with a function

Files You Will Need

EX 2-1.xlsx   EX 2-3.xlsx
EX 2-2.xlsx   EX 2-4.xlsx

Create a Complex Formula

A **complex formula** is one that uses more than one arithmetic operator. You might, for example, need to create a formula that uses addition and multiplication. In formulas containing more than one arithmetic operator, Excel uses the standard **order of precedence** rules to determine which operation to perform first. You can change the order of precedence in a formula by using parentheses around the part you want to calculate first. For example, the formula =4+2*5 equals 14, because the order of precedence dictates that multiplication is performed before addition. However, the formula =(4+2)*5 equals 30, because the parentheses cause 4+2 to be calculated first. **CASE** *You want to create a formula that calculates a 20% increase in tour expenses.*

STEPS

1. **Start Excel, open the file** EX 2-1.xlsx **from the location where you store your Data Files, then save it as** EX 2-R2G Tour Expense Analysis

2. **Select the range** B4:B11, **click the** Quick Analysis tool 📧 **that appears below the selection, then click the** Totals tab

   The Totals tab in the Quick Analysis tool displays commonly used functions, as seen in **FIGURE 2-1**.

3. **Click the** AutoSum button Σ **in the Quick Analysis tool**

   The newly calculated value displays in cell B12 and has bold formatting automatically applied, helping to set it off as a sum. This shading is temporary, and will not appear after you click a cell.

4. **Click cell** B12, **then drag the** fill handle **to cell** E12

   The formula in cell B12, as well as the bold formatting, is copied to cells C12:E12.

5. **Click cell** B14, **type** =, **click cell** B12, **then type** +

   In this first part of the formula, you are inserting a reference to the cell that contains total expenses for Quarter 1.

6. **Click cell** B12, **then type** *.2

   The second part of this formula adds a 20% increase (B12*.2) to the original value of the cell (the total expenses for Quarter 1).

7. **Click the** Enter button ✔ **on the formula bar**

   The result, 42749.58, appears in cell B14.

8. **Press [Tab], type** =, **click cell** C12, **type** +, **click cell** C12, **type** *.2, **then click** ✔

   The result, 42323.712, appears in cell C14.

9. **Drag the fill handle from cell** C14 **to cell** E14, **then save your work**

   The calculated values appear in the selected range, as shown in **FIGURE 2-2**. Dragging the fill handle on a cell copies the cell's contents or continues a series of data (such as Quarter 1, Quarter 2, etc.) into adjacent cells. This option is called **Auto Fill**.

Using Add-ins to improve worksheet functionality

Excel has more functionality than simple and complex math computations. Using the My Add-ins feature (found in the Add-ins group in the Insert tab), you can insert an add-in into your worksheet that accesses the web and adds functionality. Many of the add-ins are free or available for a small fee and can be used to create an email, appointment, meeting, contact, or task, or be a reference source, such as the Mini Calendar or Date Picker. When you click the My Add-ins button list arrow, you'll see any Recently Used Add-ins. Click See All to display the featured Add-ins for Office and to go to the Store to view available add-ins. When you find one you want, make sure you're logged in to Office.com, click the add-in, click Trust It, and the add-in will be installed. Click the My Add-ins button and your add-in should display under Recently Used Add-ins. Click it, then click Insert. The add-in will display in the Recently Used Add-ins pane when you click the My Add-ins button.

FIGURE 2-1: Totals tab in the Quick Analysis tool

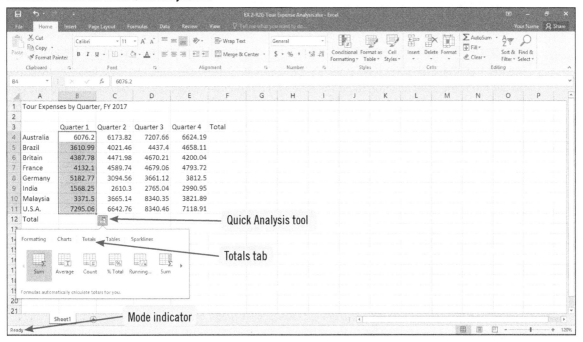

FIGURE 2-2: Results of copied formulas

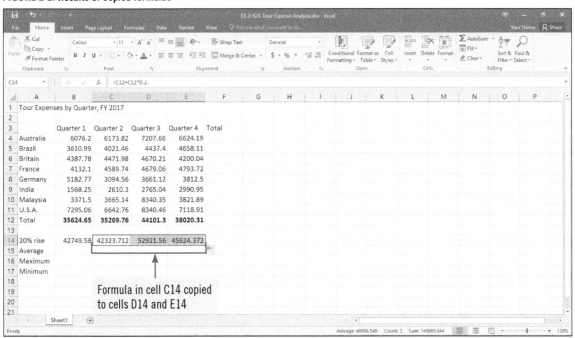

Reviewing the order of precedence

When you work with formulas that contain more than one operator, the order of precedence is very important because it affects the final value. If a formula contains two or more operators, such as 4+.55/4000*25, Excel performs the calculations in a particular sequence based on the following rules: Operations inside parentheses are calculated before any other operations. Reference operators (such as ranges) are calculated first. Exponents are calculated next, then any multiplication and division—progressing from left to right. Finally, addition and subtraction are calculated from left to right. In the example 4+.55/4000*25, Excel performs the arithmetic operations by first dividing .55 by 4000, then multiplying the result by 25, then adding 4. You can change the order of calculations by using parentheses. For example, in the formula (4+.55)/4000*25, Excel would first add 4 and .55, then divide that amount by 4000, then finally multiply by 25.

Insert a Function

Learning
Outcomes
• Use the Insert
  Function button
• Select a range for
  use in a function
• Select a function
  from the AutoSum
  list arrow

Functions are predefined worksheet formulas that enable you to perform complex calculations easily. You can use the Insert Function button on the formula bar to choose a function from a dialog box. You can quickly insert the SUM function using the AutoSum button on the Ribbon, or you can click the AutoSum list arrow to enter other frequently used functions, such as **AVERAGE**. You can also use the Quick Analysis tool to calculate commonly used functions. Functions are organized into categories, such as Financial, Date & Time, and Statistical, based on their purposes. You can insert a function on its own or as part of another formula. For example, you have used the SUM function on its own to add a range of cells. You could also use the SUM function within a formula that adds a range of cells and then multiplies the total by a decimal. If you use a function alone, it always begins with an equal sign (=) as the formula prefix. **CASE** *You need to calculate the average expenses for the first quarter of the year and decide to use a function to do so.*

STEPS

QUICK TIP
When using the
Insert Function button
or the AutoSum list
arrow, it is not
necessary to type the
equal sign (=); Excel
adds it as necessary.

1. **Click cell B15**

   This is the cell where you want to enter a calculation that averages expenses per country for the first quarter.

2. **Click the** Insert Function button f_x **on the formula bar**

   An equal sign (=) is inserted in the active cell and in the formula bar, and the Insert Function dialog box opens, as shown in FIGURE 2-3. In this dialog box, you specify the function you want to use by clicking it in the Select a function list. The Select a function list initially displays recently used functions. If you don't see the function you want, you can click the Or select a category list arrow to choose the desired category. If you're not sure which category to choose, you can type the function name or a description in the Search for a function field. The AVERAGE function is a statistical function, but you don't need to open the Statistical category because this function already appears in the Most Recently Used category.

QUICK TIP
To learn about a
function, click it in
the Select a function
list. The arguments
and format required
for the function
appear below the list.

3. **Click** AVERAGE **in the Select a function list if necessary, read the information that appears under the list, then click** OK

   The Function Arguments dialog box opens, in which you define the range of cells you want to average.

QUICK TIP
When selecting a
range, remember to
select all the cells
between and includ-
ing the two refer-
ences in the range.

4. **Click the** Collapse button 🔲 **in the Number1 field of the Function Arguments dialog box, select the range** B4:B11 **in the worksheet, then click the** Expand button 🔲 **in the Function Arguments dialog box**

   Clicking the Collapse button minimizes the dialog box so that you can select cells in the worksheet. When you click the Expand button, the dialog box is restored, as shown in FIGURE 2-4. You can also begin dragging in the worksheet to automatically minimize the dialog box; after you select the desired range, the dialog box is restored.

5. **Click** OK

   The Function Arguments dialog box closes, and the calculated value is displayed in cell B15. The average expenses per country for Quarter 1 is 4453.0813.

6. **Click cell** C15, **click the** AutoSum list arrow Σ ▾ **in the Editing group on the Home tab, then click** Average

   A ScreenTip beneath cell C15 displays the arguments needed to complete the function. The text "number1" is in boldface, telling you that the next step is to supply the first cell in the group you want to average.

7. **Select the range** C4:C11 **in the worksheet, then click the** Enter button ✓ **on the formula bar**

   The average expenses per country for the second quarter appear in cell C15.

8. **Drag the fill handle from cell** C15 **to cell** E15

   The formula in cell C15 is copied to the rest of the selected range, as shown in FIGURE 2-5.

9. **Save your work**

FIGURE 2-3: Insert Function dialog box

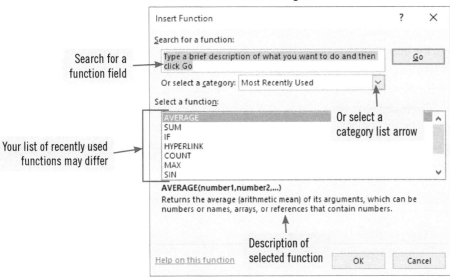

Search for a function field

Your list of recently used functions may differ

Or select a category list arrow

Description of selected function

FIGURE 2-4: Expanded Function Arguments dialog box

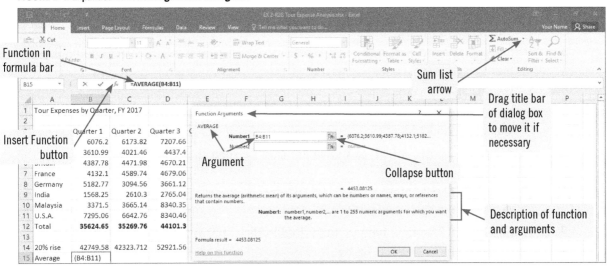

Function in formula bar

Insert Function button

Argument

Sum list arrow

Drag title bar of dialog box to move it if necessary

Collapse button

Description of function and arguments

FIGURE 2-5: Average functions used in worksheet

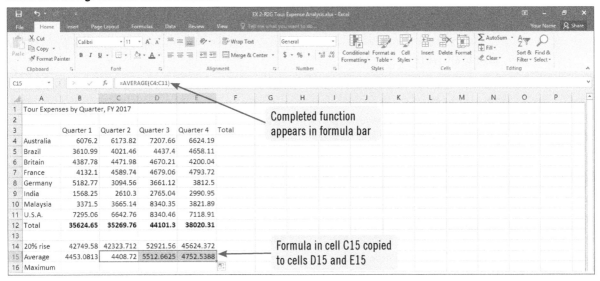

Completed function appears in formula bar

Formula in cell C15 copied to cells D15 and E15

Type a Function

Learning
Outcomes
• Select a function
  by typing
• Use AutoComplete
  to copy formulas

In addition to using the Insert Function dialog box, the AutoSum button, or the AutoSum list arrow on the Ribbon to enter a function, you can manually type the function into a cell and then complete the arguments needed. This method requires that you know the name and initial characters of the function, but it can be faster than opening several dialog boxes. Experienced Excel users often prefer this method, but it is only an alternative, not better or more correct than any other method. The Excel **Formula AutoComplete** feature makes it easier to enter function names by typing, because it suggests functions depending on the first letters you type. **CASE** *You want to calculate the maximum and minimum quarterly expenses in your worksheet, and you decide to manually enter these statistical functions.*

STEPS

1. **Click cell B16, type =, then type m**

   Because you are manually typing this function, it is necessary to begin with the equal sign (=). The Formula AutoComplete feature displays a list of function names beginning with "M" beneath cell B16. Once you type an equal sign in a cell, each letter you type acts as a trigger to activate the Formula AutoComplete feature. This feature minimizes the amount of typing you need to do to enter a function and reduces typing and syntax errors.

2. **Click MAX in the list**

   Clicking any function in the Formula AutoComplete list opens a ScreenTip next to the list that describes the function.

3. **Double-click MAX**

   > **QUICK TIP**
   > When you select the function, a ScreenTip automatically displays more detailed information about the function.

   The function is inserted in the cell, and a ScreenTip appears beneath the cell to help you complete the formula. See **FIGURE 2-6**.

4. **Select the range B4:B11, as shown in FIGURE 2-7, then click the Enter button ✓ on the formula bar**

   The result, 7295.06, appears in cell B16. When you completed the entry, the closing parenthesis was automatically added to the formula.

5. **Click cell B17, type =, type m, then double-click MIN in the list of function names**

   The MIN function appears in the cell.

6. **Select the range B4:B11, then press [Enter]**

   The result, 1568.25, appears in cell B17.

7. **Select the range B16:B17, then drag the fill handle from cell B17 to cell E17**

   The maximum and minimum values for all of the quarters appear in the selected range, as shown in **FIGURE 2-8**.

8. **Save your work**

Using the COUNT and COUNTA functions

When you select a range, a count of cells in the range that are not blank appears in the status bar. You can use this information to determine things such as how many team members entered project hours in a worksheet. For example, if you select the range A1:A5 and only cells A1, A4, and A5 contain data, the status bar displays "Count: 3." To count nonblank cells more precisely, or to incorporate these calculations in a worksheet, you can use the COUNT and COUNTA functions. The COUNT function returns the number of cells in a range that contain numeric data, including numbers, dates, and formulas. The COUNTA function returns the number of cells in a range that contain any data at all, including numeric data, labels, and even a blank space. For example, the formula =COUNT(A1:A5) returns the number of cells in the range that contain numeric data, and the formula =COUNTA(A1:A5) returns the number of cells in the range that are not empty. If you use the COUNT functions in the Quick Analysis tool, the calculation is entered in the cell immediately beneath the selected range.

FIGURE 2-6: MAX function in progress

13					
14	20% rise	42749.58	42323.712	52921.56	45624.372
15	Average	4453.0813	4408.72	5512.6625	4752.5388
16	Maximum	=MAX(			
17	Minimum	MAX(**number1**, [number2], ...)			

FIGURE 2-7: Completing the MAX function

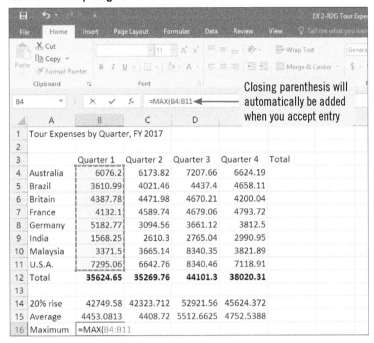

FIGURE 2-8: Completed MAX and MIN functions

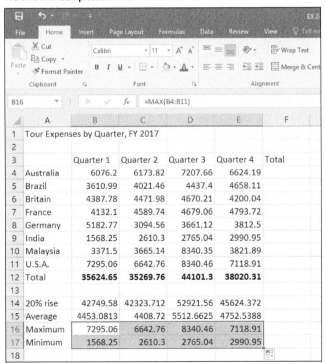

Copy and Move Cell Entries

Learning Outcomes
• Copy a range to the Clipboard
• Paste a Clipboard entry
• Empty cell contents
• Copy cell contents

There are three ways you can copy or move cells and ranges (or the contents within them) from one location to another: the Cut, Copy, and Paste buttons on the Home tab on the Ribbon; the fill handle in the lower-right corner of the active cell or range; or the drag-and-drop feature. When you copy cells, the original data remains in the original location; when you cut or move cells, the original data is deleted from its original location. You can also cut, copy, and paste cells or ranges from one worksheet to another. **CASE** *In addition to the 20% rise in tour expenses, you also want to show a 30% rise. Rather than retype this information, you copy and move selected cells.*

STEPS

QUICK TIP
To cut or copy selected cell contents, activate the cell, then select the characters within the cell that you want to cut or copy.

1. **Select the range B3:E3, then click the Copy button 📋 in the Clipboard group on the Home tab**

   The selected range (B3:E3) is copied to the **Clipboard**, a temporary Windows storage area that holds the selections you copy or cut. A moving border surrounds the selected range until you press [Esc] or copy an additional item to the Clipboard.

2. **Click the launcher ⬛ in the Clipboard group**

   The Office Clipboard opens in the Clipboard task pane, as shown in **FIGURE 2-9**. When you copy or cut an item, it is cut or copied both to the Clipboard provided by Windows and to the Office Clipboard. Unlike the Windows Clipboard, which holds just one item at a time, the Office Clipboard contains up to 24 of the most recently cut or copied items from any Office program. Your Clipboard task pane may contain more items than shown in the figure.

QUICK TIP
Once the Office Clipboard contains 24 items, the oldest existing item is automatically deleted each time you add an item.

3. **Click cell B19, then click the Paste button in the Clipboard group**

   A copy of the contents of range B3:E3 is pasted into the range B19:E19. When pasting an item from the Office Clipboard or Clipboard into a worksheet, you only need to specify the upper left cell of the range where you want to paste the selection. Notice that the information you copied remains in the original range B3:E3; if you had cut instead of copied, the information would have been deleted from its original location once it was pasted.

4. **Press [Delete]**

   The selected cells are empty. You have decided to paste the cells in a different row. You can repeatedly paste an item from the Office Clipboard as many times as you like, as long as the item remains in the Office Clipboard.

QUICK TIP
You can also close the Office Clipboard pane by clicking the launcher in the Clipboard group.

5. **Click cell B20, click the first item in the Office Clipboard, then click the Close button ✖ on the Clipboard task pane**

   Cells B20:E20 contain the copied labels.

6. **Click cell A14, press and hold [Ctrl], point to any edge of the cell until the pointer changes to ⬚, drag cell A14 to cell A21, release the mouse button, then release [Ctrl]**

   The copy pointer ⬚ continues to appear as you drag, as shown in **FIGURE 2-10**. When you release the mouse button, the contents of cell A14 are copied to cell A21.

7. **Click to the right of 2 in the formula bar, press [Backspace], type 3, then click the Enter button ✓**

8. **Click cell B21, type =, click cell B12, type *1.3, click ✓ on the formula bar, then save your work**

   This new formula calculates a 30% increase of the expenses for Quarter 1, though using a different method from what you previously used. Anything you multiply by 1.3 returns an amount that is 130% of the original amount, or a 30% increase. Compare your screen to **FIGURE 2-11**.

FIGURE 2-9: Copied data in Office Clipboard

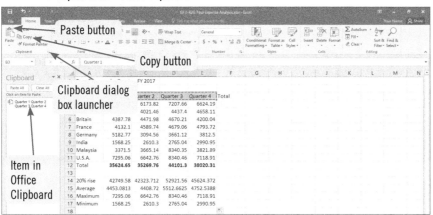

FIGURE 2-10: Copying cell contents with drag-and-drop

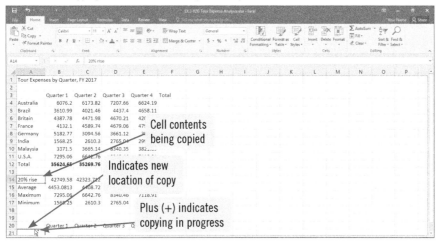

FIGURE 2-11: Formula entered to calculate a 30% increase

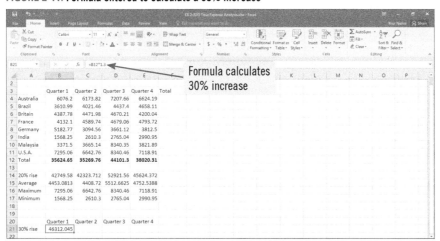

Inserting and deleting selected cells

As you add formulas to your workbook, you may need to insert or delete cells. When you do this, Excel automatically adjusts cell references to reflect their new locations. To insert cells, click the Insert list arrow in the Cells group on the Home tab, then click Insert Cells. The Insert dialog box opens, asking if you want to insert a cell and move the current active cell down or to the right of the new one. To delete one or more selected cells,

click the Delete list arrow in the Cells group, click Delete Cells, and in the Delete dialog box, indicate which way you want to move the adjacent cells. When using this option, be careful not to disturb row or column alignment that may be necessary to maintain the accuracy of cell references in the worksheet. Click the Insert button or Delete button in the Cells group to insert or delete a single cell.

Understand Relative and Absolute Cell References

As you work in Excel, you may want to reuse formulas in different parts of a worksheet to reduce the amount of data you have to retype. For example, you might want to include a what-if analysis in one part of a worksheet showing a set of sales projections if sales increase by 10%. To include another analysis in another part of the worksheet showing projections if sales increase by 50%, you can copy the formulas from one section to another and simply change the "1" to a "5". But when you copy formulas, it is important to make sure that they refer to the correct cells. To do this, you need to understand the difference between relative and absolute cell references. **CASE** ▶ *You plan to reuse formulas in different parts of your worksheets, so you want to understand relative and absolute cell references.*

DETAILS

Consider the following when using relative and absolute cell references:

- **Use relative references when you want to preserve the relationship to the formula location**

  When you create a formula that references another cell, Excel normally does not "record" the exact cell address for the cell being referenced in the formula. Instead, it looks at the relationship that cell has to the cell containing the formula. For example, in **FIGURE 2-12**, cell F5 contains the formula: =SUM(B5:E5). When Excel retrieves values to calculate the formula in cell F5, it actually looks for "the four cells to the left of the formula," which in this case is cells B5:E5. This way, if you copy the cell to a new location, such as cell F6, the results will reflect the new formula location and will automatically retrieve the values in cells B6, C6, D6, and E6. These are **relative cell references**, because Excel is recording the input cells *in relation to* or *relative to* the formula cell.

  In most cases, you want to use relative cell references when copying or moving, so this is the Excel default. In **FIGURE 2-12**, the formulas in cells F5:F12 and cells B13:F13 contain relative cell references. They total the "four cells to the left of" or the "eight cells above" the formulas.

- **Use absolute cell references when you want to preserve the exact cell address in a formula**

  There are times when you want Excel to retrieve formula information from a specific cell, and you don't want the cell address in the formula to change when you copy it to a new location. For example, you might have a price in a specific cell that you want to use in all formulas, regardless of their location. If you use relative cell referencing, the formula results would be incorrect, because the formula would reference a different cell every time you copy it. Therefore, you need to use an **absolute cell reference**, which is a reference that does not change when you copy the formula.

  You create an absolute cell reference by placing a $ (dollar sign) in front of both the column letter and the row number of the cell address. You can either type the dollar sign when typing the cell address in a formula (for example, "=C12*B16") or you can select a cell address on the formula bar and then press [F4], and the dollar signs are added automatically. **FIGURE 2-13** shows formulas containing both absolute and relative references. The formulas in cells B19 to E26 use absolute cell references to refer to a potential sales increase of 50%, shown in cell B16.

FIGURE 2-12: Formulas containing relative references

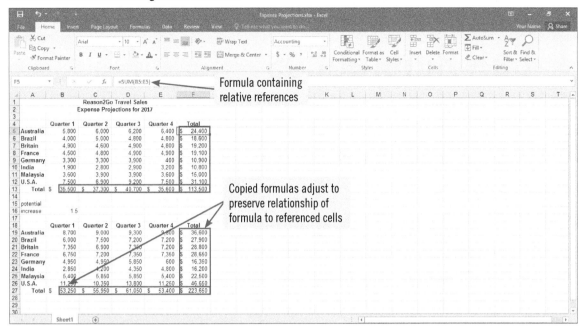

Formula containing relative references

Copied formulas adjust to preserve relationship of formula to referenced cells

FIGURE 2-13: Formulas containing absolute and relative references

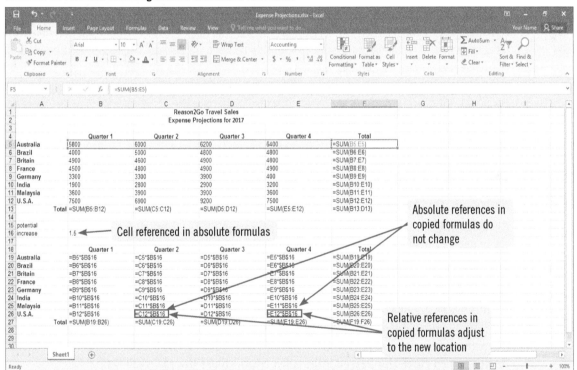

Absolute references in copied formulas do not change

Cell referenced in absolute formulas

Relative references in copied formulas adjust to the new location

Using a mixed reference

Sometimes when you copy a formula, you want to change the row reference, but keep the column reference the same. This type of cell referencing combines elements of both absolute and relative referencing and is called a **mixed reference**. For example, when copied, a formula containing the mixed reference C$14 would change the column letter relative to its new location, but not the row number. In the mixed reference $C14, the column letter would not change, but the row number would be updated relative to its location. Like an absolute reference, a mixed reference can be created by pressing the [F4] function key with the cell reference selected. With each press of the [F4] key, you cycle through all the possible combinations of relative, absolute, and mixed references (C14, C14, C$14, and $C14).

Excel 2016

Copy Formulas with Relative Cell References

Learning Outcomes
• Copy and Paste formulas with relative cell references
• Examine Auto Fill and Paste Options
• Use the Fill button

Copying and moving a cell allow you to reuse a formula you've already created. Copying cells is usually faster than retyping the formulas in them and helps to prevent typing errors. If the cells you are copying contain relative cell references and you want to maintain the relative referencing, you don't need to make any changes to the cells before copying them. **CASE** ▶ *You want to copy the formula in cell B21, which calculates the 30% increase in quarterly expenses for Quarter 1, to cells C21 through E21. You also want to create formulas to calculate total expenses for each tour country.*

STEPS

1. **Click cell B21 if necessary, then click the Copy button 📋 in the Clipboard group on the Home tab**

   The formula for calculating the 30% expense increase during Quarter 1 is copied to the Clipboard. Notice that the formula =B12*1.3 appears in the formula bar, and a moving border surrounds the active cell.

2. **Click cell C21, then click the Paste button 📋 (*not the list arrow*) in the Clipboard group**

   The formula from cell B21 is copied into cell C21, where the new result of 45850.688 appears. Notice in the formula bar that the cell references have changed so that cell C12 is referenced instead of B12. This formula contains a relative cell reference, which tells Excel to substitute new cell references within the copied formulas as necessary. This maintains the same relationship between the new cell containing the formula and the cell references within the formula. In this case, Excel adjusted the formula so that cell C12—the cell reference nine rows above C21—replaced cell B12, the cell reference nine rows above B21.

3. **Drag the fill handle from cell C21 to cell E21**

   A formula similar to the one in cell C21 now appears in cells D21 and E21. After you use the fill handle to copy cell contents, the **Auto Fill Options button** appears, as shown in **FIGURE 2-14**. You can use the Auto Fill Options button to fill the cells with only specific elements of the copied cell if you wish.

4. **Click cell F4, click the AutoSum button Σ in the Editing group, then click the Enter button ✓ on the formula bar**

5. **Click 📋 in the Clipboard group, select the range F5:F6, then click 📋**

   See **FIGURE 2-15**. After you click the Paste button, the **Paste Options button** appears.

6. **Click the Paste Options button 📋(Ctrl)▾ adjacent to the selected range**

   You can use the Paste options list to paste only specific elements of the copied selection if you wish. The formula for calculating total expenses for tours in Britain appears in the formula bar. You would like totals to appear in cells F7:F11. The Fill button in the Editing group can be used to copy the formula into the remaining cells.

7. **Press [Esc] to close the Paste Options list, then select the range F6:F11**

8. **Click the Fill button 🔽 in the Editing group, then click Down**

   The formulas containing relative references are copied to each cell. Compare your worksheet to **FIGURE 2-16**.

9. **Save your work**

Working with Formulas and Functions

FIGURE 2-14: Formula copied using the fill handle

FIGURE 2-15: Formulas pasted in the range F5:F6

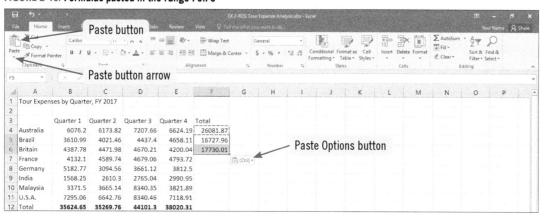

FIGURE 2-16: Formula copied using Fill Down

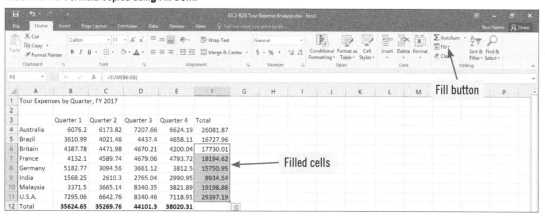

Using Paste Preview

You can selectively copy formulas, values, or other choices using the Paste list arrow, and you can see how the pasted contents will look using the Paste Preview feature. When you click the Paste list arrow, a gallery of paste option icons opens. When you point to an icon, a preview of how the content will be pasted using that option is shown in the worksheet. Options include pasting values only, pasting values with number formatting, pasting formulas only, pasting formatting only, pasting transposed data so that column data appears in rows and row data appears in columns, and pasting with no borders (to remove any borders around pasted cells).

Copy Formulas with Absolute Cell References

Learning Outcomes
• Create an absolute cell reference
• Use the fill handle to copy absolute cell references

When copying cells, you might want one or more cell references in a formula to remain unchanged. In such an instance, you need to apply an absolute cell reference before copying the formula to preserve the specific cell address when the formula is copied. You create an absolute reference by placing a dollar sign ($) before the column letter and row number of the address (for example, A1). **CASE** *You need to do some what-if analysis to see how various percentage increases might affect total expenses. You decide to add a column that calculates a possible increase in the total tour expenses, and then change the percentage to see various potential results.*

STEPS

1. **Click cell G1, type Change, then press [Enter]**

2. **Type 1.1, then press [Enter]**
   You store the increase factor that will be used in the what-if analysis in this cell (G2). The value 1.1 can be used to calculate a 10% increase: anything you multiply by 1.1 returns an amount that is 110% of the original amount.

3. **Click cell H3, type What if?, then press [Enter]**

4. **In cell H4, type =, click cell F4, type *, click cell G2, then click the Enter button ✓ on the formula bar**
   The result, 28690.1, appears in cell H4. This value represents the total annual expenses for Australia if there is a 10% increase. You want to perform a what-if analysis for all the tour countries.

5. **Drag the fill handle from cell H4 to cell H11**
   The resulting values in the range H5:H11 are all zeros, which is not the result you wanted. Because you used relative cell addressing in cell H4, the copied formula adjusted so that the formula in cell H5 is =F5*G3; because there is no value in cell G3, the result is 0, an error. You need to use an absolute reference in the formula to keep the formula from adjusting itself. That way, it will always reference cell G2.

6. **Click cell H4, press [F2] to change to Edit mode, then press [F4]**
   When you press [F2], the range finder outlines the arguments of the equation in blue and red. The insertion point appears next to the G2 cell reference in cell H4. When you press [F4], dollar signs are inserted in the G2 cell reference, making it an absolute reference. See **FIGURE 2-17**.

7. **Click ✓, then drag the fill handle from cell H4 to cell H11**
   Because the formula correctly contains an absolute cell reference, the correct values for a 10% increase appear in cells H4:H11. You now want to see what a 20% increase in expenses looks like.

8. **Click cell G2, type 1.2, then click ✓**
   The values in the range H4:H11 change to reflect the 20% increase. Compare your worksheet to **FIGURE 2-18**.

9. **Save your work**

FIGURE 2-17: Absolute reference created in formula

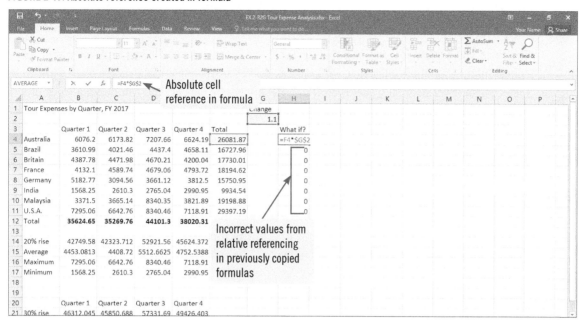

Absolute cell reference in formula

Incorrect values from relative referencing in previously copied formulas

FIGURE 2-18: What-if analysis with modified change factor

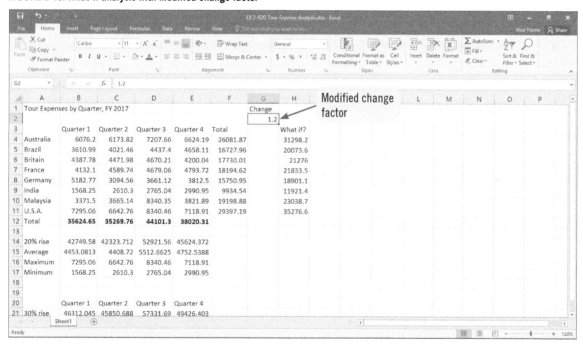

Modified change factor

Using the fill handle for sequential text or values

Often, you need to fill cells with sequential text: months of the year, days of the week, years, or text plus a number (Quarter 1, Quarter 2,...). For example, you might want to create a worksheet that calculates data for every month of the year. Using the fill handle, you can quickly and easily create labels for the months of the year just by typing "January" in a cell. Drag the fill handle from the cell containing "January" until you have all the monthly labels you need. You can also easily fill cells with a date sequence by dragging the fill handle on a single cell containing a date. You can fill cells with a number sequence (such as 1, 2, 3,...) by dragging the fill handle on a selection of two or more cells that contain the sequence. To create a number sequence using the value in a single cell, press and hold [Ctrl] as you drag the fill handle of the cell. As you drag the fill handle, Excel automatically extends the existing sequence into the additional cells. (The content of the last filled cell appears in the ScreenTip.) To choose from all the fill series options for the current selection, click the Fill button in the Editing group on the Home tab, then click Series to open the Series dialog box.

Round a Value with a Function

Learning Outcomes
• Use Formula AutoComplete to insert a function
• Copy an edited formula

The more you explore features and tools in Excel, the more ways you'll find to simplify your work and convey information more efficiently. For example, cells containing financial data are often easier to read if they contain fewer decimal places than those that appear by default. You can round a value or formula result to a specific number of decimal places by using the ROUND function. **CASE** *In your worksheet, you'd like to round the cells showing the 20% rise in expenses to show fewer digits; after all, it's not important to show cents in the projections, only whole dollars. You want Excel to round the calculated value to the nearest integer. You decide to edit cell B14 so it includes the ROUND function, and then copy the edited formula into the other formulas in this row.*

STEPS

1. **Click cell B14, then click to the right of = in the formula bar**
   You want to position the function at the beginning of the formula, before any values or arguments.

2. **Type RO**
   Formula AutoComplete displays a list of functions beginning with RO beneath the formula bar.

3. **Double-click ROUND in the functions list**
   The new function and an opening parenthesis are added to the formula, as shown in **FIGURE 2-19**. A few additional modifications are needed to complete your edit of the formula. You need to indicate the number of decimal places to which the function should round numbers, and you also need to add a closing parenthesis around the set of arguments that comes after the ROUND function.

4. **Press [END], type ,0), then click the Enter button ✓ on the formula bar**
   The comma separates the arguments within the formula, and 0 indicates that you don't want any decimal places to appear in the calculated value. When you complete the edit, the parentheses at either end of the formula briefly become bold, indicating that the formula has the correct number of open and closed parentheses and is balanced.

5. **Drag the fill handle from cell B14 to cell E14**
   The formula in cell B14 is copied to the range C14:E14. All the values are rounded to display no decimal places. Compare your worksheet to **FIGURE 2-20**.

6. **Scroll down so row 25 is visible, click cell A25, type your name, then click ✓**

7. **Save your work, preview the worksheet in the Print place in Backstage view, then submit your work to your Instructor as directed**

8. **Exit Excel**

Using Auto Fill options

When you use the fill handle to copy cells, the Auto Fill Options button appears. Auto Fill options differ depending on what you are copying. If you had selected cells containing a series (such as "Monday" and "Tuesday") and then used the fill handle, you would see options for continuing the series (such as "Wednesday" and "Thursday") or for simply pasting the copied cells. Clicking the Auto Fill Options button opens a list that lets you choose from the following options: Copy Cells, Fill Series (if applicable), Fill Formatting Only, Fill Without Formatting, or Flash Fill. Choosing Copy Cells means that the cell's contents and its formatting will be copied. The Fill Formatting Only option copies only the formatting attributes, but not cell contents. The Fill Without Formatting option copies the cell contents, but no formatting attributes. Copy Cells is the default option when using the fill handle to copy a cell, so if you want to copy the cell's contents and its formatting, you can ignore the Auto Fill Options button. The Flash Fill option allows you to create customized fill ranges on the fly, such as 2, 4, 6, 8, 10, by entering at least two values in a pattern: Excel automatically senses the pattern.

FIGURE 2-19: ROUND function added to an existing formula

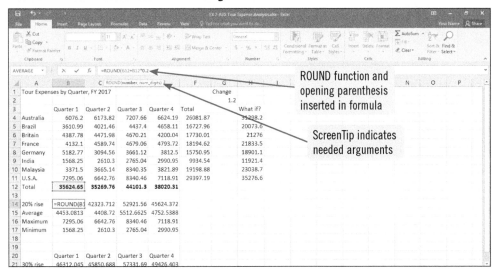

ROUND function and
opening parenthesis
inserted in formula

ScreenTip indicates
needed arguments

FIGURE 2-20: Completed worksheet

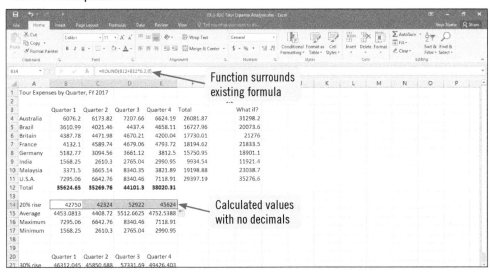

Function surrounds
existing formula

Calculated values
with no decimals

Excel 2016

Creating a new workbook using a template

Excel **templates** are predesigned workbook files intended to save time when you create common documents such as balance sheets, budgets, or time cards. Templates contain labels, values, formulas, and formatting, so all you have to do is customize them with your own information. Excel comes with many templates, and you can also create your own or find additional templates on the web. Unlike a typical workbook, which has the file extension .xlsx, a template has the extension .xltx. To create a workbook using a template, click the File tab, then click New on the navigation bar. The New place in Backstage view displays thumbnails of some of the many templates available. The Blank workbook template is selected by default and is used to create a blank workbook with no content or special formatting. To select a different template, click one of the selections in the New place, view the preview, then click Create. FIGURE 2-21 shows an example. (Your available templates may differ.) When you click

Create, a new workbook is created based on the template; when you save the new file in the default format, it has the regular .xlsx extension. To save a workbook of your own as a template, open the Save As dialog box, click the Save as type list arrow, then change the file type to Excel Template.

FIGURE 2-21: Previewing the Budget Planner template

Practice

Concepts Review

Label each element of the Excel worksheet window shown in FIGURE 2-22.

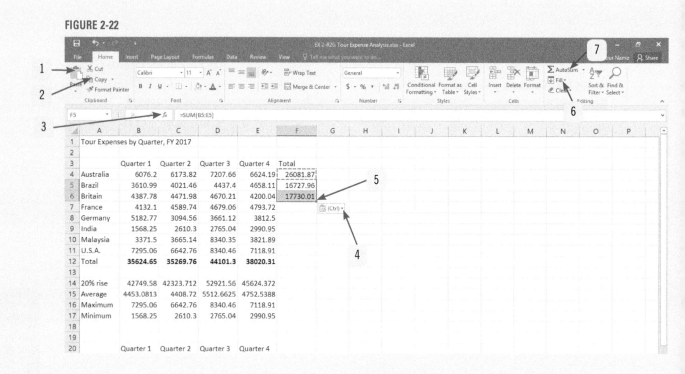

FIGURE 2-22

Match each term or button with the statement that best describes it.

8. Launcher
9. Fill handle
10. Drag-and-drop method
11. Formula AutoComplete
12. [Delete] key

a. Clears the contents of selected cells
b. Item on the Ribbon that opens a dialog box or task pane
c. Lets you move or copy data from one cell to another without using the Clipboard
d. Displays an alphabetical list of functions from which you can choose
e. Lets you copy cell contents or continue a series of data into a range of selected cells

Select the best answer from the list of choices.

13. **You can use any of the following features to enter a new function *except*:**
    a. Insert Function button.
    c. AutoSum list arrow.
    b. Formula AutoComplete.
    d. Clipboard.

14. **Which key do you press and hold to copy while dragging and dropping selected cells?**
    a. [Alt]
    c. [F2]
    b. [Ctrl]
    d. [Tab]

15. **What type of cell reference is C$19?**
    a. Relative
    c. Mixed
    b. Absolute
    d. Certain

16. **Which key do you press to convert a relative cell reference to an absolute cell reference?**
    a. [F2]
    c. [F5]
    b. [F4]
    d. [F6]

17. **What type of cell reference changes when it is copied?**
    a. Circular
    c. Relative
    b. Absolute
    d. Specified

Skills Review

1. **Create a complex formula.**
   a. Open EX 2-2.xlsx from the location where you store your Data Files, then save it as **EX 2-Construction Supply Company Inventory**.
   b. Select the range B4:B8, click the Totals tab in the Quick Analysis tool, then click the AutoSum button.
   c. Use the fill handle to copy the formula in cell B9 to cells C9:E9.
   d. In cell B11, create a complex formula that calculates a 30% decrease in the total number of cases of pylons.
   e. Use the fill handle to copy this formula into cell C11 through cell E11.
   f. Save your work.

2. **Insert a function.**
   a. Use the AutoSum list arrow to create a formula in cell B13 that averages the number of cases of pylons in each storage area.
   b. Use the Insert Function button to create a formula in cell B14 that calculates the maximum number of cases of pylons in a storage area.
   c. Use the AutoSum list arrow to create a formula in cell B15 that calculates the minimum number of cases of pylons in a storage area.
   d. Save your work.

Skills Review (continued)

3. Type a function.

   a. In cell C13, type a formula that includes a function to average the number of cases of bricks in each storage area. (*Hint*: Use Formula AutoComplete to enter the function.)

   b. In cell C14, type a formula that includes a function to calculate the maximum number of cases of bricks in a storage area.

   c. In cell C15, type a formula that includes a function to calculate the minimum number of cases of bricks in a storage area.

   d. Save your work.

4. Copy and move cell entries.

   a. Select the range B3:F3.

   b. Copy the selection to the Clipboard.

   c. Open the Clipboard task pane, then paste the selection into cell B17.

   d. Close the Clipboard task pane, then select the range A4:A9.

   e. Use the drag-and-drop method to copy the selection to cell A18. (*Hint*: The results should fill the range A18:A23.)

   f. Save your work.

5. Understand relative and absolute cell references.

   a. Write a brief description of the difference between relative and absolute references.

   b. List at least three situations in which you think a business might use an absolute reference in its calculations. Examples can include calculations for different types of worksheets, such as time cards, invoices, and budgets.

6. Copy formulas with relative cell references.

   a. Calculate the total in cell F4.

   b. Use the Fill button to copy the formula in cell F4 down to cells F5:F8.

   c. Select the range C13:C15.

   d. Use the fill handle to copy these cells to the range D13:F15.

   e. Save your work.

7. Copy formulas with absolute cell references.

   a. In cell H1, change the existing value to **1.575**.

   b. In cell H4, create a formula that multiplies F4 and an absolute reference to cell H1.

   c. Use the fill handle to copy the formula in cell H4 to cells H5 and H6.

   d. Use the Copy and Paste buttons to copy the formula in cell H4 to cells H7 and H8.

   e. Change the amount in cell H1 to **2.5**.

   f. Save your work.

Skills Review (continued)

8. **Round a value with a function.**

   a. Click cell H4.

   b. Edit this formula to include the ROUND function showing zero decimal places.

   c. Use the fill handle to copy the formula in cell H4 to the range H5:H8.

   d. Enter your name in cell A25, then compare your work to FIGURE 2-23.

   e. Save your work, preview the worksheet in Backstage view, then submit your work to your instructor as directed.

   f. Close the workbook, then exit Excel.

FIGURE 2-23

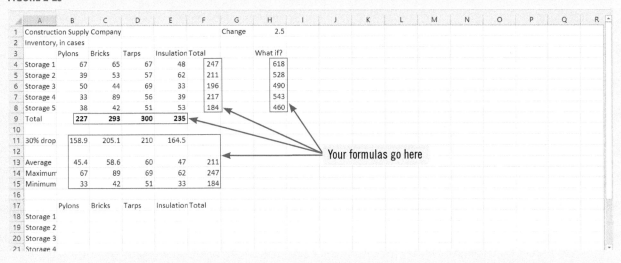

Excel 2016

Independent Challenge 1

You are thinking of starting a small coffee shop where locals can gather. Before you begin, you need to evaluate what you think your monthly expenses will be. You've started a workbook, but need to complete the entries and add formulas.

a. Open EX 2-3.xlsx from the location where you store your Data Files, then save it as **EX 2-Coffee Shop Expenses**.

b. Make up your own expense data, and enter it in cells B4:B10. (Monthly sales are already included in the worksheet.)

c. Create a formula in cell C4 that calculates the annual rent.

d. Copy the formula in cell C4 to the range C5:C10.

e. Move the label in cell A15 to cell A14.

f. Create formulas in cells B11 and C11 that total the monthly and annual expenses.

g. Create a formula in cell C13 that calculates annual sales.

h. Create a formula in cell B14 that determines whether you will make a profit or loss, then copy the formula into cell C14.

i. Copy the labels in cells B3:C3 to cells E3:F3.

j. Type **Projected Increase** in cell G1, then type **.2** in cell H2.

k. Create a formula in cell E4 that calculates an increase in the monthly rent by the amount in cell H2. You will be copying this formula to other cells, so you'll need to use an absolute reference.

l. Create a formula in cell F4 that calculates the increased annual rent expense based on the calculation in cell E4.

m. Copy the formulas in cells E4:F4 into cells E5:F10 to calculate the remaining monthly and annual expenses.

n. Create a formula in cell E11 that calculates the total monthly expenses, then copy that formula to cell F11.

o. Copy the contents of cells B13:C13 into cells E13:F13.

p. Create formulas in cells E14 and F14 that calculate profit/loss based on the projected increase in monthly and annual expenses.

q. Change the projected increase to **.17**, then compare your work to the sample in FIGURE 2-24.

r. Enter your name in a cell in the worksheet.

s. Save your work, preview the worksheet in Backstage view, submit your work to your instructor as directed, close the workbook, and exit Excel.

FIGURE 2-24

	A	B	C	D	E	F	G	H	I
1	Estim	Your formulas go here (your formula results will differ)	ɔnses				Projected Increase		
2								0.17	
3		Monthly	Annually		Monthly	Annually			
4	Rent	2500	30000		2925	35100			
5	Supplies	1600	19200		1872	22464			
6	Milk	3600	43200		4212	50544			
7	Sugar	1300	15600		1521	18252			
8	Pastries	850	10200		994.5	11934			
9	Coffee	600	7200		702	8424			
10	Utilities	750	9000		877.5	10530			
11	Total	11200	134400		13104	157248			
12									
13	Sales	24500	294000		23000	276000			
14	Profit/Loss	13300	159600		9896	118752			

Independent Challenge 2

The Office Specialists Center is a small, growing business that rents small companies space and provides limited business services. They have hired you to organize their accounting records using Excel. The owners want you to track the company's expenses. Before you were hired, one of the bookkeepers began entering last year's expenses in a workbook, but the analysis was never completed.

a. Start Excel, open EX 2-4.xlsx from the location where you store your Data Files, then save it as **EX 2-Office Specialists Center Finances**. The worksheet includes labels for functions such as the average, maximum, and minimum amounts of each of the expenses in the worksheet.

b. Think about what information would be important for the bookkeeping staff to know.

c. Using the Quick Analysis tool, create a formula in the Quarter 1 column that uses the SUM function, then copy that formula into the Total row for the remaining quarters.

d. Use the SUM function to create formulas for each expense in the Total column.

e. Create formulas for each expense and each quarter in the Average, Maximum, and Minimum columns and rows using the method of your choice.

f. Compare your worksheet to the sample shown in FIGURE 2-25.

g. Enter your name in cell A25, then save your work.

h. Preview the worksheet, then submit your work to your instructor as directed.

i. Close the workbook and exit Excel.

FIGURE 2-25

	A	B	C	D	E	F	G	H	I	J
1	Office Specialists Center									
2										
3	Operating Expenses for 2017									
4										
5	Expense	Quarter 1	Quarter 2	Quarter 3	Quarter 4	Total	Average	Maximum	Minimum	
6	Rent	10240	10240	10240	10240	40960	10240	10240	10240	
7	Utilities	9500	8482	7929	8596	34507	8626.75	9500	7929	
8	Payroll	24456	27922	26876	30415	109669	27417.3	30415	24456	
9	Insurance	9000	8594	8472	8523	34589	8647.25	9000	8472	
10	Education	4000	4081	7552	5006	20639	5159.75	7552	4000	
11	Inventory	15986	14115	14641	15465	60207	15051.8	15986	14115	
12	Total	**73182**	**73434**	**75710**	**78245**					
13										
14	Average	12197	12239	12618.3	13040.8			Your formulas go here		
15	Maximum	24456	27922	26876	30415					
16	Minimum	4000	4081	7552	5006					

Working with Formulas and Functions

Independent Challenge 3

As the accounting manager of a locally owned food co-op with multiple locations, it is your responsibility to calculate accrued sales tax payments on a monthly basis and then submit the payments to the state government. You've decided to use an Excel workbook to make these calculations.

a. Start Excel, then save a new, blank workbook to the drive and folder where you store your Data Files as **EX 2-Food Co-op Sales Tax Calculations**.

b. Decide on the layout for all columns and rows. The worksheet will contain data for six stores, which you can name by store number, neighborhood, or another method of your choice. For each store, you will calculate total sales tax based on the local sales tax rate. You'll also calculate total tax owed for all six locations.

c. Make up sales data for all six stores.

d. Enter the rate to be used to calculate the sales tax, using your own local rate.

e. Create formulas to calculate the sales tax owed for each location. If you don't know the local tax rate, use **6.5%**.

f. Create a formula to total all the accrued sales tax.

g. Use the ROUND function to eliminate any decimal places in the sales tax figures for each location and in the total due.

h. Add your name to the header, then compare your work to the sample shown in FIGURE 2-26.

i. Save your work, preview the worksheet, and submit your work to your instructor as directed.

j. Close the workbook and exit Excel.

FIGURE 2-26

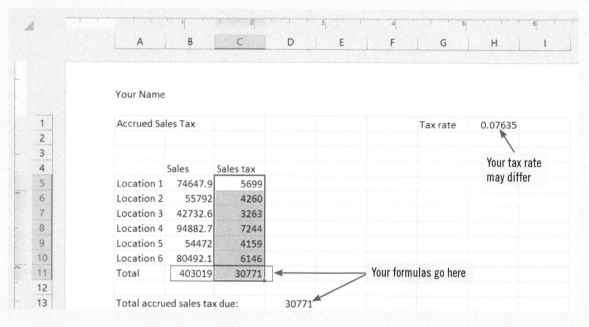

Independent Challenge 4: Explore

So many friends have come to you for help in understanding the various fees associated with purchasing a home that you've decided to create a business that specializes in helping first-time home-buyers. Your first task is to create a worksheet that clearly shows all the information a home buyer will need. Some fees are based on a percentage of the purchase price, and others are a flat fee; overall, they seem to represent a substantial amount above the purchase prices you see listed. A client has seen five houses so far that interest her; one is easily affordable, and the remaining four are all nice, but increasingly more expensive. You decide to create an Excel workbook to help her figure out the real cost of each home.

a. Find out the typical cost or percentage rate of at least three fees that are usually charged when buying a home and taking out a mortgage. (*Hint*: If you have access to the Internet, you can research the topic of home buying on the web, or you can ask friends about standard rates or percentages for items such as title insurance, credit reports, and inspection fees.)

b. Start Excel, then save a new, blank workbook to the location where you store your Data Files as **EX 2-Home Purchase Fees Worksheet**.

c. Create labels and enter data for at least five homes. If you enter this information across the columns in your worksheet, you should have one column for each house, with the purchase price in the cell below each label. Be sure to enter a different purchase price for each house.

d. Create labels for the Fees column and for an Amount or Rate column. Enter the information for each of the fees you have researched.

e. In each house column, enter formulas that calculate the fee for each item. The formulas (and use of absolute or relative referencing) will vary depending on whether the charges are a flat fee or based on a percentage of the purchase price. Make sure that the formulas for items that are based on a percentage of the purchase price (such as the fees for the Title Insurance Policy, Loan Origination, and Underwriter) contain absolute references. A sample of what your workbook might look like is shown in FIGURE 2-27.

f. Total the fees for each house, then create formulas that add the total fees to the purchase price.

g. Enter a title for the worksheet and include your client's name (or use Client 1) in the header.

h. Enter your name in the header, save your work, preview the worksheet, then submit your work to your instructor as directed.

i. Close the file and exit Excel.

FIGURE 2-27

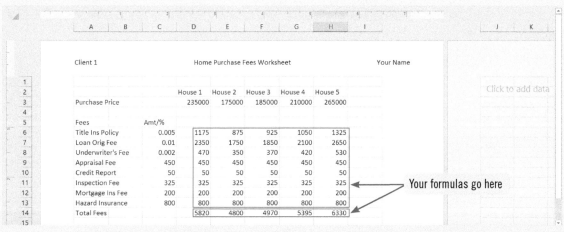

Visual Workshop

Create the worksheet shown in **FIGURE 2-28** using the skills you learned in this module. Save the workbook as **EX 2-Monthly Expenses** to the location where you store your Data Files. Enter your name and worksheet title in the header as shown, hide the gridlines, preview the worksheet, and then submit your work to your instructor as directed. (*Hint:* Change the Zoom factor to 90% by using the Zoom out button.)

FIGURE 2-28

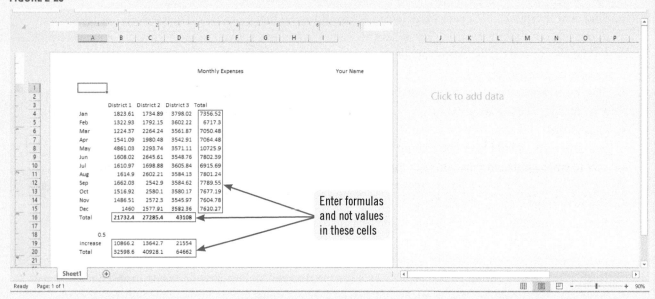

	District 1	District 2	District 3	Total
Jan	1823.61	1734.89	3798.02	7356.52
Feb	1322.93	1792.15	3602.22	6717.3
Mar	1224.37	2264.24	3561.87	7050.48
Apr	1541.09	1980.48	3542.91	7064.48
May	4861.03	2293.74	3571.11	10725.9
Jun	1608.02	2645.61	3548.76	7802.39
Jul	1610.97	1698.88	3605.84	6915.69
Aug	1614.9	2602.21	3584.13	7801.24
Sep	1662.03	2542.9	3584.62	7789.55
Oct	1516.92	2580.1	3580.17	7677.19
Nov	1486.51	2572.3	3545.97	7604.78
Dec	1460	2577.91	3582.36	7620.27
Total	21732.4	27285.4	43108	

Monthly Expenses   Your Name

0.5

increase	10866.2	13642.7	21554
Total	32598.6	40928.1	64662

Enter formulas and not values in these cells

Click to add data

Sheet1

Ready   Page: 1 of 1   90%

Working with Formulas and Functions

Formatting a Worksheet

CASE The marketing managers at Reason2Go have requested data from all R2G locations for advertising expenses incurred during the first quarter of this year. Mary Watson has created a worksheet listing this information. She asks you to format the worksheet to make it easier to read and to call attention to important data.

Module Objectives

After completing this module, you will be able to:

- Format values
- Change font and font size
- Change font styles and alignment
- Adjust column width
- Insert and delete rows and columns

- Apply colors, patterns, and borders
- Apply conditional formatting
- Rename and move a worksheet
- Check spelling

Files You Will Need

EX 3-1.xlsx   EX 3-4.xlsx
EX 3-2.xlsx   EX 3-5.xlsx
EX 3-3.xlsx

Format Values

Learning
Outcomes
• Format a number
• Format a date
• Increase/decrease
  decimals

The **format** of a cell determines how the labels and values look—for example, whether the contents appear boldfaced, italicized, or with dollar signs and commas. Formatting changes only the appearance of a value or label; it does not alter the actual data in any way. To format a cell or range, first you select it, then you apply the formatting using the Ribbon, Mini toolbar, or a keyboard shortcut. You can apply formatting before or after you enter data in a cell or range. **CASE** ▶ *Mary has provided you with a worksheet that details advertising expenses, and you're ready to improve its appearance and readability. You start by formatting some of the values so they are displayed as currency, percentages, and dates.*

STEPS

1. **Start Excel, open the file** EX 3-1.xlsx **from the location where you store your Data Files, then save it as** EX 3-R2G Advertising Expenses

   This worksheet is difficult to interpret because all the information is crowded and looks the same. In some columns, the contents appear cut off because there is too much data to fit given the current column width. You decide not to widen the columns yet, because the other changes you plan to make might affect column width and row height. The first thing you want to do is format the data showing the cost of each ad.

QUICK TIP

You can use a different type of currency, such as Euros or British pounds, by clicking the Accounting Number Format list arrow, then clicking a different currency type.

2. **Select the range** D4:D32, **then click the** Accounting Number Format button $ **in the Number group on the Home tab**

   The default Accounting **number format** adds dollar signs and two decimal places to the data, as shown in FIGURE 3-1. Formatting this data in Accounting format makes it clear that its values are monetary values. Excel automatically resizes the column to display the new formatting. The Accounting and Currency number formats are both used for monetary values, but the Accounting format aligns currency symbols and decimal points of numbers in a column.

QUICK TIP

Select any range of contiguous cells by clicking the upper-left cell of the range, pressing and holding [Shift], then clicking the lower-right cell of the range. Add a column to the selected range by continuing to hold down [Shift] and pressing →; add a row by pressing ↓.

3. **Select the range** F4:H32, **then click the** Comma Style button ⟋ **in the Number group**

   The values in columns F, G, and H display the Comma Style format, which does not include a dollar sign but can be useful for some types of accounting data.

4. **Select the range** J4:J32, **click the** Number Format list arrow, **click** Percentage, **then click the** Increase Decimal button ⬆ **in the Number group**

   The data in the % of Total column is now formatted with a percent sign (%) and three decimal places. The Number Format list arrow lets you choose from popular number formats and shows an example of what the selected cell or cells would look like in each format (when multiple cells are selected, the example is based on the first cell in the range). Each time you click the Increase Decimal button, you add one decimal place; clicking the button twice would add two decimal places.

5. **Click the** Decrease Decimal button ⬇ **in the Number group** twice

   Two decimal places are removed from the percentage values in column J.

6. **Select the range** B4:B31, **then click the** launcher ⟐ **in the Number group**

   The Format Cells dialog box opens with the Date category already selected on the Number tab.

QUICK TIP

Make sure you examine formatted data to confirm that you have applied the appropriate formatting; for example, dates should not have a currency format, and monetary values should not have a date format.

7. **Select the first** 14-Mar-12 format **in the Type list box as shown in** FIGURE 3-2, **then click** OK

   The dates in column B appear in the 14-Mar-12 format. The second 14-Mar-12 format in the list (visible if you scroll down the list) displays all days in two digits (it adds a leading zero if the day is only a single-digit number), while the one you chose displays single-digit days without a leading zero.

8. **Select the range** C4:C31, **right-click the** range, **click** Format Cells **on the shortcut menu, click** 14-Mar **in the Type list box in the Format Cells dialog box, then click** OK

   Compare your worksheet to FIGURE 3-3.

9. **Press** [Ctrl][Home], **then save your work**

FIGURE 3-1: Accounting number format applied to range

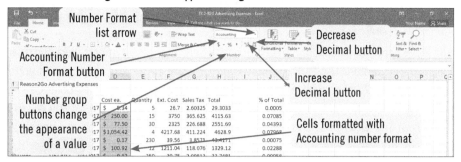

FIGURE 3-2: Format Cells dialog box

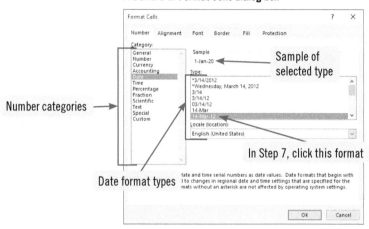

FIGURE 3-3: Worksheet with formatted values

Formatting as a table

Excel includes 60 predefined **table styles** to make it easy to format selected worksheet cells as a table. You can apply table styles to any range of cells that you want to format quickly, or even to an entire worksheet, but they're especially useful for those ranges with labels in the left column and top row, and totals in the bottom row or right column. To apply a table style, select the data to be formatted or click anywhere within the intended range (Excel can automatically detect a range of cells filled with data), click the Format as Table button in the Styles group on the Home tab, then click a style in the gallery, as shown in FIGURE 3-4. Table styles are organized in three categories: Light, Medium, and Dark. Once you click a style, Excel asks you to confirm the range selection, then applies the style. Once you have formatted a range as a table, you can use Live Preview to preview the table in other styles by pointing to any style in the Table Styles gallery.

FIGURE 3-4: Table Styles gallery

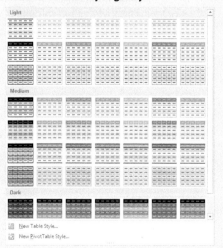

Change Font and Font Size

Learning
Outcomes
• Change a font
• Change a font size
• Use the Mini
  toolbar

A **font** is the name for a collection of characters (letters, numbers, symbols, and punctuation marks) with a similar, specific design. The **font size** is the physical size of the text, measured in units called points. A **point** is equal to 1/72 of an inch. The default font and font size in Excel is 11-point Calibri. TABLE 3-1 shows several fonts in different font sizes. You can change the font and font size of any cell or range using the Font and Font Size list arrows. The Font and Font Size list arrows appear on the Home tab on the Ribbon and on the Mini toolbar, which opens when you right-click a cell or range. **CASE** *You want to change the font and font size of the labels and the worksheet title so that they stand out more from the data.*

STEPS

QUICK TIP
When you point to an option in the Font or Font Size list, Live Preview shows the selected cells with the option temporarily applied.

1. **Click the** Font list arrow **in the Font group on the Home tab, scroll down in the Font list to see an alphabetical listing of the fonts available on your computer, then click** Times New Roman, **as shown in** FIGURE 3-5

   The font in cell A1 changes to Times New Roman. Notice that the font names on the list are displayed in the font they represent.

QUICK TIP
You can format an entire row by clicking the row indicator button to select the row before formatting (or select an entire column by clicking the column indicator button before formatting).

2. **Click the** Font Size list arrow **in the Font group, then click** 20

   The worksheet title appears in 20-point Times New Roman, and the Font and Font Size list boxes on the Home tab display the new font and font size information.

3. **Click the** Increase Font Size button A⁺ **in the Font group twice**

   The font size of the title increases to 24 point.

4. **Select the range** A3:J3, **right-click, then click the** Font list arrow **on the Mini toolbar**

   The Mini toolbar includes the most commonly used formatting tools, so it's great for making quick formatting changes.

QUICK TIP
To quickly move to a font in the Font list, type the first few characters of its name.

5. **Scroll down in the Font list and click** Times New Roman, **click the** Font Size list arrow **on the Mini toolbar, then click** 14

   The Mini toolbar closes when you move the pointer away from the selection. Compare your worksheet to FIGURE 3-6. Notice that some of the column labels are now too wide to appear fully in the column. Excel does not automatically adjust column widths to accommodate cell formatting; you have to adjust column widths manually. You'll learn to do this in a later lesson.

6. **Save your work**

TABLE 3-1: Examples of fonts and font sizes

font	12 point	24 point
Calibri	Excel	Excel
Playbill	Excel	Excel
Comic Sans MS	Excel	Excel
Times New Roman	Excel	Excel

Formatting a Worksheet

FIGURE 3-5: Font list

Font size list arrow

Font list arrow

Click a font to apply it to the selected cell

Active cell displays selected font

	A	B			F	G	H	I	J	K	L	M	N	O	P
1	Reason2Go Adve									Sales Tax	0.0975				
2															
3	Type	Inv. Da			Ext. Cost	Sales Tax	Total			% of Total					
4	USB drive	1-Jai			26.70	2.60	29.30			0.1%					
5	TV Sponsc	7-Jai			3,750.00	365.63	4,115.63			7.1%					
6	Podcasts	20-Jai			5.00	226.69	2,551.69			4.4%					
					7.68	411.22	4,628.90			8.0%					
					9.56	3.86	43.42			0.1%					
					1,211.04	118.08	1,329.12			2.3%					
					30.75	3.00	33.75			0.1%					
11	TV sponsc	15-Jai			3,750.00	365.63	4,115.63			7.1%					
12	Billboard	12-Jai			2,037.40	198.65	2,236.05			3.8%					
13	USB drive	25-Jai			32.04	3.12	35.16			0.1%					
14	USB drive	1-Fel			10.68	1.04	11.72			0.0%					
15	T-Shirts	3-Fel			1,134.00	110.57	1,244.57			2.1%					
16	TV comme	1-Fel			4,217.68	411.22	4,628.90			8.0%					
17	USB drive	1-Mar-17	31-Mar	$ 23.91	2	47.82	4.66	52.48		0.1%					

Font list: STENCIL STD, Sylfaen, Symbol, Tahoma, Tekton Pro, Tekton Pro Cond, Tekton Pro Ext, Tempus Sans ITC, Times New Roman, TRAJAN PRO, Trebuchet MS, Tw Cen MT, Tw Cen MT Condens., Tw Cen MT Condensed Extra Bold, Verdana, Viner Hand ITC, Vivaldi, Vladimir Script, Webdings, Wide Latin, Wingdings

FIGURE 3-6: Worksheet with formatted title and column labels

Font and font size of active cell or range

Title appears in 24-point Times New Roman

Column headings are now 14-point Times New Roman

	A	B	C	D	E	F	G	H	I	J	K	L	M	N	O	P
1	Reason2Go Advertising Expenses										Sales Tax	0.0975				
2																
3	Type	Inv. Date	Inv. Due	Cost ea.	Quantity	Ext. Cost	Sales Ta	Total			% of Total					
4	USB drive	1-Jan-17	31-Jan	$ 5.34	5	26.70	2.60	29.30			0.1%					
5	TV Sponsc	7-Jan-17	6-Feb	$ 250.00	15	3,750.00	365.63	4,115.63								
6	Podcasts	20-Jan-17	19-Feb	$ 77.50	30	2,325.00	226.69	2,551.69								
7	TV comme	1-Jan-17	31-Jan	$1,054.42	4	4,217.68	411.22	4,628.90								
8	Web page	13-Jan-17	12-Feb	$ 0.17	230	39.56	3.86	43.42								
9	Magazine	7-Jan-17	6-Feb	$ 100.92	12	1,211.04	118.08	1,329.12								
10	Pens	5-Jan-17	4-Feb	$ 0.12	250	30.75	3.00	33.75			0.1%					

Inserting and adjusting online pictures and other images

You can illustrate your worksheets using online pictures and other images. Office.com makes many photos and animations available for your use. To add a picture to a worksheet, click the Online Pictures button in the Illustrations group on the Insert tab. The Insert Pictures window opens. Here you can search for online pictures (or Clip Art) from a variety of popular sources such as Facebook and Flickr, through the Bing search engine, or on OneDrive. To search, type one or more **keywords** (words related to your subject) in the appropriate Search text box, then press [Enter]. For example, pictures that relate to the keyword house in a search of Office.com appear in the Office.com window, as shown in **FIGURE 3-7**. When you double-click the image you want in the window, the image is inserted at the location of the active cell. To add images on your computer (or computers on your network) to a worksheet, click the Insert tab on the Ribbon, then click the Pictures button in the Illustrations group. Navigate to

the file you want, then click Insert. To resize an image, drag any corner sizing handle. To move an image, point inside the clip until the pointer changes to ⊹, then drag it to a new location.

FIGURE 3-7: Results of Online Picture search

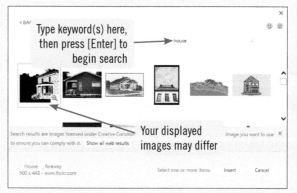

Type keyword(s) here, then press [Enter] to begin search

Your displayed images may differ

Change Font Styles and Alignment

Font styles are formats such as bold, italic, and underlining that you can apply to affect the way text and numbers look in a worksheet. You can also change the **alignment** of labels and values in cells to position them in relation to the cells' edges—such as left-aligned, right-aligned, or centered. You can apply font styles and alignment options using the Home tab, the Format Cells dialog box, or the Mini toolbar. See TABLE 3-2 for a description of common font style and alignment buttons that are available on the Home tab and the Mini toolbar. Once you have formatted a cell the way you want it, you can "paint" or copy the cell's formats into other cells by using the Format Painter button in the Clipboard group on the Home tab. This is similar to using copy and paste, but instead of copying cell contents, it copies only the cell's formatting. **CASE** *You want to further enhance the worksheet's appearance by adding bold and underline formatting and centering some of the labels.*

STEPS

1. **Press [Ctrl][Home], then click the** Bold button **B** **in the Font group on the Home tab**
   The title in cell A1 appears in bold.

2. **Click cell** A3, **then click the** Underline button **U** **in the Font group**
   The column label is now underlined.

3. **Click the** Italic button **I** **in the Font group, then click** **B**
   The heading now appears in boldface, underlined, italic type. Notice that the Bold, Italic, and Underline buttons in the Font group are all selected.

4. **Click the** Italic button **I** **to deselect it**
   The italic font style is removed from cell A3, but the bold and underline font styles remain.

5. **Click the** Format Painter button **in the Clipboard group, then select the range** B3:J3
   The formatting in cell A3 is copied to the rest of the column labels. To paint the formats on more than one selection, double-click the Format Painter button to keep it activated until you turn it off. You can turn off the Format Painter by pressing [Esc] or by clicking. You decide the title would look better if it were centered over the data columns.

6. **Select the range** A1:H1, **then click the** Merge & Center button **in the Alignment group**
   The Merge & Center button creates one cell out of the eight cells across the row, then centers the text in that newly created, merged cell. The title "Reason2Go Advertising Expenses" is centered across the eight columns you selected. To split a merged cell into its original components, select the merged cell, then click the Merge & Center button to deselect it. Occasionally, you may find that you want cell contents to wrap within a cell. You can do this by selecting the cells containing the text you want to wrap, then clicking the Wrap Text button in the Alignment group on the Home tab on the Ribbon.

7. **Select the range** A3:J3, **right-click, then click the** Center button **on the Mini toolbar**
   Compare your screen to FIGURE 3-8. Although they may be difficult to read, notice that all the headings are centered within their cells.

8. **Save your work**

FIGURE 3-8: Worksheet with font styles and alignment applied

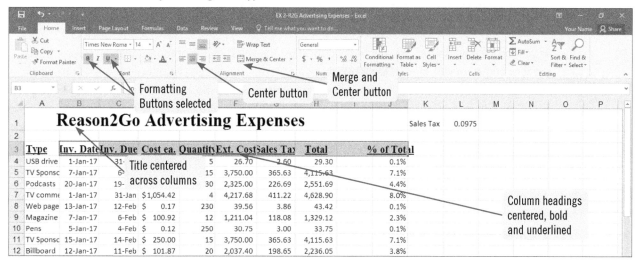

TABLE 3-2: Common font style and alignment buttons

button	description
B	Bolds text
I	Italicizes text
U	Underlines text
🔳	Centers text across columns, and combines two or more selected, adjacent cells into one cell
≡	Aligns text at the left edge of the cell
≡	Centers text horizontally within the cell
≡	Aligns text at the right edge of the cell
🔳	Wraps long text into multiple lines

Rotating and indenting cell entries

In addition to applying fonts and font styles, you can rotate or indent data within a cell to further change its appearance. You can rotate text within a cell by altering its alignment. Click the Home tab, select the cells you want to modify, then click the launcher 🔳 in the Alignment group to open the Alignment tab of the Format Cells dialog box. Click a position in the Orientation box or type a number in the Degrees text box to rotate text from its default horizontal orientation, then click OK. You can indent cell contents using the Increase Indent button 🔳 in the Alignment group, which moves cell contents to the right one space, or the Decrease Indent button 🔳, which moves cell contents to the left one space.

Adjust Column Width

Learning Outcomes
- Change a column width by dragging
- Resize a column with AutoFit
- Change the width of multiple columns

As you format a worksheet, you might need to adjust the width of one or more columns to accommodate changes in the amount of text, the font size, or font style. The default column width is 8.43 characters, a little less than 1". With Excel, you can adjust the width of one or more columns by using the mouse, the Format button in the Cells group on the Home tab, or the shortcut menu. Using the mouse, you can drag or double-click the right edge of a column heading. The Format button and shortcut menu include commands for making more precise width adjustments. TABLE 3-3 describes common column formatting commands. **CASE** *You have noticed that some of the labels in columns A through J don't fit in the cells. You want to adjust the widths of the columns so that the labels appear in their entirety.*

STEPS

1. **Position the mouse pointer on the line between the column A and column B headings until it changes to ↔**

   See FIGURE 3-9. The **column heading** is the box at the top of each column containing a letter. Before you can adjust column width using the mouse, you need to position the pointer on the right edge of the column heading for the column you want to adjust. The cell entry "TV commercials" is the widest in the column.

   QUICK TIP
   If "#######" appears after you adjust a column of values, the column is too narrow to display the values completely; increase the column width until the values appear.

2. **Click and drag the ↔ to the right until the column displays the "TV commercials" cell entries fully (approximately 15.29 characters, 1.23", or 112 pixels)**

   As you change the column width, a ScreenTip is displayed listing the column width. In Normal view, the ScreenTip lists the width in characters and pixels; in Page Layout view, the ScreenTip lists the width in inches and pixels.

3. **Position the pointer on the line between columns B and C until it changes to ↔, then double-click**

   Double-clicking the right edge of a column heading activates the **AutoFit** feature, which automatically resizes the column to accommodate the widest entry in the column. Column B automatically widens to fit the widest entry, which is the column label "Inv. Date".

4. **Use AutoFit to resize columns C, D, and J**

5. **Select the range E5:H5**

   You can change the width of multiple columns at once, by first selecting either the column headings or at least one cell in each column.

   QUICK TIP
   If an entire column rather than a column cell is selected, you can change the width of the column by right-clicking the column heading, then clicking Column Width on the shortcut menu.

6. **Click the Format button in the Cells group, then click Column Width**

   The Column Width dialog box opens. Column width measurement is based on the number of characters that will fit in the column when formatted in the Normal font and font size (in this case, 11-point Calibri).

7. **Drag the dialog box by its title bar if its placement obscures your view of the worksheet, type 11 in the Column width text box, then click OK**

   The widths of columns E, F, G, and H change to reflect the new setting. See FIGURE 3-10.

8. **Save your work**

TABLE 3-3: Common column formatting commands

command	description	available using
Column Width	Sets the width to a specific number of characters	Format button; shortcut menu
AutoFit Column Width	Fits to the widest entry in a column	Format button; mouse
Hide & Unhide	Hides or displays hidden column(s)	Format button; shortcut menu
Default Width	Resets column to worksheet's default column width	Format button

FIGURE 3-9: Preparing to change the column width

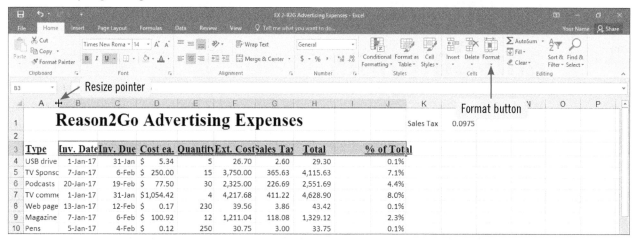

FIGURE 3-10: Worksheet with column widths adjusted

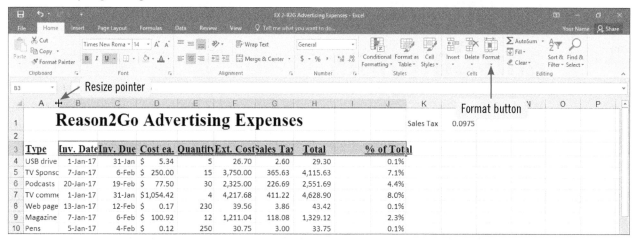

Changing row height

Changing row height is as easy as changing column width. Row height is calculated in points, the same units of measure used for fonts. The row height must exceed the size of the font you are using. Normally, you don't need to adjust row heights manually, because row heights adjust automatically to accommodate font size changes. If you format something in a row to be a larger point size, Excel adjusts the row to fit the largest point size in the row. However, you have just as many options for changing row height as you do column width. Using the mouse, you can place the ✚ pointer on the line dividing a row heading from the heading below, and then drag to the desired height; double-clicking the line AutoFits the row height where necessary. You can also select one or more rows, then use the Row Height command on the shortcut menu, or click the Format button on the Home tab and click the Row Height or AutoFit Row Height command.

Insert and Delete Rows and Columns

Learning Outcomes
• Use the Insert dialog box
• Use column and row heading buttons to insert and delete

As you modify a worksheet, you might find it necessary to insert or delete rows and columns to keep your worksheet current. For example, you might need to insert rows to accommodate new inventory products or remove a column of yearly totals that are no longer necessary. When you insert a new row, the row is inserted above the cell pointer and the contents of the worksheet shift down from the newly inserted row. When you insert a new column, the column is inserted to the left of the cell pointer and the contents of the worksheet shift to the right of the new column. To insert multiple rows, select the same number of row headings as you want to insert before using the Insert command. **CASE** *You want to improve the overall appearance of the worksheet by inserting a row between the last row of data and the totals. Also, you have learned that row 27 and column J need to be deleted from the worksheet.*

STEPS

QUICK TIP

To insert a single row or column, right-click the row heading immediately below where you want the new row, or right-click the column heading to the right of where you want the new column, then click Insert on the shortcut menu.

1. **Right-click cell A32, then click Insert on the shortcut menu**

   The Insert dialog box opens. See FIGURE 3-11. You can choose to insert a column or a row; insert a single cell and shift the cells in the active column to the right; or insert a single cell and shift the cells in the active row down. An additional row between the last row of data and the totals will visually separate the totals.

2. **Click the Entire row option button, then click OK**

   A blank row appears between the Billboard data and the totals, and the formula result in cell E33 has not changed. The Insert Options button 🖉 appears beside cell A33. Pointing to the button displays a list arrow, which you can click and then choose from the following options: Format Same As Above (the default setting, already selected), Format Same As Below, or Clear Formatting.

3. **Click the row 27 heading**

   All of row 27 is selected, as shown in FIGURE 3-12.

QUICK TIP

If you inadvertently click the Delete list arrow instead of the button itself, click Delete Sheet Rows in the menu that opens.

4. **Click the Delete button in the Cells group; *do not click the list arrow***

   Excel deletes row 27, and all rows below it shift up one row. You must use the Delete button or the Delete command on the shortcut menu to delete a row or column; pressing [Delete] on the keyboard removes only the *contents* of a selected row or column.

5. **Click the column J heading**

   The percentage information is calculated elsewhere and is no longer necessary in this worksheet.

QUICK TIP

After inserting or deleting rows or columns in a worksheet, be sure to proof formulas that contain relative cell references.

6. **Click the Delete button in the Cells group**

   Excel deletes column J. The remaining columns to the right shift left one column.

7. **Use AutoFit to resize columns F and H, then save your work**

Hiding and unhiding columns and rows

When you don't want data in a column or row to be visible, but you don't want to delete it, you can hide the column or row. To hide a selected column, click the Format button in the Cells group on the Home tab, point to Hide & Unhide, then click Hide Columns. A hidden column is indicated by a dark green vertical line in its original position. This green line disappears when you click elsewhere in the worksheet. You can display a hidden column by selecting the columns on either side of the hidden column, clicking the Format button in the Cells group, pointing to Hide & Unhide, and then clicking Unhide Columns. (To hide or unhide one or more rows, substitute Hide Rows and Unhide Rows for the Hide Columns and Unhide Columns commands.)

FIGURE 3-11: Insert dialog box

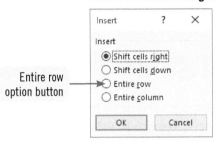

Entire row
option button

FIGURE 3-12: Worksheet with row 27 selected

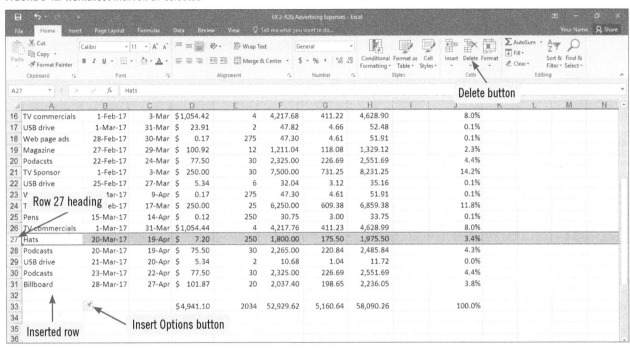

Delete button

Row 27 heading

Insert Options button

Inserted row

Excel 2016

Adding and editing comments

Much of your work in Excel may be in collaboration with teammates with whom you share worksheets. You can share ideas with other worksheet users by adding comments within selected cells. To include a comment in a worksheet, click the cell where you want to place the comment, click the Review tab on the Ribbon, then click the New Comment button in the Comments group. You can type your comments in the resizable text box that opens containing the computer user's name. A small, red triangle appears in the upper-right corner of a cell containing a comment. If comments are not already displayed in a workbook, other users can point to the triangle to display the comment. To see all worksheet comments, as shown in FIGURE 3-13, click the Show All Comments button in the Comments group. To edit a comment, click the cell containing the comment, then click the Edit Comment button in the Comments

group. To delete a comment, click the cell containing the comment, then click the Delete button in the Comments group.

FIGURE 3-13: Comments displayed in a worksheet

21	TV Sponsor	1-Feb-16	2-Mar Food Network
22	Newspaper	25-Feb-16	26-Mar Village Reader
23	Web page ads	10-Mar-16	9-Apr Advertising Concepts
24	TV Sponsor	15-Feb-16	16-Mar Food Network
25	Pens	15-Mar-16	14-Apr Mass Appeal, Inc.
26	TV commercials	1-Mar-16	31-Mar Discovery Channel
27	Podcasts	20-Mar-16	19-Apr iPodAds
28	Newspaper	1-Apr-16	1-May University Voice
29	Podcasts	10-Apr-16	10-May iPodAds
30	Billboard	28-Mar-16	27-Apr Advertising Concepts

Harriet McDonald: I think this will turn out to be a very good decision.

Will Moss: Should we continue with this market, or expand to other types of publications?

Apply Colors, Patterns, and Borders

Learning
Outcomes
• Use Live Preview
  to apply color
  to cells
• Format cells using
  the shortcut menu
• Apply a border
  and pattern to
  a cell

You can use colors, patterns, and borders to enhance the overall appearance of a worksheet and make it easier to read. You can add these enhancements by using the Borders, Font Color, and Fill Color buttons in the Font group on the Home tab of the Ribbon and on the Mini toolbar, or by using the Fill tab and the Border tab in the Format Cells dialog box. You can open the Format Cells dialog box by clicking the dialog box launcher in the Font, Alignment, or Number group on the Home tab, or by right-clicking a selection, then clicking Format Cells on the shortcut menu. You can apply a color to the background of a cell or a range or to cell contents (such as letters and numbers), and you can apply a pattern to a cell or range. You can apply borders to all the cells in a worksheet or only to selected cells to call attention to selected information. To save time, you can also apply **cell styles**, predesigned combinations of formats. **CASE** *You want to add a pattern, a border, and color to the title of the worksheet to give the worksheet a more professional appearance.*

STEPS

1. **Select cell A1, click the** Fill Color list arrow [icon] **in the Font group, then hover the pointer over the** Turquoise, Accent 2 color **(first row, sixth column from the left)**
   See **FIGURE 3-14**. Live Preview shows you how the color will look *before* you apply it. (Remember that cell A1 spans columns A through H because the Merge & Center command was applied.)

2. **Click the** Turquoise, Accent 2 color
   The color is applied to the background (or fill) of this cell. When you change fill or font color, the color on the Fill Color or Font Color button changes to the last color you selected.

3. **Right-click cell A1, then click** Format Cells **on the shortcut menu**
   The Format Cells dialog box opens.

4. **Click the** Fill tab, **click the** Pattern Style list arrow, **click the** 6.25% Gray style **(first row, sixth column from the left), then click** OK

5. **Click the** Borders list arrow [icon] **in the Font group, then click** Thick Bottom Border
   Unlike underlining, which is a text-formatting tool, borders extend to the width of the cell, and can appear at the bottom of the cell, at the top, on either side, or on any combination of the four sides. It can be difficult to see a border when the cell is selected.

6. **Select the range A3:H3, click the** Font Color list arrow [icon] **in the Font group, then click the** Blue, Accent 1 color **(first Theme Colors row, fifth column from the left) on the palette**
   The new color is applied to the labels in the selected range.

7. **Select the range J1:K1, click the** Cell Styles button **in the Styles group, click the** Neutral cell style **(first row, fourth column from the left) in the gallery, then AutoFit** column J
   The font and color change in the range, as shown in **FIGURE 3-15**.

8. **Save your work**

FIGURE 3-14: Live Preview of fill color

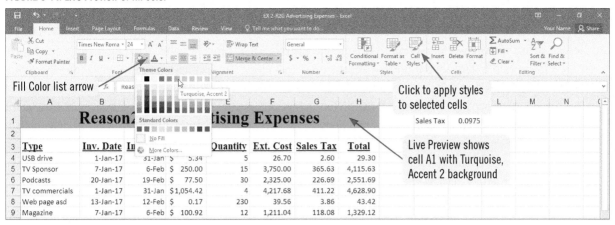

Fill Color list arrow

Click to apply styles to selected cells

Live Preview shows cell A1 with Turquoise, Accent 2 background

FIGURE 3-15: Worksheet with color, patterns, border, and style applied

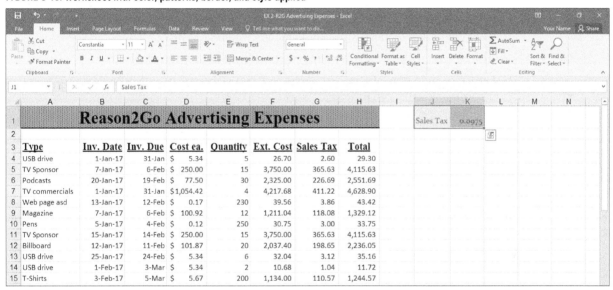

Working with themes and cell styles

Using themes and cell styles makes it easier to ensure that your worksheets are consistent. A **theme** is a predefined set of formats that gives your Excel worksheet a professional look. Formatting choices included in a theme are colors, fonts, and line and fill effects. To apply a theme, click the Themes button in the Themes group on the Page Layout tab to open the Themes gallery, as shown in **FIGURE 3-16**, then click a theme in the gallery. **Cell styles** are automatically updated if you change a theme. For example, if you apply the 20% - Accent1 cell style to cell A1 in a worksheet that has no theme applied, the fill color changes to light blue with no pattern, and the font changes to Calibri. If you change the theme of the worksheet to Ion Boardroom, cell A1's fill color changes to red and the font changes to Century Gothic, because these are the new theme's associated formats.

FIGURE 3-16: Themes gallery

Apply Conditional Formatting

So far, you've used formatting to change the appearance of different types of data, but you can also use formatting to highlight important aspects of the data itself. For example, you can apply formatting that changes the font color to red for any cells where the value is greater than $100 and to green where the value is below $50. This is called **conditional formatting** because Excel automatically applies different formats to data if the data meets conditions you specify. The formatting is updated if you change data in the worksheet. You can also copy conditional formats the same way you copy other formats. **CASE** ▶ *Mary is concerned about advertising costs exceeding the yearly budget. You decide to use conditional formatting to highlight certain trends and patterns in the data so that it's easy to spot the most expensive advertising.*

STEPS

1. **Select the range H4:H30, click the** Conditional Formatting **button in the Styles group on the Home tab, point to** Data Bars, **then point to the** Light Blue Data Bar **(second row, second from left)**

   Data bars are colored horizontal bars that visually illustrate differences between values in a range of cells. Live Preview shows how this formatting will appear in the worksheet, as shown in **FIGURE 3-17**.

2. **Point to the** Green Data Bar **(first row, second from left), then click it**

3. **Select the range F4:F30, click the** Conditional Formatting **button in the Styles group, then point to** Highlight Cells Rules

   The Highlight Cells Rules submenu displays choices for creating different formatting conditions. For example, you can create a rule for values that are greater than or less than a certain amount, or between two amounts.

4. **Click** Between **on the submenu**

   The Between dialog box opens, displaying input boxes you can use to define the condition and a default format (Light Red Fill with Dark Red Text) selected for cells that meet that condition. Depending on the condition you select in the Highlight Cells Rules submenu (such as "Greater Than" or "Less Than"), this dialog box displays different input boxes. You define the condition using the input boxes and then assign the formatting you want to use for cells that meet that condition. Values used in input boxes for a condition can be constants, formulas, cell references, or dates.

5. **Type** 2000 **in the first text box, type** 4000 **in the second text box, click the** with list arrow, **click** Light Red Fill, **compare your settings to** FIGURE 3-18, **then click** OK

   All cells with values between 2000 and 4000 in column F appear with a light red fill.

6. **Click cell** E7, **type** 3, **then press [Enter]**

   When the value in cell E7 changes, the formatting also changes because the new value meets the condition you set. Compare your results to **FIGURE 3-19**.

7. **Press [Ctrl][Home] to select cell A1, then save your work**

FIGURE 3-17: Previewing data bars in a range

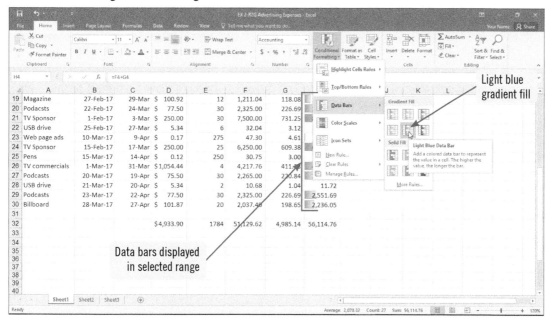

Light blue
gradient fill

Data bars displayed
in selected range

FIGURE 3-18: Between dialog box

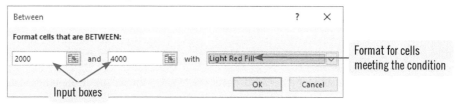

Format for cells
meeting the condition

Input boxes

FIGURE 3-19: Worksheet with conditional formatting

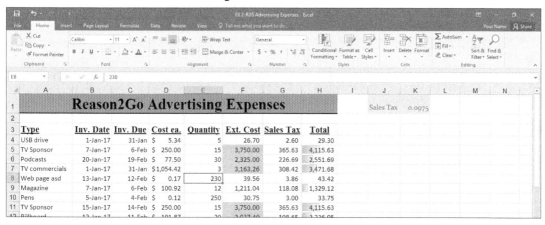

Managing conditional formatting rules

If you create a conditional formatting rule and then want to change a condition, you don't need to create a new rule; instead, you can modify the rule using the Rules Manager. Click the Conditional Formatting button in the Styles group, then click Manage Rules. The Conditional Formatting Rules Manager dialog box opens. Select the rule you want to edit, click Edit Rule, and then modify the settings in the Edit the Rule Description area in the Edit Formatting Rule dialog box. To change the formatting for

a rule, click the Format Style button in the Edit the Rule Description area, select the formatting styles you want the text to have, then click OK three times to close the Format Cells dialog box, the Edit Formatting Rule dialog box, and the Conditional Formatting Rules Manager dialog box. The rule is modified, and the new conditional formatting is applied to the selected cells. To delete a rule, select the rule in the Conditional Formatting Rules Manager dialog box, then click the Delete Rule button.

Rename and Move a Worksheet

By default, an Excel workbook initially contains one worksheet named Sheet1, although you can add sheets at any time. Each sheet name appears on a sheet tab at the bottom of the worksheet. When you open a new workbook, the first worksheet, Sheet1, is the active sheet. To move from sheet to sheet, you can click any sheet tab at the bottom of the worksheet window. The sheet tab scrolling buttons, located to the left of the sheet tabs, are useful when a workbook contains too many sheet tabs to display at once. To make it easier to identify the sheets in a workbook, you can rename each sheet and add color to the tabs. You can also organize them in a logical way. For instance, to better track performance goals, you could name each workbook sheet for an individual salesperson, and you could move the sheets so they appear in alphabetical order. **CASE** *In the current worksheet, Sheet1 contains information about actual advertising expenses. Sheet2 contains an advertising budget, and Sheet3 contains no data. You want to rename the two sheets in the workbook to reflect their contents, add color to a sheet tab to easily distinguish one from the other, and change their order.*

STEPS

1. **Click the Sheet2 tab**

   Sheet2 becomes active, appearing in front of the Sheet1 tab; this is the worksheet that contains the budgeted advertising expenses. See **FIGURE 3-20**.

2. **Click the Sheet1 tab**

   Sheet1, which contains the actual advertising expenses, becomes active again.

3. **Double-click the Sheet2 tab, type Budget, then press [Enter]**

   The new name for Sheet2 automatically replaces the default name on the tab. Worksheet names can have up to 31 characters, including spaces and punctuation.

4. **Right-click the Budget tab, point to Tab Color on the shortcut menu, then click the Bright Green, Accent 4, Lighter 40% color (fourth row, third column from the right) as shown in FIGURE 3-21**

5. **Double-click the Sheet1 tab, type Actual, then press [Enter]**

   Notice that the color of the Budget tab changes depending on whether it is the active tab; when the Actual tab is active, the color of the Budget tab changes to the green tab color you selected. You decide to rearrange the order of the sheets so that the Budget tab is to the left of the Actual tab.

6. **Click the Budget tab, hold down the mouse button, drag it to the left of the Actual tab, as shown in FIGURE 3-22, then release the mouse button**

   As you drag, the pointer changes to ▯, the sheet relocation pointer, and a small, black triangle just above the tabs shows the position the moved sheet will be in when you release the mouse button. The first sheet in the workbook is now the Budget sheet. See **FIGURE 3-23**. You can move multiple sheets by pressing and holding [Shift] while clicking the sheets you want to move, then dragging the sheets to their new location.

7. **Click the Actual sheet tab, click the Page Layout button ▤ on the status bar to open Page Layout view, enter your name in the left header text box, then click anywhere in the worksheet to deselect the header**

8. **Click the Page Layout tab on the Ribbon, click the Orientation button in the Page Setup group, then click Landscape**

9. **Right-click the Sheet3 tab, click Delete on the shortcut menu, press [Ctrl][Home], then save your work**

Formatting a Worksheet

FIGURE 3-20: **Sheet tabs in workbook**

Sheet1 tab   Sheet2 tab

FIGURE 3-21: **Tab Color palette**

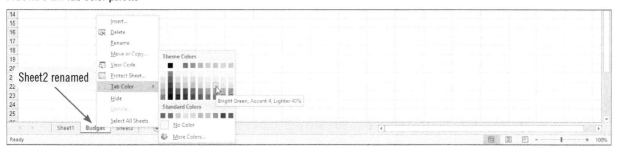

Sheet2 renamed

FIGURE 3-22: **Moving the Budget sheet**

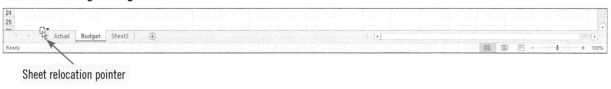

Sheet relocation pointer

FIGURE 3-23: **Reordered sheets**

Budget sheet comes
before Actual sheet

Excel 2016

Copying, adding, and deleting worksheets

There are times when you may want to copy a worksheet. For example, a workbook might contain a sheet with Quarter 1 expenses, and you want to use that sheet as the basis for a sheet containing Quarter 2 expenses. To copy a sheet within the same workbook, press and hold [Ctrl], drag the sheet tab to the desired tab location, release the mouse button, then release [Ctrl]. A duplicate sheet appears with the same name as the copied sheet followed by "(2)" indicating that it is a copy. You can then rename the sheet to a more meaningful name. To copy a sheet to a different workbook, both the source and destination workbooks must be open. Select the sheet to copy or move, right-click the sheet tab, then click Move or Copy in the shortcut menu. Complete the information in the Move or Copy dialog box. Be sure to click the Create a copy check box if you are copying rather than moving the worksheet. Carefully check your calculation results whenever you move or copy a worksheet. You can add multiple worksheets to a workbook by clicking the Home tab on the Ribbon, pressing and holding [Shift], then clicking the number of existing worksheet tabs that correspond with the number of sheets you want to add, clicking the Insert list arrow in the Cells group on the Home tab, then clicking Insert Sheet. You can delete multiple worksheets from a workbook by clicking the Home tab, pressing and holding [Shift], clicking the sheet tabs of the worksheets you want to delete, clicking the Delete list arrow in the Cells group on the Home tab, then clicking Delete Sheet.

Check Spelling

Learning
Outcomes
• Describe how spell
  checking works
• Change the
  spelling using
  a suggestion
• Replace a word
  using Find & Select

Excel includes a spell checker to help you ensure that the words in your worksheet are spelled correctly. The spell checker scans your worksheet, displays words it doesn't find in its built-in dictionary, and suggests replacements when they are available. To check all of the sheets in a multiple-sheet workbook, you need to display each sheet individually and run the spell checker for each one. Because the built-in dictionary cannot possibly include all the words that anyone needs, you can add words to the dictionary, such as your company name, an acronym, or an unusual technical term. Once you add a word or term, the spell checker no longer considers that word misspelled. Any words you've added to the dictionary using Word, Access, or PowerPoint are also available in Excel. **CASE** ▶ *Before you distribute this workbook to Mary, you check the spelling.*

STEPS

QUICK TIP
The Spelling dialog
box lists the name of
the language
currently being used
in its title bar.

1. **Click the Review tab on the Ribbon, then click the Spelling button in the Proofing group**
   The Spelling: English (United States) dialog box opens, as shown in FIGURE 3-24, with "asd" selected as the first misspelled word in the worksheet, and with "ads" selected in the Suggestions list as a possible replacement. For any word, you have the option to Ignore this case of the flagged word, Ignore All cases of the flagged word, Change the word to the selected suggestion, Change All instances of the flagged word to the selected suggestion, or add the flagged word to the dictionary using Add to Dictionary.

2. **Click Change**
   Next, the spell checker finds the word "Podacsts" and suggests "Podcasts" as an alternative.

3. **Verify that the word Podcasts is selected in the Suggestions list, then click Change**
   When no more incorrect words are found, Excel displays a message indicating that the spell check is complete.

4. **Click OK**

5. **Click the Home tab, click Find & Select in the Editing group, then click Replace**
   The Find and Replace dialog box opens. You can use this dialog box to replace a word or phrase. It might be a misspelling of a proper name that the spell checker didn't recognize as misspelled, or it could simply be a term that you want to change throughout the worksheet. Mary has just told you that each instance of "Billboard" in the worksheet should be changed to "Sign."

6. **Type Billboard in the Find what text box, press [Tab], then type Sign in the Replace with text box**
   Compare your dialog box to FIGURE 3-25.

7. **Click Replace All, click OK to close the Microsoft Excel dialog box, then click Close to close the Find and Replace dialog box**
   Excel has made two replacements.

8. **Click the File tab, click Print on the navigation bar, click the No Scaling setting in the Settings section on the Print tab, then click Fit Sheet on One Page**

9. **Click the Return button ⊙ to return to your worksheet, save your work, submit it to your instructor as directed, close the workbook, then exit Excel**
   The completed worksheet is shown in FIGURE 3-26.

Emailing a workbook

You can send an entire workbook from within Excel using your installed email program, such as Microsoft Outlook. To send a workbook as an email message attachment, open the workbook, click the File tab, then click Share on the navigation bar. With the Email option selected in the Share section in Backstage view, click Send as Attachment in the right pane. An email message opens in your default email program with the workbook automatically attached; the filename appears in the Attached field. Complete the To and optional Cc fields, include a message if you wish, then click Send.

FIGURE 3-24: **Spelling: English (United States) dialog box**

Misspelled word →

Suggested replacements for misspelled word

Click to ignore all occurrences of misspelled word

Click to add word to dictionary

FIGURE 3-25: **Find and Replace dialog box**

FIGURE 3-26: **Completed worksheet**

Your Name

Reason2Go Advertising Expenses

Sales Tax   0.0975

Type	Inv. Date	Inv. Due	Cost ea.	Quantity	Ext. Cost	Sales Tax	Total
USB drive	1-Jan-17	31-Jan	$ 5.34	5	26.70	2.60	29.30
TV Sponsor	7-Jan-17	6-Feb	$ 250.00	15	3,750.00	365.63	4,115.63
Podcasts	20-Jan-17	19-Feb	$ 77.50	30	2,325.00	226.69	2,551.69
TV commercials	1-Jan-17	31-Jan	$ 1,054.42	3	3,163.26	308.42	3,471.68
Web page ads	13-Jan-17	12-Feb	$ 0.17	230	39.56	3.86	43.42
Magazine	7-Jan-17	6-Feb	$ 100.92	12	1,211.04	118.08	1,329.12
Pens	5-Jan-17	4-Feb	$ 0.12	250	30.75	3.00	33.75
TV Sponsor	15-Jan-17	14-Feb	$ 250.00	15	3,750.00	365.63	4,115.63
Sign	12-Jan-17	11-Feb	$ 101.87	20	2,037.40	198.65	2,236.05
USB drive	25-Jan-17	24-Feb	$ 5.34	6	32.04	3.12	35.16
USB drive	1-Feb-17	3-Mar	$ 5.34	2	10.68	1.04	11.72
T-Shirts	3-Feb-17	5-Mar	$ 5.67	200	1,134.00	110.57	1,244.57
TV commercials	1-Feb-17	3-Mar	$ 1,054.42	4	4,217.68	411.22	4,628.90
USB drive	1-Mar-17	31-Mar	$ 23.91	2	47.82	4.66	52.48
Web page ads	28-Feb-17	30-Mar	$ 0.17	275	47.30	4.61	51.91
Magazine	27-Feb-17	29-Mar	$ 100.92	12	1,211.04	118.08	1,329.12
Podcasts	22-Feb-17	24-Mar	$ 77.50	30	2,325.00	226.69	2,551.69
TV Sponsor	1-Feb-17	3-Mar	$ 250.00	30	7,500.00	731.25	8,231.25
USB drive	25-Feb-17	27-Mar	$ 5.34	6	32.04	3.12	35.16
Web page ads	10-Mar-17	9-Apr	$ 0.17	275	47.30	4.61	51.91
TV Sponsor	15-Feb-17	17-Mar	$ 250.00	25	6,250.00	609.38	6,859.38
Pens	15-Mar-17	14-Apr	$ 0.12	250	30.75	3.00	33.75
TV commercials	1-Mar-17	31-Mar	$ 1,054.44	4	4,217.76	411.23	4,628.99
Podcasts	20-Mar-17	19-Apr	$ 75.50	30	2,265.00	220.84	2,485.84
USB drive	21-Mar-17	20-Apr	$ 5.34	2	10.68	1.04	11.72
Podcasts	23-Mar-17	22-Apr	$ 77.50	30	2,325.00	226.69	2,551.69
Sign	28-Mar-17	27-Apr	$ 101.87	20	2,037.40	198.65	2,236.05
			$ 4,933.90	1783	50,075.20	4,882.33	54,957.53

Practice

Concepts Review

Label each element of the Excel worksheet window shown in FIGURE 3-27.

FIGURE 3-27

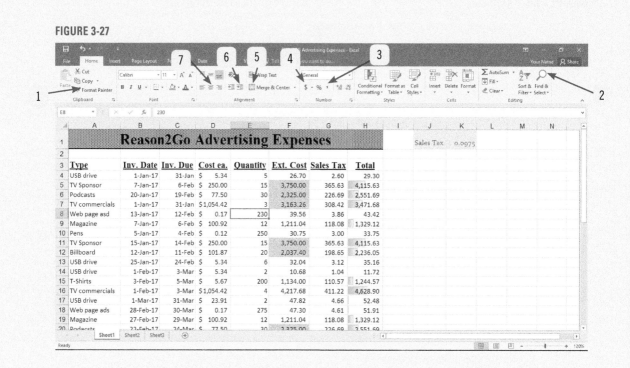

Match each command or button with the statement that best describes it.

8. **Spelling button**
9. $
10. ◇ -
11. **[Ctrl][Home]**
12. ⊞
13. **Conditional formatting**

a. Checks for apparent misspellings in a worksheet
b. Adds dollar signs and two decimal places to selected data
c. Displays fill color options for a cell
d. Moves cell pointer to cell A1
e. Centers cell contents across multiple cells
f. Changes formatting of a cell that meets a certain rule

Select the best answer from the list of choices.

14. Which of the following is an example of Accounting number format?

   a. 5555   **c.** 55.55%

   b. $5,555.55   **d.** 5,555.55

15. What is the name of the feature used to resize a column to accommodate its widest entry?

   a. AutoFormat   **c.** AutoResize

   b. AutoFit   **d.** AutoRefit

16. Which button copies multiple formats from selected cells to other cells?

   a.   **c.**

   b.   **d.**

17. Which button increases the number of decimal places in selected cells?

   a.   **c.**

   b.   **d.**

18. Which button removes the italic font style from selected cells?

   a. *I*   **c.** *I*

   b. B   **d.** U

19. What feature is used to delete a conditional formatting rule?

   a. Rules Reminder   **c.** Condition Manager

   b. Conditional Formatting Rules Manager   **d.** Format Manager

Skills Review

1. Format values.

   a. Start Excel, open the file EX 3-2.xlsx from the location where you store your Data Files, then save it as **EX 3-Health Insurance Premiums**.

   b. Use the Sum function to enter a formula in cell B10 that totals the number of employees.

   c. Create a formula in cell C5 that calculates the monthly insurance premium for the accounting department. (*Hint*: Make sure you use the correct type of cell reference in the formula. To calculate the department's monthly premium, multiply the number of employees by the monthly premium in cell B14.)

   d. Copy the formula in cell C5 to the range C6:C10.

   e. Format the range C5:C10 using Accounting number format.

   f. Change the format of the range C6:C9 to the Comma Style.

   g. Reduce the number of decimals in cell B14 to 0 using a button in the Number group on the Home tab.

   h. Save your work.

2. Change font and font sizes.

   a. Select the range of cells containing the column labels (in row 4).

   b. Change the font of the selection to Times New Roman.

   c. Increase the font size of the selection to 12 points.

   d. Increase the font size of the label in cell A1 to 14 points.

   e. Save your changes.

3. Change font styles and alignment.

   a. Apply the bold and italic font styles to the worksheet title in cell A1.

   b. Use the Merge & Center button to center the Health Insurance Premiums label over columns A–C.

   c. Apply the italic font style to the Health Insurance Premiums label.

   d. Add the bold font style to the labels in row 4.

   e. Use the Format Painter to copy the format in cell A4 to the range A5:A10.

   f. Apply the format in cell C10 to cell B14.

   g. Change the alignment of cell A10 to Align Right using a button in the Alignment group.

Skills Review (continued)

   h. Select the range of cells containing the column labels, then center them.

   i. Remove the italic font style from the Health Insurance Premiums label, then increase the font size to 14.

   j. Move the Health Insurance Premiums label to cell A3, remove the Merge & Center format, then add the bold and underline font styles.

   k. Save your changes.

4. Adjust column width.

   a. Resize column C to a width of 10.71 characters.

   b. Use the AutoFit feature to resize columns A and B.

   c. Clear the contents of cell A13 (do not delete the cell).

   d. Change the text in cell A14 to **Monthly Premium**, then change the width of the column to 25 characters.

   e. Save your changes.

5. Insert and delete rows and columns.

   a. Insert a new row between rows 5 and 6.

   b. Add a new department, **Donations**, in the newly inserted row. Enter **6** as the number of employees in the department.

   c. Copy the formula in cell C7 to C6.

   d. Add the following comment to cell A6: **New department**. Display the comment, then drag to move it out of the way, if necessary.

   e. Add a new column between the Department and Employees columns with the title **Family Coverage**, then resize the column using AutoFit.

   f. Delete the Legal row from the worksheet.

   g. Move the value in cell C14 to cell B14.

   h. Save your changes.

6. Apply colors, patterns, and borders.

   a. Add Outside Borders around the range A4:D10.

   b. Add a Bottom Double Border to cells C9 and D9 (above the calculated employee and premium totals).

   c. Apply the Aqua, Accent 5, Lighter 80% fill color to the labels in the Department column (do not include the Total label).

   d. Apply the Orange, Accent 6, Lighter 60% fill color to the range A4:D4.

   e. Change the color of the font in the range A4:D4 to Red, Accent 2, Darker 25%.

   f. Add a 12.5% Gray pattern style to cell A1.

   g. Format the range A14:B14 with a fill color of Dark Blue, Text 2, Lighter 40%, change the font color to White, Background 1, then apply the bold font style.

   h. Save your changes.

7. Apply conditional formatting.

   a. Select the range D5:D9, then create a conditional format that changes cell contents to green fill with dark green text if the value is between 150 and 275.

   b. Select the range C5:C9, then create a conditional format that changes cell contents to red text if the number of employees exceeds 10.

   c. Apply a purple gradient-filled data bar to the range C5:C9. (*Hint*: Click Purple Data Bar in the Gradient Fill section.)

   d. Use the Rules Manager to modify the conditional format in cells C5:C9 to display values greater than 10 in bold dark red text.

   e. Save your changes.

8. Rename and move a worksheet.

   a. Name the Sheet1 tab **Insurance Data**.

   b. Add a sheet to the workbook, then name the new sheet **Employee Data**.

   c. Change the Insurance Data tab color to Red, Accent 2, Lighter 40%.

Skills Review (continued)

d. Change the Employee Data tab color to Aqua, Accent 5, Lighter 40%.

e. Move the Employee Data sheet so it comes before (to the left of) the Insurance Data sheet.

f. Make the Insurance Data sheet active, enter your name in cell A20, then save your work.

9. **Check spelling.**

   a. Move the cell pointer to cell A1.

   b. Use the Find & Select feature to replace the Accounting label with **Accounting/Legal**.

   c. Check the spelling in the worksheet using the spell checker, and correct any spelling errors if necessary.

   d. Save your changes, then compare your Insurance Data sheet to FIGURE 3-28.

   e. Preview the Insurance Data sheet in Backstage view, submit your work to your instructor as directed, then close the workbook and exit Excel.

FIGURE 3-28

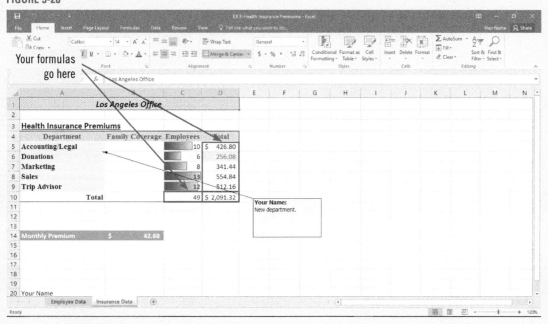

Independent Challenge 1

You run a freelance accounting business, and one of your newest clients is Fresh To You, a small local grocery store. Now that you've converted the store's accounting records to Excel, the manager would like you to work on an analysis of the inventory. Although more items will be added later, the worksheet has enough items for you to begin your modifications.

   a. Start Excel, open the file EX 3-3.xlsx from the location where you store your Data Files, then save it as **EX 3-Fresh To You Inventory**.

   b. Create a formula in cell E4 that calculates the value of the items in stock based on the price paid per item in cell B4. Format the cell in the Comma Style.

   c. In cell F4, calculate the sale value of the items in stock using an absolute reference to the markup value shown in cell H1.

   d. Copy the formulas created above into the range E5:F14; first convert any necessary cell references to absolute so that the formulas work correctly.

   e. Apply bold to the column labels, and italicize the inventory items in column A.

   f. Make sure that all columns are wide enough to display the data and labels.

   g. Format the values in the Sale Value column as Accounting number format with two decimal places.

   h. Format the values in the Price Paid column as Comma Style with two decimal places.

Excel 2016

Independent Challenge 1 (continued)

i. Add a row under Cheddar Cheese for **Whole Wheat flour**, price paid **0.95**, sold by weight (**pound**), with **23** on hand. Copy the appropriate formulas to cells E7:F7.

j. Verify that all the data in the worksheet is visible and formulas are correct. Adjust any items as needed, and check the spelling of the entire worksheet.

k. Use conditional formatting to apply yellow fill with dark yellow text to items with a quantity of less than 25 on hand.

l. Use an icon set of your choosing in the range D4:D14 to illustrate the relative differences between values in the range.

m. Add an outside border around the data in the Item column (*do not* include the Item column label).

n. Delete the row containing the Resource Coffee - decaf entry.

o. Enter your name in an empty cell below the data, then save the file. Compare your worksheet to the sample in FIGURE 3-29.

p. Preview the worksheet in Backstage view, submit your work to your instructor as directed, close the workbook, then exit Excel.

FIGURE 3-29

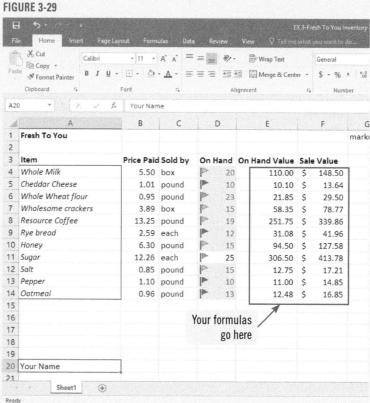

Independent Challenge 2

You volunteer several hours each week with the Assistance League of San Antonio, and you are in charge of maintaining the membership list. You're currently planning a mailing campaign to members in certain regions of the city. You also want to create renewal letters for members whose membership expires soon. You decide to format the list to enhance the appearance of the worksheet and make your upcoming tasks easier to plan.

a. Start Excel, open the file EX 3-4.xlsx from the location where you store your Data Files, then save it as **EX 3-Memphis Assistance League**.

b. Remove any blank columns.

c. Create a conditional format in the Zip Code column so that entries greater than 38249 appear in light red fill with dark red text.

d. Make all columns wide enough to fit their data and labels. (*Hint*: You can use any method to size the columns.)

e. Use formatting enhancements, such as fonts, font sizes, font styles, and fill colors, to make the worksheet more attractive.

Independent Challenge 2 (continued)

f. Center the column labels.

g. Use conditional formatting so that entries for Year of Membership Expiration that are between 2021 and 2023 appear in green fill with bold black text. (*Hint*: Create a custom format for cells that meet the condition.)

h. Adjust any items as necessary, then check the spelling.

i. Change the name of the Sheet1 tab to one that reflects the sheet's contents, then add a tab color of your choice.

j. Enter your name in an empty cell, then save your work.

k. Preview the worksheet, make any final changes you think necessary, then submit your work to your instructor as directed. Compare your work to the sample shown in FIGURE 3-30.

l. Close the workbook, then exit Excel.

FIGURE 3-30

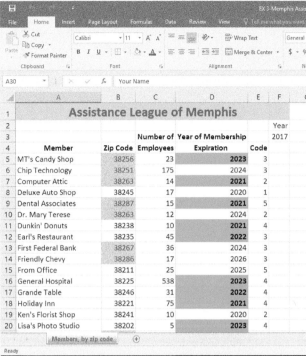

Independent Challenge 3

Advantage Calendars is a Dallas-based printer that prints and assembles calendars. As the finance manager for the company, one of your responsibilities is to analyze the monthly reports from the five district sales offices. Your boss, Joanne Bennington, has just asked you to prepare a quarterly sales report for an upcoming meeting. Because several top executives will be attending this meeting, Joanne reminds you that the report must look professional. In particular, she asks you to highlight the fact that the Northeastern district continues to outpace the other districts.

a. Plan a worksheet that shows the company's sales during the first quarter. Assume that all calendars are the same price. Make sure you include the following:

- The number of calendars sold (units sold) and the associated revenues (total sales) for each of the five district sales offices. The five sales districts are Northeastern, Midwestern, Southeastern, Southern, and Western.
- Calculations that show month-by-month totals for January, February, and March, and a 3-month cumulative total.
- Calculations that show each district's share of sales (percent of Total Sales).
- Labels that reflect the month-by-month data as well as the cumulative data.
- Formatting enhancements such as data bars that emphasize the recent month's sales surge and the Northeastern district's sales leadership.

b. Ask yourself the following questions about the organization and formatting of the worksheet: What worksheet title and labels do you need, and where should they appear? How can you calculate the totals? What formulas can you copy to save time and keystrokes? Do any of these formulas need to use an absolute reference? How do you show dollar amounts? What information should be shown in bold? Do you need to use more than one font? Should you use more than one point size?

c. Start Excel, then save a new, blank workbook as **EX 3-Advantage Calendars** to the location where you store your Data Files.

Independent Challenge 3 (continued)

d. Build the worksheet with your own price and sales data. Enter the titles and labels first, then enter the numbers and formulas. You can use the information in **TABLE 3-4** to get started.

TABLE 3-4

Advantage Calendars											
1st Quarter Sales Report											
		January		February		March		Total			
Office	Price	Units Sold	Sales	Units Sold	Sales	Units Sold	Sales	Units Sold	Sales	Total % of Sales	
Northeastern											
Midwestern											
Southeastern											
Southern											
Western											

e. Add a row beneath the data containing the totals for each column.

f. Adjust the column widths as necessary.

g. Change the height of row 1 to 33 points.

h. Format labels and values to enhance the look of the worksheet, and change the font styles and alignment if necessary.

i. Resize columns and adjust the formatting as necessary.

j. Add data bars for the monthly Units Sold columns.

k. Add a column that calculates a 25% increase in total sales dollars. Use an absolute cell reference in this calculation. (*Hint:* Make sure that the current formatting is applied to the new information.)

l. Delete the contents of cells J4:K4 if necessary, then merge and center cell I4 over column I:K.

m. Add a bottom double border to cells I10:L10.

n. Enter your name in an empty cell.

o. Check the spelling in the workbook, change to a landscape orientation, save your work, then compare your work to **FIGURE 3-31**.

p. Preview the worksheet in Backstage view, then submit your work to your instructor as directed.

q. Close the workbook file, then exit Excel.

FIGURE 3-31

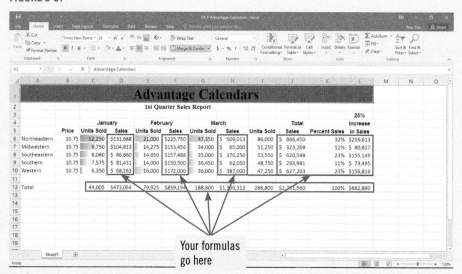

Independent Challenge 4: Explore

This Independent Challenge requires an Internet connection.

Your corporate relocation company helps employees to settle quickly and easily into new cities around the world. Your latest client plans to send employees to seven different countries. All employees will receive the same weekly budget in American currency. You need to create a worksheet to help all the employees understand the currency conversion rates in the different countries so that they can plan their spending effectively.

a. Start Excel, then save a new, blank workbook as **EX 3-Foreign Currency Rates** to the location where you store your Data Files.

b. Add a title at the top of the worksheet.

c. Think of seven countries that each use a different currency, then enter column and row labels for your worksheet. (*Hint*: You may wish to include row labels for each country, plus column labels for the country, the $1 equivalent in native currency, the total amount of native currency employees will have in each country, and the name of each country's monetary unit.)

d. Decide how much money employees will bring to each country (for example, $1,000), and enter that in the worksheet.

e. Use your favorite search engine to find your own information sources on currency conversions for the countries you have listed.

f. Enter the cash equivalent to $1 in U.S. dollars for each country in your list.

g. Create an equation that calculates the amount of native currency employees will have in each country, using an absolute cell reference in the formula.

h. Format the entries in the column containing the native currency $1 equivalent as Number number format with three decimal places, and format the column containing the total native currency budget with two decimal places, using the correct currency number format for each country. (*Hint*: Use the Number tab in the Format cells dialog box; choose the appropriate currency number format from the Symbol list.)

i. Create a conditional format that changes the font style and color of the calculated amount in the $1,000 US column to light red fill with dark red text if the amount exceeds **1000** units of the local currency.

j. Merge and center the worksheet title over the column headings.

k. Add any formatting you want to the column headings, and resize the columns as necessary.

l. Add a background color to the title and change the font color if you choose.

m. Enter your name in the header of the worksheet.

n. Spell check the worksheet, save your changes, compare your work to FIGURE 3-32, then preview the worksheet, and submit your work to your instructor as directed.

o. Close the workbook and exit Excel.

FIGURE 3-32

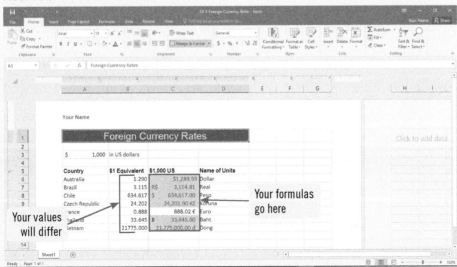

Visual Workshop

Open the file EX 3-5.xlsx from the location where you store your Data Files, then save it as **EX 3-London Employees**. Use the skills you learned in this module to format the worksheet so it looks like the one shown in FIGURE 3-33. Create a conditional format in the Level column so that entries greater than 3 appear in light red fill with dark red text. Create an additional conditional format in the Review Cycle column so that any value equal to 3 appears in black fill with white bold text. Replace the Accounting department label with **Legal**. (*Hint*: The only additional font used in this exercise is 18-point Times New Roman in row 1.) Enter your name in the upper-right part of the header, check the spelling in the worksheet, save your changes, then submit your work to your instructor as directed. (*Hint*: To match the figure exactly, remember to match the zoom level.)

FIGURE 3-33

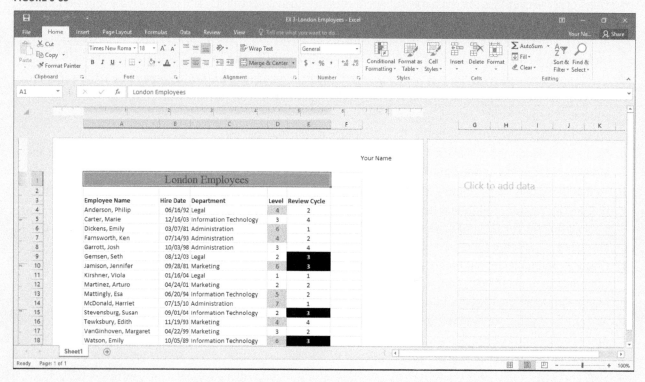

Working with Charts

CASE ▶ At the upcoming annual meeting, Yolanda Lee wants to discuss spending patterns at Reason2Go. She asks you to create a chart showing the trends in company expenses over the past four quarters.

Module Objectives

After completing this module, you will be able to:

- Plan a chart
- Create a chart
- Move and resize a chart
- Change the chart design

- Change the chart format
- Format a chart
- Annotate and draw on a chart
- Create a pie chart

Files You Will Need

EX 4-1.xlsx	EX 4-4.xlsx
EX 4-2.xlsx	EX 4-5.xlsx
EX 4-3.xlsx	EX 4-6.xlsx

Plan a Chart

Learning
Outcomes
• Prepare to create
a chart
• Identify chart
elements
• Explore common
chart types

Before creating a chart, you need to plan the information you want your chart to show and how you want it to look. Planning ahead helps you decide what type of chart to create and how to organize the data. Understanding the parts of a chart makes it easier to format and change specific elements so that the chart best illustrates your data. **CASE** ▶ *In preparation for creating the chart for Yolanda's presentation, you identify your goals for the chart and plan its layout.*

DETAILS

Use the following guidelines to plan the chart:

• **Determine the purpose of the chart, and identify the data relationships you want to communicate graphically**

You want to create a chart that shows quarterly tour expenses for each country where Reason2Go provides tours. This worksheet data is shown in **FIGURE 4-1**. You also want the chart to illustrate whether the quarterly expenses for each country increased or decreased from quarter to quarter.

QUICK TIP
The Quick Analysis tool recommends charts based on the selected data.

• **Determine the results you want to see, and decide which chart type is most appropriate**

Different chart types display data in distinctive ways. For example, a pie chart compares parts to the whole, so it's useful for showing what proportion of a budget amount was spent on tours in one country relative to what was spent on tours in other countries. A line chart, in contrast, is best for showing trends over time. To choose the best chart type for your data, you should first decide how you want your data displayed and interpreted. **TABLE 4-1** describes several different types of charts you can create in Excel and their corresponding buttons on the Insert tab on the Ribbon. Because you want to compare R2G tour expenses in multiple countries over a period of four quarters, you decide to use a column chart.

• **Identify the worksheet data you want the chart to illustrate**

Sometimes you use all the data in a worksheet to create a chart, while at other times you may need to select a range within the sheet. The worksheet from which you are creating your chart contains expense data for each of the past four quarters and the totals for the past year. You will need to use all the quarterly data except the quarterly totals.

• **Understand the elements of a chart**

The chart shown in **FIGURE 4-2** contains basic elements of a chart. In the figure, R2G tour countries are on the horizontal axis (also called the **x-axis**) and expense dollar amounts are on the vertical axis (also called the **y-axis**). The horizontal axis is also called the **category axis** because it often contains the names of data groups, such as locations, months, or years. The vertical axis is also called the **value axis** because it often contains numerical values that help you interpret the size of chart elements. (3-D charts also contain a **z-axis**, for comparing data across both categories and values.) The area inside the horizontal and vertical axes is the **plot area**. The **tick marks**, on the vertical axis, and **gridlines** (extending across the plot area) create a scale of measure for each value. Each value in a cell you select for your chart is a **data point**. In any chart, a **data marker** visually represents each data point, which in this case is a column. A collection of related data points is a **data series**. In this chart, there are four data series (Quarter 1, Quarter 2, Quarter 3, and Quarter 4). Each is made up of column data markers of a different color, so a **legend** is included to make it easy to identify them.

FIGURE 4-1: Worksheet containing expense data

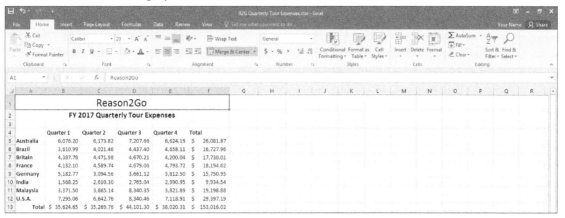

FIGURE 4-2: Chart elements

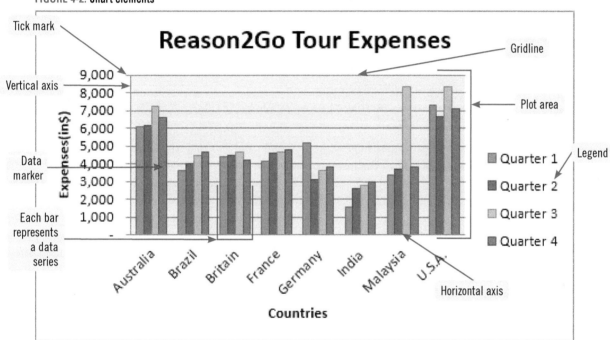

TABLE 4-1: Common chart types

type	button	description
Column		Compares data using columns; the Excel default; sometimes referred to as a bar chart in other spreadsheet programs
Line		Compares trends over even time intervals; looks similar to an area chart, but does not emphasize total
Pie		Compares sizes of pieces as part of a whole; used for a single series of numbers
Bar		Compares data using horizontal bars; sometimes referred to as a horizontal bar chart in other spreadsheet programs
Area		Shows how individual volume changes over time in relation to total volume
Scatter		Compares trends over uneven time or measurement intervals; used in scientific and engineering disciplines for trend spotting and extrapolation
Combo		Displays two or more types of data using different chart types; illustrates mixed or widely varying types of data

Create a Chart

Learning
Outcomes
• Create a chart
• Switch a chart's
  columns/rows
• Add a chart title

To create a chart in Excel, you first select the range in a worksheet containing the data you want to chart. Once you've selected a range, you can use The Quick Analysis tool or the Insert tab on the Ribbon to create a chart based on the data in the range. **CASE** *Using the worksheet containing the quarterly expense data, you create a chart that shows how the expenses in each country varied across the quarters.*

STEPS

QUICK TIP
When charting data
for a particular time
period, make sure
that all series are for
the same time period.

1. **Start Excel, open the file** EX 4-1.xlsx **from the location where you store your Data Files, then save it as** EX 4-R2G Quarterly Tour Expenses

   You want the chart to include the quarterly tour expenses values, as well as quarter and country labels. You don't include the Total column and row because the figures in these cells would skew the chart.

2. **Select the range A4:E12, click the** Quick Analysis tool 📧 **in the lower-right corner of the range, then click** Charts

   The Charts tab on the Quick Analysis tool recommends commonly used chart types based on the range you have selected. The Charts tab also includes a More Charts button for additional chart types, such as stock charts for charting stock market data.

QUICK TIP
To base a chart on
data in nonadjacent
ranges, press and
hold [Ctrl] while
selecting each range,
then use the Insert
tab to create the
chart.

3. **On the** Charts tab, **verify that** Clustered Column **is selected, as shown in** FIGURE 4-3, **then click** Clustered Column

   The chart is inserted in the center of the worksheet, and two contextual Chart Tools tabs appear on the Ribbon: Design and Format. On the Design tab, which is currently active, you can quickly change the chart type, chart layout, and chart style, and you can swap how the columns and rows of data in the worksheet are represented in the chart. When seen in the Normal view, three tools display to the right of the chart: these enable you to add, remove, or change chart elements ➕, set a style and color scheme 🖌, and filter the results shown in a chart 🔽. Currently, the countries are charted along the horizontal x-axis, with the quarterly expense dollar amounts charted along the y-axis. This lets you easily compare the quarterly expenses for each country.

4. **Click the** Switch Row/Column button **in the Data group on the Chart Tools Design tab**

   The quarters are now charted along the x-axis. The expense amounts per country are charted along the y-axis, as indicated by the updated legend. See FIGURE 4-4.

5. **Click the** Undo button ↺ ▾ **on the Quick Access Toolbar**

   The chart returns to its original design.

QUICK TIP
You can also
triple-click to select
the chart title text.

6. **Click the** Chart Title placeholder **to show the text box, click anywhere in the** Chart Title text box, **press [Ctrl][A] to select the text, type** R2G Quarterly Tour Expenses, **then click anywhere in the chart to deselect the title**

   Adding a title helps identify the chart. The border around the chart and the **sizing handles**, the small series of dots at the corners and sides of the chart's border, indicate that the chart is selected. See FIGURE 4-5. Your chart might be in a different location on the worksheet and may look slightly different; you will move and resize it in the next lesson. Any time a chart is selected, as it is now, a blue border surrounds the worksheet data range on which the chart is based, a purple border surrounds the cells containing the category axis labels, and a red border surrounds the cells containing the data series labels. This chart is known as an **embedded chart** because it is inserted directly in the current worksheet and doesn't exist in a separate file. Embedding a chart in the current sheet is the default selection when creating a chart, but you can also embed a chart on a different sheet in the workbook, or on a newly created chart sheet. A **chart sheet** is a sheet in a workbook that contains only a chart that is linked to the workbook data.

7. **Save your work**

FIGURE 4-3: Charts tab in Quick Analysis tool

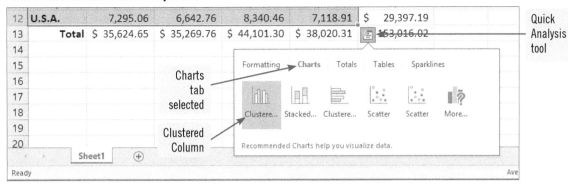

FIGURE 4-4: Clustered Column chart with different configuration of rows and columns

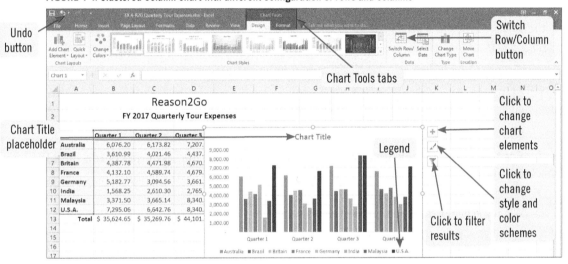

FIGURE 4-5: Chart with original configuration restored and title added

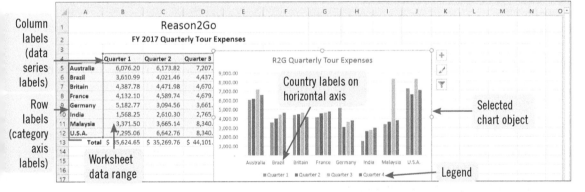

Creating sparklines

You can quickly create a miniature chart called a **sparkline** that serves as a visual indicator of data trends. You can create a sparkline by selecting a range of data, clicking the Quick Analysis tool, clicking the Sparklines tab, then clicking the type of sparkline you want. (The sparkline appears in the cell immediately adjacent to the selected range.) You can also select a range, click the Insert tab, then click the Line, Column, or Win/Loss button in the Sparklines group. In the Create Sparklines dialog box that opens, enter the cell in which you want the sparkline to appear,

then click OK. FIGURE 4-6 shows a sparkline created in a cell. Any changes to data in the range are reflected in the sparkline. To delete a selected sparkline from a cell, click the Clear button in the Group group on the Sparkline Tools Design tab.

FIGURE 4-6: Sparklines in a cell

Move and Resize a Chart

Learning
Outcomes
• Reposition a chart
• Resize a chart
• Modify a legend
• Modify chart data

A chart is an **object**, or an independent element on a worksheet, and is not located in a specific cell or range. You can select an object by clicking it; sizing handles around the object indicate it is selected. (When a chart is selected in Excel, the Name box, which normally tells you the address of the active cell, tells you the chart number.) You can move a selected chart anywhere on a worksheet without affecting formulas or data in the worksheet. Any data changed in the worksheet is automatically updated in the chart. You can even move a chart to a different sheet in the workbook, and it will still reflect the original data. You can resize a chart to improve its appearance by dragging its sizing handles. You can reposition chart objects (such as a title or legend) to predefined locations using commands using the Chart Elements button or the Add Chart Element button on the Chart Tools Design tab, or you can freely move any chart object by dragging it or by cutting and pasting it to a new location. When you point to a chart object, the name of the object appears as a ScreenTip. **CASE** *You want to resize the chart, position it below the worksheet data, and move the legend.*

STEPS

1. **Make sure the chart is still selected, then position the pointer over the chart**

   The pointer shape ⁺ᵏ indicates that you can move the chart. For a table of commonly used object pointers, refer to **TABLE 4-2**.

2. **Position ᵏ on a blank area near the upper-left edge of the chart, press and hold the left mouse button, drag the chart until its upper-left corner is at the upper-left corner of cell A16, then release the mouse button**

   When you release the mouse button, the chart appears in the new location.

3. **Scroll down so you can see the whole chart, position the pointer on the right-middle sizing handle until it changes to ⟷, then drag the right border of the chart to the right edge of column G**

   The chart is widened. See **FIGURE 4-7**.

4. **Position the pointer over the upper-middle sizing handle until it changes to ↕, then drag the top border of the chart to the top edge of row 15**

5. **Position the pointer over the lower-middle sizing handle until it changes to ↕, then drag the bottom border of the chart to the bottom border of row 26**

   You can move any object on a chart. You want to align the top of the legend with the top of the plot area.

6. **Click the Quick Layout button in the Chart Layouts group of the Chart Tools Design tab, click Layout 1 (in the upper-left corner of the palette), click the legend to select it, press and hold [Shift], drag the legend up using ᵏ so the dotted outline is approximately ¼" above the top of the plot area, then release [Shift]**

   When you click the legend, sizing handles appear around it and "Legend" appears as a ScreenTip when the pointer hovers over the object. As you drag, a dotted outline of the legend border appears. Pressing and holding the [Shift] key holds the horizontal position of the legend as you move it vertically. Although the sizing handles on objects within a chart look different from the sizing handles that surround a chart, they function the same way.

7. **Click cell A12, type United States, click the Enter button ✓ on the formula bar, use AutoFit to resize column A, then save your work**

   The axis label changes to reflect the updated cell contents, as shown in **FIGURE 4-8**. Changing any data in the worksheet modifies corresponding text or values in the chart. Because the chart is no longer selected, the Chart Tools tabs no longer appear on the Ribbon.

FIGURE 4-7: **Moved and resized chart**

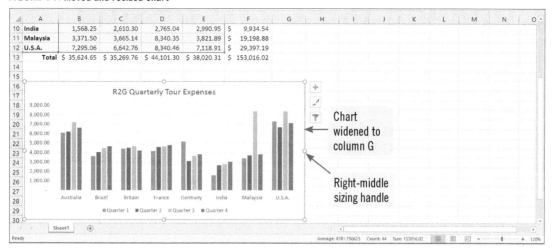

FIGURE 4-8: **Worksheet with modified legend and label**

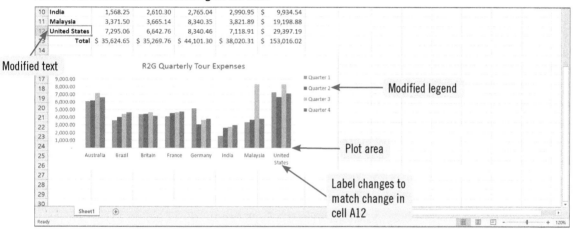

TABLE 4-2: **Common object pointers**

name	pointer	use	name	pointer	use
Diagonal resizing	⤢ or ⤡	Change chart shape from corners	I-beam	I	Edit object text
Draw	+	Draw an object	Move	⇱	Move object
Horizontal resizing	⟷	Change object width	Vertical resizing	⇕	Change object height

Moving an embedded chart to a sheet

Suppose you have created an embedded chart that you decide would look better on a chart sheet or in a different worksheet. You can make this change without recreating the entire chart. To do so, first select the chart, click the Chart Tools Design tab, then click the Move Chart button in the Location group. The Move Chart dialog box opens. To move the chart to its own chart sheet, click the New sheet option button, type a name for the new sheet if desired, then click OK. If the chart is already on its own sheet or you want to move it to a different existing sheet, click the Object in option button, click the desired worksheet, then click OK.

Change the Chart Design

Learning
Outcomes
• Change the chart
  design
• Change the chart
  type
• Apply a chart style

Once you've created a chart, you can change the chart type, modify the data range and column/row configuration, apply a different chart style, and change the layout of objects in the chart. The layouts in the Chart Layouts group on the Chart Tools Design tab offer arrangements of objects in your chart, such as its legend, title, or gridlines; choosing one of these layouts is an alternative to manually changing how objects are arranged in a chart. **CASE** *You discovered that the data for Malaysia and the United States in Quarter 3 is incorrect. After the correction, you want to see how the data looks using different chart layouts and types.*

STEPS

1. **Click cell D11, type** 5568.92, **press [Enter], type** 7107.09, **then press [Enter]**

   In the chart, the Quarter 3 data markers for Malaysia and the United States reflect the adjusted expense figures. See **FIGURE 4-9**.

2. **Select the** chart **by clicking a blank area within the chart border, click the** Chart Tools Design tab **on the Ribbon, click the** Quick Layout button **in the Chart Layouts group, then click** Layout 3

   The legend moves to the bottom of the chart. You prefer the original layout.

3. **Click the** Undo button 🔄 **on the Quick Access Toolbar, then click the** Change Chart Type button **in the Type group**

   The Change Chart Type dialog box opens, as shown in **FIGURE 4-10**. The left pane of the dialog box lists the available categories, and the right pane shows the individual chart types. A pale gray border surrounds the currently selected chart type.

4. **Click** Bar **in the left pane of the Change Chart Type dialog box, confirm that the first Clustered Bar chart type is selected in the right pane, then click** OK

   The column chart changes to a clustered bar chart. See **FIGURE 4-11**. You decide to see how the data looks in a three-dimensional column chart.

5. **Click the** Change Chart Type button **in the Type group, click** Column **in the left pane of the Change Chart Type dialog box, click** 3-D Clustered Column **(fourth from the left in the top row) in the right pane, verify that the left-most 3-D chart is selected, then click** OK

   A three-dimensional column chart appears. You notice that the three-dimensional column format gives you a sense of volume, but it is more crowded than the two-dimensional column format.

6. **Click the** Change Chart Type button **in the Type group, click** Clustered Column **(first from the left in the top row) in the right pane of the Change Chart Type dialog box, then click** OK

7. **Click the** Style 3 chart style **in the Chart Styles group**

   The columns change to lighter shades of color. You prefer the previous chart style's color scheme.

8. **Click** 🔄 **on the Quick Access Toolbar, then save your work**

Creating a combo chart

A **combo chart** presents two or more charts in one; a column chart with a line chart, for example. This type of chart is helpful when charting dissimilar but related data. For example, you can create a combo chart based on home price and home size data, showing home prices in a column chart and related home sizes in a line chart. Here a **secondary axis** (such as a vertical axis on the right side of the chart) would supply the scale for the home sizes.

To create a combo chart, select all the data you want to plot, click the Combo chart button 📊 in the Charts group in the Insert tab, click a suggested type or Create Custom Combo Chart, supply additional series information if necessary, then click OK. To change an existing chart to a combo chart, select the chart, click Change Chart Type in the Type group on the Chart Tools Design tab, then follow the same procedure.

FIGURE 4-9: Worksheet with modified data

FIGURE 4-9: Worksheet with modified data

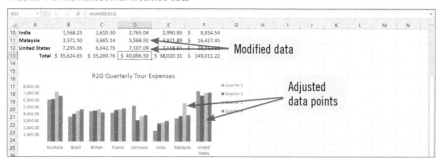

FIGURE 4-10: Change Chart Type dialog box

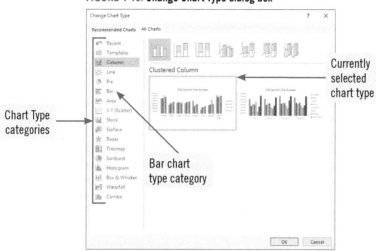

FIGURE 4-11: Column chart changed to bar chart

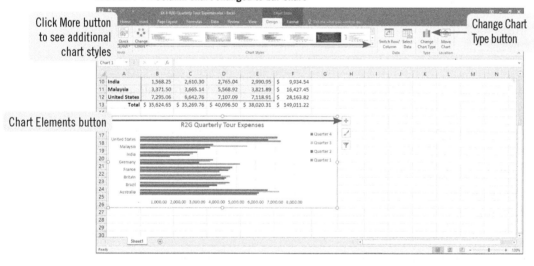

Working with a 3-D chart

Excel includes two kinds of 3-D chart types. In a true 3-D chart, a third axis, called the **z-axis**, lets you compare data points across both categories and values. The z-axis runs along the depth of the chart, so it appears to advance from the back of the chart. To create a true 3-D chart, look for chart types that begin with "3-D," such as 3-D Column. In a 3-D chart, data series can sometimes obscure other columns or bars in the same chart, but you can rotate the chart to obtain a better view. Right-click the chart, then click 3-D Rotation. The Format Chart Area pane opens with the 3-D Rotation category active. The 3-D Rotation options let you change the orientation and perspective of the chart area, plot area, walls, and floor. The 3-D Format category lets you apply three-dimensional effects to selected chart objects. (Not all 3-D Rotation and 3-D Format options are available on all charts.)

Excel 2016

Change the Chart Format

Learning
Outcomes
• Change the
  gridlines display
• Add axis titles
• Change the
  border color
• Add a shadow
  to an object

While the Chart Tools Design tab contains preconfigured chart layouts you can apply to a chart, the Chart Elements button makes it easy to add, remove, and modify individual chart objects such as a chart title or legend. Using options on this shortcut menu (or using the Add Chart Element button on the Chart Tools Design tab), you can also add text to a chart, add and modify labels, change the display of axes, modify the fill behind the plot area, create titles for the horizontal and vertical axes, and eliminate or change the look of gridlines. You can format the text in a chart object using the Home tab or the Mini toolbar, just as you would the text in a worksheet. **CASE** *You want to change the layout of the chart by creating titles for the horizontal and vertical axes. To improve the chart's appearance, you'll add a drop shadow to the chart title.*

STEPS

1. **With the chart still selected, click the** Add Chart Element button **in the Chart Layouts group on the Chart Tools Design tab, point to** Gridlines, **then click** Primary Major Horizontal **to deselect it**

   The gridlines that extend from the value axis tick marks across the chart's plot area are removed as shown in FIGURE 4-12.

2. **Click the** Chart Elements button ⊞ **in the upper-right corner** *outside* **the chart border, click the** Gridlines arrow, **click** Primary Major Horizontal, **click** Primary Minor Horizontal, **then click** ⊞ **to close the Chart Elements fly-out menu**

   Both major and minor gridlines now appear in the chart. **Major gridlines** represent the values at the value axis tick marks, and **minor gridlines** represent the values between the tick marks.

3. **Click** ⊞, **click the** Axis Titles checkbox **to select all the axis titles options, triple-click the** vertical axis title **on the chart, then type** Expenses (in $)

   Descriptive text on the category axis helps readers understand the chart.

4. **Triple-click the** horizontal axis title **on the chart, then type** Tour Countries

   The text "Tour Countries" appears on the horizontal axis, as shown in FIGURE 4-13.

5. **Right-click the** horizontal axis labels ("Australia", "Brazil", etc.), **click** Font **on the shortcut menu, click the** Latin text font list arrow **in the Font dialog box, click** Times New Roman, **click the** Size down arrow **until** 8 **is displayed, then click** OK

   The font of the horizontal axis labels changes to Times New Roman, and the font size decreases, making more of the plot area visible.

6. **Right-click the** vertical axis labels, **then click** Reset to Match

7. **Right-click the** Chart Title ("R2G Quarterly Tour Expenses"), **click** Format Chart Title **on the shortcut menu, click the** Border arrow ▶ **in the Format Chart Title pane to display the options if necessary, then click the** Solid line option button **in the pane**

   A solid border appears around the chart title with the default blue color.

8. **Click the** Effects button ⬜ **in the Format Chart Title pane, click** Shadow, **click the** Presets list arrow, **click** Offset Diagonal Bottom Right **in the Outer group (first row, first from the left), click the** Format Chart Title pane Close button ✕, **then save your work**

   A blue border with a drop shadow surrounds the title. Compare your work to FIGURE 4-14.

FIGURE 4-12: Gridlines removed from chart

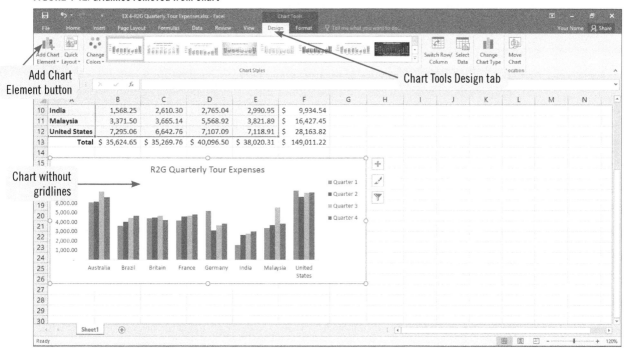

FIGURE 4-13: Axis titles added to chart

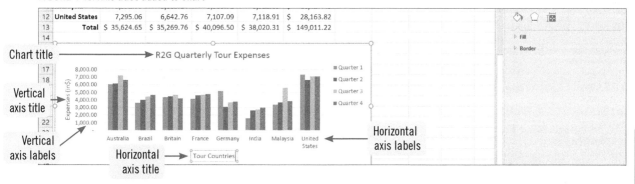

FIGURE 4-14: Enhanced chart

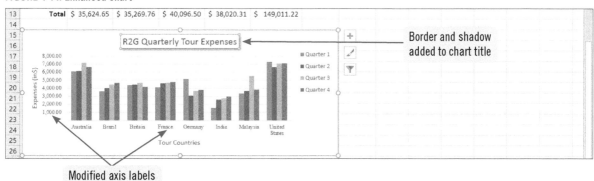

Adding data labels to a chart

There are times when your audience might benefit by seeing data labels on a chart. These labels appear next to the data markers in the chart and can indicate the series name, category name, and/or the value of one or more data points. Once your chart is selected, you can add this information to your chart by clicking the Chart Elements button in the upper-right corner outside the selected chart, clicking the Data Labels arrow, and then clicking a display option for the data labels. Once you have added the data labels, you can format them or delete individual data labels. To delete a data label, select it and then press [Delete].

Format a Chart

Learning
Outcomes
- Change the fill of
  a data series
- Use Live Preview
  to see a new data
  series color
- Apply a style to a
  data series

Formatting a chart can make it easier to read and understand. Many formatting enhancements can be made using the Chart Tools Format tab. You can change the fill color for a specific data series, or you can apply a shape style to a title or a data series using the Shape Styles group. Shape styles make it possible to apply multiple formats, such as an outline, fill color, and text color, all with a single click. You can also apply different fill colors, outlines, and effects to chart objects using arrows and buttons in the Shape Styles group. **CASE** *You want to use a different color for one data series in the chart and apply a shape style to another, to enhance the look of the chart.*

STEPS

1. **With the chart selected, click the** Chart Tools Format tab **on the Ribbon, then click any column in the** Quarter 4 data series

   Handles appear on each column in the Quarter 4 data series, indicating that the entire series is selected.

2. **Click the** Shape Fill list arrow **in the Shape Styles group on the Chart Tools Format tab**

3. **Click** Orange, Accent 6 **(first row, 10th from the left) as shown in** FIGURE 4-15

   All the columns for the series become orange, and the legend changes to match the new color. You can also change the color of selected objects by applying a shape style.

4. **Click any** column **in the** Quarter 3 data series

   Handles appear on each column in the Quarter 3 data series.

5. **Click the** More button ⌄ **on the Shape Styles gallery, then** *hover the pointer* **over the** Moderate Effect – Olive Green, Accent 3 shape style **(fifth row, fourth from the left) in the gallery, as shown in** FIGURE 4-16

   Live Preview shows the data series in the chart with the shape style applied.

6. **Click the** Subtle Effect – Olive Green, Accent 3 shape style

   The style for the data series changes, as shown in FIGURE 4-17.

7. **Save your work**

Previewing a chart

To print or preview just a chart, select the chart (or make the chart sheet active), click the File tab, then click Print on the navigation bar. To reposition a chart by changing the page's margins, click the Show Margins button ▦ in the lower-right corner of the Print tab to display the margins in the preview. You can drag the margin lines to the exact settings you want; as the margins change, the size and placement of the chart on the page change too.

FIGURE 4-15: New shape fill applied to data series

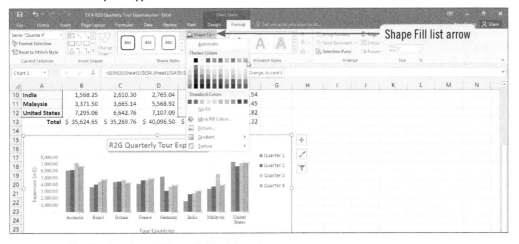

FIGURE 4-16: Live Preview of new style applied to data series

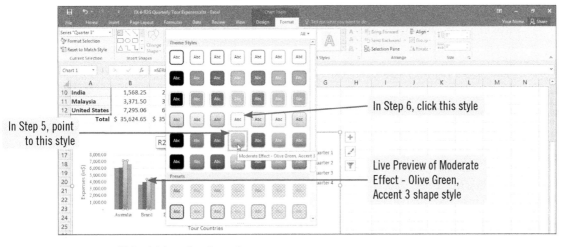

FIGURE 4-17: Style of data series changed

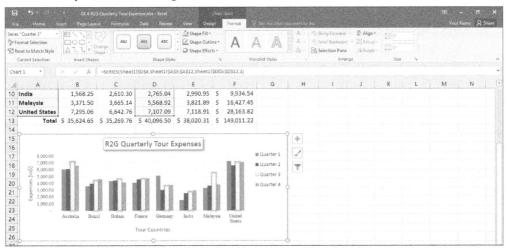

Changing alignment and angle in axis labels and titles

The buttons on the Chart Tools Design tab provide a few options for positioning axis labels and titles, but you can customize their position and rotation to exact specifications using the Format Axis pane or Format Axis Title pane. With a chart selected, right-click the axis text you want to modify, then click Format Axis or Format Axis Title on the shortcut menu. In the pane that opens, click the Size & Properties button, then select the appropriate option. You can also create a custom angle by clicking the Custom angle up and down arrows. When you have made the desired changes, close the pane.

Annotate and Draw on a Chart

Learning
Outcomes
• Type text in a text
  box
• Draw an arrow on
  a chart
• Modify a drawn
  object

You can use text annotations and graphics to point out critical information in a chart. **Text annotations** are labels that further describe your data. You can also draw lines and arrows that point to the exact locations you want to emphasize. Shapes such as arrows and boxes can be added from the Illustrations group on the Insert tab or from the Insert Shapes group on the Chart Tools Format tab on the Ribbon. The Insert group is also used to insert pictures into worksheets and charts. **CASE** *You want to call attention to the Germany tour expense decrease, so you decide to add a text annotation and an arrow to this information in the chart.*

STEPS

1. **With the chart selected and the Chart Tools Format tab active, click the Text Box button 🖾 in the Insert Shapes group, then move the pointer over the worksheet**
   The pointer changes to ↓, indicating that you will insert a text box where you next click.

2. **Click to the right of the chart (anywhere *outside* the chart boundary)**
   A text box is added to the worksheet, and the Drawing Tools Format tab appears on the Ribbon so that you can format the new object. First you need to type the text.

3. **Type Great Improvement**
   The text appears in a selected text box on the worksheet, and the chart is no longer selected, as shown in FIGURE 4-18. Your text box may be in a different location; this is not important because you'll move the annotation in the next step.

4. **Point to an edge of the text box so that the pointer changes to ✥, drag the text box into the chart to the left of the chart title, as shown in FIGURE 4-19, then release the mouse button**
   The text box is a text annotation for the chart. You also want to add a simple arrow shape in the chart.

5. **Click the chart to select it, click the Chart Tools Format tab, click the Arrow button ╲ in the Insert Shapes group, then move the pointer over the text box on the chart**
   The pointer changes to ✚, and the status bar displays "Click and drag to insert an AutoShape." When ✚ is over the text box, black handles appear around the text in the text box. A black handle can act as an anchor for the arrow.

6. **Position ✚ on the black handle to the right of the "t" in the word "improvement" (in the text box), press and hold the left mouse button, drag the line to the Quarter 2 column for the Germany category in the chart, then release the mouse button**
   An arrow points to the Quarter 2 expense for Germany, and the Drawing Tools Format tab displays options for working with the new arrow object. You can resize, format, or delete it just like any other object in a chart.

7. **Click the Shape Outline list arrow in the Shape Styles group, click the Automatic color, click the Shape Outline list arrow again, point to Weight, then click 1½ pt**
   Compare your finished chart to FIGURE 4-20.

8. **Save your work**

FIGURE 4-18: **Text box added**

Drawing
Tools
Format tab

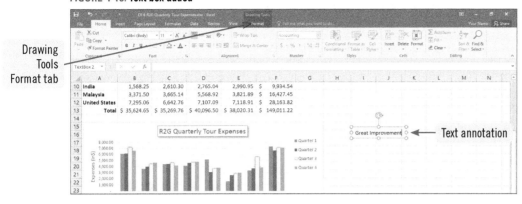

FIGURE 4-19: **Text annotation on the chart**

Text annotation

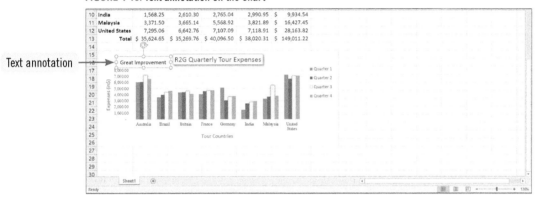

FIGURE 4-20: **Arrow shape added to chart**

Arrow drawn
and formatted

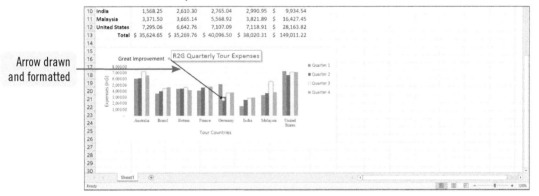

Adding SmartArt graphics

In addition to charts, annotations, and drawn objects, you can create a variety of diagrams using SmartArt graphics. **SmartArt graphics** are available in List, Process, Cycle, Hierarchy, Relationship, Matrix, Pyramid, Picture, and Office.com categories. To insert SmartArt, click the Insert a SmartArt Graphic button in the Illustrations group on the Insert tab to open the Choose a SmartArt Graphic dialog box. Click a SmartArt category in the left pane, then click a layout for the graphic in the right pane. The right pane shows sample layouts for the selected SmartArt, as shown in FIGURE 4-21. The SmartArt graphic appears in the worksheet as an embedded object with sizing handles. Depending on the type of SmartArt graphic you selected, a text pane opens next to the graphic; you can enter text into the graphic using the text pane or by typing directly in the shapes in the diagram.

FIGURE 4-21: **Choose a SmartArt Graphic dialog box**

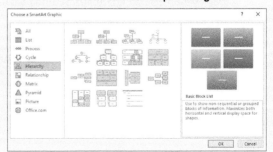

Create a Pie Chart

Learning
Outcomes
• Create a pie chart
• Explode a pie
  chart slice

You can create multiple charts based on the same worksheet data. While a column chart may illustrate certain important aspects of your worksheet data, you may find that you want to create an additional chart to emphasize a different point. Depending on the type of chart you create, you have additional options for calling attention to trends and patterns. For example, if you create a pie chart, you can emphasize one data point by **exploding**, or pulling that slice away from, the pie chart. When you're ready to print a chart, you can preview it just as you do a worksheet to check the output before committing it to paper. You can print a chart by itself or as part of the worksheet. **CASE** *At an upcoming meeting, Yolanda plans to discuss the total tour expenses and which countries need improvement. You want to create a pie chart she can use to illustrate total expenses. Finally, you want to fit the worksheet and the charts onto one worksheet page.*

STEPS

1. **Select the range** A5:A12, **press and hold** [Ctrl], **select the range** F5:F12, **click the** Insert tab, **click the** Insert Pie or Doughnut Chart button **in the Charts group, then click** 3-D Pie **in the chart gallery**

   The new chart appears in the center of the worksheet. You can move the chart and quickly format it using a chart layout.

2. **Drag the** chart **so its upper-left corner is at the upper-left corner of cell** G1, **click the** Quick Layout button **in the Chart Layouts group of the Chart Tools Design tab, then click** Layout 2

   The chart is repositioned on the page, and its layout changes so that a chart title is added, the percentages display on each slice, and the legend appears just below the chart title.

3. **Select the** Chart Title text, **then type** R2G Total Expenses, by Country

4. **Click the slice for the** India data point, **click it again so it is the only slice selected, right-click it, then click** Format Data Point

   The Format Data Point pane opens, as shown in **FIGURE 4-22**. You can use the Point Explosion slider to control the distance a pie slice moves away from the pie, or you can type a value in the Point Explosion text box.

5. **Double-click** 0 **in the** Point Explosion text box, **type** 40, **then click the** Close button ✕

   Compare your chart to **FIGURE 4-23**. You decide to preview the chart and data before you print.

6. **Click cell** A1, **switch to** Page Layout view, **type your name in the left header text box, then click cell** A1

   You decide the chart and data would fit better on the page if they were printed in landscape orientation.

7. **Click the** Page Layout tab, **click the** Orientation button **in the Page Setup group, then click** Landscape

8. **Click the** File tab, **click** Print **on the navigation bar, verify that the correct printer is selected, click the** No Scaling setting **in the Settings section on the Print tab, then click** Fit Sheet on One Page

   The data and chart are positioned horizontally on a single page, as shown in **FIGURE 4-24**. The printer you have selected may affect the appearance of your preview screen.

9. **Save and close the workbook, submit your work to your instructor as directed, then exit Excel**

FIGURE 4-22: Format Data Point pane

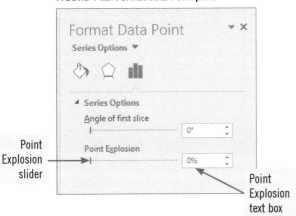

Point Explosion slider

Point Explosion text box

FIGURE 4-23: Exploded pie slice

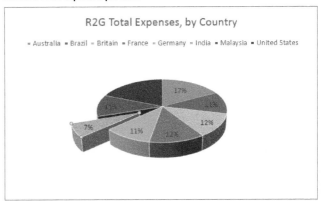

FIGURE 4-24: Preview of worksheet with charts in Backstage view

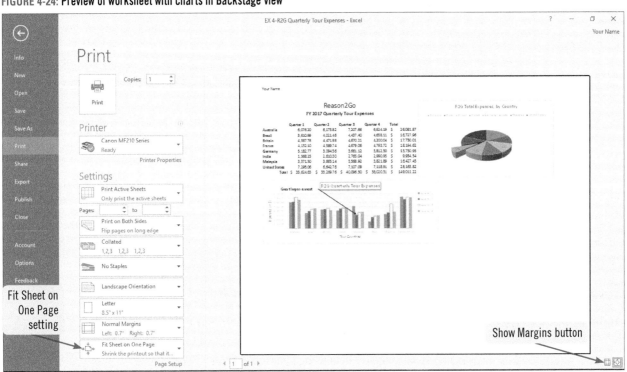

Fit Sheet on One Page setting

Show Margins button

Using the Insert Chart dialog box to discover new chart types

Excel 2016 includes five new chart types. You can explore these charts by clicking the Insert tab on the Ribbon, clicking Recommended Charts, then clicking the All Charts tab in the Insert Chart dialog box. Near the bottom of the list in the left panel are the new chart types: Treemap (which has nine variations), Sunburst, Histogram, Box & Whisker, and Waterfall. If cells are selected prior to opening the Insert Chart dialog box, you will see a sample of the chart type when you click each chart type; the sample will be magnified when you hover the mouse over the sample. The Treemap and Sunburst charts both offer visual comparisons of relative sizes. The Histogram looks like a column chart, but each column (or bin) represents a range of values. The Box & Whisker chart shows distribution details as well as the mean, quartiles, and outliers. The Waterfall chart shows results above and below an imaginary line.

Excel 2016

Practice

Concepts Review

Label each element of the Excel chart shown in FIGURE 4-25.

FIGURE 4-25

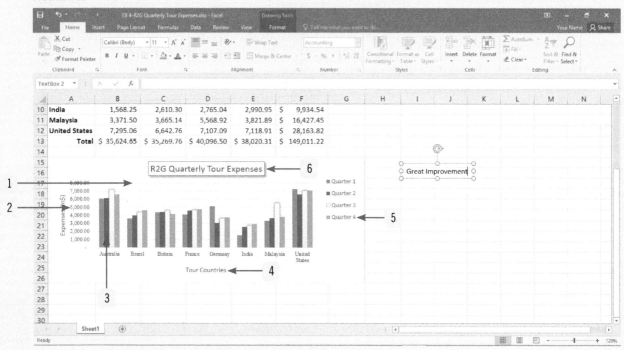

Match each chart type with the statement that best describes it.

7. Combo
8. Pie
9. Area
10. Column
11. Line

a. Displays different chart types within one chart
b. Compares trends over even time intervals
c. Compares data using columns
d. Compares data as parts of a whole
e. Shows how volume changes over time

Select the best answer from the list of choices.

12. **Which tab on the Ribbon do you use to create a chart?**
    a. Design
    b. Insert
    c. Page Layout
    d. Format

13. **A collection of related data points in a chart is called a:**
    a. Data series.
    b. Data tick.
    c. Cell address.
    d. Value title.

14. **The object in a chart that identifies the colors used for each data series is a(n):**
    a. Data marker.
    b. Data point.
    c. Organizer.
    d. Legend.

15. **How do you move an embedded chart to a chart sheet?**
    a. Click a button on the Chart Tools Design tab.
    b. Drag the chart to the sheet tab.
    c. Delete the chart, switch to a different sheet, then create a new chart.
    d. Use the Copy and Paste buttons on the Ribbon.

16. **Which is *not* an example of a SmartArt graphic?**
    a. Sparkline
    b. Basic Matrix
    c. Organization Chart
    d. Basic Pyramid

17. **Which tab appears only when a chart is selected?**
    a. Insert
    b. Chart Tools Format
    c. Review
    d. Page Layout

Skills Review

1. **Plan a chart.**
   a. Start Excel, open the Data File EX 4-2.xlsx from the location where you store your Data Files, then save it as **EX 4-Software Usage Polling Results**.
   b. Describe the type of chart you would use to plot this data.
   c. What chart type would you use to compare the number of Excel users in each type of business?

2. **Create a chart.**
   a. In the worksheet, select the range containing all the data and headings.
   b. Click the Quick Analysis tool.
   c. Create a Clustered Column chart, then add the chart title **Software Usage, by Business** above the chart.
   d. If necessary, click the Switch Row/Column button so the business type (Accounting, Advertising, etc.) appears as the x-axis.
   e. Save your work.

Skills Review (continued)

3. **Move and resize a chart.**
   a. Make sure the chart is still selected, and close any open panes if necessary.
   b. Move the chart beneath the worksheet data.
   c. Widen the chart so it extends to the right edge of column H.
   d. Use the Quick Layout button in the Chart Tools Design tab to move the legend to the right of the charted data. (*Hint*: Use Layout 1.)
   e. Resize the chart so its bottom edge is at the top of row 25.
   f. Save your work.

4. **Change the chart design.**
   a. Change the value in cell B3 to **8**. Observe the change in the chart.
   b. Select the chart.
   c. Use the Quick Layout button in the Chart Layouts group on the Chart Tools Design tab to apply the Layout 10 layout to the chart, then undo the change.
   d. Use the Change Chart Type button on the Chart Tools Design tab to change the chart to a Clustered Bar chart.
   e. Change the chart to a 3-D Clustered Column chart, then change it back to a Clustered Column chart.
   f. Save your work.

5. **Change the chart layout.**
   a. Use the Chart Elements button to turn off the primary major horizontal gridlines in the chart.
   b. Change the font used in the horizontal and vertical axis labels to Times New Roman.
   c. Turn on the primary major gridlines for both the horizontal and vertical axes.
   d. Change the chart title's font to Times New Roman if necessary, with a font size of 20.
   e. Insert **Business** as the primary horizontal axis title.
   f. Insert **Number of Users** as the primary vertical axis title.
   g. Change the font size of the horizontal and vertical axis titles to 10 and the font to Times New Roman, if necessary.
   h. Change "Personnel" in the worksheet column heading to **Human Resources**, then AutoFit column D, and any other columns as necessary.
   i. Change the font size of the legend to 14.
   j. Add a solid line border in the default color and a (preset) Offset Diagonal Bottom Right shadow to the chart title.
   k. Save your work.

6. **Format a chart.**
   a. Make sure the chart is selected, then select the Chart Tools Format tab, if necessary.
   b. Change the shape fill of the Excel data series to Dark Blue, Text 2.
   c. Change the shape style of the Excel data series to Subtle Effect – Orange, Accent 6.
   d. Save your work.

7. **Annotate and draw on a chart.**
   a. Make sure the chart is selected, then create the text annotation **Needs more users**.
   b. Position the text annotation so the word "Needs" is just below the word "Software" in the chart title.
   c. Select the chart, then use the Chart Tools Format tab to create a 1½ pt weight dark blue arrow that points from the bottom center of the text box to the Excel users in the Human Resources category.
   d. Deselect the chart.
   e. Save your work.

Skills Review (continued)

8. Create a pie chart.

a. Select the range A1:F2, then create a 3-D Pie chart.

b. Drag the 3-D pie chart beneath the existing chart.

c. Change the chart title to **Excel Users**.

d. Apply the Style 7 chart style to the chart, then apply Layout 6 using the Quick Layout button.

e. Explode the Law Firm slice from the pie chart at **25%**.

f. In Page Layout view, enter your name in the left section of the worksheet header.

g. Preview the worksheet and charts in Backstage view, make sure all the contents fit on one page, then submit your work to your instructor as directed. When printed, the worksheet should look like FIGURE 4-26. (Note that certain elements such as the title may look slightly different when printed.)

h. Save your work, close the workbook, then exit Excel.

FIGURE 4-26

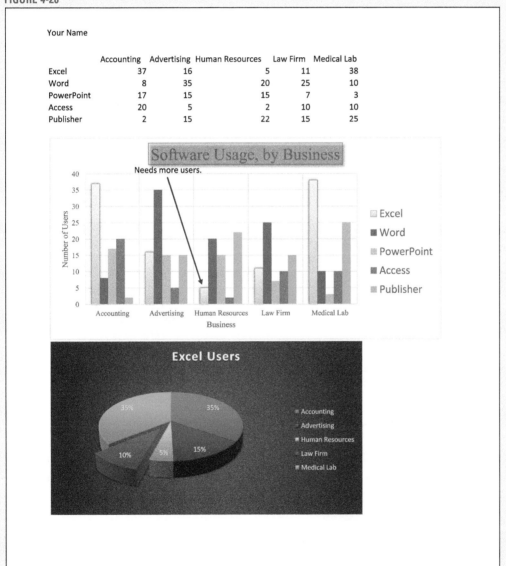

Excel 2016

Independent Challenge 1

You are the operations manager for the Chicago Arts Alliance. Each year the group revisits the number and types of activities they support to better manage their budgets. For this year's budget, you need to create charts to document the number of events in previous years.

a. Start Excel, open the file EX 4-3.xlsx from the location where you store your Data Files, then save it as **EX 4-Chicago Arts Alliance**.

b. Take some time to plan your charts. Which type of chart or charts might best illustrate the information you need to display? What kind of chart enhancements do you want to use? Will a 3-D effect make your chart easier to understand?

c. Create a Clustered Column chart for the data.

d. Change at least one of the colors used in a data series.

e. Make the appropriate modifications to the chart to make it visually attractive and easier to read and understand. Include a legend to the right of the chart, and add chart titles and horizontal and vertical axis titles using the text shown in TABLE 4-3.

TABLE 4-3

title	text
Chart title	Chicago Arts Alliance Events
Vertical axis title	Number of Events
Horizontal axis title	Types of Events

f. Create at least two additional charts for the same data to show how different chart types display the same data. Reposition each new chart so that all charts are visible in the worksheet. One of the additional charts should be a pie chart for an appropriate data set; the other is up to you.

g. Modify each new chart as necessary to improve its appearance and effectiveness. A sample worksheet containing three charts based on the worksheet data is shown in FIGURE 4-27.

h. Enter your name in the worksheet header.

i. Save your work. Before printing, preview the worksheet in Backstage view, then adjust any settings as necessary so that all the worksheet data and charts will print on a single page.

j. Submit your work to your instructor as directed.

k. Close the workbook, then exit Excel.

FIGURE 4-27

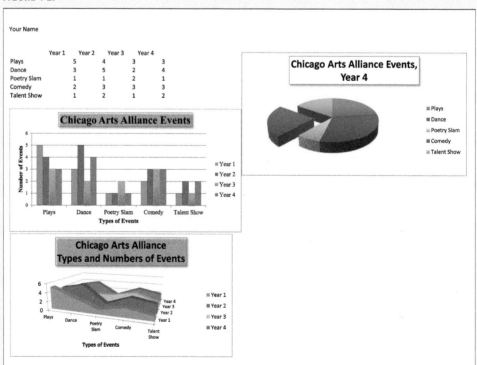

Independent Challenge 2

You work at Canine Companions, a locally owned dog obedience school. One of your responsibilities at the school is to manage the company's sales and expenses using Excel. As part of your efforts, you want to help the staff better understand and manage the school's largest sources of both expenses and sales. To do this, you've decided to create charts using current operating expenses including rent, utilities, and payroll. The manager will use these charts at the next monthly meeting.

a. Start Excel, open EX 4-4.xlsx from the location where you store your Data Files, then save it as **EX 4-Canine Companions Expense Analysis**.

b. Decide which data in the worksheet should be charted. What chart types are best suited for the information you need to show? What kinds of chart enhancements are necessary?

c. Create a 3-D Clustered Column chart in the worksheet showing the expense data for all four quarters. (*Hint*: The expense categories should appear on the x-axis. Do not include the totals.)

d. Change the vertical axis labels (Expenses data) so that no decimals are displayed. (*Hint*: Use the Number category in the Format Axis pane.)

e. Using the sales data, create two charts on this worksheet that compare the sales amounts. (*Hint*: Move each chart to a new location on the worksheet, then deselect it before creating the next one.)

f. In one chart of the sales data, add data labels, then add chart titles as you see fit.

g. Make any necessary formatting changes to make the charts look more attractive, then enter your name in a worksheet cell.

h. Save your work.

i. Preview each chart in Backstage view, and adjust any items as needed. Fit the worksheet to a single page, then submit your work to your instructor as directed. A sample of a printed worksheet is shown in FIGURE 4-28.

j. Close the workbook, then exit Excel.

FIGURE 4-28

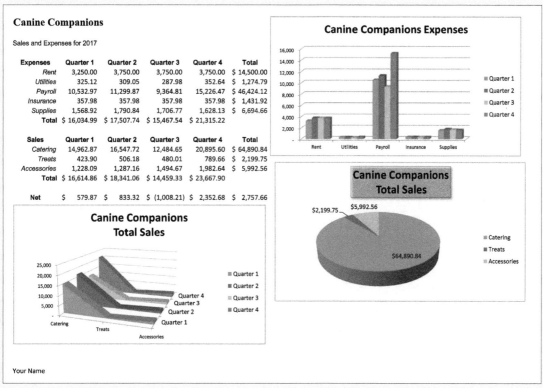

Excel 2016

Independent Challenge 3

You are working as an account representative at a clothing store called Zanzibar. You have been examining the advertising expenses incurred recently. The CEO wants to examine expenses designed to increase sales and has asked you to prepare charts that can be used in this evaluation. In particular, you want to see how dollar amounts compare among the different expenses, and you also want to see how expenses compare with each other proportional to the total budget.

a. Start Excel, open the Data File EX 4-5.xlsx from the location where you store your Data Files, then save it as **EX 4-Zanzibar Advertising Expenses**.

b. Identify three types of charts that seem best suited to illustrate the data in the range A16:B24. What kinds of chart enhancements are necessary?

c. Create at least two different types of charts that show the distribution of advertising expenses. (*Hint*: Move each chart to a new location on the same worksheet.) One of the charts should be a 3-D pie chart.

d. In at least one of the charts, add annotated text and arrows highlighting important data, such as the largest expense.

e. Change the color of at least one data series in at least one of the charts.

f. Add chart titles and category and value axis titles where appropriate. Format the titles with a font of your choice. Apply a shadow to the chart title in at least one chart.

g. Add your name to a section of the header, then save your work.

h. Explode a slice from the 3-D pie chart.

i. Add a data label to the exploded pie slice.

j. Preview the worksheet in Backstage view. Adjust any items as needed. Be sure the charts are all visible on one page. Compare your work to the sample in FIGURE 4-29.

k. Submit your work to your instructor as directed, close the workbook, then exit Excel.

FIGURE 4-29

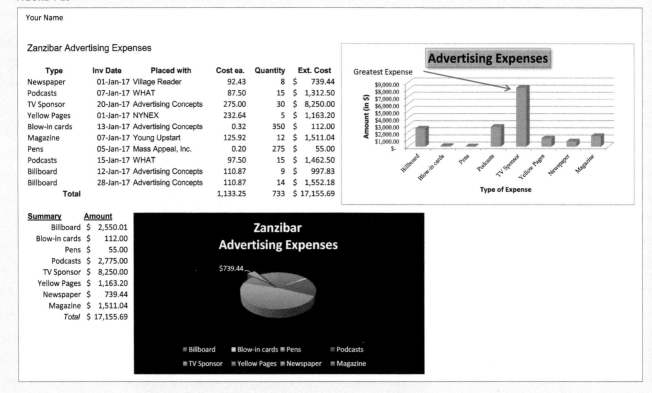

Independent Challenge 4: Explore

This Independent Challenge requires an Internet connection.

All the years of hard work and saving money have paid off, and you have decided to purchase a home. You know where you'd like to live, and you decide to use the web to find out more about houses that are currently available. A worksheet would be a great place to compare the features and prices of potential homes.

a. Start Excel, then save a new, blank workbook as **EX 4-My New House** to the location where you save your Data Files.

b. Decide on where you would like to live, and use your favorite search engine to find information sources on homes for sale in that area. (*Hint*: Try using realtor.com or other realtor-sponsored sites.)

c. Determine a price range and features within the home. Find data for at least five homes that meet your location and price requirements, and enter them in the worksheet. See **TABLE 4-4** for a suggested data layout.

d. Format the data so it looks attractive and professional.

e. Create any type of column chart using only the House and Asking Price data. Place it on the same worksheet as the data. Include a descriptive title.

TABLE 4-4

suggested data layout					
Location					
Price range					
	House 1	House 2	House 3	House 4	House 5
Asking price					
Bedrooms					
Bathrooms					
Year built					
Size (in sq. ft.)					

f. Change the colors in the chart using the chart style of your choice.

g. Enter your name in a section of the header.

h. Create an additional chart: a combo chart that plots the asking price on one axis and the size of the home on the other axis. (*Hint*: Use the Tell me what you want to do text box above the Ribbon to get more guidance on creating a Combo Chart.)

i. Save the workbook. Preview the worksheet in Backstage view and make adjustments if necessary to fit all of the information on one page. See **FIGURE 4-30** for an example of what your worksheet might look like.

j. Submit your work to your instructor as directed.

k. Close the workbook, then exit Excel.

FIGURE 4-30

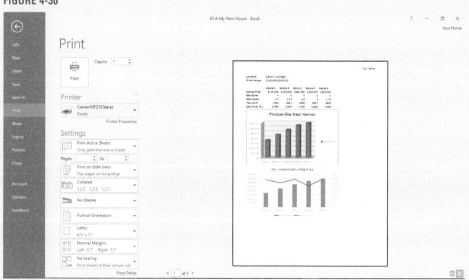

Visual Workshop

Open the Data File EX 4-6.xlsx from the location where you store your Data Files, then save it as **EX 4-Estimated Cost Center Expenses**. Format the worksheet data so it looks like FIGURE 4-31, then create and modify two charts to match the ones shown in the figure. You will need to make formatting, layout, and design changes once you create the charts. (*Hint*: The shadow used in the 3-D pie chart title is made using the Outer Offset Diagonal Top Right shadow.) Enter your name in the left text box of the header, then save and preview the worksheet. Submit your work to your instructor as directed, then close the workbook and exit Excel.

FIGURE 4-31

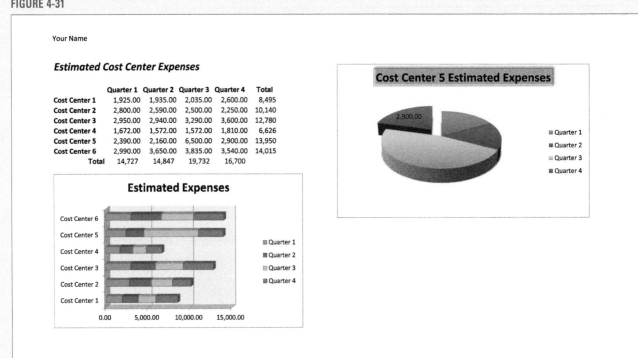

Integrating Word and Excel

CASE You are working as an operations assistant to Kevin Lawrence, the vice president of Operations for R2G. Kevin has asked you to explore the integration capabilities of Office 2016. First, you create a report in Word that includes values and a chart created in Excel, and then you embed a paragraph of text created in Word into an Excel worksheet.

Module Objectives

After completing this module, you will be able to:

- Integrate data between Word and Excel
- Copy data from Excel to Word
- Copy a chart from Excel to Word
- Create linked objects
- Embed a Word file in Excel

Files You Will Need

INT 1-1.xlsx	INT 1-9.docx
INT 1-2.docx	INT 1-10.xlsx
INT 1-3.xlsx	INT 1-11.xlsx
INT 1-4.docx	INT 1-12.docx
INT 1-5.xlsx	INT 1-13.xlsx
INT 1-6.docx	INT 1-14.docx
INT 1-7.xlsx	INT 1-15.xlsx
INT 1-8.docx	INT 1-16.docx

Integration
Module 1

Learning
Outcomes
• Define copy/paste,
  link, and embed
  integration
  options

Integrate Data Between Word and Excel

Microsoft Office programs are designed to work together through a process called **integration**. When you integrate data from multiple Office programs, you work with both a source file and a destination file. The **source file** is the file from which the information is copied or used. The **destination file** is the file that receives the copied information. You can choose from three integration methods: pasting, linking, and embedding. **CASE** ▶ *As an operations assistant, you often create documents such as reports and price lists that include data from both Word and Excel. You decide to review some of the ways in which you integrate data between the two programs.*

DETAILS

You can integrate Word and Excel by:

• **Copying and pasting data from the Clipboard**

  You use the Copy and Paste commands to duplicate **objects** such as text selections, numbers (called values in Excel), and pictures from one program and place them into another program. After you copy and paste an object, changes that you make to the object in the source file do not appear in the destination file. The report shown in **FIGURE 1-1** was created in Word and includes two objects that were copied from Excel—the photograph that appears to the right of the document title and the shaded table under the document subtitle.

• **Linking data**

  Sometimes you want to connect the data that is included in two or more files. For example, suppose you copy the contents of a cell containing a formula from an Excel worksheet and paste it into a Word document. When you change the formula values in Excel, you want the corresponding values to change in the Word document. To create a **link** between data in two files, you select one of the link options that appears when you either click the Paste button list arrow or view options in the Paste Special dialog box. You use the term **linked object** to refer to the connected data. In the report shown in **FIGURE 1-1**, the value "90" is a linked object. If this percentage changes in the Excel worksheet, the linked percentage in the Word document also changes.

• **Copying and pasting charts**

  When you copy a chart from Excel and paste it into Word using the Paste command, Word automatically creates a link between the pasted chart and the original chart. In the report shown in **FIGURE 1-1**, the column chart was copied from Excel and pasted into the Word document. When the chart values are updated in Excel, the same chart values are updated in the chart copied to Word. You can also copy a chart from the source file and then paste it into the destination file as an object that is not linked.

• **Embedding a Word file in Excel**

  You can **embed**, or place an unlinked copy of, the contents of a Word file into an Excel worksheet. You edit the embedded object by double-clicking it and using Word program tools to change text and formatting. This process changes the embedded copy of the Word object in Excel, but does not affect the original source document you created in Word. Similarly, any changes to the source Word document are not reflected in the embedded copy in Excel. In the price list shown in **FIGURE 1-2**, the text that describes the R2G tours was inserted in Excel as an embedded Word file.

FIGURE 1-1: Word report with objects copied from Excel

Table object copied from Excel

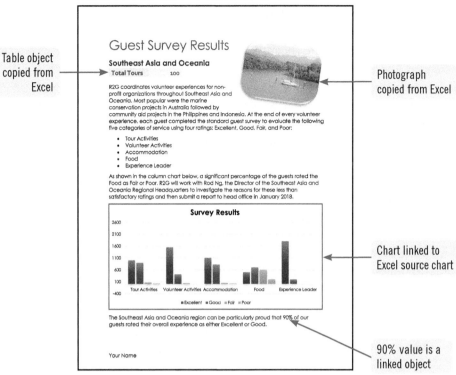

Photograph copied from Excel

Chart linked to Excel source chart

90% value is a linked object

FIGURE 1-2: Price list with embedded Word file

Embedded text inserted directly from a Word file

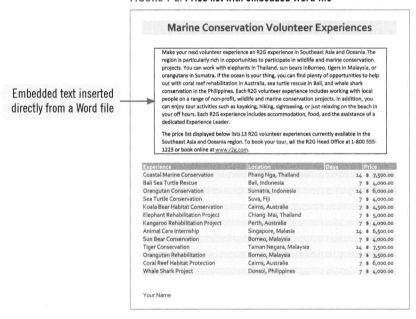

Understanding object linking and embedding (OLE)

The term **object linking and embedding (OLE)** refers to the technology that Microsoft uses to let you integrate data between programs. You create an object in one program, and then you can choose to either link the object to or embed it in another program. The difference between linking and embedding relates to where the object is stored and how you update the object after you place it in a document. A linked object in a destination file is an image of an object contained in a source file, not a copy of it. Both objects share a single source, which means you make changes to an object only in the source file.

When you embed an object that you created in another program, you include a copy of the object in a destination file. To update the object, you double-click it in the destination file and then use the tools of the source program to make changes. You cannot edit the source object using the tools of the destination program.

Copy Data from Excel to Word

You use the Copy and Paste commands when you want to copy an item from one program to another program. The item might be a line of text, a selection of cells, or an object such as a chart or a picture. The procedure is the same as the one you use to copy and paste an object from one location in a document to another location in the same document. By default, an object copied from one program to another program retains the formatting of the original object and is not linked to the original object. The exception occurs when you copy and paste a chart, which you will learn about in the next lesson. **CASE** ▶ *Kevin Lawrence, the vice president of Operations at R2G, has provided you with an Excel worksheet containing survey data from the Southeast Asia and Oceania Regional Headquarters and created a report in Word that describes the survey results. He asks you to copy two objects from the Excel worksheet and paste them into the Word report.*

STEPS

1. **Start Excel, open the file** INT 1-1.xlsx **from the location** where you store your **Data Files, then save it as** INT 1-Customer Survey Data

   The values in the range B7:F10 represent the total number of responses in each of the four rating categories for the volunteer experiences that R2G operated in Southeast Asia and Oceania.

2. **Start Word, open the file** INT 1-2.docx **from the location** where you store your **Data Files, then save it as** INT 1-Customer Survey Report

   The Word report contains text that describes the results of the survey.

3. **Move the mouse pointer over the** Excel program button **on the taskbar, as shown in** FIGURE 1-3, **then click the** Excel program button **to switch to Excel**

   When you point to the Excel program button, a picture of the worksheet and the filename appear.

4. **On the Home tab, click the** dialog box launcher 🔽 **in the Clipboard group**

   The Clipboard task pane opens to the left of the worksheet window. You use the Clipboard when you want to copy and paste more than one item from one program to another program. You can "collect" up to 24 items on the Clipboard and then switch to the other program to paste them.

5. **Click the photograph, click the** Copy button **in the Clipboard group, select the range A4:B4, then click the** Copy button

   Both items now appear on the Clipboard, as shown in FIGURE 1-4. When you place multiple items on the Clipboard, newer items appear at the top of the list and older items move down.

6. **Click the** Word program button **on the taskbar, click the** dialog box launcher 🔽 **in the Clipboard group, verify that the Insertion point appears to the left of the title, then click the photograph on the Clipboard**

7. **Click in the blank space below the subtitle Southeast Asia and Oceania, click** Total Tours 100 **on the Clipboard, then click the** Close button ❌ **on the Clipboard task pane**

   You pasted the object as a table below the document subtitle. When you use the Copy and Paste commands, the default setting is for the copied object to retain the formatting applied to it in the source file.

8. **Click the photograph in the Word document, click the** Layout Options button 🖼 **in the upper-right corner of the photograph, click the** Square option 🖼, **then drag the photograph to the right of the first paragraph using the green alignment guides, as shown in** FIGURE 1-5

9. **Click anywhere in the document to deselect the photograph, then save the document**

FIGURE 1-3: Word and Excel on the taskbar

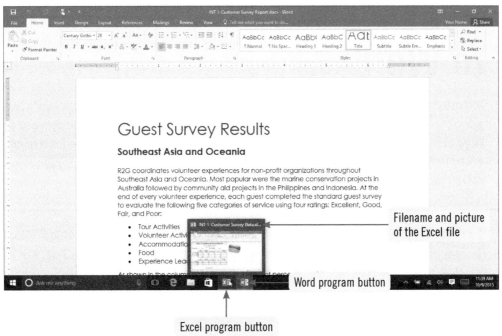

Filename and picture
of the Excel file

Word program button

Excel program button

FIGURE 1-4: Two items collected on the Clipboard

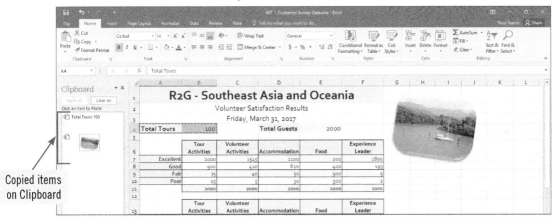

Copied items
on Clipboard

FIGURE 1-5: Picture positioned in the Word report

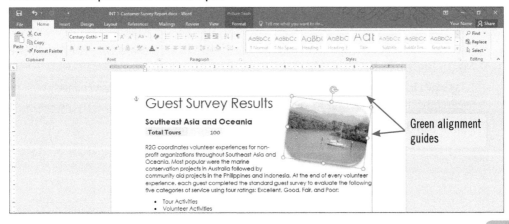

Green alignment
guides

Copy a Chart from Excel to Word

Learning
Outcomes
• Copy a chart
• View Paste options
• Update a linked
  chart

You use the Copy and Paste tools to create a link between a chart in Excel and the same chart pasted into a document in Word. When you change the data in the Excel source file, the linked data also changes in the Word destination file. By default, the copied chart will be linked to the chart in the Excel report. However, it will be formatted with the same theme applied to the destination document. **CASE** ▸ *You need to copy a column chart representing survey results from Excel and paste it into the Word report.*

STEPS

1. Click the Excel program button on the taskbar, then close the Clipboard task pane

2. Scroll down to view the column chart, click an edge of the chart to select it, then click the Copy button in the Clipboard group

   The chart in Excel is formatted with the colors of the Banded theme.

3. Switch to Word, click below the second paragraph (which ends with "January 2018"), then click the Paste button in the Clipboard group

   The chart appears in the Word document formatted with the colors of the Slice theme, because this theme was already applied to the Word document. The Paste Options button appears in the lower-right corner of the chart.

4. Click the Paste Options button ⬚ (Ctrl) ▾ outside the lower-right corner of the pasted chart, as shown in FIGURE 1-6

   A selection of paste options appears. By default, the option Use Destination Theme & Link Data is selected. The Word document is the destination file and is formatted with the Slice theme. The Excel document is the source file and is formatted with the Banded theme. As a result, the Slice theme applied to the Word file is applied to the chart. TABLE 1-1 describes the five options available for pasting a copied chart.

5. Move the mouse over each of the five Paste Options buttons to view how the formatting of the chart changes depending on which button is selected, then click the Use Destination Theme & Link Data button ⬚

6. Switch to Excel, then note the position of the bars for the Food category in the column chart

   At present, the Poor column (pink) is quite high compared to the Poor columns for the other categories.

7. Scroll up, click cell E8, type 700, press [Enter], click cell E10, type 200, then press [Enter] and scroll down to the chart

   In the chart, the Good column (lime green) in the Food category has grown, and the Poor column has shrunk.

8. Switch to Word, click the chart, click the Chart Tools Design tab, then click the Refresh Data button in the Data group

   As shown in FIGURE 1-7, the bars for the Food category in the column chart change in the linked chart to reflect the changes you made to the chart in Excel.

9. Save the document, switch to Excel, then save the workbook

FIGURE 1-6: Paste Options

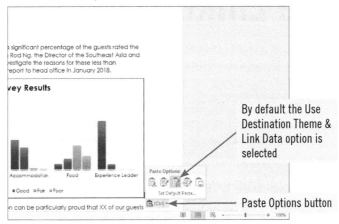

By default the Use Destination Theme & Link Data option is selected

Paste Options button

FIGURE 1-7: Linked chart updated in Word

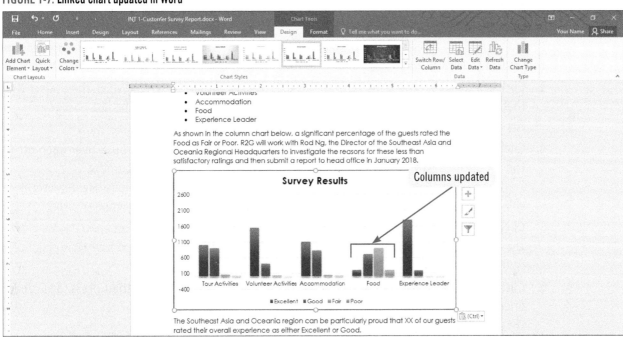

TABLE 1-1: Paste options for charts

Paste Options button	button name	description
	Use Destination Theme & Embed Workbook	The pasted chart is not linked to the source document, and the pasted chart assumes the formatting of the destination document
	Keep Source Formatting & Embed Workbook	The pasted chart is not linked to the source document, and the pasted chart keeps the same formatting as the source document
	Use Destination Theme & Link Data	This button is selected by default when a chart is pasted into the destination document; the theme of the destination document is applied to the chart, and the chart is linked to the object in the source document
	Keep Source Formatting & Link Data	The pasted chart is linked to the source document, so any changes made to the chart in the source document will be made to the copied chart in the Word document; in addition, the formatting of the source document is retained
	Picture	The chart is pasted as a picture that cannot be modified, and uses the same formatting as the chart in the source document

Create Linked Objects

Learning
Outcomes
• Use Paste Special
  to create a link
• Update a linked
  object

To link data other than a chart, you use the Copy button and the Paste Special command to create a link between the source file and the destination file. **CASE** ▸ *You need your report to include a value that represents the average customer ratings. You decide to link the report to the source file data so you can update the data in both files when new information becomes available.*

STEPS

1. **In Excel, click cell G14, type the formula** =AVERAGE(B14:F14), **press [Enter], click cell G14, then drag its fill handle to cell G17 to enter the remaining three percentages**
   The value "56%" appears in cell G14. This value indicates that, on average, 56% of the responses were Excellent. Only 3% of the responses were Poor.

2. **Click cell F18, type Good/Excellent, press [Tab], type the formula** =G14+G15 **in cell G18, then press [Enter]**
   The value "87%" appears in cell G18, indicating that 87% of guests rated their R2G volunteer experience as Good or Excellent.

3. **Click cell G18, click the Copy button in the Clipboard group, switch to Word, then select XX that appears following the phrase "can be particularly proud that" in the last paragraph**
   You will paste the contents of cell G18 from Excel over the "XX" in Word.

4. **Click the Paste list arrow in the Clipboard group, then move your mouse over each of the six options to view how the pasted object will appear in the document**
   Two options allow linking—Link & Keep Source Formatting and Link & Merge Formatting. However, both options also insert a line break, so you look for additional paste options in the Paste Special dialog box.

5. **Click Paste Special**
   The Paste Special dialog box opens, as shown in **FIGURE 1-8**. In this dialog box, you have more options for pasting the value and for controlling its appearance in the destination file.

6. **Click the Paste link option button, click Unformatted Text, click OK, then press [Spacebar] once to add a space after "87%" if necessary**
   The percentage, 87%, appears in the Word document. You decide to test the link.

7. **Switch to Excel, click cell E7, type 500, press [Enter], click cell E9, type 600, then press [Enter]**
   The Good/Excellent rating in cell G18 is now 90%.

8. **Switch to Word, right-click 87%, then click Update Link**
   The value 90% appears. The final document is shown in **FIGURE 1-9**.

9. **Type your name where indicated in the Word footer, save the document, switch to Excel, type your name where indicated in cell A37, save the workbook, submit your files to your instructor, then close the files**
   If you print the Excel workbook, make sure you fit it on one page.

FIGURE 1-8: **Paste Special dialog box**

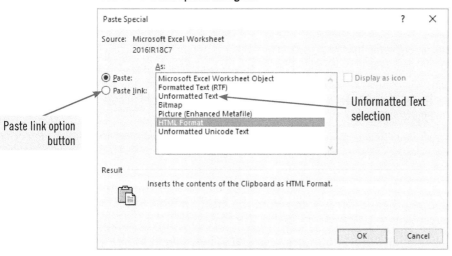

FIGURE 1-9: **Completed report**

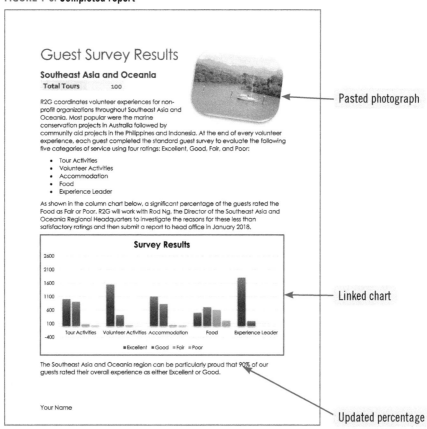

Opening linked files and reestablishing links to charts

When you open a Word file that contains links from an Excel file, a dialog box opens with a message telling you that the document contains links that may refer to other files. The message also asks if you want to update this document with the data from the linked file. Click Yes to update the document with data from the linked file. If you want to change information in both the Excel file and the Word file, you need to open the Excel workbook first, followed by the Word document.

If you make a change to a linked chart in the Excel file, you need to refresh the chart data in Word. To do so, click the chart in Word, click the Chart Tools Design tab, then click the Refresh Data button in the Data group. You also need to manually update any other links by right-clicking the link in Word and then clicking Update Link.

Embed a Word File in Excel

Learning
Outcomes
• Insert a Word file
  as an object
• Edit the Word file
  in Excel

You can embed an entire file that you create in one Office program into a document created in another Office program. You can then edit the embedded file by double-clicking it in the destination program to open the source program. You use the tools of the source program to make changes. TABLE 1-2 summarizes the four ways in which you integrated data between Word and Excel in this module. **CASE** ▶ *You have created a price list in Excel that lists the wildlife and marine conservation experiences offered in Southeast Asia and Oceania, but before you distribute it at an upcoming meeting, you decide to include some explanatory text that you have stored in a Word document.*

STEPS

1. In Excel, open the file INT 1-3.xlsx from the location where you store your Data Files, then save it as INT 1-Wildlife Conservation Price List; in Word, open the file INT 1-4.docx from the location where you store your Data Files, save it as INT 1-Wildlife Conservation, then close the document

TROUBLE
If the Object button is not visible on the Ribbon, click the down arrow in the Text group.

2. **In Excel, click cell G3, click the Insert tab, then click the Object button ▭ in the Text group**
   The Object dialog box opens. Here you can choose to either create a new object or insert an object from a file.

3. Click the Create from File tab, **click** Browse, navigate to where you stored the INT 1-Wildlife Conservation file if necessary, **double-click** INT 1-Wildlife Conservation, then click OK
   The text from the Word document appears in a box that starts in cell G3. When you insert an object from another program such as Word, you sometimes need to reposition the current worksheet contents to accommodate the inserted object.

4. Select the range A4:D20, move the mouse pointer over any border of the selection to show the ⌖, then drag the selection down to cell A18

5. Move the mouse pointer over the border of the box containing the Word text to show the ⌖ pointer, drag the selection to cell A3, click a blank cell, then compare your screen to FIGURE 1-10

6. Double-click the box containing the Word text
   Because the object is embedded, the Word Ribbon and tabs appear within the Excel window. As a result, you can use the tools from the source program (Word) to edit the text. The title bar shows "Document in INT 1-Wildlife Conservation Price List.xlsx - Excel" because you are working within the destination file to edit the embedded object.

7. Click the Select button in the Editing group, click Select All, click the dialog box launcher ▫ in the Paragraph group, select the contents of the Left text box in the Indentation section, type .2, press [Tab], type .2 in the Right text box, then click OK

8. Select 10 in the first line of paragraph 2, type 13, compare the edited object to FIGURE 1-11, then click outside the object to return to Excel
   The embedded object is updated in Excel. The text in the source file is not updated because the source file is not linked to the destination file.

9. Click the File tab, click Print, click Page Setup, click the Margins tab, click the Horizontally check box, click OK, then click ⬅ to return to the workbook
   The embedded Word object and Excel data are centered between the left and right margins of the page.

10. Type your name where indicated in cell A34, save the workbook, submit your files to your instructor, then close the workbook and exit Word and Excel

FIGURE 1-10: Embedded Word file positioned in Excel

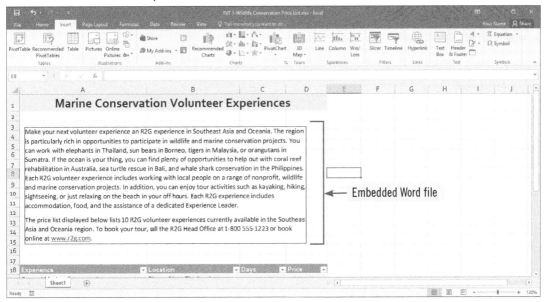

FIGURE 1-11: Embedded object updated in Excel

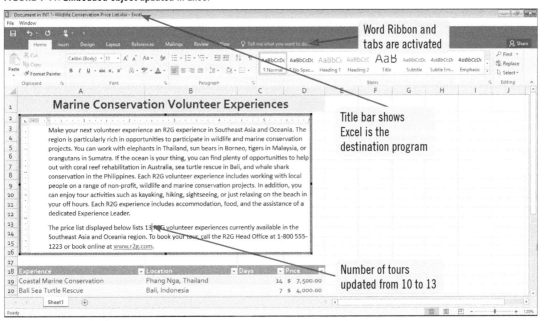

TABLE 1-2: Module 1 integration tasks

object	command	source program	destination program	result	connection	page no.
Cells	Copy/Paste	Excel	Word	Object with Excel formatting	Pasted: no link	4
Chart	Copy/Paste	Excel	Word	Object with Word formatting	Linked	6
Cell	Copy/Paste Special/Paste link	Excel	Word	Formatting varies depending on the formatting option chosen in the Paste Special dialog box	Linked	8
File	Insert/Object/ Create from File	Word	Excel	Text box containing the Word file: to update, double-click and use Word tools within the Excel destination file	Embedded: no link	10

Practice

Concepts Review

Match each term with the statement that best describes it.

1. Embedded file
2. Paste Special
3. Destination file
4. Source file
5. Linked object

a. An unlinked copy of a file placed into another file and then activated by double-clicking
b. The file containing information that is copied and often linked to a different file
c. Within a document, an element that maintains a connection to a different file
d. Used to create and format a connection between objects copied from one file to another file
e. The file that receives the information copied from a different file

Select the best answer from the list of choices.

6. **Which of the following objects is, by default, pasted as a link in the destination file?**
   a. Excel chart pasted into Word
   b. Word text pasted into Excel
   c. Excel values pasted into Word
   d. Picture pasted from Excel to Word
7. **Use the Keep Source Formatting & _____ Data option to paste a chart that you wish to connect with the source document.**
   a. Embed
   b. Paste
   c. Link File
   d. Link
8. **By default, what theme is applied to a chart when it is copied from Excel and pasted into Word?**
   a. The theme used in the source file (Excel)
   b. The Word 2016 theme
   c. The theme used in the destination file (Word)
   d. No theme is applied.
9. **In which group on the Excel Ribbon do you find the option to embed an entire file?**
   a. Insert
   b. Clipboard
   c. Text
   d. Links

Skills Review

1. **Copy data from Excel to Word.**
   a. Start Excel, open the file INT 1-5.xlsx from the location where you store your Data Files, then save it as **INT 1-Humanities Data**.
   b. Start Word, open the file INT 1-6.docx from the location where you store your Data Files, then save it as **INT 1-Humanities Report**.
   c. Switch to Excel, open the Clipboard task pane, then, if there are items on the Clipboard, click Clear All.
   d. Copy the contents of cell A1 to the Clipboard.
   e. Select the range A4:A7, then copy the contents to the Clipboard.
   f. Switch to Word, open the Clipboard task pane, paste the Humanities object at the top of the document (at the current position of the insertion point), then press [Enter] to add an additional blank line.
   g. Paste the subject areas object on the blank line below the first paragraph.
   h. Close the Clipboard task pane, then save the document.

Skills Review (continued)

2. **Copy a chart from Excel to Word.**

   a. Switch to Excel, close the Clipboard task pane, then copy the bar chart.

   b. Switch to Word, then paste the bar chart below the second paragraph of text (which ends with "and State scores").

   c. Switch to Excel, then note the position of the bars for Literature.

   d. Change the value in cell C4 to **70**, then switch to Word.

   e. Click the chart, refresh the data, if necessary, then save the document.

   f. Switch to Excel, then save the workbook.

3. **Create linked objects.**

   a. In Excel, enter the formula **=B4-C4** in cell D4.

   b. Use the Fill handle to copy the formula to the range D5:D7.

   c. Select the range A3:D7, copy it, switch to Word, then use the Paste Special command to paste the cells as a link below paragraph 3 (which ends with "state-wide"), using the Formatted Text (RTF) selection in the Paste Special dialog box.

   d. In Excel, copy cell D7, switch to Word, then use Paste Special to paste the cell over "XX" in the last paragraph as a link using the Unformatted Text option in the Paste Special dialog box. Add a space after the linked object if necessary.

   e. In Excel, change the value in cell B7 to **90**.

   f. In Word, refresh the chart if necessary.

   g. Update the link in the table and the link in the last paragraph so that "20" appears in both places.

   h. Enter your name where indicated in the footer in Word, save the Word report, compare your document to **FIGURE 1-12**, submit your file to your instructor, then close the document.

   i. In Excel, enter your name in cell A26, save the workbook, submit the file to your instructor, then close the workbook.

4. **Embed a Word file in Excel.**

   a. In Excel, open the file INT 1-7.xlsx from the location where you store your Data Files, then save it as **INT 1-Art Course Revenue**.

   b. In Word, open the file INT 1-8.docx from the location where you store your Data Files, save it as **INT 1-Art Courses**, then close it.

   c. In Excel, in cell H4, insert the Word file INT 1-Art Courses.docx as an embedded file.

   d. Select the range A6:F16, then move it to cell A14.

   e. Position the box containing the Word text so its upper-left corner is in cell A3.

   f. Change "XX" to **$65** in paragraph 1, then change "ZZ" in paragraph 1 to **80%**.

   g. Click outside the embedded object to return to Excel, compare your screen to **FIGURE 1-13**, enter your name in cell A24, save the workbook, submit the file to your instructor, then close the workbook and exit Word and Excel.

FIGURE 1-12

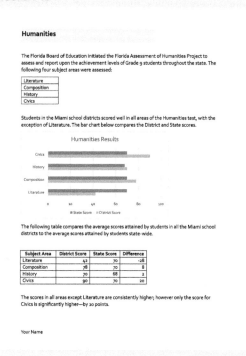

FIGURE 1-13

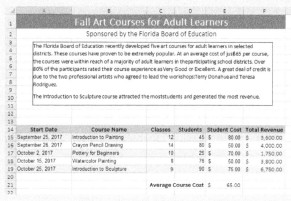

Independent Challenge 1

As a member of the Wolf Island Arts Commission in Alaska, you are responsible for compiling the minutes of the commission's quarterly meetings. You have already written most of the text required for the minutes. Now you need to insert data from Excel that shows how much money was raised from various fund-raising activities.

a. Start Word, open the file INT 1-9.docx from the location where you store your Data Files, save it as **INT 1-Wolf Island Arts Commission Minutes**, start Excel, open the file INT 1-10.xlsx from the location where you store your Data Files, then save it as **INT 1-Wolf Island Data**.

b. In Excel, open the Clipboard task pane, clear all items if necessary, then copy the photograph and cell A2.

c. In Word, open the Clipboard task pane, paste the photograph at the top of the Word document, change the text wrapping of the picture to Square, then position the photograph to the right of the first paragraph.

d. Click to the left of "Approval of Minutes," then paste cell A2.

e. Copy the Fundraising Revenue chart from Excel, then paste it in the appropriate area in the Word document.

f. In Excel, change the number of participants in the plant sale to **1000**; then in Word, refresh the data in the chart if necessary. The Plant Sale slice should be 60%.

g. In Excel, copy the contents of cell E7, switch to Word, select "XX" in the paragraph below the chart, view the paste options, then paste the value as a link using the Unformatted Text selection in the Paste Special dialog box. Add a space if necessary.

h. In Excel, click cell G7, then calculate the total funds raised by adding the contents of the range B7:F7.

i. In cell B8, enter the formula **=B7/G7**, use [F4] to make cell G7 absolute, then copy the formula to the range C8:F8.

j. Copy cell E8, switch to Word, select "ZZ" in the paragraph below the chart, then paste the value as a link using the Unformatted Text selection, adding a space if necessary.

k. In Excel, change the number of participants in the plant sale to **1200**; then in Word, verify the Plant Sale slice changed to 64% and the links updated to $60,000 and 64%. If the links do not update automatically, right-click them and click Update Link in the Word document.

l. Type your name in the Word footer, then save the Word document and Excel workbook, submit the files to your instructor, then close them.

Independent Challenge 2

You work at a summer camp in Montana that provides teens with training programs in digital literacy and community service. You have collected data about the camp enrollment from 2014 to 2019 in an Excel workbook. Now you need to prepare the workbook for distribution at an upcoming meeting with local businesspeople who are interested in sponsoring the camp. You want to include text in the workbook that you have stored in a Word document.

a. Start Excel, open the file INT 1-11.xlsx from the location where you store your Data Files, then save it as **INT 1-High Plains Camp Data**.

b. Start Word, open the file INT 1-12.docx from the location where you store your Data Files, save it as **INT 1-High Plains Camp Information**, then close it.

c. In a blank area of the Excel worksheet, insert the Camp Information file as an embedded object.

d. Adjust the positions of the Excel data and the box containing the Word text so the Word text appears above the Excel data and below the title.

e. In Excel, calculate the total enrollment for the Digital Literacy and Community Service programs in the appropriate cells.

f. To the right of "Community Service," enter and format **Total** to match the formatting for "Digital Literacy" and "Community Service," then calculate the total enrollment for both programs for each year and the total for all programs in all years.

Independent Challenge 2 (continued)

g. Copy the Total enrollment value, edit the embedded Word document so the text is indented by .3" from the left and right margins, then paste the correct total enrollment figure to replace "XX" using the Keep Text Only paste option.

h. Enter your name in cell A22 in Excel, save the Excel workbook, submit the file to your instructor, then close the workbook and exit Excel.

Independent Challenge 3

You own Garden Artist, a landscaping business in Portland, Oregon. You have entered your projected income and expenses in Excel. Now you need to link objects to the company's sales summary in Word.

a. Start Excel, open the file INT 1-13.xlsx from the location where you store your Data Files, then save it as **INT 1-Garden Artist Sales Data**.

b. In cell B14, calculate the Cost of Sales by multiplying the Sales Amount by 60%. (*Hint*: In your formula, multiply the value in cell B6 times .6.) Copy the formula to the range C14:E14.

c. In cell B16, calculate the total profit or loss by subtracting the total expenses from the total income for the month, then copy the formula to the range C16:F16. You should see $66,800 in cell F16.

d. Save the workbook, start Word, open the file INT 1-14.docx from the location where you store your Data Files, then save it as **INT 1-Garden Artist Sales Report**.

e. Select EXPENSES in the paragraph under Projected Expenses, switch to Excel, then copy the value in cell F15 and paste it as a link and as Unformatted Text in Word.

f. Use the same procedure to copy the INCOME and PROFIT amounts from Excel to the appropriate locations in the Word document. Make sure you paste the copied values as links in Unformatted Text.

g. Copy the pie chart from Excel, and paste it into the Word document below the first paragraph after Projected Expenses. Center the pie chart.

h. In Excel, note the percentages in the pie chart (for example, the April slice is 35%), then increase the salaries expense for June to **15,000** and for July to **12,000**.

i. Change the salaries for both April and May to **20,000**. Note how the April slice is now 32%.

j. In Word, update all three links, and verify that the April slice is now 32%.

k. In Excel, open the Clipboard task pane, then copy the heading in cell A1 to the Clipboard.

l. In Word, open the Clipboard task pane, paste the heading at the top of the page and center it, then change the font to Arial Black, the font size to 22 point, and the font color to Dark Green, Accent 2, Darker 25%.

m. Add your name to the document footer, compare the completed sales report to FIGURE 1-14, save the Word file, submit the file to your instructor, then close the Word file.

n. In Excel, enter your name in cell A35, save the workbook, submit the file to your instructor, then close the workbook.

FIGURE 1-14

Garden Artist

Lana Warren, our accountant at Garden Artist, has projected the income and expenses for our landscaping business for the months of April through July.

Projected Expenses
The total projected expenses is $117,200.00 for April through July. The pie chart below displays a breakdown of expenses by total amount.

Breakdown of Monthly Expenses
· April · May · June · July
14%
32%
19%
35%

In order to help decrease our expenses, Elisa Jefferson, one of our own staff members, will create a series of brochures to advertise our products and services, thereby cutting our advertising expenses by 30%.

Projected Income
The total projected income is $174,000.00 for April through July. The projected profit for Garden Artist is $56,800.00 from April through July. We plan to increase sales by charging a higher rate for our landscaping services in April and May, our busiest months.

Your Name

Visual Workshop

Using the Data Files INT 1-15.xlsx and INT 1-16.docx, create the price list shown in FIGURE 1-15. Use formulas to calculate the prices for two-packs and four-packs. Save the workbook as **INT 1-Great Organics Price List**, and save the Word document as **INT 1-Great Organics Information**. Embed the Word document into the Excel worksheet, position the inserted file and the price list in Excel as shown in FIGURE 1-15, then format the embedded Word object as shown in FIGURE 1-15. (*Hint*: The indentation on both sides of the text is .3, and the font size is 12 point.) Add your name to the Excel worksheet, save all files, submit them to your instructor, then close all files.

FIGURE 1-15

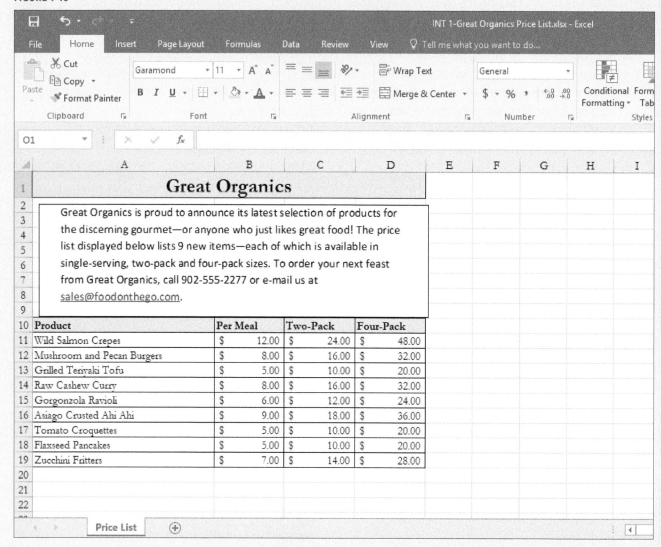

Glossary

3D printer Deposits multiple layers of material (typically heated plastic) onto a surface. To achieve the desired shape, the tool head may travel in a different direction as each layer is applied.

Absolute cell reference In a formula, a cell address that refers to a specific cell and does not change when you copy the formula; indicated by a dollar sign before the column letter and/or row number. *See also* Relative cell reference.

Accessories Simple Windows application programs (apps) that perform specific tasks, such as the Calculator accessory for performing calculations. Also called Windows accessories.

Account Log-on information including ISP, email address, and password for each person using Outlook; used to create folders in Outlook for contacts, email, and schedules. *See* also Personal account.

Action Center Opened by clicking the Notifications button on the right side of the taskbar; shows notifications, tips, and reminders. Contains Quick Actions buttons for commonly-used Windows settings.

Active The currently available document, program, or object; on the taskbar, when more than one program is open, the button for the active program appears slightly lighter.

Active cell The cell in which you are currently working.

Active window The window you are currently using; if multiple windows are open, the window in front of other open windows.

Add-in Software that works with an installed app to extend its features.

Add-ins Small programs available from the online Office Store that allow you to access information on the web without having to leave Word.

Address A sequence of drive and folder names that describes a folder's or file's location in the file hierarchy; the highest hierarchy level is on the left, with lower hierarchy levels separated by the ⟩ symbol to its right.

Address bar In a window, the area just below the Ribbon that shows the file hierarchy, or address of the files that appear in the file list below it; the address appears as a series of links you can click to navigate to other locations on your computer.

Address book A stored list of names and email addresses that you can access through an email program such as Outlook to address messages.

Adjustment handle A small yellow handle that changes the appearance of an object's most prominent feature.

Align To place objects' edges or centers on the same plane.

Alignment The placement of cell contents in relation to a cell's edges; for example, left-aligned, centered, or right-aligned.

Alignment command A command used in Layout or Design View for a form or report to left-, center-, or right-align a value within its control using the Align Left, Center, or Align Right buttons on the Home tab. In Design View, you can also align the top, bottom, right, or left edge of selected controls using the Align button.

Alternate Back Color property A property that determines the alternating background color of the selected section in a form or report.

Anchoring A layout positioning option that allows you to tie controls together so you can work with them as a group.

AND criteria Criteria placed in the same row of the query design grid. All criteria on the same row must be true for a record to appear on the resulting datasheet.

Animation emphasis effect In Sway, a special effect you can apply to an object to animate it.

Animation tag Identifies the order an object is animated on a slide during a slide show.

App An application program; Windows 10 apps are smaller apps available at the Windows store. Desktop apps, such as Microsoft Office, are more full-featured programs and are available from many software companies.

App window The window that opens after you start an app, showing you the tools you need to use the program and any open program documents.

Application developer The person responsible for building and maintaining tables, queries, forms, and reports for all of the database users.

Application program Any program that lets you work with files or create and edit files such as graphics, letters, financial summaries, and other useful documents, as well as view Web pages on the Internet and send and receive e-mail. Also called an app.

Appointment In the Outlook Calendar, an activity that does not involve inviting other people or scheduling resources.

Argument Information that a function uses to create the final answer. Multiple arguments are separated by commas. All of the arguments for a function are surrounded by a single set of parentheses.

Arithmetic operators In a formula, symbols that perform mathematical calculations, such as addition (+), subtraction (–), multiplication (*), division (/), or exponentiation (^).

Attachment A file, such as a picture, audio clip, video clip, document, worksheet, or presentation, that is sent in addition to the email message composed by typing in the message window.

AutoComplete A feature that automatically suggests text to insert.

AutoCorrect A feature that automatically detects and corrects typing errors, minor spelling errors, and capitalization, and inserts certain typographical symbols as you type.

AutoFill Feature activated by dragging the fill handle; copies a cell's contents or continues a series of entries into adjacent cells.

AutoFill Options button Button that appears after using the fill handle to copy cell contents; enables you to choose to fill cells with specific elements (such as formatting) of the copied cell if desired.

AutoFit A feature that automatically adjusts the width of a column or the height of a row to accommodate its widest or tallest entry.

Automatic page break A page break that is inserted automatically at the bottom of a page.

AutoNumber A field data type in which Access enters a sequential integer for each record added into the datasheet. Numbers cannot be reused even if the record is deleted.

Avg function A built-in Access function used to calculate the average of the values in a given field.

Background The area behind the text and graphics on a slide.

Background graphic An object placed on the slide master

Background image An image that fills an entire form or report, appearing "behind" the other controls; also sometimes called a watermark.

Backstage view View that appears when the File tab is clicked as shown. The navigation bar on the left side contains commands to perform actions common to most Office programs, such as opening a file, saving a file, and closing the file.

Backup A duplicate copy of a file that is stored in another location.

Backward-compatible Software feature that enables documents saved in an older version of a program to be opened in a newer version of the program.

Bibliography A list of sources that you consulted or cited while creating a document.

Blind courtesy copy (Bcc) A way to send an email message to recipients when the sender does not want to reveal who has received courtesy copies.

Blog An informal journal that is created by an individual or a group and available to the public on the Internet; short for weblog.

Blogger The person who creates and maintains a blog.

Bluetooth A type of wireless technology that uses short range radio waves. A Bluetooth device must first be "paired" with a computer so that it knows to trust that particular device.

Bold Formatting applied to text to make it thicker and darker.

Border A line that can be added above, below, or to the sides of a paragraph, text, or table cell; a line that divides the columns and rows of a table.

Bound control A control used in either a form or report to display data from the underlying field; used to edit and enter new data in a form.

Building block Reusable piece of formatted content or document part that is stored in a gallery.

Bullet A small graphic symbol used to identify an item in a list.

Business Intelligence tools Excel features for gathering and analyzing data to answer sophisticated business questions.

Button A small rectangle you can click in order to issue a command to an application program.

Calculation A new value that is created by an expression in a text box on a form or report.

Calculation operators Symbols in a formula that indicate what type of calculation to perform on the cells, ranges, or values.

Calendar In Outlook, provides a convenient way to manage appointments and events.

Calendar Picker A pop-up calendar from which you can choose dates for a date field.

Canvas In the Paint accessory, the area in the center of the app window that you use to create drawings.

Card A section for a particular type of content in a Sway presentation.

Case sensitive An application program's (app's) ability to differentiate between uppercase and lowercase letters; usually used to describe how an operating system evaluates passwords that users type to gain entry to user accounts.

Categories In Outlook, a feature used to tag items so you can track and organize them by specific criteria.

Category axis Horizontal axis in a chart, usually containing the names of data categories; in a 2-dimensional chart, also known as the x-axis.

Cell The box formed by the intersection of a table row and table column.

Cell address The location of a cell, expressed by cell coordinates; for example, the cell address of the cell in column A, row 1 is A1.

Cell pointer Dark rectangle that outlines the active cell.

Cell styles Predesigned combinations of formats based on themes that can be applied to selected cells to enhance the look of a worksheet.

Center Alignment in which an item is centered between the margins.

Character spacing Formatting that changes the width or scale of characters, expands or condenses the amount of space between characters, raises or lowers characters relative to the line of text, and adjusts kerning (the space between standard combinations of letters).

Chart A graphical representation of numerical data from a worksheet. Chart types include 2-D and 3-D column, bar, pie, area, and line charts.

Chart sheet A separate sheet in a workbook that contains only a chart, which is linked to the workbook data.

Charts Pictorial representations of worksheet data that make it easier to see patterns, trends, and relationships; *also called* graphs.

Check box A box that turns an option on when checked or off when unchecked.

Citation A parenthetical reference in the document text that gives credit to the source for a quotation or other information used in a document.

Click To quickly press and release the left button on the pointing device; also called single-click. The touch-screen equivalent is a tap on the screen.

Click and Type A feature that allows you to automatically apply the necessary paragraph formatting to a table, graphic, or text when you insert the item in a blank area of a document in Print Layout or Web Layout view.

Click and Type pointer A pointer used to move the insertion point and automatically apply the paragraph formatting necessary to insert text at that location in the document.

Clip A media file, such as a graphic, sound, animation, or movie.

Clip art A collection of graphic images that can be inserted into documents, presentations, Web pages, spreadsheets, and other Office files.

Clipboard A temporary storage area for items that are cut or copied from any Office file and are available for pasting. *See* Office Clipboard and System Clipboard.

Close button In a Windows title bar, the rightmost button; closes the open window, app, and/or document.

Cloud computing When data, applications, and resources are stored on servers accessed over the Internet or a private internal network rather than on a local computer.

Cloud storage location File storage locations on the World Wide Web, such as Windows OneDrive or Dropbox.

Column break A break that forces text following the break to begin at the top of the next column.

Column heading The box containing the column letter on top of the columns in the worksheet.

Column separator The thin line that separates field names to the left or right in a datasheet or the query design grid.

Combination chart Two charts in one, such as a column chart combined with a line chart, that together graph related but dissimilar data.

Combo box A bound control used to display a drop-down list of possible entries for a field. You can also type an entry from the keyboard into the control so it is a "combination" of the list box and text box controls.

Command An instruction to perform a task, such as opening a file or emptying the Recycle Bin.

Comments button A button on the PowerPoint status bar in Normal view allows you to open the Comments pane where you can create, edit, select, and delete comments.

Comparison operators In a formula, symbols that compare values for the purpose of true/false results.

Compatibility The ability of different programs to work together and exchange data.

Complex formula A formula that uses more than one arithmetic operator.

Computer network The hardware and software that make it possible for two or more computers to share information and resources.

Conditional formatting A type of cell formatting that changes based on the cell's value or the outcome of a formula.

Contact Group A named subset of the people in your Outlook Contacts folder, the named group includes the email addresses for all people in the group so you can send a message or invitation to everyone in the group at once. *See* also Distribution list.

Contacts In Outlook, all information related to people, such as business associates and personal friends.

Content control An interactive object that is embedded in a document you create from a template and that expedites your ability to customize the document with your own information.

Content placeholder A placeholder that is used to enter text or objects such as clip art, charts, or pictures.

Contextual tab A tab that appears only when a specific task can be performed; contextual tabs appear in an accent color and close when no longer needed.

Continuous section break A break that begins a new section on the same page.

Control Any element on a form or report such as a label, text box, line, or combo box. Controls can be bound, unbound, or calculated.

Control Source property A property of a bound control in a form or report that determines the field to which the control is connected.

Conversations Emails that discuss a common subject or thread.

Copy To make a duplicate copy of a file, folder, or other object that you want to store in another location.

Copy and paste To move text or graphics using the Copy and Paste commands.

Cortana The digital personal assistant that comes with Windows 10 and Windows phones; can search, give you reminders, alarms, directions, news, weather, and more.

Courtesy copy (Cc) In email, a way to send a message to a recipient who needs to be aware of the correspondence between the sender and the recipients but who is not the primary recipient of the message.

Creative Commons license A public copyright license that allows the free distribution of an otherwise copyrighted work.

Criteria Entries (rules and limiting conditions) that determine which records are displayed when finding or filtering records in a datasheet or form, or when building a query.

Criteria syntax Rules by which criteria need to be entered. For example, text criteria syntax requires that the criteria are surrounded by quotation marks (" "). Date criteria are surrounded by pound signs (#).

Crop To hide part of an object by using the Cropping tool or to delete a part of a picture.

Current record The record that has the focus or is being edited.

Cut To remove an item from a document and place it on the Clipboard.

Cut and paste To move text or graphics using the Cut and Paste commands.

Data marker A graphical representation of a data point in a chart, such as a bar or column.

Data point Individual piece of data plotted in a chart.

Data series The selected range in a worksheet whose related data points Excel converts into a chart.

Data series label Text in the first row and column of a worksheet that identifies data in a chart.

Data series marker A graphical representation of a data series, such as a bar or column.

Data type A required property for each field that defines the type of data that can be entered in each field. Valid data types include AutoNumber, Short Text, Long Text, Number, Currency, Yes/No, Date/Time, and Hyperlink.

Database designer The person responsible for building and maintaining tables, queries, forms, and reports.

Database user The person primarily interested in entering, editing, and analyzing the data in the database.

Datasheet A spreadsheet-like grid that displays fields as columns and records as rows.

Datasheet View A view that lists the records of an object in a datasheet. Tables, queries, and most form objects have a Datasheet View.

Date function A built-in Access function used to display the current date on a form or report; enter the Date function as Date().

Date Navigator A monthly calendar in the To-Do Bar that gives you an overview of the month.

Default In an app window or dialog box, a value that is automatically set; you can change the default to any valid value.

Delete To permanently remove an item from a document.

Deleted Items The folder that stores items when you delete or erase a message from any email folder, which means a deleted item, such as an email or contact card, is actually stored rather than being immediately and permanently deleted. *Also called* Trash folder.

Design View A view in which the structure of an object can be manipulated. Every Access object (table, query, form, report, macro, and module) has a Design View.

Desktop apps Application programs (apps), such as Microsoft Word, that are full-featured and that are often purchased, either from the Windows Store or from a software developer; also called traditional apps.

Destination file In integration, the file that receives the copied information. A Word file that contains an Excel file is the destination file.

Destination presentation The presentation you insert slides to when you reuse slides from another presentation.

Device A hardware component that is part of your computer system, such as a disk drive, a pointing device, or a touch screen device.

Dialog box A window with controls that lets you tell Windows how you want to complete an application program's (app's) command.

Dialog box launcher An icon you can click to open a dialog box or task pane from which to choose related commands.

Digital signature A way to authenticate a presentation files using computer cryptography. A digital signature is not visible in a presentation.

Distribute To evenly divide the space horizontally or vertically between objects relative to each other or the slide edges.

Distribution list A collection of contacts to whom you want to send the same messages; makes it possible for you to send a message to the same group without having to select each contact in the group. *See also* Contact Group.

Docs.com A Microsoft website designed for sharing Sway sites.

Document The electronic file you create using Word.

Document Inspector A PowerPoint feature that examines a presentation for hidden data or personal information.

Document properties Details about a file, such as author name or the date the file was created, that are used to describe, organize, and search for files.

Document window The portion of a application program's (app's) window in which you create the document; displays all or part of an open document.

Documents folder The folder on your hard drive used to store most of the files you create or receive from others; might contain subfolders to organize the files into smaller groups.

Double-click To quickly press and release or click the left button on the pointing device twice. The touch-screen equivalent is a double-tap on the screen.

Draft view A view that shows a document without margins, headers and footers, or graphics.

Drafts The folder that stores unfinished messages that you can finish writing at a later time; many email programs automatically save unsent messages at regular intervals in the Drafts folder as a safety measure.

Drag To point to an object, press and hold the left button on the pointing device, move the object to a new location, and then release the left button. Touch-screen users can press and hold a location, then move along the screen with a finger or stylus.

Drag and drop To move text or a graphic by dragging it to a new location using the mouse.

Drawing canvas In OneNote, a container for shapes and lines.

Drive A physical location on your computer where you can store files.

Drive name A name for a drive that consists of a letter followed by a colon, such as C: for the hard disk drive.

Drop cap A large dropped initial capital letter that is often used to set off the first paragraph of an article.

Dropbox A free online storage site that lets you transfer files that can be retrieved by other people you invite. *See also* Cloud storage location.

Edit To make a change to the contents of an active cell.

Edit mode The mode in which Access assumes you are trying to edit a particular field, so keystrokes such as [Ctrl][End], [Ctrl][Home], [↓], and [↑] move the insertion point within the field.

Edit record symbol A pencil-like symbol that appears in the record selector box to the left of the record that is currently being edited in either a datasheet or a form.

Electronic mail (email) The technology that makes it possible for you to send and receive messages through the Internet.

Electronic spreadsheet A computer program used to perform calculations and analyze and present numeric data.

Email message A message sent using email technology.

Email software A computer program that enables you to send and receive email messages over a network, within an intranet, and through the Internet.

Embed Placement of an object such as a text selection, value, or picture created in a source file into a destination file. An embedded object is edited by opening it in the destination file and then using the tools of the source file to make changes. These changes appear only in the embedded object in the destination file.

Embedded chart A chart displayed as an object in a worksheet.

Embedded object An object that is created in one application and inserted to another; can be edited using the original program file in which they were created.

Emoticon A symbol created by combining keyboard characters; used to communicate feelings in emails.

Endnote Text that provides additional information or acknowledges sources for text in a document and that appears at the end of a document.

Error indicator An icon that automatically appears in Design View to indicate some type of error. For example, a green error indicator appears in the upper-left corner of a text box in Form Design View if the text box Control Source property is set to a field name that doesn't exist.

Even page section break A break that begins a new section on the next even-numbered page.

Event In the Outlook Calendar, an activity that lasts 24 hours or longer.

Exploding Visually pulling a slice of a pie chart away from the whole pie chart in order to add emphasis to the pie slice.

Expression A combination of values, functions, and operators that calculates to a single value. Access expressions start with an equal sign and are placed in a text box in either Form Design View or Report Design View.

Field A code that serves as a placeholder for data that changes in a document, such as a page number.

Field list A list of the available fields in the table or query that the field list represents. Also, a pane that opens in Access and lists the database tables and the fields they contain.

Field name The name given to each field in a table.

Field selector The button to the left of a field in Table Design View that indicates the currently selected field. Also the thin gray bar above each field in the query grid.

File A collection of information stored on your computer, such as a letter, video, or app.

File Explorer A Windows app that allows you to navigate your computer's file hierarchy and manage your files and folders.

File extension A three- or four-letter sequence, preceded by a period, at the end of a filename that identifies the file as a particular type of document; for example, documents in the Rich Text Format have the file extension .rtf.

File hierarchy The tree-like structure of folders and files on your computer.

File list A section of a window that shows the contents of the folder or drive currently selected in the Navigation pane.

File management The ability to organize folders and files on your computer.

File syncing Changes to files stored in the Cloud are automatically synced to all devices.

File tab Provides access to Backstage view and the Word Options dialog box.

Filename A unique, descriptive name for a file that identifies the file's content.

Filter A way to temporarily display only those records that match given criteria.

Filter By Form A way to filter data that allows two or more criteria to be specified at the same time.

Filter By Selection A way to filter records for an exact match.

First line indent A type of indent in which the first line of a paragraph is indented more than the subsequent lines.

Flag A method of coding email messages by assigning different flags to the messages to categorize them or indicate their level of importance for follow up.

Flash Fill A feature that lets you fill a range of text based on samples existing in the current worksheet.

Floating graphic A graphic to which text wrapping has been applied, making the graphic independent of text and able to be moved anywhere on a page.

Focus The property that indicates which field would be edited if you were to start typing.

Folder An electronic container that helps you organize your computer files, like a cardboard folder on your desk; it can contain subfolders for organizing files into smaller groups.

Folder name A unique, descriptive name for a folder that helps identify the folder's contents.

Font The typeface or design of a set of characters (letters, numbers, symbols, and punctuation marks).

Font effect Font formatting that applies a special effect to text, such as small caps or superscript.

Font size The size of characters, measured in units called points.

Font style Format such as bold, italic, and underlining that can be applied to change the way characters look in a worksheet or chart.

Footer Information, such as text, a page number, or a graphic, that appears at the bottom of every page in a document or a section.

Footnote Text that provides additional information or acknowledges sources for text in a document and that appears at the bottom of the page on which the note reference mark appears.

Foreign key field In a one-to-many relationship between two tables, the foreign key field is the field in the "many" table that links the table to the primary key field in the "one" table.

Form An Access object that provides an easy-to-use data entry screen that generally shows only one record at a time.

Form section A location in a form that contains controls. The section in which a control is placed determines where and how often the control prints.

Form View View of a form object that displays data from the underlying recordset and allows you to enter and update data.

Form Wizard An Access wizard that helps you create a form.

Format The appearance of a cell and its contents, including font, font styles, font color, fill color, borders, and shading. *See also* Number format.

Format Painter A feature used to copy the format settings applied to the selected text to other text you want to format the same way.

Formatting Enhancing the appearance of information through font, size, and color changes.

Formatting marks Nonprinting characters that appear on screen to indicate the ends of paragraphs, tabs, and other formatting elements.

Formula A set of instructions used to perform one or more numeric calculations, such as adding, multiplying, or averaging, on values or cells.

Formula bar The area above the worksheet grid where you enter or edit data in the active cell.

Formula prefix An arithmetic symbol, such as the equal sign (=), used to start a formula.

Forwarding Sending an email message you have received to someone else.

Free response quiz A type of Office Mix quiz containing questions that require short answers.

Function A special, predefined formula that provides a shortcut for a commonly used or complex calculation, such as SUM (for calculating a sum) or FV (for calculating the future value of an investment).

Gallery A collection of choices you can browse through to make a selection. Often available with Live Preview.

Gesture An action you take with your finger (or fingers) directly on the screen, such as tapping or swiping.

Graphic image *See* Image.

Gridlines Evenly spaced horizontal and vertical lines on the slide that help you align objects.

Group A PowerPoint feature in which you combine multiple objects into one object.

Grouping A way to sort records in a particular order, as well as provide a section before and after each group of records.

Groups Areas of the Ribbon that arrange commands based on their function, for example, text formatting commands such as Bold, Underline, and Italic are located on the Home tab, in the Font group.

Gutter Extra space left for a binding at the top, left, or inside margin of a document.

Hanging indent A type of indent in which the second and subsequent lines of a paragraph are indented more than the first.

Hard disk A built-in, high-capacity, high-speed storage medium for all the software, folders, and files on a computer. Also called a hard drive.

Hard page break *See* Manual page break.

have not yet been sent.

Header Information, such as text, a page number, or a graphic, that appears at the top of every page in a document or a section.

Highlighted Describes the changed appearance of an item or other object, usually a change in its color, background color, and/or border; often used for an object on which you will perform an action, such as a desktop icon.

Highlighting Transparent color that can be applied to text to call attention to it.

Horizontal ruler A ruler that appears at the top of the document window in Print Layout, Draft, and Web Layout view.

Horizontal scroll bar *See* Scroll bar.

Hub A pane in Microsoft Edge that provides access to favorite websites, a reading list, browsing history, and downloaded files.

Hyperlink Text or a graphic that opens a file, Web page, or other item when clicked. *Also called* a link.

I-beam pointer The pointer used to move the insertion point and select text.

Icon A small image that represents an item, such as the Recycle Bin on your Windows desktop; you can rearrange, add, and delete desktop icons.

Image A nontextual piece of information such as a picture, piece of clip art, drawn object, or graph. Because images are graphical (andnot numbers or letters), they are sometimes referred to as graphical images.

Inactive window An open window you are not currently using; if multiple windows are open, the window(s) behind the active window.

Inbox An email folder that stores all incoming email.

Indent The space between the edge of a line of text or a paragraph and the margin.

Indent marker A marker on the horizontal ruler that shows the indent settings for the active paragraph.

Infinity symbol The symbol that indicates the "many" side of a one-to-many relationship.

Ink annotations A freehand drawing on the screen in Slide Show view made by using the pen or highlighter tool.

Ink to Math tool The OneNote tool that converts handwritten mathematical formulas to formatted equations or expressions.

Ink to Text tool The OneNote tool that converts inked handwriting to typed text.

Inked handwriting In OneNote, writing produced when using a pen tool to enter text.

Inking Freehand pen and highlighter marks you can draw on a slide in Normal view to emphasize information.

Inking toolbar In Microsoft Edge, a collection of tools for annotating a webpage.

Inline graphic A graphic that is part of a line of text.

Insertion point A blinking vertical line that appears when you click in a text box; indicates where new text will be inserted.

Integrate To incorporate a document and parts of a document created in one program into another program; for example, to incorporate an Excel chart into a PowerPoint slide, or an Access table into a Word document.

Integration Term used to describe the process of combining objects and data from two or more applications. For example, a report created in Word can include a chart copied from Excel, or a presentation created in PowerPoint can include a table copied from Access.

Interface The look and feel of a program; for example, the appearance of commands and the way they are organized in the program window.

Is Not Null A criterion that finds all records in which any entry has been made in the field.

Is Null A criterion that finds all records in which no entry has been made in the field.

Italic Formatting applied to text to make the characters slant to the right.

Join line The line identifying which fields establish the relationship between two related tables. Also called a link line.

Junk email Unwanted email that arrives from unsolicited sources. *Also called* spam. Also a default folder in Outlook for junk email.

Justify Alignment in which an item is flush with both the left and right margins.

Key symbol The symbol that identifies the primary key field in each table.

Keyboard shortcut A combination of keys or a function key that can be pressed to perform a command.

Keyword A descriptive word or phrase you enter to obtain a list of results that include that word or phrase. *Also called* shortcut key.

Label control An unbound control that displays text to describe and clarify other information on a form or report.

Label Wizard A report wizard that precisely positions and sizes information to print on a vast number of standard business label specifications.

Labels Descriptive text or other information that identifies data in rows, columns, or charts, but is not included in calculations.

Landscape Page orientation in which the contents of a page span the length of a page rather than its width, making the page wider than it is tall.

Landscape orientation Page orientation in which the page is wider than it is tall.

Launch To open or start a program on your computer.

Launcher An icon you click to open a dialog box or task pane.

Layout A way to group several controls together on a form or report to more quickly add, delete, rearrange, resize, or align controls.

Layout View An Access view that lets you make some design changes to a form or report while you are browsing the data.

Left function An Access function that returns a specified number of characters, starting with the left side of a value in a Text field.

Left indent A type of indent in which the left edge of a paragraph is moved in from the left margin.

Left-align Alignment in which the item is flush with the left margin.

Legend Text box feature in a chart that provides an explanation about the data presented in a chart.

Like operator An operator used in a query to find values in a field that match the pattern you specify.

Line spacing The amount of space between lines of text.

Link A connection created between a source file and a destination file. When an object created in a source file is inserted into or copied to a destination file, any changes made to the object in the source file also appear in the object contained in the destination file.

Link line The line identifying which fields establish the relationship between two related tables.

Linked object An object such as a text selection, value, or picture that is contained in a destination file and linked to a source file. When a change is made to the linked object in the source file, the change also occurs in the linked object in the destination file.

List box A box that displays a list of options from which you can choose (you may need to scroll and adjust your view to see additional options in the list).

Live Preview A feature that lets you point to a choice in a gallery or palette and see the results in the document or object without actually clicking the choice.

Live tile Updated, "live" content that appears on some apps' tiles on the Windows Start menu, including the Weather app and the News app.

Lock screen The screen that appears when you first start your computer, or after you leave it unattended for a period of time, before the sign-in screen.

Log in To select a user account name when a computer starts up, giving access to that user's files. Also called sign in.

Logical view The datasheet of a query is sometimes called a logical view of the data because it is not a copy of the data, but rather, a selected view of data from the underlying tables.

Macro An Access object that stores a collection of keystrokes or commands such as those for printing several reports in a row or providing a toolbar when a form opens.

Mail In Outlook, lets you manage all email.

Major gridlines In a chart, the gridlines that represent the values at the tick marks on the value axis.

Manual page break A page break inserted to force the text following the break to begin at the top of the next page.

Map It An Outlook feature on a Contact card that lets you view a contact's address on a map.

Margin The blank area between the edge of the text and the edge of a page.

Masters One of three views that stores information about the presentation theme, fonts, placeholders, and other background objects. The three master views are Slide Master view, Handout Master view, and Notes Master view.

Maximize button On the right side of a window's title bar, the center button of three buttons; used to expand a window so that it fills the entire screen. In a maximized window, this button changes to a Restore button.

Maximized window A window that fills the desktop.

Meeting In the Outlook Calendar, an activity you invite people to or reserve resources for.

Menu A list of related commands.

Merge A feature in PowerPoint used to combine multiple shapes together; provides you a way to create a variety of unique geometric shapes that are not available in the Shapes gallery.

Message body In an email message, where you write the text of your message.

Message header Contains the basic information about a message including the sender's name and email address, the names and email addresses of recipients and Cc recipients, a date and time stamp, and the subject of the message.

Message threading Allows you to navigate through a group of messages, seeing all replies and forwards from all recipients; includes all emails that discuss a common subject.

Metadata Another name for document properties that includes the author name, the document subject, the document title, and other personal information.

Microsoft account A web service that lets users sign on to one web address so they can use Windows 10 computers as well as Outlook com.

Microsoft Edge New in Windows 10, the Microsoft Web browser that is intended to replace Internet Explorer.

Microsoft OneDrive A Microsoft Web site where you can obtain free file storage space, using your own account, that you can share with others; you can access OneDrive from a laptop, tablet computer, or smartphone.

Microsoft OneNote Mobile app The lightweight version of Microsoft OneNote designed for phones, tablets, and other mobile devices.

Microsoft Store A website, accessible from the Store icon in the Windows 10 taskbar, where you can purchase and download apps, including games, productivity tools, and media software.

Microsoft Windows 10 An operating system.

Mini toolbar A small toolbar that appears next to selected text that contains basic text-formatting commands.

Minimize button On the right side of a window's title bar, the leftmost button of three buttons; use to reduce a window so that it only appears as an icon on the taskbar.

Minimized window A window that is visible only as an icon on the taskbar.

Minor gridlines In a chart, the gridlines that represent the values between the tick marks on the value axis.

Mirror margins Margins used in documents with facing pages, where the inside and outside margins are mirror images of each other.

Mixed reference Cell reference that combines both absolute and relative cell addressing.

Mode indicator An area on the left end of the status bar that indicates the program's status. For example, when you are changing the contents of a cell, the word 'Edit' appears in the mode indicator.

Module An Access object that stores Visual Basic programming code that extends the functions of automated Access processes.

Mouse pointer A small arrow or other symbol on the screen that you move by manipulating the pointing device; also called a pointer.

Move To change the location of a file, folder, or other object by physically placing it in another location.

Multilevel list A list with a hierarchical structure; an outline.

Multiuser A characteristic that means more than one person can enter and edit data in the same Access database at the same time.

Name box Box to the left of the formula bar that shows the cell reference or name of the active cell.

Name property A property that uniquely identifies each object and control on a form or report.

Navigate To move around in a worksheet; for example, you can use the arrow keys on the keyboard to navigate from cell to cell, or press [Page Up] or [Page Down] to move one screen at a time.

Navigate down To move to a lower level in your computer's file hierarchy.

Navigate up To move to a higher level in your computer's file hierarchy.

Navigation buttons Buttons in the lower-left corner of a datasheet or form that allow you to quickly navigate between the records in the underlying object as well as add a new record.

Navigation mode A mode in which Access assumes that you are trying to move between the fields and records of the datasheet (rather than edit a specific field's contents), so keystrokes such as [Ctrl][Home] and [Ctrl][End] move you to the first and last field of the datasheet.

Navigation Pane A pane in the Access program window that provides a way to move between objects (tables, queries, forms, reports, macros, and modules) in the database.

Negative indent A type of indent in which the left edge of a paragraph is moved to the left of the left margin. *Also called* outdent.

Next page section break A break that begins a new section on the next page.

Normal style The default style for text and paragraphs in Word.

Normal view Default worksheet view that shows the worksheet without features such as headers and footers; ideal for creating and editing a worksheet, but may not be detailed enough when formatting a document.

Note In OneNote, a small window that contains text or other types of information.

Note reference mark A mark (such as a letter or a number) that appears next to text to indicate that additional information is offered in a footnote or endnote.

Notebook In OneNote, the container for notes, drawings, and other content.

Notes In Outlook, the electronic version of the sticky notes you buy at your local stationery store; a convenient way to quickly jot down a reminder or an idea.

Notes button A button on the status bar in PowerPoint that opens the Notes pane.

Notes Page view A presentation view that displays a reduced image of the current slide above a large text box where you can type notes.

Notes pane The area in Normal view that shows speaker notes for the current slide; also in Notes Page view, the area below the slide image that contains speaker notes.

Notification area An area on the right side of the Windows 10 taskbar that displays the current time as well as icons representing selected information; the Notifications button displays pop-up messages when a program on your computer needs your attention. Click the Notifications button to display the Action Center. *See also* Action Center.

Number format A format applied to values to express numeric concepts, such as currency, date, and percentage.

Object A table, query, form, report, macro, or module in an Access database.

Object Linking and Embedding (OLE) The term used to refer to the technology Microsoft uses to allow the integration of data between programs. The difference between linking and embedding relates to where the object is stored and how the object is updated after placement in a document. A linked object in a destination file is an image of an object contained in a source file. Both objects share a single source, which means the object is updated only in the source file.

Odd page section break A break that begins a new section on the next odd-numbered page.

Office Clipboard A temporary storage area shared by all Office programs that can be used to cut, copy, and paste multiple items within and between Office programs. The Office Clipboard can hold up to 24 items collected from any Office program. *See also* System Clipboard.

Office Mix A free add-in application integrated to the PowerPoint Ribbon that allows you to create interactive content.

Office Online Apps Versions of the Microsoft Office applications with limited functionality that are available online from Microsoft OneDrive. Users can view documents online and then edit them in the browser using a selection of functions.

Off-site backup Duplicate storage of computer data at a remote location other than your home or office. The backup may be stored on a removable hard drive or sent over the Internet to a Cloud service.

OneDrive An online storage and file sharing service. Access to OneDrive is through a Microsoft account.

One-to-many line The line that appears in the Relationships window and shows which field is duplicated between two tables to serve as the linking field. The one-to-many line displays a "1" next to the field that serves as the "one" side of the relationship and displays an infinity symbol next to the field that serves as the "many" side of the relationship when referential integrity is specified for the relationship. Also called the one-to-many join line.

One-to-many relationship The relationship between two tables in an Access database in which a common field links the tables together. The linking field is called the primary key field in the "one" table of the relationship and the foreign key field in the "many" table of the relationship.

Online collaboration The ability to incorporate feedback or share information across the Internet or a company network or intranet.

Open To use one of the methods for opening a document to retrieve it and display it in the document window.

Operating system A program that manages the complete operation of your computer and lets you interact with it.

Option button A small circle in a dialog box that you click to select only one of two or more related options.

OR criteria Criteria placed on different rows of the query design grid. A record will be selected for the resulting datasheet if it is true for any single row.

Order of precedence Rules that determine the order in which operations are performed within a formula containing more than one arithmetic operator.

Orphan The first line of a paragraph when it appears alone at the bottom of a page.

Orphan record A record in the "many" table of a one-to-many relationship that doesn't have a matching entry in the linking field of the "one" table. Orphan records cannot be created if referential integrity is enforced on a relationship.

Outbox A temporary storage folder for email messages that have not yet been sent.

Outdent *See* Negative indent.

Outline view A view in PowerPoint where you can enter text on slides in outline form. Includes three areas. The Outline pane where you enter text, the Slide pane for the main slide, and the Notes pane where you enter notes.

Outlook Today A feature in Outlook that shows your day at a glance, like an electronic version of a daily planner book; when it is open, you can see what is happening in the Calendar, Tasks, and Messages for the day.

Padding The space between controls.

Page In OneNote, a workspace for inserting notes and other content, similar to a page in a physical notebook.

Page break *See* Automatic page break or Manual page break.

Page Break Preview A worksheet view that displays a reduced view of each page in your worksheet, along with page break indicators that you can drag to include more or less information on a page.

Page Layout view Provides an accurate view of how a worksheet will look when printed, including headers and footers.

Pane A section of a window, such as the Navigation pane in the File Explorer window.

Paragraph spacing The amount of space between paragraphs.

Password A special sequence of numbers and letters that users can employ to control who can access the files in their user account area; keeping the password private helps keep users' computer information secure.

Paste To place a copied item from the Clipboard to a location in a document.

Paste Options button Button that appears onscreen after pasting content; enables you to choose to paste only specific elements of the copied selection, such as the formatting or values, if desired.

Path An address that describes the exact location of a file in a file hierarchy; shows the folder with the highest hierarchy level on the left and steps through each hierarchy level toward the right. Locations are separated by small triangles or by backslashes.

Peek A feature in Outlook that opens a small window when you mouse over an event, task, or some activity and shows you a snapshot of the details for the item.

People In Outlook, where you manage all your business and personal contact information.

People Pane Available in several Outlook views; shows you any social media information available for the person sending the current message and included files, appointments, and notes related to that person.

Personal account In Outlook, identifies you as a user with information such as your email address and password, the type of Internet service provider (ISP) you are using, and the incoming and outgoing email server address for your ISP. *See also* Account.

Photos app A Windows 10 app that lets you view and organize your pictures.

Picture A digital photograph, piece of line art, or other graphic that is created in another program and is inserted into PowerPoint.

Pixel (picture element) One pixel is the measurement of one picture element on the screen.

Plot area In a chart, the area inside the horizontal and vertical axes.

Point A unit of measure used for font size and row height. One point is equal to 1/72nd of an inch.

Pointer *See* Mouse pointer.

Pointing device A device that lets you interact with your computer by controlling the movement of the mouse pointer on your computer screen; examples include a mouse, trackball, touchpad, pointing stick, on-screen touch pointer, or a tablet.

Pointing device action A movement you execute with your computer's pointing device to communicate with the computer; the five basic pointing device actions are point, click, double-click, drag, and right-click.

Portrait Page orientation in which the contents of a page span the width of a page, so the page is taller than it is wide.

Portrait orientation A printout that is 8.5 inches wide by 11 inches tall.

Power button The physical button on your computer that turns your computer on.

PowerPoint window A window that contains the running PowerPoint application including the Ribbon, panes, and tabs.

Presentation software A software program used to organize and present information typically as part of an electronic slide show.

Presenter view A PowerPoint view you access while in Slide Show view. Typically you use this view when showing a presentation through two monitors, one that you see as the presenter and one that the audience sees.

Preview pane A pane on the right side of a File Explorer window that shows the actual contents of a selected file without opening an app; might not work for some types of files, such as databases.

Previewing Prior to printing, seeing onscreen exactly how the printed document will look.

Primary key field A field that contains unique information for each record. A primary key field cannot contain a null entry.

primary recipient of the message.

Print area The portion of a worksheet that will be printed; can be defined by selecting a range and then using the Print Area button on the Page Layout tab.

Print Layout view A view that shows a document as it will look on a printed page.

Print Preview An Access view that shows you how a report or other object will print on a sheet of paper.

Program A set of instructions written for a computer, such as an operating system program or an application program; also called an application or an app.

Property A characteristic that further defines a field (if field properties), control (if control properties), section (if section properties), or object (if object properties).

Property Sheet A window that displays an exhaustive list of properties for the chosen control, section, or object on a form or report.

Query An Access object that provides a spreadsheet-like view of the data, similar to that in tables. It may provide the user with a subset of fields and/or records from one or more tables. Queries are created when the user has a "question" about the data in the database.

Query design grid The bottom pane of the Query Design View window in which you specify the fields, sort order, and limiting criteria for the query.

Query Design View The window in which you develop queries by specifying the fields, sort order, and limiting criteria that determine which fields and records are displayed in the resulting datasheet.

Quick Access buttons Buttons that appear at the bottom of the Windows Action Center; single-click to perform common actions such as turning WiFi on or off.

Quick Access toolbar A customizable toolbar that contains buttons you can click to perform frequently used commands.

Quick Access view A list of frequently-used folders and recently used files that appears when you first open File Explorer.

Quick Analysis tool An icon that is displayed below and to the right of a range that lets you easily create charts and other elements.

Quick Part A reusable piece of content that can be inserted into a document, including a field, document property, or a preformatted building block.

Quick Style Determines how fonts, colors, and effects of the theme are combined and which color, font, and effect is dominant. A Quick Style can be applied to shapes or text.

RAM (Random Access Memory) The storage location that is part of every computer, that temporarily stores open apps and document data while a computer is on.

Range A selection of two or more cells, such as B5:B14.

Read Mode view A document view that hides the tabs and Ribbon and is useful for reading long documents.

Reading view In Microsoft Edge, the display of a webpage that removes ads and most graphics and uses a simple format for the text.

Read-only An object property that indicates whether the object can read and display data, but cannot be used to change (write to) data.

Record A row of data in a table.

Record source The table or query that defines the field and records displayed in a form or report.

Recycle Bin A desktop object that stores folders and files you delete from your hard drive(s) and enables you to restore them.

Reference operators In a formula, symbols which enable you to use ranges in calculations.

Referential integrity A set of Access rules that govern data entry and help ensure data accuracy. Setting referential integrity on a relationship prevents the creation of orphan records.

Relational database software Software such as Access that is used to manage data organized in a relational database.

Relative cell reference In a formula, a cell address that refers to a cell's location in relation to the cell containing the formula and that automatically changes to reflect the new location when the formula is copied or moved; default type of referencing used in Excel worksheets. *See also* Absolute cell reference.

Removable storage Storage media that you can easily transfer from one computer to another, such as DVDs, CDs, or USB flash drives.

Report An Access object that creates a professional printout of data that may contain such enhancements as headers, footers, and calculations on groups of records.

Report Wizard An Access wizard that helps you create a report.

Responsive design A way to provide content so that it adapts appropriately to the size of the display on any device.

Restore Down button On the right side of a maximized window's title bar, the center of three buttons; use to reduce a window to its last non-maximized size. In a restored window, this button changes to a Maximize button.

Ribbon In many Microsoft app windows, a horizontal strip near the top of the window that contains tabs (pages) of grouped command buttons that you click to interact with the app.

Ribbon Display Options button A button on the title bar that is used to use to hide or show the Ribbon and the Ribbon tabs and commands.

Rich Text Format (RTF) The file format that the WordPad app uses to save files.

Right indent A type of indent in which the right edge of a paragraph is moved in from the right margin.

Right-align Alignment in which an item is flush with the right margin.

Right-click To press and release the right button on the pointing device; use to display a shortcut menu with commands you issue by left-clicking them.

Rotate handle A small round arrow at the top of a selected object that you can drag to turn the selected object.

Row heading The box containing the row number to the left of the row in a worksheet.

RTF *See* Rich Text Format.

Rule In Outlook, enables you to organize your email by setting parameters for incoming email; for example, you can specify that all email from a certain person goes into the folder for a specific project.

Ruler A vertical or horizontal guide that appears in Form and Report Design View to help you position controls.

Sandbox A computer security mechanism that helps to prevent attackers from gaining control of a computer.

Sans serif font A font (such as Calibri) whose characters do not include serifs, which are small strokes at the ends of letters.

Save To store a file permanently on a disk or to overwrite the copy of a file that is stored on a disk with the changes made to the file.

Save As Command used to save a file for the first time or to create a new file with a different filename, leaving the original file intact.

Save As command A command on the File tab that saves the entire database (and all objects it contains) or only the current object with a new name.

Screen capture An electronic snapshot of your screen, as if you took a picture of it with a camera, which you can paste into a document.

Screen clipping In OneNote, an image copied from any part of a computer screen.

Screen recording In Office Mix, a video you create by capturing your desktop and any actions performed on it.

ScreenTip A label that identifies the name of the button or feature, briefly describes its function, conveys any keyboard shortcut for the command, and includes a link to associated help topics, if any.

Scroll To use the scroll bars or the arrow keys to display different parts of a document in the document window.

Scroll arrow A button at each end of a scroll bar for adjusting your view in a window in small increments in that direction.

Scroll bar A vertical or horizontal bar that appears along the right or bottom side of a window when there is more content than can be displayed within the window, so that you can adjust your view.

Scroll bars Bars on the right edge (vertical scroll bar) and bottom edge (horizontal scroll bar) of the document window that allow you to move around in a document that is too large to fit on the screen at once.

Scroll box A box in a scroll bar that you can drag to display a different part of a window.

Search criteria Descriptive text that helps identify the application program (app), folder, file, or Web site you want to locate when conducting a search.

Search Tools tab A tab that appears in the File Explorer window after you click the Search text box; lets you specify a specific search location, limit your search, repeat previous searches, save searches, and open a folder containing a found file.

Secondary axis In a combination chart, an additional axis that supplies the scale for one of the chart types used.

Section A location of a form or report that contains controls. The section in which a control is placed determines where and how often the control prints.

Section break A formatting mark inserted to divide a document into sections.

Section tab In OneNote, a divider for organizing a notebook.

Select To change the appearance of an item by clicking, double-clicking, or dragging across it, to indicate that you want to perform an action on it.

Select pointer The mouse pointer shape that looks like a white arrow pointing toward the upper-left corner of the screen.

Selection box A dashed border that appears around a text object or placeholder, indicating that it is ready to accept text.

Selection pointer A pointer used to click a button or another element of the Word program window.

Sent Items When you send an email message, a copy of the message is stored in this folder to help you track the messages you send out.

Serif font A font (such as Times New Roman) whose characters include serifs, which are small strokes at the ends of letters.

Service provider The organization or company that provides email or Internet access.

Shading A background color or pattern that can be applied to text, tables, or graphics.

Share button A button on the Ribbon that is used to save a document to the Cloud.

Sheet tab scrolling buttons Allow you to navigate to additional sheet tabs when available; located to the left of the sheet tabs.

Sheet tabs Identify the sheets in a workbook and let you switch between sheets; located below the worksheet grid.

Shortcut An icon that acts as a link to an app, file, folder, or device that you use frequently.

Shortcut key *See* Keyboard shortcut.

Shortcut menu A menu of context-appropriate commands for an object that opens when you right-click that object.

Shut down To exit the operating system and turn off your computer.

Sign in To select a user account name when a computer starts up, giving access to that user's files. Also called log in.

Simple Query Wizard An Access wizard that prompts you for information it needs to create a new query.

Single-click *See* Click.

Single-factor authentication Security protocol in which an individual provides only one credential (password) to verify their identity.

Sizing handles Small series of dots at the corners and edges of a chart indicating that the chart is selected; drag to resize the chart.

Slide layout This determines how all of the elements on a slide are arranged, including text and content placeholders.

Slide Library A folder that you and others can access to open, modify, and review presentation slides.

Slide Notes In Office Mix, the written and displayed version of notes typically used to recite narration while creating a slide recording.

Slide pane The main section of Normal view that displays the current slide.

Slide recording In Office Mix, a video you create by recording action with a webcam, a camera attached or built into a computer.

Slide Show view A view that shows a presentation as an electronic slide show; each slide fills the screen.

Slide Sorter view A view that displays a thumbnail of all slides in the order in which they appear in a presentation; used to rearrange slides and slide transitions.

Slide thumbnail *See* Thumbnail.

Slide timing The amount of time each slide is visible on the screen during a slide show.

Slide transition The special effect that moves one slide off the screen and the next slide on the screen during a slide show. Each slide can have its own transition effect.

Slides tab On the left side of the Normal view, displays the slides in the presentation as thumbnails.

Smart Guides A feature in PowerPoint used to help position objects relative to each other and determine equal distances between objects.

SmartArt A professional quality graphic diagram that visually illustrates text.

SmartArt graphics Predesigned diagram types for the following types of data: List, Process, Cycle, Hierarchy, Relationship, Matrix, and Pyramid.

SmartArt Style A pre-set combination of formatting options that follows the design theme that you can apply to a SmartArt graphic.

Snap assist feature The Windows 10 feature that lets you drag a window to the left or right side of the screen, where it "snaps" to fill that half of the screen and displays remaining open windows as thumbnails you click to fill the other half.

Soft page break *See* Automatic page break.

Sort Change the order of, such as the order of files or folders in a window, based on criteria such as date, file size, or alphabetical by filename.

Source file In integration, the file from which the information is copied or used. An Excel file that is inserted into a file that contains a Word report is the source file.

Source presentation The presentation you insert slides from when you reuse slides from another presentation.

Spam Unwanted email that arrives from unsolicited sources. *Also called* junk email.

Spamming The sending of identical or near-identical unsolicited messages to a large number of recipients. Many email programs have filters that identify this email and place it in a special folder.

Sparkline A quick, simple chart located within a cell that serves as a visual indicator of data trends.

Spin box A text box with up and down arrows; you can type a setting in the text box or click the arrows to increase or decrease the setting.

Split form A form split into two panes; the upper pane allows you to display the fields of one record in any arrangement, and the lower pane maintains a datasheet view of the first few records.

SQL (Structured Query Language) A language that provides a standardized way to request information from a relational database system.

Start button A clickable button at in the lower left corner of the Windows 10 screen that you click to open the Start menu.

Start menu Appears after you click the Start button; provides access to all programs, documents, and settings on the computer.

Status bar The bar at the bottom of the Word program window that shows information about the document, including the current page number, the total number of pages in a document, the document word count, and the on/off status of spelling and grammar checking, and contains the view buttons, the Zoom level button and the Zoom slider.

Storyline In Sway, the workspace for assembling a presentation.

Style A named collection of character and paragraph formats that are stored together and can be applied to text to format it quickly.

Subdatasheet A datasheet that is nested within another datasheet to show related records. The subdatasheet shows the records on the "many" side of a one-to-many relationship.

Subfolder A folder within another folder.

Subject line Meaningful text in the subject text box of an email message providing recipients with an idea of the message content.

Subscript A font effect in which text is formatted in a smaller font size and placed below the line of text.

Subtitle text placeholder A box on the title slide reserved for subpoint text.

Suite A group of programs that are bundled together and share a similar interface, making it easy to transfer skills and program content among them.

Sum function A mathematical function that totals values in a field.

Superscript A font effect in which text is formatted in a smaller font size and placed above the line of text.

Sway site A website Sway creates to share and display a Sway presentation.

Symbol A special character that can be inserted into a document using the Symbol command.

Sync In OneNote, to save a new or updated notebook so that all versions of the notebook, such as a notebook on OneDrive and a copy on a hard drive, have the same contents.

Syntax Rules for entering information such as query criteria or property values.

System Clipboard A clipboard that stores only the last item cut or copied from a document. See also Clipboard and Office Clipboard.

System on a Chip (SoC) Consolidates the functions of the CPU, graphics and sound cards, memory, and more onto a single silicon chip. This miniaturization allows devices to become increasingly compact.

Tab A page in an application program's Ribbon, or in a dialog box, that contains a group of related commands and settings.

Tab Index property A form property that indicates the numeric tab order for all controls on the form that have the Tab Stop property set to Yes.

Tab leader A line that appears in front of tabbed text.

Tab order property A form property that determines the sequence in which the controls on the form receive the focus when the user presses [Tab] or [Enter] in Form view.

Tab stop A location on the horizontal ruler that indicates where to align text.

Tab Stop property A form property that determines whether a field accepts focus.

Table A collection of records for a single subject, such as all of the customer records; the fundamental building block of a relational database because it stores all of the data.

Table Design View A view of a table that provides the most options for defining fields.

Table styles Predesigned formatting that can be applied to a range of cells or even to an entire worksheet; especially useful for those ranges with labels in the left column and top row, and totals in the bottom row or right column. See also Table.

Tabs Organizational unit used for commands on the Ribbon. The tab names appear at the top of the Ribbon and the active tab appears in front.

Task In Outlook, an item in Tasks.

Task view A new Windows 10 area, accessible from the Task view button on the taskbar, that lets you switch applications and create multiple desktops (also called virtual desktops).

Taskbar The horizontal bar at the bottom of the Windows 10 desktop; displays icons representing apps, folders, and/or files on the left, and the Notification area, containing the date and time and special program messages, on the right.

Tasks In Outlook, the electronic to-do list, whereby each task has a subject, a start and end date, priority, and a description.

Tell Me box A text box on the Ribbon that is used to find a command or access the Word Help system.

Template A predesigned, formatted file that serves as the basis for a new workbook; Excel template files have the file extension .xltx.

Text Align property A control property that determines the alignment of text within the control.

Text annotations Labels added to a chart to draw attention to or describe a particular area.

Text box An area in a Windows program that you click to enter text.

Text concatenation operators In a formula, symbols used to join strings of text in different cells.

Text effect Formatting that applies a visual effect to text, such as a shadow, glow, outline, or reflection.

Text placeholder A box with a dotted border and text that you replace with your own text.

Text wrapping Formatting applied to a graphic to make it a floating graphic.

Text wrapping break Forces the text following the break to begin at the beginning of the next line.

Theme A predefined set of colors, fonts, line and fill effects, and other formats that can be applied to an Access database and give it a consistent, professional look.

Theme colors The set of 12 coordinated colors that make up a PowerPoint presentation; a theme assigns colors for text, lines, fills, accents, hyperlinks, and background.

Theme effects The set of effects for lines and fills.

Theme fonts The set of fonts for titles and other text.

Thumbnail A small image of a slide. Thumbnails are visible on the Slides tab and in Slide Sorter view.

Tick marks Notations of a scale of measure on a chart axis.

Tile A shaded rectangle on the Windows 10 Start menu that represents an app. See also App and Application program.

Title bar Appears at the top of every Office program window; displays the document name and program name.

Title placeholder A box on a slide reserved for the title of a presentation or slide.

Title slide The first slide in a presentation.

To Do tag In OneNote, an icon that helps you keep track of your assignments and other tasks.

Toggle button A button that turns a feature on and off.

Toolbar In an application program, a set of buttons, lists, and menus you can use to issue program commands.

Trash folder *See* Deleted Items folder.

Two-factor authentication (2FA) Security protocol in which an individual provides two credentials (often a pre-established password plus a one-time, randomly-generated code sent to a mobile phone) to verify their identity.

Ultraportable computer A type of laptop that is generally smaller and less powerful.

Unbound control A control that does not change from record to record and exists only to clarify or enhance the appearance of the form, using elements such as labels, lines, and clip art.

Universal apps *See* Windows 10 apps.

USB (Universal Serial Bus) Data communications standard designed to replace the need for earlier interfaces such as parallel and serial ports.

USB flash drive A removable storage device for folders and files that you plug into a USB port on your computer; makes it easy to transport folders and files to other computers. Also called a pen drive, flash drive, jump drive, keychain drive, or thumb drive.

User account A special area in a computer's operating system where users can store their own files and preferences.

User interface A collective term for all the ways you interact with a software program.

Username The first part of an email address that identifies the person who receives the email that is sent to this email address.

Vacation response An automatically-generated email message you can have sent in response to received emails when you are away; most email programs allow you to create a vacation response.

Value axis In a chart, the axis that contains numerical values; in a 2-dimensional chart, also known as the y-axis.

Values Numbers, formulas, and functions used in calculations.

Variant A custom variation of the applied theme that uses different colors, fonts, and effects.

Vertical alignment The position of text in a document relative to the top and bottom margins.

Vertical ruler A ruler that appears on the left side of the document window in Print Layout view.

Vertical scroll bar *See* scroll bar.

View Each Access object has different views for different purposes. For example, you work with data in Datasheet View. You modify the design of the object in Layout and Design Views. You preview a printout in Print Preview. Common views include Datasheet View for a table or query, or Design View for any Access object.

View buttons Buttons on the status bar that are used to change document views.

View Shortcuts The buttons at the bottom of the PowerPoint window on the status bar that you click to switch among views.

Wearables Computer devices that may be worn on a person's wrist or incorporated into clothing.

Web Layout view A view that shows a document as it will look when viewed with a Web browser.

Web Note In Microsoft Edge, an annotation on a webpage.

Web-based email Web site that provides free email addresses and service.

What-if analysis A decision-making tool in which data is changed and formulas are recalculated, in order to predict various possible outcomes.

Widow The last line of a paragraph when it is carried over to the top of the following page, separate from the rest of the paragraph.

Wildcard A special character used in criteria to find, filter, and query data. The asterisk (*) stands for any group of characters. For example, the criteria I* in a State field criterion cell would find all records where the state entry was IA, ID, IL, IN, or Iowa. The question mark (?) wildcard stands for only one character.

Window A rectangular-shaped work area that displays an app or a collection of files, folders, and Windows tools.

Window control buttons The set of three buttons on the right side of a window's title bar that let you control the window's state, such as minimized, maximized, restored to its previous open size, or closed.

Windows 10 apps Apps (application programs) for Windows 10 that often have a single purpose, such as Photos, News, or OneDrive.

Windows 10 desktop An electronic work area that lets you organize and manage your information, much like your own physical desktop.

Windows 10 UI The Windows 10 user interface. *See also* User interface.

Windows accessories Application programs (apps), such as Paint or WordPad, that come with the Windows 10 operating system.

Windows Action Center A pane that appears in the lower right corner of the Windows 10 screen that lets you quickly view system notifications and selected settings; also has Quick Action buttons to perform common actions in one click.

Windows app Small program available for free or for purchase in the Windows Store; can run on Windows desktops, laptops, tablets, and phones.

Windows Search The Windows feature that lets you look for files and folders on your computer storage devices; to search, type text in the Search text box in the title bar of any open window, or click the Start button and type text in the search text box.

Word art A drawing object that contains text formatted with special shapes, patterns, and orientations.

Word processing program A software program that includes tools for entering, editing, and formatting text and graphics.

Word program window The window that contains the Word program elements, including the document window, Quick Access toolbar, Ribbon, and status bar.

Word wrap A feature that automatically moves the insertion point to the next line as you type.

WordArt A set of decorative styles or text effects that is applied to text.

Workbook A collection of related worksheets contained within a single file which has the file extension xlsx.

Works cited A list of sources that you cited while creating a document.

Worksheet A single sheet within a workbook file; also, the entire area within an electronic spreadsheet that contains a grid of columns and rows.

Worksheet window Area of the program window that displays part of the current worksheet; the worksheet window displays only a small fraction of the worksheet, which can contain a total of 1,048,576 rows and 16,384 columns.

X-axis The horizontal axis in a chart; because it often shows data categories, such as months or locations, *also called* Category axis.

XML Acronym that stands for eXtensible Markup Language, which is a language used to structure, store, and send information.

Y-axis The vertical axis in a chart; because it often shows numerical values, *also called* Value axis.

Z-axis The third axis in a true 3-D chart, lets you compare data points across both categories and values.

Zoom level button A button on the status bar that is used to change the zoom level of the document in the document window.

Zoom slider A slider on the status bar that is dragged to enlarge or decrease the display size of the document in the document window.

Zooming A feature that makes screen information appear larger but shows less of it on screen at once, or shows more of a document on screen at once but at a reduced size; does not affect actual document size.

Zooming in A feature that makes a printout appear larger but shows less of it on screen at once; does not affect the actual size of the printout.

Zooming out A feature that shows more of a printout on screen at once but at a reduced size; does not affect the actual size of the printout.

Index

word-processing software, ECC 24, ECC 25. *See also* Microsoft Word
workbooks, ECC 24, EX 2
   emailing, EX 68
   new, creating using templates, EX 41
   recovering unsaved changes, EX 10
worksheet(s), ECC 24, ECC 25, EX 2, EX 3, PPT 56
   adding, EX 67
   add-ins to improve functionality, EX 26
   copying, EX 67
   deleting, EX 66, EX 67
   formatting. *See* formatting worksheets
   importing into Access, INT 18, INT 19, INT 20–21
   moving between, EX 66
   navigating, EX 9
   renaming, EX 66
   size, EX 14
   switching views, EX 14–15
worksheet window, EX 4, EX 5
workstations, ECC 18
World Wide Web (Web or WWW), ECC 18
   uses, ECC 2
worms, ECC 20
WWW. *See* World Wide Web (Web or WWW)

X Y charts, PPT 57
x-axis, EX 80, EX 81

y-axis, EX 80, EX 81
Yes/No data type, AC 7

Z

z-axis, EX 80, EX 87
Zoom In button, Microsoft Office 2016, OFF 6, OFF 7
Zoom level button, WD 4, WD 5
Zoom Out button, Microsoft Office 2016, OFF 6, OFF 7
Zoom slider, EX 16, WD 4, WD 5
   PowerPoint window, PPT 6, PPT 7